Ruby Ann Poulson

SIGNPOSTS IN A STRANGE LAND

D1166039

Ruby Ann Poulson

ALSO BY WALKER PERCY

NOVELS

THE MOVIEGOER (1961)

THE LAST GENTLEMAN (1966)

LOVE IN THE RUINS (1971)

LANCELOT (1977)

THE SECOND COMING (1980)

THE THANATOS SYNDROME (1987)

NONFICTION

THE MESSAGE IN THE BOTTLE (1975)

LOST IN THE COSMOS (1983)

SIGNPOSTS IN A STRANGE LAND

WALKER PERCY

EDITED WITH AN INTRODUCTION
BY
PATRICK SAMWAY

PICADOR
FARRAR, STRAUS AND GIROUX
NEW YORK

SIGNPOSTS IN A STRANGE LAND. Copyright © 1991 by Mary Bernice Percy. Introduction copyright © 1991 by Patrick Samway. All rights reserved. Printed in the United States of America. No part of this book may be used or reproduced in any manner whatsoever without written permission except in the case of brief quotations embodied in critical articles or reviews. For information, address Picador, 175 Fifth Avenue, New York, N.Y. 10010.

www.picadorusa.com

Picador® is a U.S. registered trademark and is used by Farrar, Straus and Giroux under license from Pan Books Limited.

For information on Picador Reading Group Guides, as well as ordering, please contact the Trade Marketing department at St. Martin's Press.
Phone: 1-800-221-7945 extension 763
Fax: 212-677-7456
E-mail: trademarketing@stmartins.com

Library of Congress Cataloging-in-Publication Data

Percy, Walker.
    Signposts in a strange land / Walker Percy : edited with an introduction by Patrick Samway.
        p. cm.
    Includes bibliographical references.
    ISBN 0-312-25419-9 (pbk)
    1. Percy, Walker, 1916–1990—Interviews. 2. Novelists, American—20th century—Interviews. 3. Southern states—Civilization.
4. Fiction—Authorship. I. Title.

PS3566.E612S27 2000
813'.54—dc21
[B]   98-089573
                                                 CIP

First published in the United States by Farrar, Straus and Giroux

D10 9 8 7 6 5

INSTEAD OF CONSTRUCTING A PLOT AND CREATING
A CAST OF CHARACTERS FROM A WORLD FAMILIAR
TO EVERYBODY, HE [THE NOVELIST] IS MORE APT
TO SET FORTH WITH A STRANGER IN A STRANGE LAND
WHERE THE SIGNPOSTS ARE ENIGMATIC BUT WHICH
HE SETS OUT TO EXPLORE NEVERTHELESS.

[NOTES FOR A NOVEL ABOUT THE END OF THE WORLD]

Contents

❧

Introduction

❧

When Walker Percy, M.D., died at his home in Covington, Louisiana, on May 10, 1990, he left a considerable legacy of uncollected nonfiction, including three unpublished essays—"Is a Theory of Man Possible?," "Culture, the Church, and Evangelization," and "Another Message in the Bottle"—as well as two unpublished talks—his acceptance speech on receiving the National Book Award for *The Moviegoer* and his remarks "Concerning *Love in the Ruins*"—all of which appear here for the first time. In addition, there is the 18th Annual Jefferson Lecture, entitled "The Fateful Rift: The San Andreas Fault in the Modern Mind," which he delivered in Washington, D.C., on May 3, 1989, at the invitation of the National Endowment for the Humanities and which has never before been published in its complete and final form.

All the writings in this book cover a wide range of topics which fall, as I discovered, into three categories reflecting the basic dimensions of Percy's thought: life in the South; science, language, and literature; morality and religion. The earliest piece here (written in 1935, during his undergraduate days at the University of North Carolina at Chapel Hill), entitled "The Movie Magazine: A Low 'Slick,' " prefigures motifs in his first novel, *The Moviegoer*. His thoughtful and extended Jefferson Lecture, on the other hand, was his last public statement.

One of my tasks as editor was to narrow down and arrange

these writings so as to allow Percy's related ideas and nuanced speculations to assume their proper intertextual weight and importance. For obvious reasons, I have excluded the fifteen essays that Percy collected and published in his book *The Message in the Bottle* (1975), as well as juvenilia, book reviews, panel discussions in which he took part, unfinished essays, and (with one exception) the interviews published in *Conversations with Walker Percy* (1985).

Walker Percy's place in American fiction not only is firmly established in this country, but the steadily increasing number of translations of his novels, as well as the conference on his fiction and nonfiction held in the summer of 1989 in Sandbjerg, Denmark, indicate that international interest in his books is continuing to grow. It is my hope that *Signposts in a Strange Land* will provide readers with a wider range of texts essential for an understanding of Percy's thought than has yet been available.

My task would have been more difficult had it not been for the conversations we had in his home overlooking the peaceful Bogue Falaya in Covington. On one occasion, as he talked about his nonfiction—while tracking out of the corner of his eye the movements of a solitary egret wading in the muddy bayou—Dr. Percy lowered his voice and looked at me directly. For a brief moment, his congenial at-home smile uncharacteristically disappeared: he was explaining how difficult it had been for him to search within himself and articulate his most deeply felt views. His careful and meticulous preparation of these writings became particularly palpable as he described the writing of his Jefferson Lecture. His health was then declining and he knew this lecture would probably be his last opportunity to discuss in detail his belief that the view of the world we get consciously or unconsciously from modern science is radically incoherent. As for his earlier nonfiction, the corrected and emended manuscripts and typescripts that I have examined and worked with leave no doubt that he was equally assiduous in the preparation of all his texts.

Walker Percy was born on May 28, 1916, in Birmingham, Alabama, where his parents, LeRoy and Martha Susan Percy, were part of the social elite of the community. After his father's death from self-inflicted wounds on July 9, 1929, Mrs. Percy took young

Walker and his two brothers to live for a year with her mother in Athens, Georgia. When second cousin William Alexander Percy—a poet, lawyer, plantation owner, and the author of *Lanterns on the Levee* (1941)—invited Mrs. Percy and her boys to move into his home in Greenville, Mississippi, they accepted. Mrs. Percy, tragically, died in an automobile accident on April 2, 1932. Though subsequently adopted by "Uncle" Will, Walker and his brothers nevertheless had a double loss to bear; yet Uncle Will did everything possible in assisting the Percy boys to cope with their grief. Above all, he wanted each of them to receive an excellent education. Walker graduated from Greenville High School in 1933, the University of North Carolina at Chapel Hill in 1937, and the College of Physicians and Surgeons of Columbia University in 1941. While an intern at Bellevue Hospital in New York City, he contracted tuberculosis and was sent to a sanatorium in Saranac Lake, New York, to recuperate. Eventually Dr. Percy returned South, married Mary Bernice Townsend, and moved with her to Covington to raise a family and pursue his new career as a writer. His published work includes six novels—*The Moviegoer* (1961), which won the National Book Award in 1962, *The Last Gentleman* (1966), *Love in the Ruins* (1971), *Lancelot* (1977), *The Second Coming* (1980), and *The Thanatos Syndrome* (1987)—in addition to two works of nonfiction, *The Message in the Bottle* and *Lost in the Cosmos* (1983).

The first section of *Signposts in a Strange Land*, on life in the South, begins with a personal statement: why Percy, in a joint decision with his wife, chose to live in Covington. "Technically speaking," he writes, "Covington is a nonplace in a certain relation to a place (New Orleans), a relation that allows one to avoid the horrors of total placement or total nonplacement or total misplacement." As an ideal nonplace, Covington offered the friendly privacy he needed to write, where one "can sniff the ozone from the pine trees, visit the local bars, eat crawfish, and drink Dixie beer and feel as good as it is possible to feel in this awfully interesting century." (I remember sensing the casual hospitality of Covington the first time I drove through town on a sunny fall day in 1978 to have lunch with the Percys at their home.) Percy once wrote that when a fellow Covingtonian asked him what he did for a living, he said that he wrote books. But when the townsman pressed him as to what he *really* did, Percy answered, "Nothing"—and both were pleased with the response. Covington is one of the last sleepy towns in Louisiana before one crosses the long causeway to the Big Easy, with a vibrant mixture of Spanish and French history and a culture all its own; clearly, Covington offered Percy the best of all possible worlds.

The other essays in this section trace the people, customs, historical events, ideas, and locales in the South important for an understanding of Percy's landscape and mindscape: New Orleans with its "lively" and "exotic" cemeteries; reflections on returning to Athens, Georgia; life with Uncle Will in Greenville; the significance of the Civil War, particularly one hundred years after Appomattox; the decline of what can be considered the noble and gracious Old Stoa in the South; modest proposals concerning race relations; and thoughts on the quality of education in Louisiana. This section ends with his own upbeat short history of Bourbon whiskey, complete with "Cud'n Walker's Uncle Will's Favorite Mint Julep Receipt."

The second and third sections in this collection have similar modes of development. In "Is a Theory of Man Possible?," for example, a talk Percy gave to a group interested in mental health at Louisiana State University in Baton Rouge, as a result of an appointment there during the 1974–75 academic year, he asks a key philosophical question. In the long run, Percy's answer (and he says that a positive answer to this question *can* be given) actually demanded for him an analysis of the philosophy of man, the sciences, semiotics, literature, and psychiatry, as well as reflections on his life as a physician and novelist. As a diagnostician of the modern malaise that affects us all, Percy does not limit this investigation to one discipline; rather, he synthesizes a wide body of knowledge, often using his own experience from medicine and science as touchstones to arrive at the truth of the matter. In "The State of the Novel," originally delivered as the 1977 Hopwood Lecture at the University of Michigan in Ann Arbor, he expresses one of his important assumptions: "Art is cognitive; that is, it discovers and knows and tells, tells the reader how things are, how we are, in a way that the reader can confirm with as much certitude as a scientist taking a pointer-reading." Further, in his Jefferson Lecture, relying on the work of the noted semiotician and pragmatist Charles Sanders Peirce (1839–1914), he develops the idea that science as we know it cannot utter a single word about what is distinctive in human behavior, language, art, and thought itself—in short, what it is to be born, to live, and to die as a human being. Percy would have us look to the humanities, "the elder brother of the sciences," and grapple more and more with what Peirce characterizes as "interpreter," "asserter," "mind," "ego," even "soul"—words and concepts not in fashion in many academic circles today.

By using, however tentatively, the seemingly religious word "soul" in the Jefferson Lecture, Percy showed once again that he tried not to compartmentalize his life and work. As with Teilhard de Chardin, S.J., a scientist and priest whose works (as he once told me) he admired, Percy himself strove for greater unity of vision in his life. And as a convert to Catholicism, he grew steadily in knowledge and love of his adopted religious heritage.

Yet no one could have been more surprised than he when he was the sole American to receive an invitation to participate in a symposium at the Vatican sponsored by the Pontifical Council for Culture in January 1988. In his address to this council on "Culture, the Church, and Evangelization," Percy stated his views about secularism in American society and suggested that the Roman Catholic Church could more effectively use television in its efforts to evangelize. Percy never backed away from his faith, and though he once told his novelist friend and fellow convert Mary Lee Settle that the Roman Catholic Church was a "very untidy outfit," he often made it clear that this was where he wanted to be. Not surprisingly, he took the trouble to state his opposition to abortion both in an Op Ed article (1981) in *The New York Times* and in an unpublished letter (1988) to the same newspaper.

No matter how he perceived evil—and Father Smith's "Confession" and "Footnote" in *The Thanatos Syndrome* provide imaginative clues to Percy's belief, as a novelist, that personified evil exists in our society—he did not feel obliged to write edifying stories in which virtue wins out. In fact, his 1987 talk entitled "Another Message in the Bottle" at an educational conference in New

Orleans, in which he makes some remarkable connections between the novel form and Catholicism, contains honest and direct advice for teachers of today's students: if students do not make a breakthrough into reading—and Percy is thinking about reading in very broad terms—then they probably will not make breakthroughs into other areas of life. Percy believed profoundly in the simple "holiness of the ordinary" in all its facets. The protagonists of his novels, everyday wayfarers whose lives are mysterious, dramatically reflect this.

A word about the titles of some of his essays and talks that might seem to have been omitted from *Signposts in a Strange Land* but are not. Percy would occasionally repeat a talk or an essay and rework it under a different title. The 1978 Phinizy Lecture at the University of Georgia, for example, was reprinted in a slightly different version as "Random Thoughts on Southern Literature, Southern Politics, and the American Future" in *The Georgia Review* (Fall 1978) and the following year as "Southern Comfort" in *Harper's* (January 1979). Likewise, his tribute to William Alexander Percy, here entitled "Uncle Will," appeared with variations as " 'Uncle Will' and His South" in *Saturday Review / World* (November 1973) and as an abbreviated introduction to *Sewanee* (1982). The 1977 Chekhov Lecture at Cornell University, issued as "Diagnosing the Modern Malaise" by the Faust Publishing Company (1985), also appeared as "Novelist as Diagnostician of the Modern Malaise" in *Chekhov and Our Age*, edited by James McConkey, and in a revised version as "The Diagnostic Novel: On the Uses of Modern Fiction" in *Harper's* (June 1986). "Mississippi: The Fallen Paradise" first appeared in a special issue of *Harper's* and later appeared with some interesting additions in a book entitled *The South Today*, edited by Willie Morris.

The epilogue contains Zoltán Abádi-Nagy's probing interview and ends with Percy's delightful self-interview, "Questions They Never Asked Me." Here he responds more directly to the felt difficulties of his readers and fills in the gaps of some of his essays, particularly when he discusses his own fiction. This self-interview, a masterly example of the genre, allows Percy to give marvelous expression to the breadth of his personality. In commenting (see page 422) on the portrait of himself painted by Lyn Hill, Percy perceptively notes that his figure is standing outside the painting's frame, "somewhat out of it, out of the world that is framed off behind him." At the same time, this image carries on an implied dialogue, which never violates the freedom of the beholder: *"You and I know something, don't we? Or do we? . . . True, this is a strange world I'm in, but what about the world you're in? Have you noticed it lately? Are we onto something, you and I? Probably not."* This is his personal invitation to explore undiscovered worlds—an invitation he repeatedly offers his readers in both his fiction and his nonfiction.

In conclusion, I would like to thank the following persons for their encouragement and assistance: Joseph L. Blotner and the late Yvonne Blotner, John F. Desmond, Rhoda K. Faust, Shelby Foote, Ben and Nadine Forkner, Robert Giroux, Diana Gonzalez, Linda Whitney Hobson, Lewis A. Lawson, Joseph P. Parkes, S.J., Louis D. Rubin, Jr., Mary Lee Settle, Eudora Welty, and especially Mrs. Mary Bernice Percy.

PATRICK H. SAMWAY, S.J.

One

LIFE IN

THE SOUTH

WHY I LIVE
WHERE I LIVE

❧

The reason I live in Covington, Louisiana, is not because it was listed recently in *Money* as one of the best places in the United States to retire to. The reason is not that it is a pleasant place but rather that it is a pleasant nonplace. Covington is in the Deep South, which is supposed to have a strong sense of place. It does, but Covington occupies a kind of interstice in the South. It falls between places.

Technically speaking, Covington is a nonplace in a certain relation to a place (New Orleans), a relation that allows one to avoid the horrors of total placement or total nonplacement or total misplacement.

Total placement for a writer would be to live in a place like Charleston or Mobile, where one's family has lived for two hundred years. A pleasant enough prospect, you might suppose, but not for a writer—or not for this writer. Such places are haunted. Ancestors perch on your shoulder while you write. Faulkner managed to do it but only by drinking a great deal and by playing little charades, like pretending to be a farmer. It is necessary to escape the place of one's origins and the ghosts of one's ancestors but not too far. You wouldn't want to move to Tucumcari.

Total nonplacement would be to do what Descartes did, live anonymously among the burghers of Amsterdam. Or do what Kierkegaard did, live in the business district of Copenhagen, pop out into the street every half hour, and speak to the shopkeepers so one will be thought an idler. It pleased Kierkegaard to be thought an idler at the very time he was turning out five books a year. On the other hand, a writer in the United States doesn't have to go to such lengths to be taken for an idler. Another type of nonplacement for a Southern writer is to live in a nondescript Northern place like Waterbury, Connecticut, or become writer in residence at Purdue. This is a matter of taste. It works for some very good writers, like Styron (in Connecticut), for whom the placeness of the South becomes too suffocating. Indeed, more often than not, it is only possible to write about the South by leaving it. For me, I miss the South if I am gone too long. I prefer to live in the South but on my own terms. It takes some doing to insert oneself in such a way as not to succumb to the ghosts of the Old South or the happy hustlers of the new Sunbelt South.

A popular and often necessary form of nonplacement is to hook up with academe, teaching or visiting in universities. This works for some writers. Indeed, it can be a godsend for serious writers who can rarely support themselves by writing. It works if one (*a*) is a good teacher or (*b*) is a bad teacher who doesn't care or (*c*) can both teach and write. For me, teaching is harder work than writing. It is hard enough to deal with words but having to deal with words and students overtaken as they are by their terrible needs, vulnerability, likability, intelligence, and dumbness wears me out. How I respect and envy the gifted teacher!

Total misplacement is to live in another place, usually an exotic place, which is so strongly informed by its exoticness that the writer, who has fled his haunted place or his vacant nonplace and who feels somewhat ghostly himself, somehow expects to become informed by the exotic identity of the new place. A real bummer if you ask me, yet it has worked for some. Hemingway in Paris and Madrid. Sherwood Anderson in New Orleans, Malcolm Lowry in Mexico, Vidal in Italy, Tennessee Williams in Key West, James Jones on the Ile St.-Louis in Paris. Such a remove is a reasonable alternative to Northern ghostliness but unfortunately only a temporary one. Even James Baldwin and Richard Wright had to come home. Northern (by Northern, I mean upper North Hemisphere—North America, England, Sweden, Germany) ghostliness tends to evacuate a Latin neighborhood, like a drop of acid on a map of Mexico.

There is a species of consumption at work here. Places are consumed nowadays. The more delectable the place, the quicker it is ingested, digested, and turned to feces. Once I lived in Santa Fe, a lovely placid place, but after a while the silver-and-turquoise jewelry, the Pueblo Indians, the mesquite, the Sangre de Cristo Mountains, became as commonplace, *used up*, as Dixie beer, good old boys, and Nashville music. After a sojourn in the desert, memories of Louisiana green become irresistible.

Another sort of nonplacement traditionally available to writers, and paradoxically felicitous, is enforced placement in a nonplace—that is, exile or imprisonment. I don't have to tell you how well Cervantes and some other writers have done in jail. My own suspicion is that many American writers secretly envy writers like Solzhenitsyn, who get sent to the Gulag camps for their writings, keep writing on toilet paper, take on the whole bloody state—and win. The total freedom of writers in this country can be distressing. What a burden to bear, that the government not only allows us complete freedom—even freedom for atrocities like *MacBird!*—but, like ninety-five percent of Americans, couldn't care less what we write. Oh, you lucky Dostoevskys, with your firing squads (imagine shooting an American writer!), exiles, prison camps, nuthouses. True, American writers are often regarded as nuts but as harmless ones. So the exile has to be self-imposed—which has its drawbacks. One goes storming off, holes up in Montmartre or Algiers, cursing McCarthyism, racism, TV, shopping centers, consumerism, and no one pays the slightest attention. Months, years, later, one saunters back, hands in pockets, eyes averted—but no one is looking now either. Mailer and Vidal write books reviling the establishment—and make main selection of Book-of-the-Month.

Free people have a serious problem with place, being in a place, using up a place, deciding which new place to rotate to. Americans ricochet around the United States like billiard balls. Swedes, Americans, Germans, and the English play musical chairs with places, usually Southern places (all but the French, who think they live in the Place). But for writers, place is a special problem because they never fitted in in the first place. The problem is to choose a place where one's native terror is not completely neutralized (like a writer who disappears into Cuernavaca and coke happily and forever) but rendered barely tolerable.

Here in Covington, one is able to insert oneself into the South, a region celebrated for its strong sense of place and roots, which most Southern writers can't stand and have to get away from and so go North, where they can sit in desolate bars and go on about how lovely the South looks—from there. Witness the writers of the Agrarian Movement in the South, nearly all of whom ended up in Northern universities. What makes the insertion possible is that Covington is a nonplace but the right sort of nonplace. Here is one place in the South where a writer can live as happily as a bug in a crack in the sidewalk, where he can mosey out now and then and sniff the air just to make sure this is not just any crack in any sidewalk.

The pleasantest things about Covington are its nearness to New Orleans—which is very much of a place, drenched in its identity, its history, and its rather self-conscious exotica—and its own attractive lack of identity, lack of placeness, even lack of history. Nothing has ever happened here, no great triumphs or tragedies. In fact, people seldom die. The pine trees are supposed to secrete a healthful ozone that has given Covington the reputation of being the "second healthiest place on earth" (I never found out what the first was). I thought this was part of the local moonshine until my friend Steve Ellis, judge and historian, showed me newspaper clippings for a year of a yellow-fever outbreak in New Orleans. Even though Covington received refugees by the hundreds that year, nobody died of yellow fever and only a few people died of any cause.

Covington is a cheerfully anomalous place. Its major streets have New England names—Boston, New Hampshire, Vermont, Rutland—and nobody seems to know why or care. It is the seat of the parish (what counties are called in Louisiana) of St. Tammany. This name, thought up by the first American governor of Louisiana, was probably a joke or a jibe at the French practice of using saints' names, like St. John the Baptist Parish.

When I first saw Covington, having driven over from New

Orleans one day, I took one look around, sniffed the ozone, and exclaimed unlike Brigham Young: "This is the nonplace for me!" It had no country clubs, no subdivisions, no Chamber of Commerce, no hospitals, no psychiatrists (now it has all these). I didn't know anybody, had no kin here. A stranger in my own country. A perfect place for a writer! I bought a house the following week.

Another attraction is Covington's rather admirable tradition of orneriness and dissent, its positive genius for choosing the wrong side in the issues of the day, and its abiding indifference to the currents of history. It is a backwater of a backwater. Yet the region was a refuge for Tories in full flight from the crazy American revolutionaries. Shortly thereafter, when several local parishes revolted against Spain to set up their own republic—capital at St. Francisville, flag with one star, which lasted three months— Covington was against it. It liked the Spanish. Then when the United States and Louisiana proposed to annex the Republic of West Florida, we voted against it. We didn't like Louisiana. When Louisiana voted to secede from the Union in 1861, we voted against that, too. We liked the Union. Yet when the war was over, slave owners kept their slaves as if the Emancipation Proclamation never occurred. During the years of Prohibition, the Little Napoleon bar served drinks.

Things have changed in recent years. We have joined the Sunbelt with a vengeance, are in fact one of the fastest-growing counties in the country. It is worrisome to be written up by *Money* magazine, but more ominous is the plan afoot to build a "theme park" here, like Walt Disney World but bigger.

Covington is now threatened by progress. It has become a little jewel in the Sunbelt and is in serious danger of being written up in *Southern Living*, what with its restored shotgun cottages, live oaks, nifty shops, converted depot. Its politics, no longer strange, have become standard Sunbelt Reagan. There are as many Carter jokes as there used to be Roosevelt and Kennedy jokes in Mississippi. The level of political debate lies somewhere between Genghis Khan and the Incredible Hulk. The center is holding only too well, about ninety degrees to the right of center—which is not necessarily bad. Whenever I get depressed about living in a place where the main political issue is Reagan versus Connally, I have only to imagine what it would be like to live in a McGovernite community. Southern conservatives, in my experience, are more tolerant than Northern liberals. That is to say, they put up with "liberal" writers with better grace than Berkeley would put up, say, with Buckley. A Southern writer is allowed his eccentricities. The prevailing attitude is a kind of benevolent neglect. As the saying goes in these parts: He may be a son of a bitch, but he's *our* son of a bitch. A minor cultural note: In my opinion, local Yankee racists are worse than Southern racists; they don't even like Uncle Toms and Aunt Jemimas. One can only wonder how Abraham Lincoln ever talked these people into fighting a war to free slaves. And the main difference between local country-clubbers (affluent, often Midwestern) and the local Klan (poor, Southern) is that the former tolerate Jews and Catholics, probably because there are so few Jews and the Catholics are generally as conservative as country-club WASPs.

But these are minor matters. The worst of it is that Covington may be in danger of losing its peculiar distinction of being a pleasant backwater lost, but not too lost, in the interstices of place and time. One of the first things to attract me to Covington was the complaint of a former resident: "My God, you could live back in those pine trees for twenty years and never meet your neighbor— it's as bad as New York." Hmm. Sounds like my kind of place. The best of both worlds: a small Southern town, yet one can live as one pleases. There are all manner of folk here—even a writer can make good friends—indeed, an unusual and felicitous mix of types, Mississippi WASPs, Creole Catholics, Cajun Catholics, natives, pleasant blacks (who, for reasons that escape me, have remained pleasant), theosophists, every variety of Yankee. Any one group might be hard to take as a majority, but put together the lump gets leavened.

Covington is strategically located on the border between the Bible Belt and the Creole–French–Italian–German South. The two cultures interpenetrate. Good old Mississippi types march in Mardi Gras parades. Cajun types drive Ford Ranger pickups and listen to Loretta Lynn. I FOUND IT! bumper stickers abound (in case you didn't know, IT is Jesus Christ). But there is also the sardonic Catholic rejoinder, I NEVER LOST IT. And then there are stickers

in the old eccentric tradition: I LOST MY ANOMIE IN ST. TAM-
MANY. As well as: GOAT ROPERS NEED LOVE TOO. True.

So it is possible to live in both cultures without being suffocated
by the one or seduced by the other. New Orleans may be too
seductive for a writer. Known hereabouts as the Big Easy, it may
be too easy, too pleasant. Faulkner was charmed to a standstill and
didn't really get going until he returned to Mississippi and invented
his county. The occupational hazard of the writer in New Orleans
is a variety of the French flu, which might also be called the Vieux
Carré syndrome. One is apt to turn fey, potter about a patio, and
write feuilletons and vignettes or catty romans à clef, a pleasant
enough life but for me too seductive.

On the other hand, it is often a good idea to go against
demographic trends, reverse the flight to the country, return to
the ruined heart of the city. When the French Quarter is completely
ruined by the tourists—and deserted by them—it will again be a
good place to live. I'm sick of cutting grass. Covington lies at the
green heart of green Louisiana, a green jungle of pines, azaleas,
camellias, dogwood, grapevines, and billions of blades of grass.
I've begun to hear the grass growing at night. It costs $25 to get
my lawn mower fixed. If my wife would allow it, I would end my
days in a French cottage on Rue Dauphine with a small paved
patio and not a single blade of grass.

A Chinese curse condemns one to live in interesting and
eventful times. The best thing about Covington is that it is in a
certain sense out of place and time but not too far out and
therefore just the place for a Chinese scholar who asks nothing
more than being left alone. One can sniff the ozone from the pine
trees, visit the local bars, eat crawfish, and drink Dixie beer and
feel as good as it is possible to feel in this awfully interesting
century. And now and then, drive across the lake to New Orleans,
still an entrancing city, eat trout amandine at Galatoire's, drive
home to my pleasant, uninteresting place, try to figure out how
the world got into such a fix, shrug, take a drink, and listen to the
frogs tune up.

1980

NEW ORLEANS
MON AMOUR

✷

If the American city does not go to hell in the next few years, it will not be the likes of Dallas or Grosse Pointe which will work its deliverance, or Berkeley or New Haven, or Santa Fe or La Jolla. But New Orleans might. Just as New Orleans hit upon jazz, the only unique American contribution to art, and hit upon it almost by accident and despite itself, it could also hit upon the way out of the hell which has overtaken the American city.

My tiny optimism derives not from sociological indices—which after all didn't help much in Detroit and New Haven. It has rather to do with a quality of air, which often smells bad; with a property of space, which is often cramped; and with a certain persisting nonmalevolence, although New Orleans has the highest murder rate in the United States and kills more people with cars than Caracas.

The space in question is not the ordinary living space of individuals and families but rather the interstices thereof. In New York millions of souls carve out living space on a grid like so many circles on graph paper. These lairs are more or less habitable. But the space between is a horrid thing, a howling vacuum. If you fall ill on the streets of New York, people grumble about having to step over you or around you. In New Orleans there is still a chance, diminishing perhaps, that somebody will drag you into the neighborhood bar and pay the innkeeper for a shot of Early Times.

Mobile, Alabama, unlike New York, has no interstices. It is older than New Orleans. It has wrought iron, better azaleas, an older Mardi Gras. It appears easygoing and has had no riots. Yet it suffers from the spiritual damps, Alabama anoxia. Twenty-four hours in Mobile and you have the feeling a plastic bag is tied around your head and you're breathing your own air. Mobile's public space is continuous with the private space of its front parlors. So where New York is a vacuum, Mobile is a pressure cooker.

Philadelphia is suffocating but in a different way. I speak from experience. Once I spent an hour in Philadelphia. I had got lost driving and instead of zipping by on the turnpikes, I found myself in the middle of town. I parked and got out and stood on a street corner near Independence Hall, holding my map and looking for a street sign and also sniffing the air to smell out what manner of place this was. Some young Negroes were moping around, no doubt sons of sons of the South. They looked at me sideways. I asked a fellow for directions but he hurried away. I hummed a tune and swung my arms to keep warm. Meanwhile, all around us, ringing us 360 degrees around like a besieging army, were three or four million good white people sitting in their good homes reading *The Bulletin.* I got to thinking: I don't know a single soul in Philadelphia, black or white. What is more, I never heard of anyone coming from Philadelphia except Benjamin Franklin and Connie Mack, or of anything ever happening in Philadelphia except the signing of the Declaration of Independence. What have all these people been doing here all these years? What are they doing now? They must be waiting. Waiting for what? For something to happen. Let me out of here!

Somebody said that the only interesting thing about New Orleans was that it smelled different. There are whiffs of ground coffee and a congeries of smells which one imagines to be the "naval stores" that geography books were always speaking of. Yet the peculiar flavor of New Orleans is more than a smell. It has something to do with the South and with a cutting off from the South, with the River and with history. New Orleans is both intimately related to the South and yet in a real sense cut adrift not only from the South but from the rest of Louisiana, somewhat like Mont-St.-Michel awash at high tide. One comes upon it, moreover, in the unlikeliest of places, by penetrating the depths of the Bible Belt, running the gauntlet of Klan territory, the pine barrens of south Mississippi, Bogalusa, and the Florida parishes of Louisiana. Out and over a watery waste and there it is, a proper enough American city, and yet within the next few hours the tourist is apt to see more nuns and naked women than he ever saw before. And when he opens the sports pages to follow the Packers, he comes across such enigmatic headlines as HOLY ANGELS SLAUGHTER SACRED HEART. It is as if Marseilles had been plucked up off the Midi, monkeyed with by Robert Moses and Hugh Hefner, and set down off John O'Groats in Scotland.

The River confers a peculiar dispensation upon the space of New Orleans. Arriving from Memphis or Cincinnati, one feels the way Huck Finn did shoving off from Illinois, going from an encompassed place to an in-between zone, a sector of contending or lapsing jurisdictions. On New Orleans's ordinary streets one savors a sense both of easement and of unspecified possibilities, in fine a latitude of which notoriety and raffishness—particularly its well-known sexual license—are only the more patent abuses.

Steeped in official quaintness and self-labeled the "most interesting city in America," New Orleans conceives of itself in the language of the old Fitzpatrick Traveltalks as a city of contrasts: thriving metropolis, quaint French Quarter, gracious old Garden District. Actually, the city is a most peculiar concoction of exotic and American ingredients, a gumbo of stray chunks of the South, of Latin and Negro oddments, German and Irish morsels, all swimming in a fairly standard American soup. What is interesting is that none of the ingredients has overpowered the gumbo, yet each has flavored the others and been flavored. The Negro hit upon jazz not in Africa but on Perdido Street, a lost nowhere place, an interstice between the Creoles and the Americans where he could hear not only the airs of the French Opera House but also the hoedowns of the Kaintucks, and the salon music uptown. Neither Creole nor Scotch-Irish quite prevailed in New Orleans and here perhaps was the luck of it.

If the French had kept the city, it would be today a Martinique, a Latin confection. If the Americans had got there first, we'd have Houston or Jackson sitting athwart the great American watershed. As it happened, there may have occurred just enough of a cultural standoff to give one room to turn around in, a public space which is delicately balanced between the Northern vacuum and the Southern pressure cooker.

What makes New Orleans interesting is not its celebrated quaint folk, who are all gone anyway—Johnny Crapaud, the Kaintucks, the Louis Armstrongs—but the unquaint folk who followed them. The Creoles now are indistinguishable from the Americans except by name. There is very little difference between Congressman Hébert and Senator Claghorn of the old Fred Allen program. Every time McNamara closed down a base, say, an army-mule installation in Hébert's district, the act would go on: "This strikes, I say, this strikes a body blow to the morale of the Armed Forces!"

The grandsons and -daughters of Louis Armstrong's generation have gone the usual Negro route, either down and out to the ghetto or up into the bourgeoisie. The boy has likely dropped out of school and is in Vietnam; the girl maybe goes to college and talks like an actress on soap opera. Neither would touch a banjo or trumpet with a ten-foot pole.

Yet, being unquaint in New Orleans is still different from being unquaint in Dallas. Indeed, the most recent chunk added to the gumbo are the unquaint emigrés from the heartland who, ever since Sherwood Anderson left Ohio, have come down in droves. What happens to these pilgrims? Do they get caught upon the wheel of the quaint, use up New Orleans, and move on to Cuernavaca? Do they inform the quaint or are they informed? Those who stay often follow a recognizable dialectic, a reaction against the seedy and a reversion to the old civic virtues of Ohio which culminates in a valuable proprietorship of the quaint, a curator's zeal to preserve the best of the old and also to promote new "cultural facilities." It is often the ex-heartlanders who save jazz, save the old buildings, save the symphony. Sometimes an outlander, a member of the business-professional establishment, who has succeeded in the Protestant ethic of hard work and corporate wheeling-and-dealing, even gets to be king of Mardi

Gras these days, replacing the old Creoles for whom Fat Tuesday bore the traditional relation to Ash Wednesday. There has occurred a kind of innocent repaganization of Mardi Gras in virtue of which the successful man not only reaps the earthly reward of money but also achieves his kingdom here and now. The life of the American businessman in New Orleans is ameliorated by the quasi-liturgical rhythm of Mardi Gras, two months of carnival and ten months of Lent.

Here, in the marriage of George Babbitt and Marianne, has always resided the best hope and worst risk of New Orleans. The hope, often fulfilled, is that the union will bring together the virtues of each, the best of the two life-styles, industry and grace, political morality and racial toleration. Of course, as in the projected marriage of George Bernard Shaw and his lady admirer, the wrong genes can just as easily combine. Unfortunately and all too often, the Latins learned Anglo-Saxon racial morality and the Americans learned Latin political morality. The fruit of such a mismatch is something to behold: Baptist governors and state legislators who loot the state with Catholic gaiety and Protestant industry. Transplant the worst of Mississippi to the Delta and what do you get? Plaquemines Parish, which is something like Neshoba County run by Trujillo. Reincarnate Senator Eastland in the Latin tradition and you end up with Leander Perez, segregationist boss of the lowlands between New Orleans and the Gulf.

Yet things get better. There were times when Louisiana was like a banana republic governed by a redneck junta. Now New Orleans has people like Congressman Hale Boggs, who is actually a statesman; that is to say, a successful, able, moderate, responsible politician. And the Baptist North produces Governor John Mc-Keithen, who may well turn out to be a populist genius.

Moreover, despite the bad past, the slavery, the Latin sexual exploitation, the cheerless American segregation, the New Orleans Negro managed to stake out a bit of tolerable living space. Unlike the Choctaws, who melted away like bayou mist before the onslaught of the terrible white man, the Negro was not only tough but creative. He survived and it is not a piece of Southern foolery to say that there are many pleasant things about his life. Even now it wouldn't take much to make New Orleans quite habitable for him. Here is the tantalizing thing: that New Orleans is by providence or good luck fairly close to making it, to being a habitable place for everybody, and yet is doing little or nothing to close the gap—while in cities like Detroit the efforts are strenuous but the gap is so wide that it has not been closed.

Thus, the relative serenity of New Orleans—and the South, for that matter—is subject to dangerous misinterpretation from both sides. The black militant says that the New Orleans Negro has not tried to burn the city down because he is afraid to. The mayor and most whites would reply that the local Negro is better off and knows it, that there is still a deep long-standing affection and understanding between the races, etc., etc. Both are right and wrong. The New Orleans Negro is afraid but he still doesn't want to burn anything down—yet. Despite all, he has something his uprooted and demoralized brother in Watts does not have, no thanks to the whites, and which he himself is hard put to define. Said one Negro phoning into a recent radio talk program while the panelists were congratulating themselves on the excellent race relations in tolerant old New Orleans: "Man, who are you kidding? I've lived in New Orleans all my life and I know better and you know better. I know and you know that every Japanese and Greek sailor getting off a ship and walking down Canal Street is better off than I am and can do things and go places I can't go right here in my hometown. But where I'm going? Harlem? Man, look out!"

New Orleans can perhaps take comfort in the fact that this man still wants to live here, still has the sense of being at home, still has not turned nasty. He is still talking and is, in fact, not ill-humored. Treat him like a Greek or Japanese today and you have the feeling New Orleans could make it. But tomorrow? That is something else.

The only trouble is that as long as the Negro does not lose his temper nobody is apt to do anything about him and when he does it is too late. It is a piece of bad luck that the Negro, for whatever reason—and of course there are reasons—is like a piece of litmus paper which turns suddenly from blue to red. He takes it, looks as if he is going to keep taking it, then all of a sudden does not take it. There does not intervene in his case the political solidarity of the Irish and Italians. So, with the Negro, the blue litmus is always open to a misreading.

For any number of reasons, New Orleans should be less habitable than Albany or Atlanta. Many of its streets look like the alleys of Warsaw. In one subdivision, feces empty into open ditches. Its garbage collection is whimsical and sporadic. Its tax-assessment system is absurd. It spends more money on professional football and less on its public library than any other major city. It has some of the cruelest slums in America and blood-sucking landlords right out of Dickens, and its lazy complacent city judges won't put them in jail. It plans the largest air-conditioned domed sports stadium in the world and has no urban renewal to speak of. Its Jefferson Parish is the newest sanctuary for Mafia hoods. Its Bourbon Street is as lewd and joyless a place as Dante's Second Circle of Hell, lewd with that special sad voyeur lewdness which marks the less felicitous encounters between Latin permissiveness and Anglo-Saxon sex morality.

Its business establishment and hotelmen-restaurateurs are content that lewdness be peddled with one hand and Old World charm with the other—Bourbon Street for the conventioner, Royal Street for his wife—while everyone looks ahead with clear-eyed all-American optimism for new industry and the progress of the port. Yet there are even now signs that cynical commercialization will kill the goose. The Chamber of Commerce type reasons so: If all these tourists like the Vieux Carré, the patio-cum-slave-quarter bit, let's do it up brown with super slave quarters, huge but quaint hives of hundreds of cells laced with miles of wrought iron and lit by forests of gas lamps. An elevated expressway is planned along the riverbank in front of Jackson Square and St. Louis Cathedral, with a suitable decor, perhaps a wrought-iron façade and more gas lamps. Twenty years from now and the Vieux Carré may well be a Disneyland Française of high-rise slave quarters full of Yankee tourists looking out at other Yankee tourists, the whole nestled in the neutral ground between expressways. The only catch is that the Yankee is not that dumb. When he wants synthetic charm he can buy it in Anaheim and he can find the real thing in Mexico.

If New Orleans has the good sense of St. Louis and Pittsburgh, which had much less to work with, it will at whatever cost save the Quarter and open it up to the River, thus creating the most charming European enclave, indeed the only one, in the country.

These are some of the troubles, and there are many others. But the luck of New Orleans is that its troubles usually have their saving graces. New Orleans was the original slave market, a name to frighten Tidewater Negroes, the place where people were sold like hogs, families dismembered, and males commercially exploited, the females sexually exploited. And yet it was New Orleans which hit upon jazz, a truly happy and truly American sound which bears little relation to the chamber music of Brubeck and Mulligan.

There is nearly always an *and yet*. Take the mass media. One might have supposed that New Orleans, with its history of colorful journalistic dissent, its high-toned Creole literary journals, its pistol-toting American editors, would be entitled to the liveliest journalism in the South. What has happened here instead is that the national trend toward newspaper monopoly has taken a particularly depressing form. The *Times-Picayune* is a fat, dull, mediocre newspaper which might as well be the house organ of its advertisers. Even the local Catholic archdiocesan weekly, hardly an exciting genre, offers a more provocative sampling of opinion on its editorial page. It runs Buckley next to Ralph McGill. The great debate in the *Picayune* is generally carried on between David Lawrence and Russell Kirk. It is not as bad as the Jackson *Clarion-Ledger* or the Dallas *Morning News* but it is not as good a newsgatherer as Hodding Carter's small-town daily up the River. The best that can be said of the *Picayune* is that, being money-oriented, it does have money virtues. It is against stealing. In Louisiana this is not a virtue to be sneezed at. And even though the *Picayune* supported Governor Jimmy Davis, composer of "You Are My Sunshine," and the most lugubrious disaster ever to overtake any state, it has served over the years as the sole deterrent to the merry thieves both in Baton Rouge and in New Orleans who otherwise would have stolen everything.

And yet. And yet there is WDSU-TV, owned by the Stern family, a sparkling oasis in the wasteland. It actually performs the duties of a medium. Its news staff is one of the best in the country.

It cries when foul is committed and holds its nose when something stinks.

One might have supposed, too, that the old Jesuit-owned CBS outlet, WWL, would shed some of John XXIII's sweetness and light among rancorous Louisiana Christians, to say nothing of the Ku Klux Klansmen to the north. But although WWL radio is a powerful clear-channel station which covers the entire Southeast, its most enduring contribution to the national morale has been its broadcast of H. L. Hunt's *Lifelines*, twice a day, year after year. Millions of farmers get the word about the wicked United States government while they milk their cows in the morning and thousands of taxi drivers hear it on their way home at night. If the South once again secedes from the Union and throws in with Rhodesia and South Africa, the Jesuits are entitled to a share of the credit.

And yet there is Jesuit Father Louis Twomey, who has done more than any one man hereabouts to translate Catholic social principles into meaningful action. His Institute of Human Relations has performed valuable services in labor-management conciliation, in its campaign for social justice for the Negro, and in the education of the unskilled.

And there is Loyola University, which under new leadership is doing some admirable things in science and the humanities. As one professor expressed it: "We may be broke and we may not make it, but if we go down, we're going down in style."

Loyola sits cheek and jowl with Tulane University, which is in a fair way of becoming the first first-class university in the Deep South, although it has money problems, too, and it will probably never be able to compete for scholars and professors with Princeton and Stanford. What Tulane and Loyola should do is capitalize on the unique Creole-American flavor of their city and merge to form Greater Tulane University on the Oxford model, of which Loyola would be the Catholic college. It would be like Beauregard's Zouaves joining the Army of Northern Virginia. Clerical and anti-clerical elements would be embroiled in a fruitful melee without which either party tends to become slack and ingrown. Such an institution would be as unique as New Orleans itself, or as the Napoleonic Code of Louisiana and the civil "parish." It could well be more catholic than a Catholic school and less dogmatic than a secular school.

New Orleans has the ideological flavor of a Latin enclave in a Southern Scotch–Irish mainland. There is a certain inner rigidity softened at the edges by Southern social amiability. Catholics tend often to be more Catholic than the Pope. There are always jokes going around about how Pope John XXIII had to die in his sleep to get to heaven (i.e., awake, he'd be selling out to the Communists). Protestants are more conscious of being *not* Catholic, are indeed like Protestants of old. Unitarians are more anti-Trinitarian, anti-clericals more anti-clerical; Freudians more Freudian; anti-fluoridationists more passionate.

For all their orthodoxy, the churches—and synagogues—have not exactly distinguished themselves in the recent years of racial turmoil. William Styron said that the Negro was betrayed in the South by those two institutions best equipped to help him, the law and religion. In New Orleans the law has somewhat redeemed itself. The homegrown judges of the Fifth Circuit Court of Appeals have shouldered almost the entire burden of racial justice. The Catholics, like everybody else, have been content to yield moral leadership to the federal bench. Parochial schools integrate only when public schools are forced to. Protestants and Jews are by and large silent. The Episcopalians throughout the state have had their hands full with a different sort of problem, namely, staving off a coup d'église by their own Birchers.

And yet. The first Negro Catholic bishop in the United States was recently installed in New Orleans and has been received warmly. It is something to see him go into a Birchy parish and confirm a mixed bag of little blacks and whites and afterwards stand outside with his shepherd's crook, shaking hands with the parishioners and talking with them in the kinfolk idiom Southerners use. "Let me see now, Bishop Perry, where did you say you come from? New Iberia? Do you know so-and-so?"

The new white archbishop, Philip M. Hannan, moreover, is a man acutely aware of the needs of the poor and of the scandal of preaching the Gospel in air-conditioned churches to people who do not have inside toilets.

And yet again. The Protestant political hegemony in Louisiana has produced John McKeithen. He is in the Huey Long populist tradition but without the Long megalomania and he seems to be honest in the bargain. Recently McKeithen ran for governor against a wild segregationist (a native of Indiana), came out flat for equal opportunity, and beat his man overwhelmingly.

The peculiar virtue of New Orleans, like St. Theresa, may be that of the Little Way, a talent for everyday life rather than the heroic deed. If in its two hundred and fifty years of history it has produced no giants, no Lincolns, no Lees, no Faulkners, no Thoreaus, it has nurtured a great many people who live tolerably, like to talk and eat, laugh a good deal, manage generally to be civil and at the same time mind their own business. Such virtues may have their use nowadays. Take food, the everyday cooking and eating thereof. It may be a more reliable index of a city's temper than mean family income. If New Orleans has no great restaurants, it has many good ones. From France it inherited that admirable institution, the passable neighborhood restaurant. I attach more than passing significance to the circumstance that a man who stops for a bite in Birmingham or Detroit or Queens, spends as little time eating as possible and comes out feeling poisoned, evil-tempered, and generally ill-disposed toward his fellowman; and that the same man can go around the corner in New Orleans, take his family and spend two hours with his bouillabaisse or crawfish bisque (which took two days to fix). It is probably no accident that it was in Atlanta, which has many civic virtues but very bad food, that a dyspeptic restaurateur took out after Negroes with an ax handle and was elected governor by a million Georgians ulcerated by years of Rotary luncheons.

But it is Mardi Gras which most vividly illustrates the special promise of New Orleans and its special problems. Despite the accusations leveled against it—of commercialization, discrimination, homosexual routs—Mardi Gras is by and large an innocent and admirable occasion. Unlike other civic-commercial shows, Macy's parade, cotton carnivals, apple and orange festivals (and a noteworthy Midwestern dairy fete which crowns its queen Miss Artificial Insemination), Mardi Gras is in fact celebrated by nearly everybody in a good-sized city. As the day dawns, usually wet and cold, one can see whole families costumed and masked beginning the trek to Canal Street from the remotest suburbs, places which are otherwise indistinguishable from Levittown.

The carnival balls which have been going on now every night for the past two months end tonight with the Comus and Rex balls. There is a widespread resentment of the parades and balls among tourists and folk recently removed from Michigan and Oklahoma who discover they can't get in. The balls and parades are private affairs put on by "krewes." A "krewe" is a private social group, sometimes an eating club, which stages a ball and perhaps a parade. Some seventy balls, elaborate, expensive affairs, are held between Twelfth Night and Ash Wednesday. The older krewes are quite snooty but even they are not socially exclusive in the same sense, as, say, poor-but-proud Charleston society. In New Orleans money works, too. Here, where Protestant business ethic meets Creole snobbishness, the issue is a kind of money pedigree. Like Bourbon whiskey, the money can't be too green, but on the other hand it doesn't have to be two hundred years old.

The carnival ball itself is a mildly preposterous formal charade. It is a singular occasion for one good reason. Unlike the rest of American society, the balls, the parades, the krewes, the entire carnival season, even the decorating, are managed by men. Women have nothing to say about it. Even the queens are chosen by the all-male krewes at sessions which can be as fierce as a GM proxy fight. New Orleanians may joke about politics and war, heaven and hell, but they don't joke about society. This male dominance is probably more admirable than otherwise in a national culture where most males seem content to be portrayed as drudge and boob, a nitwitted Dagwood who leaves everything to Mama.

What is right and valuable about carnival in New Orleans is that it is a universal celebration of a public occasion by private, social, and neighborhood groups. It is thus an organic, viable folk festival, perhaps the only one in the United States.

What is wrong seems to have gone wrong inadvertently and almost by bad luck. It is this: while the unquaint white Protestant businessman is now very much a part of it, the emerging Negro, the sober unquaint middle-class Negro, is left out. Mardi Gras is the least of the Negro's troubles but is nevertheless a neat instance of his finding himself curiously invisible, present yet unaccounted for. For there is hardly a place for him in the entire publicly sponsored "official" celebration of Mardi Gras. White Orleanians will point out that the Negroes have their own Mardi Gras over on Dryades Street. They do. There is, moreover, a Negro parade, headed by King Zulu, who traditionally gets drunk and falls off the float while the parade founders. These doings were all quite innocent and unself-conscious and pleased everyone, black and white, though for different reasons. It was only a few years ago, in fact, that Louis Armstrong consented to be King Zulu. But for better or worse, times have changed. It is harder and harder to find a Negro to play the happy-go-lucky clown who, in a symbolically appropriate role, loses his way and passes out cold in the street.

New Orleans's people—black and white—may yet manage to get on the right road. The city may still detour hell but it will take some doing. *Le craps* was introduced to the New World by a Creole. Now the stakes are too high to let ride on the roll of the dice. If they do, Johnny Crapaud and his American cousin will surely crap out.

1968

THE CITY OF
THE DEAD

The title is not quite ironic and only slightly ambiguous. It refers mainly of course to the remarkable cemeteries of New Orleans, true cities of the dead, and to a certain liveliness about them. But it also refers to my own perception of New Orleans as being curiously dispirited in those very places where it advertises itself as being most alive; for example, its business community and its official celebration, Mardi Gras. Compared with Dallas and Houston and Atlanta, New Orleans is dead from the neck up, having no industry to speak of except the port and the tourists— happily for some of us who wouldn't have it otherwise, unhappily for half the young blacks who are unemployed. As for Mardi Gras, boredom sets in early when Rex—"Lord of Misrule," as he is called, though he never quite looks the part, a middle-aged businessman—toasts his queen at the Boston Club, daughter of another middle-aged businessman. The boredom approaches deep coma at the famous balls, which are as lively as high-school tableaux. The real live festival of Mardi Gras takes place elsewhere, in the byways, in the neighborhood truck parades. As for famous old Bourbon Street, it is little more now than standard U.S. sleaze, the same tired old strippers grinding away, T-shirt shops, New Orleans jazz gone bad, art gone bad, same old $32 painting of same old bayou.

The cemeteries, true cities of the dead, seem at once livelier and more exotic to the visitor newly arrived, say, from the upper Protestant South where cemeteries are sedate "memorial gardens," or from New York City, where mile after mile of Queens is strewn with gray stone, a vast gloomy moraine. A New Orleans cemetery is a city in miniature, streets, curbs, iron fences, its tombs above ground—otherwise, the coffins would float out of the ground—little two-story dollhouses complete with doorstep and lintel. The older cemeteries are more haphazard, tiny lanes as crooked as old Jerusalem, meandering aimlessly between the cottages of the dead. I remember being a pallbearer at St. Louis No. 1, one of the oldest cemeteries, stepping across corners and lots like Gulliver in Lilliput. The tombs are generally modest duplexes, one story per tenant, for good and practical reasons. It could actually accommodate an extended Creole family, for, given a decent interval when presumably coffin and tenant had gone to dust, the bones were shoved back into a deep crypt at the rear, room for one and all. After all these years a bothersome question of my childhood was answered: Where will people live when cemeteries take up all the space on earth?

They, the little cities, are liveliest on All Saints' and All Souls' Day when families turn out to fix up the family tomb, polishing or whitewashing the stone, scrubbing the doorstep for all the world like Baltimore housewives scrubbing the white steps of row houses. Not many years ago the lady of the house might be directing black servants in this annual housekeeping, as much mistress here of the dead as of the living at home. There are still iron benches in place where Creole ladies, dressed in the highest winter fashion, received friends all day. Even now, All Saints' and All Souls' have a more festive air than otherwise—should they not?—startlingly different from the unctuous solemnity of Forest Lawn. Crowds throng the tiny streets, housekeeping for the dead, setting out flowers real and plastic, perhaps regilding the lettering, while vendors hawk candy and toys for the children, and on All Souls' saying a not noticeably sad prayer or two for the dead.

Mark Twain once said that New Orleans had no architecture to speak of except in the cemeteries. As usual, he exaggerated, because the Spanish houses and their courtyards in the "French" Quarter and the little Victorian cottages, "shotguns," all over town are charming and unique. But on approaching New Orleans, one might well agree with Mark Twain. The major architectural addition in the past hundred years is the Superdome and the skyline looks like standard U.S. glass high-rises set like Stonehenge around a giant Ban roll-on. Not so in the cemeteries, where every conceivable style is rendered by taste or whim, from the simple two-storied "beehive" to toy Greek and Egyptian temples and even miniature cathedrals—to a small artificial mountain containing the mauseoleum of the Army of the Tennessee, General Albert Sydney Johnston atop, astride his horse and still in command. The great Texas general gazes at Robert E. Lee himself atop his column across town. It is easy to imagine a slightly bemused expression on the faces of these stern Anglo-Saxon commanders as they contemplate between them this their greatest city and yet surely the one place in the South most foreign to them.

1984

GOING BACK TO
GEORGIA

&

It is a pleasure and an honor to be invited here to Athens for the Ferdinand Phinizy Lecture. I may as well make a clean breast of it at the outset and admit that I am a member of the Phinizy family and that it is probably nepotism that got me here—even though nepotism implies a nephew relationship and I am not Phinizy Spalding's nephew. Actually, we're first cousins. But perhaps there are instances where nepotism is not only pardonable but justified. And this is surely one of them. I mean, how else can a poor novelist living in the boondocks of Louisiana be expected to support himself if not by kinship relations and occasional largesse from Georgia, which has emerged as the leading state of the Sunbelt, mother of Presidents, major source of national political leadership, to say nothing of Georgia–Arab banking alliances from which Louisiana is altogether excluded. (Lacking Georgia expertise, we in Louisiana have been trying for years to sell the Superdome to the Arabs, with a singular lack of success.)

Georgia, that is to say, has changed, and what I propose to talk about briefly, and a little more seriously, has to do with the nature of this extraordinary phenomenon of change, change in the South, the United States, as well as in Georgia. It is impossible, for example, to drive through Atlanta without thinking about this phenomenon—especially if one had been used to the Atlanta of the 1930s. I avoid the Chamber of Commerce word "progress" because it does not do sufficient justice to the ambiguity of the change.

I'd like to give you two small personal instances of what I mean. I used to live here in Athens. It was a long time ago and I've been here only occasionally since. When I thought of coming back to Athens, two oddly assorted memories came to mind. Driving in, we passed the place on Milledge Avenue where I used to live. It was my grandmother's house, a fine old 1890 Victorian mansion, now vanished, gone with the wind, replaced by a sorority house apparently conceived as a Hollywood–Selznick version of Tara. Now, I have nothing against sororities, and this building is undoubtedly better suited to the needs of sorority life. Yet there is a certain ambiguity about the change. It is a change in this case from the reality of a slowly recovering South of the 1890s, a business-minded and mercantile South, a reality we shared with the rest of the country—back to a reality of a more dubious character, a reality with certain mythic and romantic components which may or may not do us much good.

The other thing I remembered about living in Athens was the time I met and shook the hand of the great Catfish Smith, All-American end for the University of Georgia. I was a small boy and I was flying a model airplane in Sanford Stadium. It flew into the middle of a Georgia scrimmage. A player brought it over to me, none other than the legendary Catfish Smith; he said a few words, admired the plane, shook my hand, and went back to the game.

I mention this extremely nonmemorable event in order to call attention to the magnitude of the change which has occurred since. You know, historical change can be so profound, so swift, so all-encompassing that those caught up in it may in a sense lose their reference points and so may not be able to grasp its significance. It may take another hundred years before somebody can look back and see what is really happening now. What I am saying is that it struck me at the time as a memorable event to meet an All-American end from Georgia. Now a Georgian is President of the United States and no one gives it a second thought. If anybody had proposed in the 1930s that a Southerner, even a Northern Southerner, a Virginian, or Kentuckian, could be elected President of the United States in our lifetime, no one would have taken him seriously.

What is notable is that people all over the country either like or dislike President Carter but almost invariably do so for reasons which have nothing to do with his Southern origins.

But there is another related change, or rather possibility of change, which I think has been insufficiently noticed, but which we had better be aware of if we are to have anything to say about the future course of the change. For, beyond a doubt, the change is occurring and has already occurred—again so momentous a change that we are, I think, only vaguely aware of its implications.

The change can be expressed by two simple propositions, one of which seems to me axiomatic, the other perhaps a bit more problematic. One, the South has entered the mainstream of American life for the first time in perhaps a hundred and fifty years; that is, in a sense in which it had not been the case since perhaps the 1820s or 1830s. Not only that, but through a strange repetition of history and conjunction of circumstances, perhaps a faltering of national purpose, perhaps the ongoing economic and political power shift to the Southern Rim, perhaps also because of a Southern talent for politics, the burden of national leadership may well fall to the South for better or worse, just as it did in the early 1800s, then certainly for better. The question now is: Which is it going to be now, better or worse? The question also is: Are we even aware of what is happening? We know something is changing, and changing fast, but do we know what it is?

You drive through Atlanta (or, for that matter, Dallas or Houston) and take a look around, and up, and you wonder, what is this place? Is this a place? What's going on here? Is this place trying to outdo New York or be something new under the sun? Is this progress, and if it is progress, is progress good or bad or both, and if both, how do you tell the good from the bad?

Like most great historical changes, the change happens before our inkling of it and before its consequences begin to dawn on us. It is really a bit too much to take in, considering the history of the past one hundred and fifty years. The South in its present state might be compared to a man who has had a bad toothache for as long as he can remember and has all of a sudden gotten over it.

So constant and nagging had been the pain that he had long since come to accept it as the normal unpleasant condition of his existence. In fact, he could not imagine life without it. How does such a man spend his time, energies, talents, mental capacities? In seeking relief from the pain, by drugs, anesthesia, distraction, war, whatever—or, failing that, by actually enjoying the pain, the way one probes an aching tooth with one's tongue.

Then one morning he wakes to find the pain gone. At first he doesn't know what has happened, except that things are different, radically different. Then he realizes what has happened and takes pleasure in it. He can't believe his good fortune. But, as time goes on, he discovers that he is faced with a new and somewhat unsettling problem. The problem is, what is he going to do with himself now that he no longer has the pain to worry about, the tooth to tongue?

What has happened, of course, is that for the first time in a hundred and fifty years the South and Southerners, and I mean both black and white Southerners, no longer suffer the unique onus, the peculiar burden of race which came to be part of the very connotation of the word "South." I am not going to argue about what was good and what was bad about the South's racial experience—we're only interested here in what was uniquely oppressive for both white and black and which has now vanished. And to say that it has vanished is not to suggest that there do not remain serious, even critical, areas of race relations in all of American society, the South included.

Such troubles are well known. What is not at all well known is the consequence of this particular historical change. Now that this peculiar preoccupation which engaged Southern energies for so long has been removed, what will be the impact of this suddenly released energy? Or will there be an impact?

But first let me give you an instance or two of what I mean by the siphoning off of Southern talent, by the obsessive tonguing of this particular tooth. The figure "a hundred and fifty years" I got from the history books. But from my own experience, say the past fifty years, I can give you a simple example of what I have in mind. During my lifetime and up until a few years ago, I cannot recall a single talented Southern politician (and only the rare writer) who was not obsessed with the problem of the relation of white people and black people. It was in fact for better or worse the very condition of being Southern.

To give you the first names that come to mind: Senator Richard Russell of Georgia, an extraordinarily able and talented man, a man of great character and rectitude. Yet during the many years I recall reading about him, what he was mainly noted for was his skill in devising parliamentary tactics to defeat or delay this or that voting-rights bill.

I think next of my own kinsman, William Alexander Percy, who devoted a large part of his autobiography to defending the South against "Northern liberals." He wrote a whole chapter in defense of sharecropping. Again, I am not interested in arguing the issue, pro or con, though I feel sure that in his place and his time I'd have felt the same defensiveness and would probably have written similar polemics.

Then I think of the novelist Richard Wright, who never really came to terms with his Southernness, his Americanness, or for that matter his blackness.

The point of course is that the South does not now need defending. That is the astounding dimension of the change. The virtues and defects of the South are the virtues and defects of the nation. At least as far as writers are concerned, it does not now occur to a serious writer in the North to attack the South or to a serious Southern writer to defend the South. I think it is a healthy thing that, as a writer, I feel free to satirize both South and North.

Now it is possible for a black writer like Toni Morrison to write a novel which is not about North and South as such, nor about white or black as such, nor about white versus black, but about people.

I cannot speak for the politician, but to a writer it appears that what needs not so much defending as understanding, transforming, reconciling, healing, or affirming is not the Southern experience but the American experience. And since every writer must write of his own experience—or else he doesn't write at all—the Southern writer necessarily writes of the South, but he writes of it in terms which are translatable to the American experience and, if he is any good, ultimately to the human experience.

Consider, for example, two Southern novelists who lived during this period of the long Southern obsession and who were great enough to transcend it. They are William Faulkner and Flannery O'Connor. And they had their problems. O'Connor succeeded, I think, largely by steering clear of it—with a couple of notable exceptions. Mainly she stuck to whites, figuring, I guess, that whites had enough troubles with themselves without dragging in white-black troubles. Faulkner wobbled. He was at his best in *The Sound and the Fury* with Dilsey and her relationship with the Compsons—no one will ever surpass him on these grounds. But he could also drift into sentimental paternalism and even at times sound like a Mississippi secessionist.

This brings us to what is, to me at least, the central and most intriguing question of all and one to which I do not pretend to have an answer. It is this: How, into what channels, will Southern energies be directed now that the obsession is behind us? Will Southerners have a distinctive contribution to make—say, in politics or literature? Or will they simply meld into the great American flux?

One possible future is fairly obvious, is indeed already upon us. To many, this is the future which is not only expected but also, it seems to go without saying, desirable. It is of course the ongoing shift in population and economic power to the Sunbelt. One can simply extrapolate the future from what is happening here and now in the Southern United States, from Hilton Head to Dallas and indeed—and this is what worries me—on to Phoenix and Los Angeles. The likeliest and, to me, the not wholly desirable future of the region is an ever more prosperous Southern Rim stretching from coast to coast, an L.A.–Dallas–Atlanta axis (the Atlanta of the Omni and the Peachtree Plaza); an agribusiness–sports–vacation–retirement–show-biz culture with its spiritual center perhaps at Oral Roberts U., its economic capital in Dallas–Houston, its media center in Atlanta, its entertainment industry shared by Disney World, the Superdome, and Hollywood. In this scenario the coastal plain of the old Southeast will be preserved as a kind of historical museum, much like Williamsburg.

I don't say that this prospect is all bad. It is probably better than the hard times suffered by the South from 1865 to 1935. I only wish to take note of what is already happening. And one doesn't have to be a prophet to predict with considerable confidence that sooner or later the failing Northern cities must either be abandoned or be bailed out by some kind of domestic Marshall Plan—and why not, after all? Everyone else has benefited: Germany, Italy, Japan, Guatemala—everyone except of course the defeated Confederacy after the Civil War. The great cities must be saved and they will be, and guess who will be paying the freight for the next twenty or thirty years; that is, guess who will be paying more than their share of federal taxes while Detroiters, New Yorkers, Bostonians pay less? The taxpayers of the Southern Rim. And perhaps this is not only as it should be but, I must confess, it gives a certain satisfaction if it should come to that, the South having to save the Union. After all, it is our turn.

So far, we are talking about economics and climate and such simple home truths as the fact that a great many people who live in Michigan or Cleveland or Buffalo would rather live in Florida or Georgia or Tucson and that many have in fact moved, and that it costs less to run a factory in Louisiana and Texas than it does in New England or Ohio.

Undoubtedly then, the lower Mississippi between Baton Rouge and New Orleans will become, is already becoming, the American equivalent of the Ruhr Valley. In the year 2000, Peachtree Street may have replaced Madison Avenue. Pittsburgh may well be known as the Birmingham of the North.

I find these possibilities quite likely but not terribly interesting and certainly not decisive insofar as the real issues of the future are concerned. They represent economic inevitabilities, more or less what was bound to happen once the South with its advantages in climate, resources, and energy got past the historic disaster which befell it, mainly as a piece of extreme bad luck when two unrelated events turned up at the same time, the invention of the cotton gin and the availability of slave labor, and when it came to pass that the two, put together, were extremely profitable— profitable to some, that is, at the expense of a great many others. When I say expense, I am thinking not merely of economic exploitation but of the massive expenditure of political, intellectual, literary, and emotional energies required to defend the old system.

But what is more interesting than the present economic resurgence of the South is the question I hinted at earlier: How will Southern talent, brains, and energy express themselves apart from business enterprise, which we already know about and which is not only all to the good but indispensable—because, for one thing, and from the point of view of a writer, if businessmen and -women did not prosper and make money, who would buy our books?—but how will these energies be expressed in such fields as politics and literature now that the old burden is removed? In a word and in the case of those of you who are the future Richard Russells and Walter Georges and William Faulkners and Flannery O'Connors and Allen Tates—what will you be doing twenty years from now? If you are going to be successful businessmen and -women, well and good, but we already know that. It is the future of the other enterprises that we don't know.

One thing is certain: you will not have Southern slavery or Southern racial segregation either to defend or to attack; in short, to be preoccupied with. You won't be able to blame Northern liberals for your troubles. And if you're a Northern liberal, you won't have the South to blame. We whites can blame the blacks if we want to and the blacks can blame the whites, but it won't really work as well in the future as it did in the past.

In this context and in speculating about what the future holds, one can't help but wonder what it was like to live in the South before the bad thing happened, however one might wish to express the bad thing: getting seduced by the economics of cotton and slavery, or, as Faulkner would have put it in stronger language, the country committing what amounted to its own Original Sin and suffering the commensurate curse. I am thinking of the times in both colonial and revolutionary America and in the early 1800s when Southerners felt free to develop their talents and energies, both as Southerners and as Americans, business and agricultural talents, political talents, technical talents, artistic and creative talents. I suspect they felt much as Southerners are beginning to feel now; that is, conscious of being Southerners, yes, and glad of it, not especially self-consciously so, but rather as members of a new society where one is both challenged by a remarkable new world and remarkably free to respond to the challenge.

I am no historian but I take it as a commonplace that the early Southern political and juridical talent was unusual. One thinks of the Virginians—Jefferson, Madison, Monroe, Marshall—but also of Oglethorpe, and there were many others. It is not difficult in fact to defend the thesis that the U.S. Constitution as well as the Declaration of Independence were largely Southern creations.

If there were such a thing as a Southern gift for politics in the larger sense, not just the knack of getting elected or of filibustering in the Senate, but in the sense of discerning what is the greater good of the people, that is, the commonweal, and how best to bring it to pass, I wonder if we have not now come into a new age when these same energies are once again free to do just that.

The case for the arts is less clear and always was. If one tries to think, for example, of writers of the first rank in the early South—or for that matter the South before the publication of *The Sound and the Fury* and the Vanderbilt poets and critics—that is, of writers who were not overwhelmed by the political obsession which overwhelmed every Southern politician from Senator Calhoun to Senator Russell, it is difficult to get beyond Edgar Allan Poe, and perhaps the only thing that saved him was his preoccupation with his own personal demons.

The fact is, there was never any question about the political talent of the South, even when it was badly sidetracked, and even now there is no difficulty in seeing signs of a renascence in a new breed of Southern politicians, white and black.

But it also seems to be the case that the South has not yet had the time—paradoxically enough, for the republic is two hundred years old—to produce those ultimate incarnations of great cultures, its true cultural heroes—and I'm not talking about politicians and generals. In this connection, I'd like to quote a man I greatly admire, James McBride Dabbs of South Carolina. Some years ago he wrote: "The South could create neither poets nor saints—I mean, great region-shaping poets and saints. For it is such persons as these that shape a region, though first the region must have, by the grace of God, sufficient energy and unconscious purpose to create the poets and saints. They, as they come into being, offer a criticism of life. They create in art, and in life itself, the image of their world, of their time and their region, seen under the aspect of eternity. They substantiate, and they make substantial, the soul of their people. Looking at them and their works, their fellows see where they are trying to go, wherein they have succeeded and wherein they have failed. The poets and saints offer us a criticism of life, not just of life in the abstract but of our life now. The poets see our world; the saints—usually—live in it, in all its richness, complexity, and ambiguity, against a simplicity that lies at the heart both of the world and of themselves . . . Since the South was never able to create poets in prose or verse, or saints, *it never really quarreled with itself.* As we shall see when we come to discuss politics, it became, on the contrary, adept at quarreling with others, and for this purpose it developed the instruments of rhetoric and eloquence."

I think he is probably right. Lee was the nearest thing we had to a saint—and it is no accident that our saint was a general. Faulkner and Tate are perhaps the nearest we have to great cosmos-shaping poets and it is no accident that what they achieved was done so almost in spite of the political passions to which they periodically fell prey.

But since Dabbs wrote these words, it has become a new ball game. Somewhere, in the sixties maybe and thanks to white people like Dabbs and black people like Martin Luther King, we got back on the track we either left of our own accord or got pushed off in the 1830s.

I am not qualified to talk about sanctity, but what about the present state and the future of literature in the South? The so-called Southern renascence is over—that is, the remarkable thirty years or so when writers like Faulkner, O'Connor, Welty, Richard Wright, and Caldwell traded on the very exoticness, the uniqueness of the Southern phenomenon. It was a rich vein to mine and Faulkner, Warren, O'Connor, Tate-and-company pretty well mined it out. So, the Southern novelist today finds himself in a transition period analogous to the political situation of the South itself. Now he, too, like his fellow novelists in the Western world, is faced with the larger questions about the dilemma, not of the poor white or the poor black, decadent gentry, but of modern urban and suburban man. He can't imitate Faulkner and O'Connor, or at least he'd better not try. In the present context, that of the political reentry of the South into the American mainstream, the writer's dilemma takes on a peculiar and even paradoxical coloration. I'll give you one example of this rather baffling divergence of attitudes. President Carter has often said that the American people are good, fundamentally sound, sensible, and generous; in a word, much better than their politicians, who often fail to live up to them. I find it hard to disagree with him. On the other hand, the American novelist seems to be saying something quite different; namely, that something has gone badly wrong with Americans and with American life, indeed modern life, and that people are suffering from a deep dislocation in their lives, alienation from themselves, dehumanization, and so on—and I'm not talking about poverty, racial discrimination, and women's rights.

I'm talking about the malaise which seems to overtake the very people who seem to have escaped these material and social evils—the successful middle class. What engages the novelist's attention now is not the Snopeses or the denizens of Tobacco Road or Flannery O'Connor's half-mad backwoods preachers or a black underclass. It is rather the very people who have overcome these particular predicaments and find themselves living happily ever after in their comfortable exurban houses and condominiums. Or is it happily ever after? Either the novelists are all crazy or something has gone badly wrong here, something which has nothing to do with poverty or blackness or whiteness. The characters in most current novels are not nearly as nice as the people President Carter describes.

Then who is right, President Carter or the novelists? It is possible that both are, that it is the politician's function from Jefferson to Carter to inspire people to live up to the best that is in them, and that it is the novelist's vocation from Dostoevsky to Faulkner to explore the darker recesses of the human heart, there to name and affirm the strange admixture of good and evil, the action of the demonic, the action of grace, of courage and cowardice, of courage coming out of cowardice and vice versa; in a word, the strange human creature himself—an admixture now that is perhaps stranger than ever.

So now we'll see. I have no idea whether in the year 2000 we—and by "we" I mean you of the Southeast, the old Confederacy—will simply have become a quaint corner of the teeming prosperous Southern Rim, some hundred million people with its population center and its spiritual heartland somewhere between Dallas and L.A., whether your best writers will be doing soap opera in Atlanta, your best composers country-and-Western in Nashville, your best film directors making sequels to *Walking Tall* and *Macon County Line* in Hollywood, whether our supreme architectural achievement will be the Superdome, our supreme cultural achievement will be the year Alabama ranked number one, the Falcons won the Super Bowl, and another Bobby Jones made it a grand slam at Augusta.

There is nothing wrong with any of these achievements. The name of the game is always excellence, excellence in business, politics, literature, or sports—which is why I admired Catfish Smith. The difference is that now the door is open to all fields and the South, like the rest of the country, has no excuses.

Of course, something else could happen in the old Southeast, something besides the building of new Hyatts and Hiltons and the preserving of old buildings, something comparable to the astonishing burst of creative energy in Virginia two hundred years ago.

I will say this: We have at least gotten past the point Mr. Dabbs spoke of when he said the trouble with the South was that it could not quarrel with itself. Not only do I feel free to quarrel with the South, or the North, or the United States, but as a Southerner and glad to be one, I feel obliged to.

One nice lady in my home town said to me the other day: "You're just like certain other Southern writers—no sooner do you get published in New York than you turn on the South and criticize it." I didn't have the nerve but I felt like saying: "You're damn right, lady. I sure do."

But whichever way it goes, Sunbelt or Southeastern renascence, one thing is certain: the Southerner will be, is already, much more like his ancestor in 1830 than he is like his ancestor in 1930. That is, he is both Southern and American, but much more like other Americans than he is different. If he is black, he may discover to his amazement that he is much more like his white countrymen, for better and worse, than he is like Ugandans. He, like most of us, is out to make a life for himself, to make money, build a house, raise a family, buy an RV, a Sony Trinitron, whatever.

Well and good. Whether he gets around to doing anything else with his time, time will tell. I can only speak for myself: it would be nice to think he might once in a while write a book or read one, or at least buy one.

1978

MISSISSIPPI: THE FALLEN PARADISE

❧

A little more than one hundred years ago, a Mississippi regiment dressed its ranks and started across a meadow toward Cemetery Ridge, a minor elevation near Gettysburg. There, crouched behind a stone wall, the soldiers of the Army of the Potomac waited and watched with astonishment as the gray-clads advanced as casually as if they were on parade. The Mississippians did not reach the wall. One soldier managed to plant the regimental colors within an arm's length before he fell. The University Grays, a company made up of students from the state university, suffered a loss of precisely one hundred percent of its members killed or wounded in the charge.

These were good men. It was an honorable fight and there were honorable men on both sides of it. The issue was settled once and for all, perhaps by this very charge. The honorable men on the losing side, men like General Lee, accepted the verdict.

One hundred years later, Mississippians were making history of a different sort. If their record in Lee's army is unsurpassed for valor and devotion to duty, present-day Mississippi is mainly renowned for murder, church burning, dynamiting, assassination, night-riding, not to mention the lesser forms of terrorism. The students of the university celebrated the Centennial by a different sort of warfare and in the company of a different sort of general. It is not frivolous to compare the characters of General Edwin

Walker and General Lee, for the contrast is symptomatic of a broader change in leadership in this part of the South. In any event, the major claim to fame of the present-day university is the Ole Miss football team and the assault of the student body upon the person of one man, an assault of bullying, spitting, and obscenities. The bravest Mississippians in recent years have not been Confederates or the sons of Confederates but rather two Negroes, James Meredith and Medgar Evers.

As for the Confederate flag, once the battle ensign of brave men, it has come to stand for raw racism and hoodlum defiance of the law. An art professor at Ole Miss was bitterly attacked for "desecrating" the Stars and Bars when he depicted the flag as it was used in the 1962 riot—with curses and obscenities. The truth was that it had been desecrated long before.

No ex-Mississippian is entitled to write with any sense of moral superiority of the tragedy which has overtaken his former state. For he cannot be certain in the first place that if he had stayed he would not have kept silent—or worse. And he strongly suspects that he would not have been counted among the handful, an editor here, a professor there, a clergyman yonder, who not only did not keep silent but fought hard.

What happened to this state? Assuredly it faced difficult times after the Supreme Court decision of 1954 and subsequent court injunctions which required painful changes in customs of long standing. Yet the change has been made peacefully in other states of the South. In Georgia before the 1965 voting bill was passed by Congress, over thirty-nine percent of Negroes of voting age were registered to vote. In Mississippi the figure was around six percent.

What happened is both obvious and obscure. What is obvious is that Mississippi is poor, largely rural, and has in proportion the largest Negro minority in the United States. But Georgia shares these traits. Nor is it enough to say that Mississippi is the state that refused to change, although this is what one hears both inside and outside the state. On the contrary, Mississippi has changed several times since the Civil War. There have been times, for example, when dissent was not only possible but welcome. In 1882 George

Washington Cable, novelist and ex-Confederate cavalryman, addressed the graduating class at the University of Mississippi:

> We became distended—mired and stuffed with conservatism to the point of absolute rigidity. Our life had little or nothing to do with the onward movement of the world's thought. We were in danger of becoming a civilization that was not a civilization, because there was not in it the element of advancement.

His address was warmly received by the newspapers of the region. It is interesting to speculate how these remarks would be received today at Ole Miss, if indeed Cable would be allowed to speak at all.

Two significant changes have occurred in the past generation. The most spectacular is the total defeat of the old-style white moderate and the consequent collapse of the alliance between the "good" white man and the Negro, which has figured more or less prominently in Mississippi politics since Reconstruction days. Except for an oasis or two like Greenville, the influential white moderate is gone. To use Faulkner's personae, the Gavin Stevenses have disappeared and the Snopeses have won. What is more, the Snopeses' victory has surpassed even the gloomiest expectations of their creator. What happened to men like Gavin Stevens? With a few exceptions, they have shut up or been exiled or they are running the local White Citizens' Council. Not even Faulkner foresaw the ironic denouement of the tragedy: that the Compsons and Sartorises not only should be defeated by the Snopeses but in the end should join them.

Faulkner lived to see the defeat of his Gavin Stevens—the old-style good man, the humanist from Harvard and Heidelberg—but he still did not despair, because he had placed his best hope in the youth of the state. Chick Mallison in *Intruder in the Dust*, a sort of latter-day Huck Finn, actually got the Negro Lucas Beauchamp out of jail while Gavin Stevens was talking about the old alliance. But this hope has been blasted, too. The melancholy fact is the Chick Mallisons today are apt to be the worst lot of all. Ten years of indoctrination by the Citizens' Councils, racist politicians, and the most one-sided press north of Cuba has produced a generation of good-looking and ferocious young bigots.

The other change has been the emigration of the Negro from Mississippi, reducing the Negro majority to a minority for the first time in a hundred years. At the same time, great numbers of Negroes from the entire South were settling in Northern ghettos. The chief consequence has been the failure of the great cities of the North to deal with the Negro when he landed on their doorstep, or rather next door. Mississippi has not got any better, but New York and Boston and Los Angeles have got worse.

Meanwhile, there occurred the Negro revolution, and the battle lines changed. For the first time in a hundred and fifty years, the old sectional division has been blurred. It is no longer "North" versus "South" in the argument over the Negro. Instead, there has occurred a diffusion of the Negro and a dilution of the problem, with large sections of the South at least tolerating a degree of social change at the very time Northern cities were beginning to grumble seriously. It seems fair to describe the present national mood as a grudging inclination to redress the Negro's grievances—with the exception of a few areas of outright defiance like northern Louisiana, parts of Alabama, and the state of Mississippi.

It is only within the context of these social changes, I believe, that the state can be understood and perhaps some light shed upon a possible way out. For, unfavorable as these events may be, they are nevertheless ambiguous in their implication. The passing of the moderate and the victory of the Snopeses may be bad things in themselves. Yet, history being the queer business that it is, such a turn of events may be the very condition of the state's emergence from its long nightmare.

During the past ten years Mississippi as a society reached a condition which can only be described, in an analogous but exact sense of the word, as insane. The rift in its character between a genuine kindliness and a highly developed individual moral consciousness on the one hand and on the other a purely political and amoral view of "states' rights" at the expense of human rights led at last to a sundering of its very soul. Kind fathers and loving husbands, when they did not themselves commit crimes against the helpless, looked upon such crimes with indifference. Political campaigns, once the noblest public activity in the South, came to be conducted by incantation. The candidate who hollers "nigger" loudest and longest usually wins.

The language itself has been corrupted. In the Mississippi standard version of what happened, noble old English words are used, words like "freedom," "sacredness of the individual," "death to tyranny," but they have subtly changed their referents. After the Oxford riot in 1962, the Junior Chamber of Commerce published a brochure entitled *A Warning for Americans*, which was widely distributed and is still to be found on restaurant counters in Jackson along with the usual racist tracts, mammy dolls, and Confederate flags. The pamphlet purports to prove that James Meredith was railroaded into Ole Miss by the Kennedys in defiance of "normal judicial processes"—a remarkable thesis in itself, considering that the Meredith case received one of the most exhaustive judicial reviews in recent history. The "warning" for Americans was the usual contention that states' rights were being trampled by federal tyranny. "Tyranny is tyranny," reads the pamphlet. "It is the duty of every American to be alert when his freedom is endangered."

Lest the reader be complacent about Mississippi as the only state of double-think, the pamphlet was judged by the *national* Jay Cees to be the "second most worthy project of the year."

All statements become equally true and equally false, depending on one's rhetorical posture. In the end, even the rhetoric fails to arouse. When Senator Eastland declares, "There is no discrimination in Mississippi," and "All who are qualified to vote, black or white, exercise the right of suffrage," these utterances are received by friend and foe alike with a certain torpor of spirit. It does not matter that there is very little connection between Senator Eastland's utterances and the voting statistics of his home county: that of a population of 31,020 Negroes, 161 are registered to vote. Once the final break is made between language and reality, arguments generate their own force and lay out their own logical rules. The current syllogism goes something like this: 1. There is no ill-feeling in Mississippi between the races; the Negroes like things the way they are; if you don't believe it, I'll call my cook out of the kitchen and you can ask her. 2. The trouble is caused by outside agitators who are Communist-inspired. 3. Therefore, the real issue is between atheistic Communism and patriotic, God-fearing Mississippians.

Once such a system cuts the outside wires and begins to rely on its own feedback, anything becomes possible. The dimensions of the tragedy are hard to exaggerate. The sad and still incredible fact is that many otherwise decent people, perhaps even the majority of the white people in Mississippi, honestly believed that President John F. Kennedy was an enemy of the United States, if not a Communist fellow traveler.

How did it happen that a proud and decent people, a Protestant and Anglo-Saxon people with a noble tradition of freedom behind them, should have in the end become so deluded that it is difficult even to discuss the issues with them, because the common words of the language no longer carry the same meanings? How can responsible leadership have failed so completely when it did not fail in Georgia, a state with a similar social and ethnic structure?

The answer is far from clear, but several reasons suggest themselves. For one thing, as James Dabbs points out in his recent book *Who Speaks for the South?*, Mississippi was part of the Wild West of the Old South. Unlike the seaboard states, it missed the liberal eighteenth century altogether. Its tradition is closer to Dodge City than to Williamsburg. For another, the Populism of the eastern South never amounted to much here; it was corrupted from the beginning by the demagogic racism of Vardaman and Bilbo. Nor did Mississippi have its big city, which might have shared, for good and ill, in the currents of American urban life. Georgia had its Atlanta and Atlanta had the good luck or good sense to put men like Ralph McGill and Mayor Hartsfield in key positions. What was lacking in Mississippi was the new source of responsible leadership, the political realists of the matured city. The old moderate tradition of the planter-lawyer-statesman class had long since lost its influence. The young industrial interests have been remarkable chiefly for their discretion. When, for example, they did awake to the folly of former Governor Barnett's two-bit rebellion, it was too late. And so there was no one to head off the collision between the civil-rights movement and the racist coalition between redneck, demagogue, and small-town merchant. The result was insurrection.

The major source of racial moderation in Mississippi even until recent times has been, not Populism, but the white conservative tradition, with its peculiar strengths and, as it turned out, its fatal weakness. There came into being after Reconstruction an extraordinary alliance, which persisted more or less fitfully until the last world war, between the Negro and the white conservative, an alliance originally directed against the poor whites and the Radical Republicans. The fruits of this "fusion principle," as it is called, are surprising. Contrary to the current mythology of the Citizens' Councils, which depicts white Mississippians throwing out the carpetbaggers and Negroes and establishing our present "way of life" at the end of Reconstruction, the fact is that Negroes enjoyed considerably more freedom in the 1880s than they do now. A traveler in Mississippi after Reconstruction reported seeing whites and Negroes served in the same restaurants and at the same bars in Jackson.

This is not to say that there ever existed a golden age of race relations. But there were bright spots. It is true that the toleration of the Old Captains, as W. J. Cash called them, was both politically motivated and paternalistic, but it is not necessarily a derogation to say so. A man is a creature of his time—after all, Lincoln was a segregationist—and the old way produced some extraordinary men. There were many felicities in their relation with the Negro —it was not all Uncle Tomism, though it is unfashionable to say so. In any case, they lost; segregation was firmly established around 1890 and lynch law became widespread. For the next fifty years the state was dominated, with a few notable exceptions, by a corrupt Populism.

What is important to notice here is the nature of the traditional alliance between the white moderate and the Negro, and especially the ideological basis of the former's moderation, because this spirit has informed the ideal of race relations for at least a hundred years. For, whatever its virtues, the old alliance did not begin to have the resources to cope with the revolutionary currents of this century. Indeed, the world view of the old-style "good" man is almost wholly irrelevant to the present gut issue between the Negro revolt and the Snopes counterrevolution.

For one thing, the old creed was never really social or political but purely and simply moral in the Stoic sense: if you are a good man, then you will be magnanimous toward other men and especially toward the helpless and therefore especially toward the Negro. The Stoic creed worked very well—if you were magnanimous. But if one planter was just, the next might charge eighty percent interest at the plantation store, the next take the wife of his tenant, the next lease convict labor, which was better than the sharecropper system because it did not matter how hard you worked your help or how many died.

Once again, in recent years, dissent became possible. During the depression of the 1930s and afterwards there were stirrings of liberal currents not only in the enthusiasm for the economic legislation of the Roosevelt Administration but also in a new awareness of the plight of the Negro. Mississippi desperately needed the New Deal and profited enormously from it. Indeed, the Roosevelt farm program succeeded too well. Planters who were going broke on ten-cent cotton voted for Roosevelt, took federal money, got rich, lived to hate Kennedy and Johnson and vote for Goldwater—while still taking federal money. Yet there was something new in the wind after the war. Under the leadership of men like Hodding Carter in the Delta, a new form of racial moderation began to gather strength. Frank Smith, author of the book *Congressman from Mississippi*, was elected to Congress. Described by Edward Morgan as a "breath of fresh air out of a political swamp," Smith was one of the few politicians in recent years who tried to change the old racial refrain and face up to the real problems of the state. But he made the mistake of voting for such radical measures as the Peace Corps and the United Nations appropriation, and he did not conceal his friendship with President Kennedy. What was worse, he addressed mail to his constituents with a Mr. and Mrs., even when they were Negroes. Smith was euchred out of his district by the legislature and defeated in 1962 by the usual coalition of peckerwoods, super-patriots, and the Citizens' Councils.

But the most radical change has occurred in the past few years. As recently as fifteen years ago, the confrontation was still a three-cornered one, among the good white man, the bad white man, and the Negro. The issue was whether to treat the Negro well or badly. It went without saying that you could do either. Now one of the parties has been eliminated and the confrontation is face to face. "I assert my right to vote and to raise my family decently," the Negro is beginning to say. His enemies reply with equal simplicity: "We'll kill you first."

Yet the victory of the Snopeses is not altogether a bad thing. At least the choice is clarified. It would not help much now to have Gavin Stevens around with his talk about "man's struggle to the stars."

The old way is still seductive, however, and evokes responses from strange quarters. Ex-Governor Ross Barnett was recently revealed as a mellow emeritus statesman in the old style, even hearkening to the antique summons of noblesse oblige. A newspaper interview reported that the governor was a soft touch for any Negro who waylaid him in the corridor with a "Cap'n, I could sho use a dollar." The governor, it was also reported, liked to go hunting with a Negro friend. "We laugh and joke," the governor reminisced, "and he gets a big kick out of it when I call him Professor. There's a lot in our relationship I can't explain." No doubt, mused the interviewer, the governor would get up at all hours of the night to get Ol' Jim out of jail. It is hard to imagine what Gavin Stevens would make of this new version of the old alliance. Unquestionably, something new has been added. When Marse Ross dons the mantle of Marse Robert, Southern history has entered upon a new age. And perhaps it is just as well. Let Governor Barnett become the new squire. It simplifies matters further.

Though Faulkner liked to use such words as "cursed" and "doomed" in speaking of his region, it is questionable that Mississippians are very different from other Americans. It is increasingly less certain that Minnesotans would have performed better under the circumstances. There is, however, one peculiar social dimension wherein the state does truly differ. It has to do with the distribution, as Mississippians see it, of what is public and what is private. More precisely, it is the absence of a truly public zone, as the word is understood in most places. One has to live in Mississippi to appreciate it. No doubt, it is the mark of an almost homogeneous white population, a Protestant Anglo-Saxon minority (until recently), sharing a common tragic past and bound together by kinship bonds. This society was not only felicitous in many ways; it also commanded the allegiance of Southern intellectuals on other grounds. Faulkner saw it as the chief bulwark against the "coastal spew of Europe" and "the rootless ephemeral cities of the North." In any case, the almost familial ambit of this society came to coincide with the actual public space which it inhabited. The Negro was either excluded, shoved off into Happy Hollow, or admitted to the society on its own terms as good old Uncle Ned. No allowance was made—it would have been surprising if there had been—for a truly public sector, unlovely as you please and defused of emotional charges, where black and white might pass without troubling each other. The whole of the Delta, indeed of white Mississippi, is one big kinship lodge. You have only to walk into a restaurant or a bus station to catch a whiff of it. There is a sudden kindling of amiability, even between strangers. The salutations, "What you say now?" and "Y'all be good," are exchanged like fraternal signs. The presence of fraternity and sorority houses at Ole Miss always seemed oddly superfluous.

One consequence of this peculiar social structure has been a chronic misunderstanding between the state and the rest of the country. The state feels that unspeakable demands are being made upon it, while the nation is bewildered by the response of rage to what seem to be the ordinary and minimal requirements of the law. Recall, for example, President Kennedy's gentle appeal to the university the night of the riot when he invoked the tradition of L. Q. C. Lamar and asked the students to do their duty even as he was doing his. He had got his facts straight about the tradition of valor in Mississippi. But, unfortunately, the Kennedys had no notion of the social and semantic rules they were up against. When they entered into negotiations with the governor to get Meredith on the campus, they proceeded on the reasonable assumption that even in the arena of political give and take—i.e., deals—words bear some relation to their referents. Such was not the case.

Governor Barnett did not double-cross the Kennedys in the usual sense. The double cross, like untruth, bears a certain relation to the truth. More serious, however, was the cultural confusion over the word "public." Ole Miss is not, or was not, a public school as the word is usually understood. In Mississippi as in England, a public school means a private school. When Meredith finally did walk the paths at Ole Miss, his fellow students cursed and reviled him. But they also wept with genuine grief. It was as if he had been quartered in their living room.

It is this hypertrophy of pleasant familial space at the expense of a truly public sector which accounts for the extraordinary apposition in Mississippi of kindliness and unspeakable violence. Recently, a tourist wrote the editor of the Philadelphia, Mississippi, newspaper that, although he expected the worst when he passed through the town, he found the folks in Philadelphia as nice as they could be. No doubt it is true. The Philadelphia the tourist saw is as pleasant as he said. It is like one big front porch.

How can peace be restored to Mississippi? One would like to be able to say that the hope lies in putting into practice the Judeo-Christian ethic. In the end, no doubt, it does. But the trouble is that Christendom of a sort has already won in Mississippi. There is more church news in the Jackson papers than news about the Ole Miss football team. Political cartoons defend God against the Supreme Court. On the outskirts of Meridian, a road sign announces: THE LARGEST PERCENTAGE OF CHURCHGOERS IN THE WORLD. It is a religion, however, which tends to canonize the existing social and political structure and to brand as atheistic any threat of change. "The trouble is, they took God out of everything," said W. Arsene Dick of Summit, Mississippi, founder of Americans for the Preservation of the White Race. A notable exception to the general irrelevance of religion to social issues is the recent action of Millsaps College, a Methodist institution in Jackson, which voluntarily opened its doors to Negroes.

It seems more likely that progress will come about—as indeed it is already coming about—not through the impact of the churches upon churchgoers but because after a while the ordinary citizen gets sick and tired of the climate of violence and of the odor of disgrace which hangs over his region. Money has a good deal to do with it, too; money, urbanization, and the growing concern of politicians and the business community with such things as public images. Governor Johnson occasionally talks sense. Last year the mayor and the business leaders of Jackson defied the Citizens' Councils and supported the token desegregation of the schools. It could even happen that Governor Johnson, the man who campaigned up and down the state with the joke about what NAACP means (niggers, alligators, apes, coons, possums), may turn out to be the first governor to enforce the law. For law enforcement, it is becoming increasingly obvious, is the condition of peace. It is also becoming more likely every day that federal intervention, perhaps in the form of local commissioners, may be required in places like Neshoba County where the Ku Klux Klan has been in control and law enforcement is a shambles. Faulkner at last changed his mind about the durability of the old alliance and came to prefer even enforced change to a state run by the Citizens' Councils and the Klan. Mississippians, he wrote, will not accept change until they have to. Then perhaps they will at last come to themselves: "Why didn't someone tell us this before? Tell us this in time?"

Much will depend on the residue of good will in the state. There are some slight signs of the long-overdue revolt of the ordinary prudent man. There must be a good many of this silent breed. Hazel Brannon Smith, who won a Pulitzer Prize as editor of the Lexington *Advertiser*, recently reported that in spite of all the abuse and the boycotts, the circulation of the paper continues to rise. The Mississippi Economic Council, the state's leading businessmen's group, issued a statement urging compliance with the 1964 Civil Rights Act and demanding that registration and voting laws be "fairly and impartially administered for all." In McComb, several hundred leading citizens, after a reign of terror which lasted for a good part of 1964, demanded not only law and order but "equal treatment under the law for all citizens."

It may be that the corner has been turned. Mississippi, in the spring of 1965, looks better than Alabama. But who can say what would have happened if Martin Luther King had chosen Greenwood instead of Selma? Mississippi may in fact *be* better just because of Selma—though at this very writing Ole Miss students are living up to form and throwing rocks at Negroes. Nor can one easily forget the 1964 national election. The bizarre seven-to-one margin in favor of Senator Goldwater attests to the undiminished obsession with race. It would not have mattered if Senator Goldwater had advocated the collectivization of the plantations and open saloons in Jackson; he voted against the 1964 Civil Rights Bill and that was that.

Yet there is little doubt that Mississippi is even now beginning to feel its way toward what might be called the American Settlement of the racial issue, a somewhat ambiguous state of affairs which is less a solution than a more or less tolerable impasse. There has come into being an entire literature devoted to an assault upon the urban life wherein this settlement is arrived at, and a complete glossary of terms, such as alienation, depersonalization, and mass man. But in the light of recent history in Mississippi, the depersonalized American neighborhood looks more and more tolerable. A giant supermarket or eighty thousand people watching a pro ball game may not be the most creative of institutions, but at least they offer a modus vivendi. People generally leave each other alone.

A Southerner may still hope that someday the Southern temper, black and white, might yet prove to be the sociable yeast to leaven the American lump. Indeed, he may suspect in his heart of hearts that the solution, if it comes, may have to come from him and from the South. And with good reason: the South, with all the monstrous mythologizing of its virtues, nevertheless has these virtues—a manner and a grace and a gift for human intercourse. And despite the humbuggery about the perfect love and understanding between us white folks and darkies down in Dixie, whites and blacks in the South do in fact know something about getting along with each other which the rest of the country does not know. Both black and white Southerner can help the country a great deal, though neither may choose to do so; the Negro for fear of being taken for Uncle Tom, the white from simple vengefulness: "All right, Yankee, you've been preaching at us for a hundred years and now you've got them and you're making a mess of it and it serves you right." It may well come to lie with the South in the near future, as it lay with the North in 1860, to save the Union in its own way. Given enough trouble in

New York and Chicago, another ten years of life in the subways and urine in the streets, it might at last dawn on him, the Southerner, that it is not the South which is being put upon but the *country* which is in trouble. Then he will act as he acted in 1916 and 1941.

Someday a white Mississippian is going to go to New York, make the usual detour through Harlem, and see it for the foul cheerless warren that it is; and instead of making him happy as it does now, it is going to make him unhappy. Then the long paranoia, this damnable sectional insanity, will be one important step closer to being over.

1965

UNCLE WILL

❧

I remember the first time I saw him. I was thirteen and he had come to visit my mother and me and my brothers in Athens, Georgia, where we were living with my grandmother after my father's death.

We had heard of him, of course. He was the fabled relative, the one you liked to speculate about. His father was a United States senator and he had been a decorated infantry officer in World War I. Besides that, he was a poet. The fact that he was also a lawyer and a planter didn't cut much ice—after all, the South was full of lawyer-planters. But how many people did you know who were war heroes and wrote books of poetry? One had heard of Rupert Brooke and Joyce Kilmer, but they were dead.

The curious fact is that my recollection of him even now, after meeting him, after living in his house for twelve years, and now thirty years after his death, is no less fabled than my earliest imaginings. The image of him that takes form in my mind still owes more to Rupert Brooke and those photographs of young English officers killed in Flanders than to a flesh-and-blood cousin from Greenville, Mississippi.

I can only suppose that he must have been, for me at least, a personage, a presence, radiating that mysterious quality we call charm, for lack of a better word, in such high degree that what comes to mind is not that usual assemblage of features and habits which make up our memories of people but rather a quality, a temper, a set of mouth, a look through the eyes.

For his eyes were most memorable, a piercing gray-blue and strangely light in my memory, as changeable as shadows over water, capable of passing in an instant, we were soon to learn, from merriment—he told the funniest stories we'd ever heard—to a level gray gaze cold with reproof. They were beautiful and terrible eyes, eyes to be careful around. Yet now, when I try to remember them, I cannot see them otherwise than as shadowed by sadness.

What we saw at any rate that sunny morning in Georgia in 1930, and what I still vividly remember, was a strikingly handsome man, slight of build and quick as a youth. He was forty-five then, an advanced age, one would suppose, to a thirteen-year-old, and gray-haired besides, yet the abiding impression was of a youthful-ness—and an exoticness. He had in fact just returned from the South Seas—this was before the jet age and I'd never heard of anybody going there but Gauguin and Captain Bligh—where he had lived on the beach at Bora Bora.

He had come to invite us to live with him in Mississippi. We did, and upon my mother's death not long after, he adopted me and my two brothers. At the time what he did did not seem remarkable. What with youth's way of taking life as it comes—how else can you take it when you have no other life to compare it with?—and what with youth's incapacity for astonishment or gratitude, it did not seem in the least extraordinary to find oneself orphaned at fifteen and adopted by a bachelor-poet-lawyer-planter and living in an all-male household visited regularly by other poets, politicians, psychiatrists, sociologists, black preachers, folk singers, itinerant harmonica players. One friend came to seek advice on a book he wanted to write and stayed a year to write it. It was, his house, a standard stopover for all manner of people who were trying to "understand the South," that perennial Amer-ican avocation, and whether or not they succeeded, it was as valuable to me to try to understand them as to be understood. The observers in this case were at least as curious a phenomenon as the observed.

Now, belatedly, I can better assess what he did for us and I

even have an inkling what he gave up to do it. For him, to whom
the world was open and who felt more at home in Taormina than
in Jackson—for, though he loved his home country, he had to
leave it often to keep loving it—and who in fact could have stayed
on at Bora Bora and chucked it all like Gauguin (he told me once
he was tempted), for him to have taken on three boys, age fourteen,
thirteen, and nine, and raised them, amounted to giving up the
freedom of bachelorhood and taking on the burden of parenthood
without the consolations of marriage. Gauguin chucked it all, quit,
cut out and went to the islands for the sake of art and became a
great painter if not a great human being. Will Percy not only did
not chuck anything; he shouldered somebody else's burden. Fortunately for us, he did not subscribe to Faulkner's precept that a
good poem is worth any number of old ladies—for, if grandmothers
are dispensable, why not second cousins? I don't say we did him
in (he would laugh at that), but he didn't write much poetry
afterwards and he died young. At any rate, whatever he lost or
gained in the transaction, I know what I gained: a vocation and
in a real sense a second self; that is, the work and the self which,
for better or worse, would not otherwise have been open to me.

For to have lived in Will Percy's house, with "Uncle Will" as
we called him, as a raw youth from age fourteen to twenty-six, a
youth whose only talent was a knack for looking and listening, for
tuning in and soaking up, was nothing less than to be informed
in the deepest sense of the word. What was to be listened to,
dwelled on, pondered over for the next thirty years was of course
the man himself, the unique human being, and when I say unique
I mean it in its most literal sense: he was one of a kind: I never
met anyone remotely like him. It was to encounter a complete,
articulated view of the world as tragic as it was noble. It was to be
introduced to Shakespeare, to Keats, to Brahms, to Beethoven—
and unsuccessfully, it turned out, to Wagner whom I never liked,
though I was dragged every year to hear Flagstadt sing Isolde—
as one seldom if ever meets them in school.

"Now listen to this part," he would say as Gluck's *Orfeo* played—
the old 78s not merely dropped from a stack by the monstrous
Capehart, as big as a sideboard, but then picked up and turned
over by an astounding hoop-like arm—and you'd make the alto-

gether unexpected discovery that music, of all things, can convey the deepest and most unnamable human feelings and give great pleasure in doing so.

Or: "Read this," and I'd read or, better still, he'd read aloud, say, Viola's speech to Olivia in *Twelfth Night*:

> *Make me a willow cabin at your gate,*
> *And call upon my soul within the house . . .*
> *And make the babbling gossip of the air*
> *Cry out "Olivia!"*

"You see?" he'd as good as say, and what I'd begin to see, catch on to, was the great happy reach and play of the poet at the top of his form.

For most of us, the communication of beauty takes two, the teacher and the hearer, the pointer and the looker. The rare soul, the Wolfe or Faulkner, can assault the entire body of literature single-handedly. I couldn't or wouldn't. I had a great teacher. The teacher points and says, "Look"; the response is, "Yes, I see."

But he was more than a teacher. What he was to me was a fixed point in a confusing world. This is not to say I always took him for my true north and set my course accordingly. I did not. Indeed, my final assessment of *Lanterns on the Levee* must register reservations as well as admiration. The views on race relations, for example, diverge from my own and have not been helpful, having, in my experience, played into the hands of those whose own interest in these matters is deeply suspect. But even when I did not follow him, it was usually in *relation* to him, whether with him or against him, that I defined myself and my own direction. Perhaps he would not have had it differently. Surely it is the highest tribute to the best people we know to use them as best we can, to become, not their disciples, but ourselves.

It is the good fortune of those who did not know him that his singular charm, the unique flavor of the man, transmits with high fidelity in *Lanterns on the Levee*. His gift for communicating, communicating himself, an enthusiasm, a sense of beauty, moral outrage, carries over faithfully to the cold printed page, although for those who did not know him the words cannot evoke—or can they?—the mannerisms, the quirk of mouth, the shadowed look, the quick Gallic shrug, the inspired flight of eyebrows at an absurdity, the cold Anglo-Saxon gaze. (For he was this protean: one time I was reading *Ivanhoe*, the part about the fight between Richard and Saladin, and knowing Richard was one of Uncle Will's heroes, I identified one with the other. But wait: wasn't he actually more like Saladin, not the sir-knight defender of the Christian West, but rather the subtle Easterner, noble in his own right? I didn't ask him, but if I had, he'd have probably shrugged: both, neither . . .)

There is not much doubt about the literary quality of *Lanterns on the Levee*, which delivers to the reader not only a noble and tragic view of life but the man himself. But other, nonliterary questions might be raised here. How, for example, do the diagnostic and prophetic dimensions of the book hold up after thirty years? Here, I think, hindsight must be used with the utmost circumspection. On the one hand, it is surely justifiable to test the prophetic moments of a book against history itself; on the other hand, it is hardly proper to judge a man's views of the issues of his day by the ideological fashions of another age. Perhaps in this connection it would not be presumptuous to venture a modest hope. It is that *Lanterns on the Levee* will survive both its friends and its enemies; that is, certain more clamorous varieties of each.

One is all too familiar with both.

The first, the passionate advocate: the lady, not necessarily Southern, who comes bearing down at full charge, waving *Lanterns on the Levee* like a battle flag. "He is right! The Old South was right!" What she means all too often, it turns out, is not that she prefers agrarian values to technological but that she is enraged at having to pay her cook more than ten dollars a week; that she prefers, not merely segregation to integration, but slavery to either.

The second, the liberal enemy: the ideologue, white or black, who polishes off *Lanterns on the Levee* with the standard epithets: racist, white supremacist, reactionary, paternalist, Bourbon, etc., etc. (they always remind me of the old Stalinist imprecations: Fascist, cosmopolitan, imperialist running dog).

Lanterns on the Levee deserves better and, of course, has better readers. Its author can be defended against the more extreme reader, but I wonder if it is worth the effort. Abraham Lincoln was a segregationist. What of it? Will Percy was regarded in the Mississippi of his day as a flaming liberal and nigger-lover and reviled by the sheriff's office for his charges of police brutality. What of that? Nothing much is proved except that current categories and names, liberal and conservative, are weary past all thinking of it. Ideological words have a way of wearing thin and then, having lost their meanings, being used like switchblades against the enemy of the moment. Take the words "paternalism," "noblesse oblige," dirty words these days. But is it a bad thing for a man to believe that his position in society entails a certain responsibility toward others? Or is it a bad thing for a man to care like a father for his servants, spend himself on the poor, the sick, the miserable, the mad who come his way? It is surely better than watching a neighbor get murdered and closing the blinds to keep from "getting involved." It might even beat welfare.

Rather than measure *Lanterns on the Levee* against one or another ideological yardstick, it might be more useful to test the major themes of the book against the spectacular events of the thirty years since its publication. Certainly the overall pessimism of *Lanterns on the Levee*, its gloomy assessment of the spiritual health of Western civilization, is hard to fault these days. It seems especially prescient when one considers that the book was mostly written in the between-wars age of optimism when Americans still believed that the right kind of war would set things right once and for all. If its author were alive today, would he consider his forebodings borne out? Or has the decline accelerated even past his imaginings? Would he see glimmerings of hope? Something of all three, no doubt, but mainly, I think, he'd look grim, unsurprised, and glad enough to have made his exit.

Certainly, nothing would surprise him about the collapse of the old moralities; for example, the so-called sexual revolution, which he would more likely define in less polite language as alley-cat morality. I can hear him now: "Fornicating like white trash is one thing, but leave it to this age to call it the new morality." Nor would he be shocked by the cynicism and corruption, the stealing, lying, rascality ascendant in business and politics—though even he might be dismayed by the complacency with which they are received: "There have always been crooks, but we've not generally made a practice of reelecting them, let alone inviting them to dinner." All this to say nothing of the collapse of civil order and the new jungle law which rules the American city.

Nothing new here then for him: if the horrors of the Nazi Holocaust would have dismayed him and the moral bankruptcy of the postwar world saddened him, they would have done so only by sheer dimension. He had already adumbrated the *Götterdämmerung* of Western values.

But can the matter be disposed of so simply: decline and fall predicted, decline and fall taking place? While granting the prescience of much of *Lantern on the Levee's* pessimism, we must, I think, guard against a certain seductiveness which always attends the heralding of apocalypse, and we must not overlook some far less dramatic but perhaps equally significant counterforces. Yes, Will Percy's indictment of modern life has seemed to be confirmed by the Holocaust of the 1940s and by American political and social morality in the 1970s. But what would he make of some very homely yet surely unprecedented social gains which have come to pass during these same terrible times? To give the plainest examples: that for the first time in history a poor boy, black or white, has a chance to get an education, become what he wants to become, doctor, lawyer, even read *Lanterns on the Levee* and write poetry of his own, and that not a few young men, black and white, have done just that? Also: that for the first time in history a working man earns a living wage and can support his family in dignity. How do these solid social gains square with pronouncements of decline and fall? I ask the question and, not knowing the answer, can only wonder how Will Percy would see it now. As collapse? Or as contest? For it appears that what is upon us is not a twilight of the gods but a very real race between the powers of light and darkness, that time is short and the issue very much in doubt. So I'd love to ask him, as I used to ask him after the seven o'clock news (Ed Murrow: *This*—is London): "Well? What do you think?"

The one change that would astonish him, I think, is the spectacular emergence of the South from its traditional role of loser and scapegoat. If anyone had told him in 1940 that in thirty

years the "North" (i.e., New York, Detroit, California) would be
in the deepest kind of trouble with race, violence, and social decay
while the South had become, by contrast, relatively hopeful and
even prosperous, he would not have believed it. This is not to say
that he would find himself at home in the new Dallas or Atlanta.
But much of *Lanterns on the Levee*—for example, the chapter on
sharecropping—was written from the ancient posture of Southern
apologetics. If his defense of sharecropping against the old enemy,
the "Northern liberal," seems quaint now, it is not because there
was not something to be said for sharecropping—there was a good
deal to be said—and it is not because he wasn't naïve about the
tender regard of the plantation manager for the helpless sharecropper—he was naïve, even about his own managers. It is rather
because the entire issue and its disputants have simply been
bypassed by history. The massive social and technological upheavals
in the interval have left the old quarrel academic and changed the
odds in the new one. It is hard, for example, to imagine a serious
Southern writer nowadays firing off his heaviest ammunition at
"Northern liberals." Not the least irony of recent history is that
the "Northern liberal" has been beleaguered and the "Southern
planter" rescued by the same forces. The latter has been dispensed
by technology from the ancient problem, sharecroppers replaced
by Farmall and Allis-Chalmers, while the former has fallen out
with his old wards, the blacks. The displaced sharecroppers moved
to the Northern cities and the liberals moved out. The South in a
peculiar sense, a sense Will Percy would not necessarily have
approved (though he could hardly have repressed a certain satisfaction), may have won after all.

So Will Percy's strong feelings about the shift of power from
the virtuous few would hardly be diminished today, but he might
recast his villains and redress the battle lines. Old-style demagogue,
for example, might give way to new-style image manipulator and
smooth amoral churchgoing huckster. When he spoke of the
"bottom rail on top," he had in mind roughly the same folks as
Faulkner's Snopeses, a lower-class, itchy-palmed breed who had
dispossessed the gentry, who had in turn been the true friends of
the old-style "good" Negro. The upshot: an unholy hegemony of
peckerwood politicians, a white hoi polloi keeping them in office,

and a new breed of unmannerly Negroes misbehaving in the streets. But if he—or Faulkner, for that matter—were alive today, he would find the battleground confused. He would find most members of his own "class" not exactly embattled in a heroic *Götterdämmerung*, not exactly fighting the good fight as he called it, but having simply left, taken off for the exurbs, where, barricaded in patrolled subdivisions and country clubs and private academies, they worry about their kids and drugs. Who can blame them, but is this the "good life" Will Percy spoke of? And when some of these good folk keep *Lanterns on the Levee* on the bed table, its author, were he alive today, might be a little uneasy. For meanwhile, doing the dirty work of the Republic in the towns and cities of the South, in the schools, the school boards, the city councils, the factories, the restaurants, the stores, are to be found, of all people, the sons and daughters of the poor whites of the 1930s and some of those same uppity Negroes who went to school and ran for office, and who together are not doing so badly and in some cases very well indeed.

So it is not unreasonable to suppose that Will Percy might well revise his view of the South and the personae of his drama, particularly in favor of the lower-class whites for whom he had so little use. In this connection I cannot help but think of another book about the South, W. J. Cash's *The Mind of the South*, published, oddly enough, the same year by the same publisher as *Lanterns on the Levee*. Cash's book links Southern aristocrat and poor white much closer than the former ordinarily would have it. Both books are classics in their own right, yet they couldn't be more different; their separate validities surely testify to the diversity and complexity of this mysterious region. Yet, in this case, I would suppose that Will Percy would today find himself closer to Cash in sorting out his heroes and villains, that far from setting aristocrat against poor white and both against the new Negro, he might well choose his present-day heroes—and villains—from the ranks of all three. He'd surely have as little use for black lawlessness as for white copping out. I may be wrong, but I can't see him happy as the patron saint of Hilton Head or Paradise Estates-around-the-Country Club.

For it should be noted, finally, that despite conventional assessments of *Lanterns on the Levee* as an expression of the "aristocratic" point of view of the Old South, Will Percy had no more use than Cash for genealogical games, the old Southern itch for coats of arms and tracing back connections to the English squire-archy. Indeed, if I know anything at all about Will Percy, I judge that insofar as there might be a connection between him and the Northumberland Percys, they, not he, would have to claim kin. He made fun of his ancestor Don Carlos, and if he claimed Harry Hotspur, it was a kinship of spirit. His own aristocracy was a meritocracy of character, talent, performance, courage, and quality of life.

It is just that, a person and a life, which comes across in *Lanterns on the Levee*. And about him I will say no more than that he was the most extraordinary man I have ever known and that I owe him a debt which cannot be paid.

1973

UNCLE WILL'S HOUSE

2

It was a singular house to grow up in. I doubt if anyone ever spent his youth in such a house. It belonged to my cousin, the poet William Alexander Percy—"Uncle Will," we called him. There he lived alone, and there my brothers and I, ages eight to fourteen, went to live after our parents died. This man—bachelor, poet, planter, lawyer—was, if nothing else, extremely brave. How many bachelors would take upon themselves the rearing of three orphaned cousins?

The house and household did not seem remarkable to me at the time. Indeed, nothing seems remarkable to a child, who is programmed precisely not to find things remarkable, but to get used to them.

But it was not an ordinary house. It was in Greenville, Mississippi, a few blocks from the levee that had broken three years earlier, flooding the town and the entire Delta. For four months the house rose from a fetid brown sea ten-feet deep. Dead mules floated into the front gallery.

Hardly distinguished architecturally, the house had been the sort of bastard Greek Revival popular in the late 1800s, a tall, frame, gabled pile with a portico and two-story Ionic columns. Evidently it was somewhat ramshackle even in the 1920s, for Uncle Will's parents turned it over to a contractor-renovator-decorator to fix up, and departed for a Grand Tour of Europe—they must have had a great cotton crop that year. Upon their return, they found it as I first saw it in 1930: stuccoed (!), the portico and columns knocked off, a large bungalow-shaped porte cochere stuck on one side, and a sun parlor, as it was then called, stuck on the other.

Children notice things first, people later. People are to be dealt with, accepted, pleased, gotten along with. But things are to be explored. What things there were in that house! It had an elevator. I had never heard of such a thing, an elevator in a house. Most especially, there was the attic, a vast, dusty, rambling place littered with World War I souvenirs: spiked German helmets, binoculars, Springfield rifles, cartridge belts, puttees, and bayonets.

Downstairs in the great living room was the Capehart, a huge automatic phonograph, one of the first of its kind and surely the only one in town, and an even larger record cabinet packed with albums of 78s, from Bach to Brahms. Uncle Will wasn't much for twentieth-century music. He would play Stravinsky's *Le Sacre du printemps* and shake his head. I welcomed the job of setting up a concert for him, stacking the 78s in proper order and monitoring the marvelous machine. The Capehart would drop a record from the stack, play one side, turn it over and play the second side, then drop the next record; but sometimes it would have a fit, take a dislike to Tchaikovsky and sling records every which way.

There were dozens of rooms in the house, odd, angled-off rooms serving no known purpose. I found one, and with my friend Shelby Foote set up shop, building model airplanes—Spads, Sopwith Camels, and finally my masterpiece, a flying scale model of the Lockheed *Winnie Mae* flown by the ill-fated Wiley Post.

Off the living room was Uncle Will's library, which began with the eighteenth-century collection of our common ancestor—including a three-volume Wilson's *American Ornithology*, wondrous indeed had it not been got at by some later brat-ancestors with crayons and scissors on a rainy day. In his library, too, he barely reached the twentieth century, with Edna St. Vincent Millay and Sara Teasdale, but had not much use for the "moderns," as he called them, not even his distinguished contemporaries and fellow Southerners, the Nashville poets Allen Tate, John Crowe Ransom, and company.

What was memorable, of course, was not the house and the things, but the people—visitors, friends, kinfolk, strangers who came there. He was a literary figure and something of a spokesman for the South. As a consequence, his house became a standard stopover for all manner of folk who had set forth to make sense of this mysterious region—poets, journalists, sociologists, psychiatrists. I remember Carl Sandburg, who broke out his guitar and sang, not too well, for hours. A better musician, a black harmonica player, showed up one night from God knows where—he was on the road; it was the Great Depression—and played the blues on his harmonica as I have never heard the blues played before or since. Faulkner came for tennis. Whether distracted by literary inspiration or by bourbon, he never managed once to bring racket into contact with ball. Langston Hughes came for a visit and a speech. Uncle Will introduced him.

Harry Stack Sullivan stayed for three weeks. Perhaps this country's most eminent psychiatrist, he explained with some diffidence that he was being paid by a foundation to study race relations in the Mississippi Delta. Canny enough to know that no one can make sense of any kind of human relations in three weeks, he nevertheless and none too seriously made the best of it, and in his own sly way hit upon the best place and the best method for his case studies. The place: the pantry, a large room with bar, between kitchen and dining room, between the white folks in the front and the cook and her friends and friends of the cook's friends in the back. There in the pantry the traffic was heaviest and race relations liveliest. Uncle Will cannot be said to have run a tight ship, and did not know how many guests were fed in the kitchen or who they were. One encountered total strangers. Dr. Sullivan's methodology: Early each afternoon he made himself a pitcher of vodka martinis—no one had ever heard of such a drink in Mississippi in the 1930s—and set up shop in the pantry, listened and talked to any and all comers. I never did find out what this brilliant and sardonic upstate New Yorker made of race relations in Uncle Will's pantry.

And visitors! In those days, and especially in the South, a visit was a thing of noble dimensions. A would-be writer showed up one weekend, an ex-Greenvillian who, having succeeded in business in New Orleans, decided to retire and write a book. He came for advice from Uncle Will about the business of writing, stayed for a year, and wrote his book. He was David Cohn, a good writer, and the book was *God Shakes Creation*.

A young newspaperman from Louisiana, named Hodding Carter, came to talk, having made himself persona non grata with Huey Long in Louisiana. Uncle Will, not having a high opinion of the local paper, thought it might be a good idea to start another paper. They did. There in Greenville, Hodding Carter published his paper, won the Pulitzer Prize, and lived the rest of his life.

But it was the man, of course, not his house and not his visitors, who meant the most to my brothers and me. What to say of him here? Very little, for he said it much better in his autobiography, *Lanterns on the Levee*. It is enough to make a simple acknowledgment. Without him I do not think I would have been introduced to the world of books, of music, of art. I am sure it would not have crossed my mind to become a writer.

I remember him in his garden—a famous one—hands in pockets, frowning down at something, perhaps an iris with root rot. He took solace in his garden and from it drew human lessons. Once, as he put aluminum sulphate on his azaleas, because azaleas, of course, need acid soil, it came to him in a flash: some people, too, require acid soil! Of course! This explained a friend of ours, Miss A__, who for reasons that escaped everybody thrived on tragedy and controversy. Thereafter, Miss A__ was no mystery. Uncle Will gave her controversy cheerfully, acid soil aplenty, and the two of them got along famously ever after.

It's all gone now, house, garden, Capehart, Beethoven quartets in Victor 78s, pantry, Lorenzo de Medici in bronze, Venus in marble. In its place, I think, are neat little condo-villas of stained board-and-batten siding. Only the garden wall remains. I am not complaining. I have what he left me, and I don't mean things.

1984

A BETTER
LOUISIANA

❧

As the question goes these days, what's wrong with Louisiana? Who am I to presume to address myself to this question? Offhand I can think of only one credential which might set me somewhat apart and give me leave. I am a writer by profession and, unlike most Louisianians, can live anywhere I choose, starting tomorrow. Unlike most Louisianians, I chose Louisiana, thirty-eight years ago, and do not intend to live anywhere else.

The state is beautiful, unique, and there are no better people anywhere. If the United States takes pride in being a melting pot, in the sense that many ethnic types tolerate each other, that is, generally don't kill each other as they do in Lebanon, here in Louisiana an amazing mix of people not only tolerate each other but by and large get along well and have a good time.

But I don't like what has happened to this state. The facts are melancholy and all too familiar. One need not dwell on them. Here's a state richer in mineral resources than any other Southern state, the top gas producer in the country, possessed of the largest port, endowed with a natural wealth which in its use might have been expected to yield manifold benefits for its people.

The upshot? Depletion of its known oil and gas reserves, its marshes plundered and polluted, one of the highest cancer rates in the country, the loss of fifty square miles of wetlands yearly. And so on and on. Mineral-rich, strategically located Louisiana is in fact one of the poorest states in the country in per-capita income, vies only with Mississippi for the honor of being dead last in the quality of public education.

How did this sorry state of affairs come to pass? Here again, at least part of the answer is no great mystery. Ever since the palmy days of the Perezes fifty years ago, when Judge Leander Perez acquired royalty interests in public land drilled by major oil companies, some Louisiana politicians and the big oil-and-gas corporations seemed to have enjoyed an extended love-in, a mutually beneficial arrangement, but not necessarily beneficial to the people of the state.

But there is no use dwelling on the past. The question now is what to do.

One of the more astonishing reactions to this dilemma, to judge from some responses to the front-page editorial in this newspaper [*Times-Picayune*] on March 10, is that even asking such a question is seen as negative thinking and bad for the state's image—as if the state's image could get any worse. One should think positively; if one is a passenger on the *Titanic* and the ship begins to list, one should praise the deck chairs.

So what to do? Governor Edwin Edwards, whatever his faults and his ultimate culpability, is surely right on target with his education reform plan, which amounts to a program of massive support of public education, with rewards for excellence in teachers and provisions to get rid of incompetents.

But there's a Catch-22 here, entirely apart from the little matter of where the money's coming from. It is the nagging doubt in the taxpayer's mind about all such proposals—for he's heard them before. Just what are the real priorities of the educational establishment, the National Education Association, the administrators, the teachers' unions? Are these groups really interested in getting the best teachers into the classroom and the incompetents out? Will throwing more money at the public schools ensure better education? Teachers' unions are very vocal about higher salaries and job security, and they are right. But when you ask them how they propose to go about rewarding merit and throwing out the dumbbells, the silence is deafening.

Just as there was evidently no compelling reason why Louisiana politicians and the oil companies should place the public interest first, one wonders how educators can be moved to strive as hard for excellence, both in teachers and in pupils, as they do for more money.

It does not take a prophet to predict what is going to happen if the public schools are not supported massively and the educators do not get their act together.

Either the schools will continue to decline in quality until they become a de facto adjunct of the welfare system where children of the poor will be warehoused for twelve years, then dumped into society, ill prepared, a more or less permanent underclass.

Or taxpayers will finally get fed up with an expensive system turning out an inferior product and demand that the public schools be opened to free-market competition, perhaps by a voucher system which would give poor parents the same freedom of choice of schools as the more affluent. Such a system might have its disadvantages, but you may be sure it would get the attention of the public-school bureaucracy. Why are GM cars getting better? Not because of increased government subsidies or higher salaries. Because of Toyota.

There is another subtle factor at work which may defeat all such reforms. It is a trait peculiar to the state, part of its peculiar charm but also part of its peculiar weakness. It is summarized by that dubious expression, *Laissez le bon temps rouler*, which can be read as referring to the genuine joy of Louisiana life. But it also translates into that old Louisiana penchant for voting for flamboyant types, upcountry good ol' boys and Cajun slickers who are long on show biz and short on ethics. As long as the party lasted, the oil flowed, and the good times rolled, it didn't seem to matter.

Well, folks, the party's over. The *bon temps* have just about *roulered* out.

But I am hopeful. There are some young, honest, and able politicians on the horizon. Education is surely the key. There are plenty of dedicated teachers. And there is an ever-increasing number of informed, sobered-up, and disquieted voters. This is an economic, not a racial issue. It is the children of poor families, black and white, who are suffering from an inferior education. But there is plenty of black pride and white pride around. All it takes is good teachers and the rest of us to support them and all of us to communicate the pride of excellence to the young. It's too bad Jesse Jackson left PUSH, where he was doing an extraordinary job, and became an ordinary politician.

As the saying goes, people get the kind of government they deserve. Time will tell. We'll either continue our present course and become a somewhat comic, albeit slightly sleazy playground for tourists and conventioneers—as indeed Louisiana is already perceived by much of the country. Or we can realize our unique potential, keep the good times, but conserve our natural wealth and that greatest wealth of all—our young people. There's the hope.

1985

THE
AMERICAN
WAR

❧

What are the reasons for the current revival of interest in the Civil War? That there is such a revival is undeniable. Books on the War pour off the presses every week—some of them, incidentally, of a very high order, such as Bruce Catton's *This Hallowed Ground* and Shelby Foote's *Shiloh!* What is at once noticeable about the current literature is its frankly nonpolitical character and the absence of the old rancor. The race issue may be still very much an issue, but Northern and Southern historians have achieved a common view of the War itself. When Catton from Michigan and Foote from Mississippi write about the battle of Shiloh, it sounds like the same battle. Catton is never more eloquent than when he is appraising Lee's generalship; Foote is just as impressed by the fighting qualities of the Northern soldier. Indeed, from this distance the underdog psychology probably kindles the reader's enthusiasm more readily than do the social issues—and perhaps this is just as well.

The general impression outside the South seems to be that it is the rest of the country which has rediscovered the Civil War, that the South has never stopped looking back. This is mistaken, I believe, and is due to an understandable optical illusion. The truth is, at least in my experience, that the Southerner never thinks about the Civil War—until he finds himself among Northerners. Then, for some reason—perhaps because the Northerner insists on casting him in his historical role and the Southerner is perfectly willing to oblige, or because, lost in the great cities of the North, he feels for the first time the need of his heritage—he breaks out the Stars and Bars. I remember traveling from Alabama to summer camp in Wisconsin in the twenties. The train would stop in Chicago to pick up more boys. We from Alabama had heard as little about the Civil War as about the Boer War and cared less, but every time the Illinois boys got on in Chicago the War started, a real brawl yet not really bad-tempered. The same sort of thing must have happened during World War I when an Alabama division suddenly found itself in a donnybrook with the Fighting 69th at Plattsburg.

The truth of it is, I think, that the whole country, South included, is just beginning to see the Civil War whole and entire for the first time. The thing was too big and too bloody, too full of suffering and hatred, too closely knit into the fabric of our meaning as a people, to be held off and looked at—until now. It is like a man walking away from a mountain. The bigger it is, the farther he's got to go before he can see it. Then one day he looks back and there it is, this colossal thing lying across his past.

A history of the shifting attitudes toward the War would be enlightening. There would probably emerge a pattern common to such great events, a dialectic of loss-recovery: the long period of recollection, of intense partisan interest which is followed by a gradual fading of the Event into a dusty tapestry. (Lee and Grant at Appomattox taking their place beside Washington Crossing the Delaware.) Then, under certain circumstances, there is the recovery. Perhaps Washington will never be recovered, having been ossified too long in grammar-school tableaux. But Lincoln and Grant and McClellan and even the legendary Lee, who, after all, are closer in time to Washington than to us, have come very much alive. Why, then, their recovery, and what exactly has been recovered?

What has been recovered, it seems clear, is not the politics or the sociology of the War, or even the slavery issue, but the fight itself. The tableau I remember from school was the Reconciliation, Grant and Lee in the McLean house, Lee healing the wounds at Washington College. Little was said about the War, except that it was tragic, brother fighting against brother, etc. Undoubtedly, this was the necessary if somewhat boring emphasis for the textbooks. Now, after ninety years of Reconciliation, we can take a look at the fight itself.

What a fight it was! The South is a very big place, yet there is hardly a district that didn't have its skirmish, its federal gunboat sunk in a bayou—where some old-timer won't tell you, "Yes, they came through here." It is startling to realize that there were more casualties in the Civil War than in all the American forces of World War II, and more than in all other American wars put together. Of 3,000,000 men under arms, 2,300,000 for the Union, 750,000 for the Confederacy, 618,222 died, with total casualties probably going well past a million. For sheer concentrated fury, there are few events even in modern warfare to equal that terrible September 17 at Antietam Creek when over twenty thousand men fell—or the May–June of '64 when, beginning with the Battle of the Wilderness, Grant lost on the average of two thousand men a day for thirty days, culminating in the slaughter at Cold Harbor, when over eight thousand men fell in about ten minutes! There were murderous battles in the West which one never heard of, like Stone's River with over 25,000 casualties.

Yet, terrible as it was, it is impossible to read of the Army of Northern Virginia or of the Army of the Potomac without being caught up in the tremendous drama. The armies were big enough so that the action took place on an epic scale, yet the War was, as much as were the Punic Wars, a personal encounter of the opposing leaders. Lee was very much aware of this grim beauty when the fog rose over Fredericksburg, showing Burnside's entire army facing his, battle flags flying. "It is well that war is so terrible," he said, "else we should grow too fond of it." But what gave the Civil War the tragic proportions of the *Iliad* was the fact, apparent after Shiloh, that the American soldier, Union and Confederate, was not going to be beaten until he could literally fight no longer or was killed. When his leader was great, he was almost invincible; when his leader was mediocre, he was still superb. Pickett's charge is justly famous, but just as heartbreaking was the Union assault on Longstreet's position in the sunken road at Fredericksburg. The difference was that, where Pickett's men had every confidence in Lee, Couch's men knew very well that Burnside was wrong. Yet they attacked all day long, and only stopped when the field was piled so high with dead that they could no longer run over them.

As in all tragedies, a great deal seemed to depend upon fate. Small mischances become as important as Thetis's oversight when she dipped Achilles—all but his heel—into the Styx. A Confederate courier loses some battle orders; they are found wrapped around three cigars and brought to McClellan; the direct result is the Battle of Antietam. One can't read of that War without playing the fascinating game of what-if . . . What if Jackson had lived through Chancellorsville? What if McClellan had listened to Phil Kearny (instead of to the Pinkerton detectives) during the Seven Days? What if Jeb Stuart had tended to business at Gettysburg? Lee was always just missing his Cannae and Lincoln's generals were always just short of ordinary competence—until he got Grant.

Besides the great failures, there were the great successes, the heroes' deeds which are always irresistible to the human spirit and so pass over immediately into the legend of the race. There was Chancellorsville when Lee, facing Hooker's 85,000, divided his battered army of 43,000, sent Jackson to the left, leaving him in front of Hooker with 17,000 men—and attacked and very nearly destroyed the Army of the Potomac. There was the Union's "Pap" Thomas's assault on Missionary Ridge at Chattanooga and the subsequent demoralization of Bragg. And there was the fateful decision at Spotsylvania when, after taking a fearful mauling, Grant, instead of falling back toward Washington as the army had been doing for the past three years, retreated—*south*, sliding around Lee's right.

Therein lies the tragedy. If Lee had been a little more or a little less—if he had gotten his Cannae or if he had only been just competent and been whipped by McClellan in '62—the results would still have been notable, but they would not have approached the terror and piteousness of what actually did happen. The summer of 1864 has a *Götterdämmerung* quality. With the issue hardly in doubt after Gettysburg, the fighting nevertheless increased in fury with both sides attacking steadily, without the usual remissions between battles.

Yet, with all the horror, or perhaps because of it, there was always the feeling then, and even now as we read about it, that the things a man lived through were somehow twice as real, twice as memorable as the peace that followed. Peace is better than war, yet it is a sad fact that some of the heroes of the War, like Grant and Longstreet and many a lesser man, found the peace a long descent into mediocrity. In the ordeal the man himself seemed to become more truly himself, revealing his character or the lack of it, than at any time before or after. If a man was secretly cowardly or secretly brave, stupid or shrewd, that was what he was shown to be. The War infallibly discovered his hidden weakness and his hidden strength. Hooker the braggart was reduced to impotence simply by having Lee's small army in front of him (and understandably, for the veterans of the Army of the Potomac used to say to replacements fresh from victories in the West: "Wait till you meet Bobby Lee"). Grant the ne'er-do-well matured in defeat and became a noble and sensitive human being by having Lee at his mercy. It is no wonder that there was the temptation, especially in the ruined South, to enshrine those four years as the four years of truth and to discount all other times, even the future.

Then there were the thousand and one lesser encounters, any one of which, if it had happened at another time, would have its own literature and its own historians: the Confederate raiders, Farragut's capture of New Orleans, the battle of the ironclads, Forrest's miniature Cannae at Brice's Cross Roads, James Andrews's stealing the Confederate train, and so on. It was the last of the wars of individuals, when a single man's ingenuity and pluck not only counted for something in itself but could conceivably affect the entire issue. Forrest himself is quite unbelievable. It is as if Lancelot had been reborn in Memphis. He carried into battle a cavalry saber sharpened to a razor edge and actually killed men with it. He actually did fool a Yankee commander into surrendering by parading a single cannon back and forth in the distance as they parleyed. He actually did have twenty-nine horses shot from under him.

There is an ambiguity about this new interest in the Civil War. On the one hand, it is the past recaptured, the authentic recovery of the long agony during which this nation came to be what it is. Yet there is also the temptation to yield to a historical illusion by which the past seems to gain in stature and authenticity as it recedes and the present to be discounted because it is the here and now. We sense the illusion in the words of the old-timer, "Yes, they came through here," in which it is somehow implied that this place has existed in a long trivial aftermath after its one day of glory. Perhaps the North is in for a mild case of the same romanticism which the South recovered from over fifty years ago.

The increased emphasis upon the fighting at the expense of ideology is probably good. One does well, anyway, not to apply ideology too closely to that war. James Truslow Adams can talk about the March of Democracy and Bruce Catton can call the Union Army a truly revolutionary army and perhaps they are right. Perhaps the War was really and truly fought over slavery. But the other case can be made, too. It is difficult to see the yeoman farmers who largely made up the Army of the Tennessee and the Army of Northern Virginia as Southern Bourbons. The South had some reason to regard the fight as a continuation of the American Revolution. After all, it was her soil which was being invaded and her independence which was being denied. The South might even have the better of the constitutional argument; yet what won out seems to transcend all the arguments. For it is that extraordinary thing, the American Union.

1957

RED, WHITE,
AND BLUE-GRAY

⚘

On it goes, the second Civil War, hundreds of books, millions of words, dozens of Pickett's charges. Yet the "war" has only just started. There are four more years of it.

Many people are already bored with it. Some are uneasy about it. Yet it continues to be a literary Comstock lode. If a writer doesn't want to take on the whole War, or a campaign, or even a general, he can still browse around and take his choice among an assortment of goodies, like the Cruise of the Alabama or the War in Idaho, write a book, have a good time doing it, and stand a good chance of making money, which is more than most novelists can say.

There is a paradox about current Civil War Centennial literature. It commemorates mainly the fighting, the actual front-line killing—which was among the bloodiest and bitterest in modern history. Yet it is all very good-natured. Illinois historians say nice things about Forrest; Mississippians, if not Georgians, speak well of Sherman.

In the popular media the War is so friendly that the fighting is made to appear as a kind of sacrament of fire by which one side expresses its affection for the other. After skirting the Civil War for years—showing a few bushwhackers or jayhawkers in Kansas or a skirmish or two in Santa Fe—television finally took the plunge and put on the War itself, taking care first to turn it into a love match. In *The Americans* the only bad blood is between good Yankees and bad Yankees, good rebels and scalawags. The fighting itself is either scanted or, when it does take place, it consists mainly of chivalric gestures toward the enemy: Yankees catch a young reb on his first patrol and slip him back through the lines so he won't disgrace the family name. Yet the reconciliation is all to the good, even when it is reinforced by a concern for the Trendex rating in Alabama or Vermont.

Myth requires distance, either in space or in time. The TV Western takes place Nowhere. So perhaps that War is still a bit touchy for myth-making. One hundred years may not be enough time. But someday a scriptwriter is going to show a Civil War soldier with but a single thought: he has no trouble with his girl; he is not trying to cover up for his alcoholic colonel; his men are reliable; all he wants to do is kill as many blue-bellies (or rebs) as possible—and *Gunsmoke* will be out of business.

Bruce Catton treats the War as a kind of mystical experience, a national rite of passage in the course of which a lot of sweaty young men killed each other with unsurpassed dedication and skill and in so doing presided over the rebirth of the American character. No doubt, he is right. Something of the sort did happen.

Anyhow, since the War was fought and the time has come to say something on the subject, one might as well put on it the best complexion possible. The Union was saved, and though it was by no means a self-evident axiom that the Union should be saved, it is no doubt well that it was (despite some disgruntled liberals who are beginning to wonder whether it was a good idea after all, since it meant keeping the South—like Groucho Marx who dared to wonder whether the show must go on). The slaves were freed and this was a good thing, though they would undoubtedly have been freed anyhow.

But the fighting itself makes for some very good reading. There was a high order of courage and performance on both sides and there is now some very good writing about it.

The South has certain tactical advantages in the present "war" (like the North's industry and population in the first) and has accordingly won a species of literary revenge. The two great figures of the Civil War were Lincoln and Lee, and since most of the literature is about the fighting, Lee is bound to get the better of it. And what with the American preference for good guys and underdogs, and especially underdog good guys, and Lee's very great personal qualities and the undistinguished character of his opponents, and finally the Army of Northern Virginia which was always outnumbered and nearly always won—it looks as if the next hundred years will see the South not only running the Senate but taking over the national myth along with it.

There is an innocence about combat. For one thing, the soldiers were or anyhow seemed more admirable than the politicians. There is also a finality: somebody wins, somebody loses, and it is over.

But what was settled? The Union was saved for good. The Negro's place in society was supposed to be settled, but it wasn't after all.

The Centennial literature may be good-natured, but there is an unease among liberals about the whole business. This is understandable enough, since it derives from the concern that commemoration of that particular sectional division can only damage the current struggle for civil rights. Therefore, the less said about the whole thing, the better. But such a queasiness would seem to award by default a more ominous significance to the Civil War than it deserves.

It is true that a lot of Confederate flags are being waved in the South. But if it weren't the flag, it would be something else. Racism has no sectional monopoly. Nor was the Confederate flag a racist symbol. But it is apt to be now. The symbol is the same, but the referent has changed. Now when the Stars and Bars flies over a convertible or a speedboat or a citizens' meeting, what it signifies is not a theory of government but a certain attitude toward the Negro.

A peculiarity of civil war is the destruction not only of armies and nations but of ideologies. The words and slogans may remain the same, but they no longer mean the same thing.

There is a great deal to be said for the traditional Southern position on states' rights. Not being a historian, I don't know what the cause of that War was, whether it was fought purely and simply over slavery, or over states' rights, or, as Allen Tate once said, because the South didn't want to be put in Arrow collars. Certainly, states' rights once signified a healthy sense of local responsibility.

Nowadays in the South, however, the expression signifies a lack of responsibility, plus a certain attitude toward the Negro. When a politician mentions states' rights, it's a better than even bet that in the next sentence it will become clear what kind of states' rights he is talking about. It usually comes down to the right to keep the Negro in his place.

There is another phrase: the Southern Way of Life. Now, there was and is such a thing and it had and has nothing to do either with Negroes or with a planter aristocracy. The Northerner can sneer all he wants to, but he didn't have it and never will and doesn't even know what it is. But I don't like to hear the phrase now, "A Southern Way of Life," because I know what is coming next. It usually means segregation and very little else. In New Orleans, which has a delightful way of life, the "Southern Way of Life" usually means "Let's Keep McDonough No. 6 Segregated."

But the bitterest fruits of defeat are the latter-day defenders of the lost cause. Historians like to contrast the pre-War hotheads like Yancey and Rhett with soldiers like Lee and Grant. But our present-day hotheads are an even sorrier lot, because their heads only get hot around election time.

When Lee and the Army of Northern Virginia laid down the Confederate flag in 1865, no flag had ever been defended by better men. But when the same flag is picked up by men like Ross Barnett and Jimmy Davis, nothing remains but to make panties and pillowcases with it.

Still and all, there is no need to worry about the Reconciliation. It was very largely an Anglo-Saxon war, and Anglo-Saxon has been reconciled to Anglo-Saxon. But to whom is the Negro reconciled?

It is a discouraging fact that after one hundred years there is greater unanimity on the subject of segregation in the South than there ever was on the subject of slavery. Virginia almost abolished slavery before the Civil War. There were all shades of opinion on the question. But now it is impossible to imagine a Sparkman or a Fulbright uttering a simple forthright statement against public segregation—not that I believe that such a statement from Senator Javits or Keating is motivated by a higher brand of political courage.

Yet there is nothing left to be reconciled between North and South. The North did win and did put the South in Arrow collars. The sections are homogenized. Everybody watches the same television programs. In another hundred years, everybody will talk like Art Linkletter.

The South has gotten rich and the North has gotten Negroes, and the Negro is treated badly in both places. The Northerners won and freed the slaves and now are fleeing to the suburbs to get away from them.

Here is the Centennial nobody celebrates: the War was fought, to free the slaves according to the North; according to the South, to preserve the Southern way of life, which was better for both black and white; a million people were killed; a hundred years have passed; the North and the South are reconciled—and the country has still not made up its mind what to do about the Negro.

The Centennial is worth celebrating but there is a ghost at the feast. It is true that one can point to progress in the race problem; progress has been made North and South. But this is not saying much. For it is not gainsaying the embarrassing fact that the Negro is not treated as a man in the North or the South, and if you think the North is better, ask James Baldwin. Setting aside everything else, this state of affairs is an interesting anomaly in the first and greatest of the revolutionary democracies and the largest and most Christian nation in Christendom (Meridian, Mississippi, has the largest percentage of churchgoers in the world, and Cicero, Illinois, is not far behind).

Catton says that we still don't understand the meaning of the Civil War and we have not calculated its impact on history. This is true, and one of the most incalculable effects has been the effect of the sectional division on the Negro.

Sectionalism allows each section to dispense itself by using the other as a scapegoat. The North, after all, freed the slaves and afterwards the Northerner wore an aura of righteousness which he would still be wearing if only the slaves' descendants had stayed in the South. Who would have supposed that a hundred years later Northern cities would have large, undigested, and mostly demoralized black ghettos, which Conant recently described as the most explosive element of American life?

The South, on the other hand, has always managed to comfort itself by pointing to the hypocrisy of the North—not realizing that it is a sorry game in which the highest score is a tie: "Look, they're as bad as we are!"

The Northerner is apt to see nothing amiss in moving from uptown Manhattan to Scarsdale to get away from Harlem and deploring Faubus all the way. Southerners talk a great deal about freedom these days, usually freedom to retain segregation. In the South we attend "Christian anti-Communist crusades," segregated. Many Southerners really and truly believe that the Communists are behind the movement to get rid of segregation.

The Centennial should be celebrated and it is well that the War is over and a hundred years have passed and the country is stronger than ever. But there could be an even happier issue: perhaps the country will be sufficiently reconciled so that it may one day wake up and face the one intractable problem with which it has been beset from the very beginning. With the country reconciled and with Negroes living in Tucson and Newburgh, it could even happen that the white man will decide what to do about the black man.

1961

STOICISM IN
THE SOUTH

🍂

It is always hard to generalize about the South, harder perhaps
for the Southerner, for whom the subject is living men, himself
among them, than for the Northerner who, in proportion to his
detachment, can the more easily deal with ideas. Yet I think it is
possible to record at firsthand a momentous change which has
taken place in a single generation—and I do not mean the obvious
changes, the New South of the magazines, the Negro emigration,
or the Supreme Court decision. The change is this: until a few
years ago, the champion of Negro rights in the South, and of fair-
mindedness and toleration in general, was the upper-class white
Southerner. He is their champion no longer. He has, by and large,
unshouldered his burden for someone else to pick up. What has
happened to him? With a few courageous exceptions, he is either
silent or he is leading the Citizens' Councils.

He will not deny the charge but will reply that it is not he
who has changed but the Supreme Court, that he is still fighting
to preserve the same way of life he defended when he opposed
the Klan thirty years ago. Has not pressure from the North
rendered the moderate position untenable? Is he not now fighting
the same good fight as his fathers, who kicked out the scalawags
and carpetbaggers and rescued the South from one of the most
shameful occupations in history?

But it is not the same fight and he has changed. (Again let

me say I only feel free to say this because no white Southerner can write a *j'accuse* without making a *mea culpa*; no more is the average Northerner, either by the accident of his historical position or by his present performance, entitled to a feeling of moral superiority.)

The fact is that neither the ethos nor the traditional worldview of the upper-class white Southerner is any longer adequate to the situation. No longer able to maintain a steadfast and temperate position, he finds himself caught up in violent and even contradictory cross-movements. There is nothing atypical about Faulkner's crying the South's guilt to the high heavens one moment and the next condoning street fighting to perpetuate it. The old alliance of Negro and white gentry has broken up. During the last gubernatorial primary in Louisiana an extraordinary thing happened, the significance of which has been largely missed. The considerable Negro vote went en bloc to its traditional enemy, the poor-white candidate.

What is the reason for this dissolution of the old alliance? Is it simply a result of the Decision, or does the cause lie much deeper? Does it not, in fact, reflect a profound cultural change which, as it has turned out, cannot be accommodated within the ethos of the upper-class white?

The greatness of the South, like the greatness of the English squirearchy, had always a stronger Greek flavor than it ever had a Christian. Its nobility and graciousness was the nobility and graciousness of the Old Stoa. How immediately we recognize the best of the South in the words of the Emperor: "Every moment think steadily, as a Roman and a man, to do what thou hast in hand with perfect and simple dignity, and a feeling of affection, and freedom, and justice." And how curiously foreign to the South sound the Decalogue, the Beatitudes, the doctrine of the Mystical Body. The South's virtues were the broadsword virtues of the clan, as were her vices, too—the hubris of *noblesse* gone arrogant. The Southern gentleman did live in a Christian edifice, but he lived there in the strange fashion Chesterton spoke of, that of a man who will neither go inside nor put it entirely behind him but stands forever grumbling on the porch. From this vantage point he caught sight of Pericles and Hector and the Emperor, and recognized them as his heart's elect. Where was to be found their like? In Abraham? In Paul? He thought not. When he named a city Corinth, he did not mean Paul's community. How like him to go into Chancellorsville or the Argonne with Epictetus in his pocket; how unlike him to have had the Psalms.

It is true that he was raised on the Christian chivalry of Walter Scott, but it was a Christianity which was aestheticized by medieval trappings and a chivalry which was abstracted from its sacramental setting. If *Ivanhoe* and *The Talisman* were his favorite novels, Richard Coeur de Lion and Saladin were his favorite characters, just because in them greatheartedness and soldierly generosity transcended everything, even religious differences.

If the Stoic way was remarkably suited to the Empire of the first century, it was quite as remarkably suited to the agrarian South of the last century. The Colonel Sartoris who made himself responsible for his helpless "freedmen," and the Lucas Beauchamps who accepted his leadership, formed between them a bond such as can only exist between one man in his dignity and another. It was a far nobler relationship than what usually passes under the name of paternalism. The nobility of Sartoris—and there were a great many Sartorises—was the nobility of the natural perfection of the Stoics, the stern inner summons to man's full estate, to duty, to honor, to generosity toward his fellow men and above all to his inferiors—not because they were made in the image of God and were therefore lovable in themselves, but because to do them an injustice would be to defile the inner fortress which was oneself. Whatever its abuses, whatever its final sentimental decay, there was such a thing as *noblesse oblige* on the one side and an extraordinary native courtesy and dignity on the other, by which there occurred, under almost impossible conditions, a flowering of human individuality such as this hemisphere has rarely seen.

Yet, like the Stoa of the Empire, the Stoa of the South was based on a particular hierarchical structure and could not survive the change. Nor did it wish to survive. Its most characteristic mood was a poetic pessimism which took a grim satisfaction in the dissolution of its values—because social decay confirmed one in his original choice of the wintry kingdom of self. He is never more himself than when in a twilight victory of evil, of Modred over

Arthur. And of course he is in good company in his assessment of the modern world. It is not just Faulkner who bears witness to the coming of the mass man, to the alienation and vulgarization of the urban consumer. Ortega y Gasset and Marcel are neither Southern nor Stoic.

The difference is that for the Southern Stoic the day has been lost and lost for good. It seems to him that the Snopeses have won, not only the white Snopeses, but the black Snopeses as well: the white man has lost his *oblige*, the black man has lost his manners, and insolence prevails. For Southern society was above all a society of manners, an incredible triumph of manners, and a twilight of manners seems a twilight of the world. For the Stoic there is no real hope. His finest hour is to sit tight-lipped and ironic while the world comes crashing down around him.

It must be otherwise with the Christian. The urban plebs is not the mass which is to be abandoned to its own barbaric devices, but the lump to be leavened. The Christian is optimistic precisely where the Stoic is pessimistic. What the Stoic sees as the insolence of his former charge—and this is what he can't tolerate, the Negro's demanding his rights instead of being thankful for the squire's generosity—is in the Christian scheme the sacred right which must be accorded the individual, whether deemed insolent or not. For it was not the individual, after all, who was intrinsically precious in the Stoic view—rather, it was one's own attitude toward him, and this could not fail to be specified by the other's good manners or lack of them. If he became insolent, very well: let him taste the bitter fruits of his insolence. The Stoic has no use for the clamoring minority; the Christian must have every use for it.

We in the South can no longer afford the luxury of maintaining the Stoa beside the Christian edifice. In the past we managed the remarkable feat of keeping both, one for living in, the other for dying in. But the Church is no longer content to perform rites of passage; she has entered the arena of the living and must be reckoned with. The white Southerner, Catholic and Protestant, has been invited either to go inside the edifice he has built or to consider what he is doing on the porch at all.

Unfortunately, the Catholic laity of the South have not yet realized this. Rather, it is, to some extent, the other way around—

Catholics have absorbed the local prejudices of the community. Two days before last Good Friday, a membership blank appeared in the New Orleans *Times-Picayune* inviting "Roman Catholics of the Caucasian Race" to join an "Association of Catholic Laymen" for the purpose of "investigating and studying the problems of compulsory integration; to seek out, make known and denounce Communist infiltration, if there be any, in the integration movement," etc. "Roman Catholics of the Caucasian Race"—what a tragic distortion to connect the word Catholic with the miserable euphemism of the Sugar Bowl ticket: "For members of the Caucasian race only." Archbishop Rummel's pastoral letter of February 19 is a hard saying for Louisiana Catholics. No one yet knows what their final reaction will be; there is evidence both of loyalty to and disaffection from this luminous message of Christian charity. Here again the upper-class white Catholic has not distinguished himself. The truth is that the Catholic Church and the twentieth century have caught up with the white Catholics of the South. They can no longer afford the luxury of Creole Catholicism à la Lafcadio Hearn, of Tante Marie going to daily Mass at the Cathedral on a segregated streetcar and seeing God's will in it.

The Stoic-Christian Southerner is offended when the Archbishop of New Orleans calls segregation sinful (or discusses the rights of labor). He cannot help feeling that religion is overstepping its allotted area of morality. In the comfortable modus vivendi of the past, he had been willing enough to allow Christianity a certain say-so on the subject of sin—by which he understood misbehavior in sexual matters, or in drinking and gambling. He is therefore confused and obscurely outraged when Christian teaching is applied to social questions. It is as if a gentleman's agreement had been broken. He does not want the argument on these grounds, but prefers to talk about a "way of life," "states' rights," and legal precedents, or to murmur about Communism, left-wing elements, and infiltration.

Yet, eventually, he must come to terms with his own Christian heritage. So far, Archbishop Rummel has been answered only by having his name booed by the Citizens' Council and by having a cross burned in his front yard. The secular press is silent; the Sartorises are silent if they are not booing; many of his Protestant colleagues are silent; more sadly, his own flock wavers. But sooner or later the archbishop must be answered. And the good pagan's answer is no longer good enough for the South.

1956

A SOUTHERN

VIEW

Dear Editor:

In reading "Climate of the South" by Stephen P. Ryan in the June 15, 1957, issue of *America*—I have always found Mr. Ryan's articles on the Louisiana situation valuable and informative—I was surprised to come across my name given as an example of one of those backsliding Southern liberals who have betrayed the cause by affirming certain values of the South while continuing to oppose segregation.

Mr. Ryan finds it unbelievable that anyone living in 1957 could maintain that the South might have had better constitutional grounds in 1860 for seceding than Lincoln had for invading. (Lincoln himself wasn't quite so sure; he had to wait for something better than his constitutional position and he got it: Sumter fired on.) I made this subversive remark in an otherwise patriotic and pro-Union article in *Commonweal*; but I did not really expect anyone to take offense, since it was my impression that the issue has always been one of the great mooted constitutional questions, a question relevant, of course, to the South's prerogatives in 1860, not in 1957. I would tend to agree with Mr. Ryan that we got whipped and that, whatever the merits of the case, the issue was settled for once and all, and that it was even for the best.

It hardly seems worthwhile to renew this particular argument, since I do not regard it as applicable to the present situation. But

Mr. Ryan's article does raise another issue which is of the utmost importance in the race question. It has to do with the grounds upon which one bases his indictment of segregation.

Let us begin by agreeing on two more points: 1. Segregation is sinful, because, as Archbishop Rummel of New Orleans has said, it is a denial of the unity and solidarity of the human race; it is sinful as openly practiced in the South; it is at least as sinful as covertly practiced in the North. 2. The decision of the U.S. Supreme Court is the law of the land and should be obeyed by all Americans.

This double-barreled blast against segregation is extraordinarily effective in the South and will eventually prevail, however much the South may dislike the verdict. These two charges are directly sanctioned by two traditions deeply rooted in the Southern consciousness: Christianity and the majesty of the law.

In respect of the latter, incidentally, it seems particularly unfortunate that the Supreme Court should have relied so heavily on sociopsychological theory in its decision against segregation when there were ample grounds, according to some jurists, for a purely legal decision. Sociopsychological theories change much more rapidly than Anglo-Saxon law.

But what seems to me nothing less than monstrous is to couple the case against segregation with an ideological hatred of the South and Southern tradition. Mr. Ryan says he doesn't understand how a Southerner can oppose segregation and at the same time cherish his heritage. I don't understand how a Southerner can do anything else. Mr. Ryan sneers at Southern tradition, at "that breed of men, indigenous to the South, who are capable of approving integration and then, in practically the same breath, falling into a state of almost religious ecstasy as they hysterically extol the glories of the Old South of slavery, of mocking birds, hominy grits and bourbon whiskey . . ." This really seems to me to be gratuitously offensive. If Mr. Ryan wonders why the Southern integrationist is discouraged, he needn't look any further. If the rite of initiation into liberalism requires one to swear a blood oath against his native land, then the proposed initiate is going to take another look at the club.

In the first place, even the best-disposed Southerner knows that this sort of charge is not only insulting; it is false. There *is* a

Southern heritage, and it has nothing to do with the colonel in the whiskey ad. It has to do with the conservative tradition of a predominantly agrarian society, a tradition which at its best enshrined the humane aspects of living for rich and poor, black and white. It gave first place to a stable family life, sensitivity and good manners between men, chivalry toward women, an honor code, and individual integrity.

If one wishes to sneer at such values, let him; but I can't help wondering if the sneer does not conceal a contempt for all traditions. It is a tradition which even Wilbur J. Cash recognized as stemming not from the Virginia aristocracy but from the frontier and the farm, and which, Cash goes on to say, possessed a prevalent democratic temper that to an amazing degree destroyed class feeling.

To tell the truth, I can't believe that Mr. Ryan is altogether serious in this old-fashioned Yankee broadside against the entire South. At any rate, it is difficult for me to take it as a sober contribution to the problem, or as anything but a sort of wry, seriocomic piece of rhetoric. Certainly, Mr. Ryan must realize how an attack on segregation mounted on the battleground of enlightened liberal North versus depraved reactionary South must play directly into the hands of those Southerners who like nothing better than drawing a bead on Northern culture.

Nothing is easier than to set forth the major contributions of the North to world culture as the automobile, Levittown, and the split-level home—in which there is no sense of the past, or of real community, or even of one's own identity. Nothing is easier than to let the Northerner describe the Northern ideologist: the ritualistic liberal who sacrifices the human encounter for the abstract liberal passion, who prefers the company of Jews and Negroes, not because of the personal qualities of this or that Jew or Negro, but because they are Jews and Negroes, because of the ritual value of the gesture.

It is just as easy for a really unreconstructed Southerner like Donald Davidson to point out that Mississippi, with very low sociological indexes, has produced William Faulkner and Eudora Welty; while Illinois and Ohio and New Jersey, with very high sociological indexes, produce professors who write books about

William Faulkner. This kind of polemic takes us back to 1860 . . . Many of us had hoped by now that the days of *The New Republic* diatribes against the South were over and that men of good will in both sections would be able to approach the problem in the spirit of national unity and a plight shared in common rather than the spirit of Northern righteousness against Southern iniquity. If the Negro emigration to the North is accomplishing nothing else, it is accomplishing this: the universalizing of the problem. It is no longer a regional problem nor even a national problem, but the problem of human frailty trapped by historical circumstance. What we are faced with now are not "democratic ideals" but religious ultimates: is there any real reason, beyond democratic values, why a man should not be cruel to another man?

Surely it would be better to cherish rather than destroy the cultural cleavage between the North and the South, a cleavage which accounts for the South's preeminence in creative literature and the North's in technics, social propaganda, and objective scholarship. The difference has been traced to a Southern preoccupation with the concrete, the historical, the particular, the immediate; and the Northern passion for the technical, the abstract, the general, the ideological. I see no reason why either tradition should not be enriched rather than reviled by the other.

Here are three simple facts and one deduction which can be drawn from them. The South is a conservative society which openly practices segregation. Segregation is both sinful and illegal. Political conservatism is neither sinful nor illegal—though sometimes one wonders if liberals don't think it is. This being the case, the most effective way to fight segregation is to distinguish between it and the conservative tradition which seeks to conserve, to keep what is good in the past; and the least effective way to fight segregation is to attack not only it but the society that practices it.

Meanwhile, it is the Negro who continues to suffer, in both North and South. Mr. Ryan speaks of the Negro who "can't wait to get out of the lousy South." Has Mr. Ryan heard of the Negro who did get out and who found himself in the North, which was not only lousy but confusing? It is the Negro who is being required to play the heroic role and to transcend the hatreds of both the segregationist and the liberal—and who sometimes, incredibly, succeeds. The tactics of the Reverend Martin Luther King seem to me as wise and as successful as the sometimes arrogant tactics of the NAACP seemed designed precisely to bring about the defeat of its declared objective.

The argument from religion and the law is in the long run unanswerable. The Southern segregationist knows in his bones that he can't continue to profess Christ on Sunday and then draw a racial line to keep his fellow Christians in their place—and his churches are beginning to move. He knows in his bones that the Supreme Court decision will never be reversed and must in the end be obeyed. He has a bad conscience. But the one sure way to give him ground to stand on and to salve his conscience is to attack not only segregation but him, his people, and his past.

Mr. Ryan asks "what is to be done" about the Louisiana Catholic who defies his archbishop and promotes segregation. Well, I don't know what is to be done with him, any more than I know what is to be done with the Illinois Catholic who stones the Negro who moves into his neighborhood. I would presume that if one is a Catholic, one does not "do" anything with him. One follows St. Paul and, instead of despising him as an enemy, corrects him as a brother, all the while in fear and trembling for one's own salvation.

But I cannot close without a salute to Mr. Ryan. We need more like him. Anyhow, this is no time for integrationists to fall out, even if one of them happens to be one of those "Southern particularists." But perhaps particularism is not entirely evil. Perhaps the best imaginable society is not a countrywide Levittown in which everyone is a good liberal ashamed of his past, but a pluralistic society, rich in regional memories and usages. I sincerely believe that the worst fate that could overtake the struggle against segregation would be its capture by a political orthodoxy of the left. I share Mr. Ryan's dismay at the present mood of the South. Maybe this failure of militant liberalism might serve as an occasion for remembering what St. Francis de Sales said about catching flies with honey instead of vinegar.

WALKER PERCY, M.D.
COVINGTON, LA.

1957

THE SOUTHERN
MODERATE

~

To the moderate everywhere it must seem that important public issues are forever being corrupted by extremists. Such an issue was the matter of internal subversion after the war. The people were dismayed when conspiracy came to light and they were forced to recognize the fact that Americans in high places had betrayed their country. It was a necessary cause, the anti-Communism of the early 1950s—something needed to be done and wasn't being done—even though it was open to demagogic exploitation. Overnight, the situation polarized, with intemperate, flag-waving anti-Communists in one camp and anti-anti-Communists in the other. The moderate was pulled left or right against his better judgment, or was stranded, speechless as usual, in the middle.

A similar fate has overtaken another good cause, states' rights. Surely one of the pressing needs of the day is a strengthening of local government and a revival of local responsibility in the face of growing federal power and federal money. States' rights is in the best tradition of both parties. Yet the cause has been so abused of late that it is in danger of being lost for good. The word is coming more and more to mean the right claimed by Citizens' Councils to deny a man something because of his race.

Yet there usually comes a time when the moderate can state a few hard facts and make some modest proposals. Perhaps such a time is at hand in the issue of segregation, judging from the caliber of men appointed to the Civil Rights Commission and from the generally favorable reception the appointments met with.

The Southern moderate, let us say, is a man of good will who is aware of the seriousness of the problem, is searching for a solution, but disagrees that the solution is simple and can be effected overnight. From the point of view of either Marvin Griffin or the NAACP, the solution is relatively simple. One sees it simply as a question of obeying the law, and failing this, of enforcing the law. The other sees it simply as a question of leaving to the states the rights guaranteed them by the Constitution; in short, of letting us alone.

What the NAACP doesn't realize, or will not admit, is that what it proposes is not possible. The entire U.S. Army could not enforce school integration in the South; the South would only close the schools. (The problem of the schools is, of course, the real impasse. The other problems, voting, buses, etc., are trivial by comparison.) All that would be accomplished is the destruction of the public-school system. What the segregationist doesn't realize or doesn't admit to realizing is that racial segregation is increasingly intolerable as the twentieth century wears on. As an editorial in *America* pointed out, segregation is no wronger now than it was a hundred years ago, but times change and the same wrong may become more obvious and more hurtful. Racial segregation is more hurtful now in the time of world crisis and more demoralizing to Negroes and also, I believe, to whites in a time of heightened social consciousness. The moderate is aware both of the enormous difficulty of the problem and of the pressing need to do something about it. But the greatest need, to him, is the exercise of responsibility. What disturbs him is what he regards as the irresponsibility of both sides which has largely erased the hard-won gains of the past fifty years, the irresponsibility of a Faubus and the irresponsibility of those Northern politicians who, for the sake of the Negro vote, support any and every proposal of federal intervention.

Perhaps the most serious consequence of the hardening of attitudes has been the waste of energies, with much of Northern liberal thought preoccupied with Southern intransigence and nearly all the best minds of the South enlisted in the defense.

Instead of being constructively concerned with race questions, as the South was ten years ago, Southern brains are now committed to circumventing the Supreme Court and to cataloguing the failings of the North.

The quarrel has the nightmarish quality of a feud; the same old charges and countercharges have been revived in every dreary particular—with one difference. Rapid social changes are taking place which can only have the effect of radically altering the character of the problem, if not of solving it. Like most social changes, they are ambiguous. They may even be regarded as social evils, but they are evils from which good can come. Indeed, they hold out the first real promise of ridding the country of its greatest curse.

One change is the rapidly ongoing emigration of the Negro from the South. What is taking place is not merely the national distribution of the Negro but the national distribution of the problem of racial injustice. For the first time, the Gallup Poll reports that the race question is now regarded as the number-one American problem. This means, as I understand it, that the American dilemma is no longer what shall we do about the South, but what shall we do about the Negro. The change would seem at first sight to be only the spread of an evil and nothing to rejoice over—certainly, the increasing racial difficulties of the North are a sorry comfort to the South—but paradoxically a great good can come of it. One can only imagine what reserves of energies and good will might be tapped, North and South, if at long last the problem were shared in common. It could even mean the beginning of the end of the two complementary American failings, the neurotic guilt of the South and the triumphant Pharisaism of the North.

The country has been so long preoccupied with the wrangle that perhaps no one has an inkling of a future free of it, free, not of the problem, but of the sterile divisiveness in the face of the problem. The other night, as my daughter was reading aloud from her fifth-grade history about Revolutionary times, I could not help wondering what it was like to live as a Virginian or Carolinian or New Yorker without the old bloody reflex, one arm ever upraised to strike or defend. It may be the suffering Negro himself who will save us all from what we have done to him.

The other change in progress is an economic one. As Harry Ashmore expressed it, a pattern is emerging in which the South will accommodate its dwindling Negro population as it moves from second- to first-class citizenship, a pattern which has nothing to do with the harsh words and extremist laws, which is imperfect but bids fair to be effective. Racial injustice is bad business. There is no segregation in the stores. Let us hope the Christian conscience will be decisive, but, failing this, let us be glad that for once the pocketbook is its ally.

These changes indicate possible areas of settlement; they also indicate social dangers which could make the cure worse than the disease. Perhaps the real role of the moderate is, not to press for a quick solution, but to humanize, to moderate, the solution which is surely coming.

Let us not forget the stubborn fact that, whatever the shortcomings of the North, a man may sit where he pleases on the subway, attend the closest school; he may not always live where he pleases if he is a Negro, and he doesn't even know which hotels and restaurants he may enter. Nevertheless, it is the de jure segregation of the South, and the sign FOR WHITES ONLY, which the Negro must find increasingly humiliating. This being the case, and in the face of our present national embarrassment in world affairs, a cynical solution has been proposed. The obvious answer, the suggestion goes, is the Northern answer, de jure integration for the record and de facto segregation where it really counts. Even throw in the buses and drinking fountains; there are ways and means of zoning suburbs and school districts. The proposal is unmeriting. I mention it because it unwittingly provides clues to sociological realities which are usually overlooked in the heat of polemics and which, if examined closely, provide areas for real progress toward a settlement.

First, there is such a thing as a de facto segregation in the public schools of the North. It is partly racial but mostly ecological, a natural consequence, whatever the morality of it, of the economic organization of the city. Professor Frazier of Howard University suggests that if the South really wants to do something about de jure segregation, a knowledge of this state of affairs would go a long way toward countering the usual argument that desegregation would mean racial mixing. The fact is that, even after integration, the white schools would remain largely white and the colored schools largely colored.

Second, it illustrates the nature of the Southern protest. Southerners are frankly concerned about the social and sexual consequences of integration. If, instead of scouting this fear as exaggerated or neurotic, one takes it at face value, one will discover that it reflects a very real social phenomenon in the South and that the fear is more or less appropriate to the phenomenon. This phenomenon is the peculiar social role which the public schools play in the life of the community.

But, before making a proposal, let us first understand the gravity of the problem of school desegregation. Serious enough under the best conditions, it has become immeasurably more serious through a concurrence of bad luck, bad timing, and federal stupidity. Only such a combination, plus political irresponsibility, could have brought to pass a national disaster like Little Rock.

The difficulty of the school problem is the difficulty of any enforced cultural change. The bad luck is that the most important cultural change should be in the area of education, where those exposed to the change are children. Even Southerners who believe the change to be ultimately for the best are disturbed about subjecting their children to a culturally retarded group, however temporary the lag. But, worse luck, the group most affected must be the co-educational high school and junior high, where the problem necessarily takes on a sexual coloration. The problem of co-education at this level is itself a moot one. That it should intersect with the racial problem is unfortunate, to say the least. But the incredible bad luck is that the crisis of school integration should coincide with the crisis of juvenile morality and with the upturn of crime statistics among urban Negro populations.

But federal stupidity was the last straw. Of all possible educational levels, postgraduate, college, high school, junior high, grammar school, kindergarten, the Justice Department had to choose as the arena of its major test the co-educational high school with its full complement of explosive ingredients! As Walter Lippmann put it, this was the worst imaginable place to join the issue.

And all this at the most critical period of America's leadership in world affairs! Our enemies could not have done a better job of assembling our every fault into the ugliest possible façade for the world to see.

One has other regrets. It is perhaps a necessary evil that major changes have to be announced in an authoritative language that commands obedience. For unquestionably a great deal of the furor is engendered by words, or rather the space between word and deed which encourages myth. To give one example: I have seen white Catholics in Louisiana attend unsegregated barbecues and horse shows at "mission" churches and never think twice about it because no one advertised the affair as an "integrated horse show"— some of them Catholics who, when Archbishop Joseph F. Rummel announced his intention of integrating the parochial schools, were bitterly opposed to mixing the races. The announcement of a change encourages all sorts of specters, in this case the specter of the abstract Negro delinquent put together from newspaper headlines.

Once we appreciate the seriousness of the impasse, however, it becomes possible to make realistic suggestions. A clue to the kind of settlement the situation calls for is to be found in the nature of the Southern protest. The opposition to integration of the schools is almost invariably expressed in social terms, social, that is, in the sense of personal intercourse. This protest stems from a sociological reality which is a characteristic of Southern life. This reality is the zone of social encounter. Anyone who has gone to school North and South knows what I mean. In the North the zone of obligatory social encounter usually stops at one's front door. A public high school is a place where one goes primarily to acquire certain services, just as the A & P is a place to acquire certain goods. One may, of course, make friends in school, have dates, but this is far more of an option, far more segregated, if you will, from the business at hand.

A public high school in the South is at least as social an institution as it is educational. The social body almost coincides with the student body. This is a particular manifestation of a more general phenomenon. The same social dimension includes as well the people upstairs, next door, the corner drugstore, and so on. The agreeable state of affairs in the South was made possible, of course, by the highly homogenous character of the non-Negro population. Except for a few coastal areas and river ports, it was and is white, Protestant, and Anglo-Saxon. The schools were never seen quite as public institutions, as the word is used in the rest of the country to mean a tax-supported service provided for any person at all. That is why so many Southern schools never had sororities and fraternities—the whole school was a white, Protestant, Anglo-Saxon fellowship. Nor is this said in criticism—on the contrary: the small-town high school in the South is an extremely pleasant, humane, democratic institution.

Perhaps a similar distinction might be drawn between the small-town and big-city schools of the North. I don't know but I doubt it.

This very phenomenon—and what is happening to it—may, like the economic changes Harry Ashmore talks about, suggest its own "solution." It is an ambiguous solution. It means the passing of a unique way of life. The change is inevitable but perhaps the loss is not. One hopes that the South's genius for graceful and humane relations between people may not be forgotten in the coming urbanization.

What must take place if we are ever to have interracial peace is a shrinkage of the zone of personal intercourse. No doubt, it would be preferable to achieve racial accord by an implementing of Christian teachings. But if men do not wish to love one another, then let them at least strive for neutrality. We must, for better or worse, see the public school for what it is, a public place, as public as a post office or a department-store elevator. In spite of the physical intimacy of an elevator, the passengers do not feel they are sharing the same living space.

Once this happens, and once it is realized that desegregation does not necessarily mean a substantial mixing of the races, the greatest fear of the segregationist is removed—the fear of the necessary social, ergo sexual, encounter which, of course, is not being required of anyone. It is this difference in the social roles of the schools which leads to a major misunderstanding. The Northerner is mystified by the massive defiance of the South in this matter because to him there is no qualitive difference between sitting next to a person in the subway and sitting next to him in the classroom. For the Southerner it is very different. School integration means the lowering of two barriers, not one: the public and the social.

No doubt, human brotherhood is better than a depersonalized society. But a depersonalized society is better than one threatened by violence.

The shrinkage of the social zone is already going on apace as the South becomes urbanized and suburbanized, along with the general convergence of all regions upon a way of life in which locales are more and more indistinguishable. Television, the automobile, the suburban home, and the shopping center are much the same the country over. We have heard a great deal about the growing anonymity of American life. Even a liberal Southerner cannot fail to regret the passing of an era of true intimacy between Negro and white and cannot help contrasting it with what he sees as somewhat shallow friendships between educated whites and Negroes.

Yet the growing depersonalization of Southern life may not be such a bad thing, after all. God writes straight with crooked lines. If the shrinkage of social intercourse to patio and barbecue pit serves no other purpose, it might yet provide a truly public zone outside where people are free to move about in a kind of secure anonymity until the time comes when they might wish to be friends.

1957

BOURBON

This is not written by a connoisseur of Bourbon. Ninety-nine percent of Bourbon drinkers know more about Bourbon than I do. It is about the aesthetic of Bourbon drinking in general and in particular of knocking it back neat.

I can hardly tell one Bourbon from another, unless the other is very bad. Some bad Bourbons are even more memorable than good ones. For example, I can recall being broke with some friends in Tennessee and deciding to have a party and being able to afford only two-fifths of a $1.75 Bourbon called Two Natural, whose label showed dice coming up 5 and 2. Its taste was memorable. The psychological effect was also notable. After knocking back two or three shots over a period of half an hour, the three male drinkers looked at each other and said in a single voice: "Where are the women?"

I have not been able to locate this remarkable Bourbon since.

Not only should connoisseurs of Bourbon not read this article, neither should persons preoccupied with the perils of alcoholism, cirrhosis, esophageal hemorrhage, cancer of the palate, and so forth—all real enough dangers. I, too, deplore these afflictions. But, as between these evils and the aesthetic of Bourbon drinking, that is, the use of Bourbon to warm the heart, to reduce the anomie of the late twentieth century, to cut the cold phlegm of

Wednesday afternoons, I choose the aesthetic. What, after all, is the use of not having cancer, cirrhosis, and such, if a man comes home from work every day at five-thirty to the exurbs of Montclair or Memphis and there is the grass growing and the little family looking not quite at him but just past the side of his head, and there's Cronkite on the tube and the smell of pot roast in the living room, and inside the house and outside in the pretty exurb has settled the noxious particles and the sadness of the old dying Western world, and him thinking: "Jesus, is this it? Listening to Cronkite and the grass growing?"

If I should appear to be suggesting that such a man proceed as quickly as possible to anesthetize his cerebral cortex by ingesting ethyl alcohol, the point is being missed. Or part of the point. The joy of Bourbon drinking is not the pharmacological effect of C_2H_5OH on the cortex but rather the instant of the whiskey being knocked back and the little explosion of Kentucky U.S.A. sunshine in the cavity of the nasopharynx and the hot bosky bite of Tennessee summertime—aesthetic considerations to which the effect of the alcohol is, if not dispensable, at least secondary.

By contrast, Scotch: for me (not, I presume, for a Scot), drinking Scotch is like looking at a picture of Noel Coward. The whiskey assaults the nasopharynx with all the excitement of paregoric. Scotch drinkers (not all, of course) I think of as upward-mobile Americans, Houston and New Orleans businessmen who graduate from Bourbon about the same time they shed seersuckers for Lilly slacks. Of course, by now these same folk may have gone back to Bourbon and seersucker for the same reason, because too many Houston oilmen drink Scotch.

Nothing, therefore, will be said about the fine points of sour mash, straights, blends, bonded, except a general preference for the lower proofs. It is a matter of the arithmetic of aesthetics. If one derives the same pleasure from knocking back 80-proof Bourbon as 100-proof, the formula is both as simple as $2 + 2 = 4$ and as incredible as non-Euclidean geometry. Consider. One knocks back five one-ounce shots of 80-proof Early Times or four shots of 100-proof Old Fitzgerald. The alcohol ingestion is the same:

$$5 \times 40\% = 2$$
$$4 \times 50\% = 2$$

Yet, in the case of the Early Times, one has obtained an extra quantum of joy without cost to liver, brain, or gastric mucosa. A bonus, pure and simple, an aesthetic gain as incredible as two parallel lines meeting at infinity.

An apology to the reader is in order, nevertheless, for it has just occurred to me that this is the most unedifying and even maleficent piece I ever wrote—if it should encourage potential alcoholics to start knocking back Bourbon neat. It is also the unfairest. Because I am, happily and unhappily, endowed with a bad GI tract, diverticulosis, neurotic colon, and a mild recurring nausea, which make it less likely for me to become an alcoholic than my healthier fellow Americans. I can hear the reader now: Who is he kidding? If this joker has to knock back five shots of Bourbon every afternoon just to stand the twentieth century, he's already an alcoholic. Very well. I submit to this or any semantic. All I am saying is that if I drink much more than this I will get sick as a dog for two days and the very sight and smell of whiskey will bring on the heaves. Readers beware, therefore, save only those who have stronger wills or as bad a gut as I.

The pleasure of knocking back Bourbon lies in the plane of the aesthetic but at an opposite pole from connoisseurship. My preference for the former is or is not deplorable depending on one's value system—that is to say, how one balances out the Epicurean virtues of cultivating one's sensory end organs with the greatest discrimination and at least cost to one's health, against the virtue of evocation of time and memory and of the recovery of self and the past from the fogged-in disoriented Western world. In Kierkegaardian terms, the use of Bourbon to such an end is a kind of aestheticized religious mode of existence, whereas connoisseurship, the discriminating but single-minded stimulation of sensory end organs, is the aesthetic of damnation.

Two exemplars of the two aesthetics come to mind:

Imagine Clifton Webb, scarf at throat, sitting at Cap d'Antibes on a perfect day, the little wavelets of the Mediterranean sparkling in the sunlight, and he is savoring a 1959 Mouton Rothschild.

Then imagine William Faulkner, having finished *Absalom, Absalom!*, drained, written out, pissed-off, feeling himself over the edge and out of it, nowhere, but he goes somewhere, his favorite hunting place in the Delta wilderness of the Big Sunflower River and, still feeling bad with his hunting cronies and maybe even a little phony, which he was, what with him trying to pretend that he was one of them, a farmer, hunkered down in the cold and rain after the hunt, after honorably passing up the does and seeing no bucks, shivering and snot-nosed, takes out a flat pint of any Bourbon at all and flatfoots about a third of it. He shivers again but not from the cold.

Bourbon does for me what the piece of cake did for Proust.

1926: As a child watching my father in Birmingham, in the exurbs, living next to number-6 fairway of the New Country Club, him disdaining both the bathtub gin and white lightning of the time, aging his own Bourbon in a charcoal keg, on his hands and knees in the basement sucking on a siphon, a matter of gravity requiring cheek pressed against cement floor, the siphon getting going, the decanter ready, the first hot spurt into his mouth not spat out.

1933: My uncle's sun parlor in the Mississippi Delta and toddies on a Sunday afternoon, the prolonged and meditative tinkle of silver spoon against crystal to dissolve the sugar; talk, tinkle, talk; the talk mostly political: "Roosevelt is doing a good job; no, the son of a bitch is betraying his class."

1934: Drinking at a Delta dance, the boys in bi-swing jackets and tab collars, tough-talking and profane and also scared of the girls and therefore safe in the men's room. Somebody passes around bootleg Bourbon in a Coke bottle. It's awful. Tears start from eyes, faces turn red. "Hot damn, that's good!"

1935: Drinking at a football game in college. UNC versus Duke. One has a blind date. One is lucky. She is beautiful. Her clothes are the color of the fall leaves and her face turns up like a flower. But what to *say* to her, let alone what to do, and whether she is "nice" or "hot"—a distinction made in those days. But what to *say?* Take a drink, by now from a proper concave hip flask (a long way from the Delta Coke bottle) with a hinged top. Will she have a drink? No. But it's all right. The taste of the Bourbon

(Cream of Kentucky) and the smell of her fuse with the brilliant Carolina fall and the sounds of the crowd and the hit of the linemen in a single synesthesia.

1941: Drinking mint juleps, famed Southern Bourbon drink, though in the Deep South not really drunk much. In fact, they are drunk so seldom that when, say, on Derby Day somebody gives a julep party, people drink them like cocktails, forgetting that a good julep holds at least five ounces of Bourbon. Men fall face-down unconscious, women wander in the woods disconsolate and amnesiac, full of thoughts of Kahlil Gibran and the limberlost.

Would you believe the first mint julep I had I was sitting not on a columned porch but in the Boo Snooker bar of the New Yorker Hotel with a Bellevue nurse in 1941? The nurse, a nice upstate girl, head floor nurse, brisk, swift, good-looking; Bellevue nurses, the best in the world and this one the best of Bellevue, at least the best-looking. The julep, an atrocity, a heavy syrupy Bourbon and water in a small glass clotted with ice. But good!

How could two women be more different than the beautiful languid Carolina girl and this swift handsome girl from Utica, best Dutch stock? One thing was sure. Each was to be courted, loved, drunk with, with Bourbon. I should have stuck with Bourbon. We changed to gin fizzes because the bartender said he came from New Orleans and could make good ones. He could and did. They were delicious. What I didn't know was that they were made with raw egg albumen and I was allergic to it. Driving her home to Brooklyn and being in love! What a lovely fine strapping smart girl! And thinking of being invited into her apartment where she lived alone and of her offering to cook a little supper and of the many kisses and the sweet love that already existed between us and was bound to grow apace, when on the Brooklyn Bridge itself my upper lip began to swell and little sparks of light flew past the corner of my eye like St. Elmo's fire. In the space of thirty seconds my lip stuck out a full three-quarter inch, like a shelf, like Mortimer Snerd. Not only was kissing out of the question but my eyes swelled shut. I made it across the bridge, pulled over to the curb, and fainted. Whereupon this noble nurse drove me back to Bellevue, gave me a shot, and put me to bed.

Anybody who monkeys around with gin and egg white deserves

what he gets. I should have stuck with Bourbon and have from
that day to this.

POSTSCRIPT: *Reader, just in case you don't want to knock it back
straight and would rather monkey around with perfectly good Bourbon,
here's my favorite recipe, "Cud'n Walker's Uncle Will's Favorite Mint Julep
Receipt."*

You need excellent Bourbon whiskey; rye or Scotch will not
do. Put half an inch of sugar in the bottom of the glass and merely
dampen it with water. Next, very quickly—and here is the trick in
the procedure—crush your ice, actually powder it, preferably in a
towel with a wooden mallet, so quickly that it remains dry, and,
slipping two sprigs of fresh mint against the inside of the glass,
cram the ice in right to the brim, packing it with your hand.
Finally, fill the glass, which apparently has no room left for anything
else, with Bourbon, the older the better, and grate a bit of nutmeg
on the top. The glass will frost immediately. Then settle back in
your chair for half an hour of cumulative bliss.

1975

Two

SCIENCE,

LANGUAGE,

LITERATURE

IS A THEORY
OF MAN POSSIBLE?

❧

The answer is "yes," I think so. But a more interesting question to me is whether the question makes any sense to you. I can't help but wonder how you respond: Is a theory of man possible? Do you shrug and say to yourself: But I thought that was settled. Or do you tend to regard the question, as well as any answer, as hopelessly grandiose in our present state of knowledge? Or does the question stir memories of ancient and boring quarrels about the nature of man which you would as soon not rehash?

The question suggests that a theory of man does not presently exist or at least that traditional theories of man have been seriously challenged. Yet I suspect that most of us, whether we consciously profess it or not, are already equipped with a theory of man. Indeed, it is hard to imagine how one can live one's life and work with other people day in and day out unless one has already made certain assumptions about one's own nature as well as other people's. It may be as impossible for us *not* to have a theory of man as it is impossible for primitive man not to have a theory of the world and its origins.

The next question is whether the theories we more or less unconsciously profess make any sense, or are of any help to us as students of behavior.

Some of us, for example, would reflexly refer this question to certain traditional Greek and Judeo-Christian teachings about the nature of man which are implicit in Western civilization itself. Thus, if one is a professing Christian or Jew, or even if one is not, it still comes second-nature to us to think of man in such terms as body and soul, flesh and spirit, mind and matter, matter and form, the mental and the physical, and so on.

By the same token, some of us may find it equally natural to think of man in quite different terms—terms which are nevertheless as much part and parcel of this same Western tradition, or at least the last two hundred years of it. I mean, of course, that for a person who has spent his entire intellectual life in the scientific tradition, with, say, twenty-six years of schooling culminating in a degree in medicine or psychology or sociology or med tech or nursing or whatever, it may be quite natural to think of man as you think of rats or chimpanzees, as an organism, a biological energy system, not qualitatively different from other such energy systems. True, it is generally recognized that the human species does seem to possess certain unique properties such as language, abstract thinking, complex tool using, art, culture, and so on. Surely everyone would admit, even the most mechanistic behaviorist, that men write books about chimpanzees and dolphins but that chimpanzees and dolphins do not write books about men.

Yet these differences may not shake one's conviction that man is still an organism among organisms, responding to his environment just as other organisms do, and that these unusual traits are the consequences of evolutionary and genetic changes which have befallen man and which may appear different but are not qualitatively different from the behavior of other organisms—just as one thinks of a bird's flight as a successful genetic adventure which has worked because, under the dispensation of the natural laws of evolution, it gives the organism a better chance of occupying this or that ecological niche in its environment.

In the case of man, what is more natural than to think of man's peculiar gifts of language, culture, and technology as but yet another evolutionary stratagem not only for adapting to an environment but also for conquering it? If we overlook some of man's perverse traits, his peculiar penchant for making war against his own species, his discovery of suicide, and his vulnerability to psychosis and such, what more spectacular proof do we have of

Darwin's naturalistic theory than man's conquest of the earth through a few mutations such as upright gait, opposition of thumb and fingers, language, and cognitive process?

Does it not, in fact, offend one's sense of the continuity of science if somebody suggests that man is truly unique—unique in a sense not allowed by the organismic view of man?

What I wish to suggest to you is that these two traditional Western ways of thinking about man, the Greco-Judeo-Christian and the scientific-organismic, may presently do us a disservice as far as a workable behavioral theory is concerned. That is to say, they may very well conceal more than they reveal. For both traditions make some basic and unexamined assumptions about the nature of man and so give all the appearance of theory without being able to do what valuable theory does; namely, shed light and provide groundwork where questions can be asked and coherent answers looked for.

Ignorance, if recognized, is often more fruitful than the appearance of knowledge. Thus, if I were to raise with you the question of the nature of the red spot on the planet Jupiter, you might be curious, because we don't know what causes the red spot on Jupiter and we know we don't know. But if one raises the question of the nature of man, about which we know even less than we know about the red spot on Jupiter, one is apt to encounter blank looks, shrugs. That is, until recent years, when things began to fall apart. At least, nowadays, people are becoming aware of the incoherence of the present theories.

It is not difficult to demonstrate that there does not presently exist a coherent theory of man in the scientific sense—the sense in which we have a coherent theory about the behavior of rats and, more recently, a theory about what causes the red spot on Jupiter. I suspect that most of us hold to both traditions, man as body-mind and man as organism, without exactly knowing how he can be both—for if man is yet another organism in an environment, he is a very strange organism indeed, an organism which has the unusual capacity for making himself unhappy for no good reason, for existing as a lonely and fretful consciousness which never quite knows who he is or where he belongs.

I hasten to add that I do not presume to call into question

the value and truth of either the Judeo-Christian or the Darwinian-naturalistic concept of man. As a matter of fact, I happen to subscribe to the former theologically and to the latter scientifically, regarding it as an extremely useful and well-established theory and a valuable method of accounting for the immense variety of structure and function in the over two million earth species.

What I am suggesting is that it is of little help to us scientifically to regard man as a composite of body, mind, and soul, and that it is a positive hindrance if we think this explains anything. And it is equally stifling to scientific curiosity if we imagine that we have explained anything at all, let alone man in all his perversity and uniqueness, if we take this or that laboratory hypothesis—say, learning theory as applied to organisms in a laboratory environment—and by verbal sleight-of-hand stick the label onto man. Then we find ourselves stuck with some all-too-familiar still-born monsters. We may say, for example, that organism A endowed with genetic constitution B and subjected to environmental stimulus C will respond with behavior D if it has been rewarded by reinforcing stimulus E. Now, we know from many arduous and painstaking experiments that this model is a useful way of thinking about the behavior of many organisms. The damage is done, however, and science is affronted and curiosity depressed when in the next breath one hears something like this: Human being A endowed with brain B responds with pleasure to experience C—say, viewing the Mona Lisa in the Louvre—with behavior D, the exclamation "Beautiful!" because human being A has learned through operant conditioning E that such an expression is met with approval and an increase in status among one's peers.

Or, if we do not have the modesty of Freud, it is all too easy to play psychological parlor games and to pretend to account for Dostoevsky's *The Gambler* or Kafka's *The Castle* as an expression of such-and-such libidinal energies.

But the main error, it seems to me, of both the armchair behaviorist and the armchair psychologist is not the quick extrapolation from the simple hypothesis to complex human reality but rather the willingness of both to accept the age-old split of the human creature into this strange Janus monster comprising body and mind.

The biologist and learning theorist can't get hold of mind and usually don't want to. The Freudian psychologist, on the other hand, has trouble getting out of the psyche—his own psyche and that of his patients.

The question I am trying to raise with you is whether or not we have settled for a view of man which is grossly incoherent by any scientific canon. That is to say, I wonder if through a kind of despair or through sheer weariness we have not given up the attempt to put man back together again, if indeed he was ever whole, or whether man isn't like Humpty Dumpty, who fell off the wall three hundred years ago, or rather was pushed by Descartes, who split man into body and mind—two disparate pieces which, incidentally, Descartes believed were connected through the pineal body. As a matter of fact, I'm not sure we've made a better connection between the two since.

To bring matters closer to home and to our own interests and concerns, I would propose to you this little hospital as a kind of microcosm of this schism in Western consciousness which we accept as a matter of course. I am wondering whether, like the rest of us, in doing work here, treatment, teaching, research, you have not already proceeded on the tacit assumption that man is composed of body and mind, and that between the two there is only a nodding acquaintance.

Indeed, this hospital strikes me as an excellent model both of the virtues of modern medical and psychotherapeutic practice and of the schism we have accepted, consisting as it does of two stories, an upstairs-downstairs world where somatic disorders are treated on the ground floor where medical theory is well grounded, and psychic dysfunctions are treated on the second story. I wonder if the planners of this arrangement didn't unconsciously know what they were doing when they put the psychotherapist somewhat up in the air, so to speak? This is not to impugn either physicians or psychotherapists, but only to suggest that we laymen tend to think of the internist and surgeon as dealing with matters rather firmly grounded in the biological sciences, while we think of the psychotherapist as treating disorders which are no less real but which are notoriously hard to get hold of and even harder to connect up with the great body of the physical sciences.

To get down to cases, wouldn't it strike us all as inappropriate if a patient walked in with a case of hemorrhoids and had to get on the elevator and go upstairs for treatment—while a patient suffering from free-floating anxiety was sent down to the basement? It offends our sense of the order of things.

This is only to assert what is surely a commonplace; namely, that the medical and surgical disciplines attempt and often succeed in dealing with matter in interaction and so generally preserve a degree of continuity with the well-established laws of the chemical, physical, and biological sciences. Whereas in the case of the psychiatric and psychotherapeutic disciplines, through no fault of theirs, and however they choose to define themselves, nearly all of them address themselves—must address themselves—to mental or subjective realities. A standard textbook of psychotherapy published over ten years ago lists ten different schools of psychotherapy, running from Freud's psychoanalysis to Sullivan's theory of interpersonal relations—and this does not include the more recent and promising schools of transactional analysis and Gestalt therapy. As diverse as all these systems are, they share one trait in common: they all deal, by and large, with subjective, mental, or emotional entities, events and states which cannot be seen or measured but can only be reported by the patient. Even the stimulus-and-response therapy of Dollard and Miller stretches the term "response" to include what they call "subjectively observable responses"—in short, any mental state the patient chooses to report.

It is also surely a commonplace to say that to many physicians and surgeons such a proliferation of theory suggests that the subject matter of psychiatry and psychotherapy is both more difficult and, in a real sense, harder to get hold of by the scientific method, and that a single "correct" theory has not yet been hit upon in the sense that, say, a single theory of the mechanics of ovulation or renal function is generally agreed to exist.

I mention these well-known and fundamental divergences between the subject matters of the medical sciences and the psychiatric sciences to raise nagging questions; namely, whether this split of the human species into body and mind is not intractable, whether it is not in the very nature of things that we shall always be dealing with somatic complaints on the first floor and emotional complaints on another floor or another wing, and whether the two will ever have much more to do with each other than they do now—and to raise an even more distressing question: Is the very nature of mindstuff such that we will never be able to get hold of it, converge on it, and that schools of psychotherapy will continue to proliferate?

I mention this all too familiar state of affairs to bring to your attention the glimmer of a new way of looking at things. This is not to suggest that Humpty Dumpty can be put back together again. If modern man was split in two by Descartes's mind-body theory three hundred years ago, it is unlikely that he can be pasted back together by yet another theory. But it may be possible that we can at least see the fragments, Humpty Dumpty's fragments, not as disparate parts, body and mind, which never seem to have fit together, but at least as parts of the same creature.

By a "new way of looking at things," I refer to what is called variously triadic theory, semiotics, semiosis. It is not new, being in the main the discovery of the American logician and philosopher Charles Peirce some seventy-five years ago.

Charles Peirce's triadic theory applies mainly to man's strange and apparently unique capacity to use symbols and, in particular, to his gift of language.

It might be well to begin with what I take to be a growing consensus about the nature of language itself—which is central to our thesis. A curious swing-back of the pendulum has occurred in recent years. To oversimplify the case, one might describe the traditional view of man, say, up to one hundred years ago, as the centerpiece of creation, made in the image of God, distinguished from the beasts in being endowed with soul, intellect, free will, reason, and the gift of language. He could name things, think about things, was free to do all he wanted, convey his thoughts by words which could be understood by other men.

At the opposite swing of the pendulum—say, thirty to fifty years ago, following the victory of early Darwinism, at the full tide of Pavlovian and Watsonian behaviorism and with the gathering impetus of Freud's discovery of the power of the irrational forces of the unconscious—man was not only dethroned from his lordship of creation, but his very reason, and the autonomy of his consciousness, was called into question. And as for the one faculty which even Darwin admitted seemed to set him apart from the beasts, the gift of language, even that seemed explainable, or was held explainable, at least in principle, as a response, the learned response of an organism, admittedly more complex than the response of a rat to a signal, but not qualitatively different.

Now, let me quickly summarize what I take to be the present position of some recent writers, linguistic theorists, psycholinguists, semioticists, and the like. I have in mind not only Charles Peirce but Suzanne Langer, Ernst Cassirer, and Noam Chomsky.

The consensus, it seems fair to state, is: Man's capacity for language and the use of symbols does indeed seem to be unique among species. It cannot be explained by the known laws of learning theory or any refinement of adaptation of these laws. The contrast is dramatic. Take a human child and the most intelligent of the nonhuman primates, a young chimpanzee. Following the most rigorous training, months and years of input, a chimpanzee can be taught perhaps seventy-five hand signals by means of which he can communicate this or that need, "Want banana, hug me, tickle me," and so on. In the case of the human child, during this same period of time and without anybody taking much trouble about it, the child will learn to utter and understand an infinite number of new sentences in his language. Chomsky actually uses the word "infinite" to describe this language competence.

This capacity for language seems to be, in the evolutionary scale, a relatively recent, sudden, and explosive development. A few years ago, it was thought to have begun to happen with Homo erectus perhaps a million years ago. Now, as Julian Jaynes at Princeton, among others, believes, it appears to have occurred in Neanderthal man as recently as the fourth glaciation, which lasted from about 75,000 to 35,000 years ago. During this same period, especially around 40,000 years ago, there occurred an explosive increase in the use and variety of new tools. The human brain increased in weight about fifty-four percent, much of this increase occurring in the cortex, especially in those areas around the Sylvan fissure implicated in the perception and production of speech.

There are new structures, not present or else extremely rudimentary in even the highest apes. Moreover, recent experiments have shown that if one destroys this cortical region in other primates, it has no effect on vocalization, which is mediated not by a cortical but rather by the limbic system.

What does this mean? It means, for one thing, that there occurred in the evolution of man an extraordinary and unprecedented event which in the scale of evolutionary time was as sudden as biblical creation and whose consequences we are just beginning to explore. A fifty-four percent increase in brain weight in a few thousand years is, evolutionarily speaking, almost an instantaneous event. Anatomically speaking, it is perhaps not too much to say that this spectacular quantum jump is what made man human.

What is important to notice is that this change is not merely yet another evolutionary adaptation or adventure, however extraordinary. Man is not merely another organism which has learned to utter and understand sounds. Language is apparently an all-or-none threshold. As the linguist Edward Sapir said, there is no such thing as a primitive language. Language is unlike bird's flight. Some birds are superb flyers; others are lousy. But every normal human has the capacity for uttering and understanding an infinite number of sentences in his language, no matter what the language is. As Helen Keller said, once she discovered that the word "water" was the name of the liquid, she then had to know what everything else was.

What I am saying, along with Peirce, Langer, Cassirer, and Chomsky, is that once man has crossed the threshold of language and the use of other symbols, he literally lives in a new and different world. If a Martian were to visit earth, I think the main thing he would notice about earthlings is that they spend most of their time in one kind of symbolic transaction or other, talking or listening, gossiping, reading books, writing books, making reports, listening to lecturers, delivering lectures, telling jokes, looking at paintings, watching TV, going to movies. Even at night, asleep, his mind is busy with dreams, which are, of course, a very tissue of symbols.

So sweepingly has his very life and his world been transformed by his discovery of symbols that it seems more accurate to call man not Homo sapiens—because man's folly is at least as characteristic as his wisdom—but Homo symbolificus, man the symbol-mongerer, or Homo loquens, man the talker. To paraphrase William Faulkner: Even if the world should come to an end and there are only two survivors, what do you think they would be doing most of the time? Talking, talking about what happened and what they plan to do about it.

Assuming, then, that this is the case, that man is truly a different kind of creature, something new under the sun, a symbol-mongerer, does that bring us any closer to the beginnings of a minimal theory of man; that is to say, a model of man which would do justice to his uniqueness while at the same time giving a coherent account of his place in the hierarchy of creatures, an account, in other words, which might be acceptable both to behavioral scientists and to theologians?

Charles Peirce's idea is quite simple really, like all important ideas so simple, in fact, that it is hard to get hold of, so ingrained has become our customary way of thinking about natural phenomena, whether these phenomena are the chemical reactions in a test tube or the metabolism within a cell or the Freudian model of libidinal energies transacting within a psyche.

Peirce believed that there are at least two kinds of natural phenomena, and by this he did not mean physical and mental phenomena. He referred to the two as dyadic and triadic events. He made this discovery almost a hundred years ago, but so unfashionable was it that no one paid serious attention until recently. Times have changed. Semiotics is currently the hottest item around, not only in the study of transactions between humans but, in Europe especially, as a new method of literary criticism.

To make the distinction as briefly as possible: by dyadic events, Peirce meant nothing more or less than the phenomena studied by the conventional sciences, whether the collision of subatomic particles, or the reaction of NaOH with H_2SO_4, or the response of an amoeba to a change in pH, or the performance of a rat in learning to thread a maze.

The model which fits any of these events according to Peirce is simply the dyad

whether A is a subatomic particle or an electrical impulse jumping a synapse in a rat's brain. Thus, Peirce would probably agree with most behaviorists that when one of Skinner's pigeons responds to a blue light by doing a figure 8, no matter how complicated the brain event is, no matter how many neurones and synapses are in a neural web, the event can still be set forth as a series of dyads:

Event A———————>Event B———————>Event C———> and so on

But there is one kind of natural phenomenon which, according to Peirce, cannot be so explained. It is man's transactions with symbols, of which, of course, the prime example is his use of language.

Thus, when a two-year-old child learns from his father that the sound "ball" uttered by his father is the *name* of the round object there on the floor, Peirce would insist that this event, the child naming the ball, cannot be explained as any series or combinations of dyads; that is, by any stimulus-and-response psychology, however elaborated and refined.

Thus, language in particular and all of man's transactions with symbols in general are not dyadic but triadic behavior. Three elements are involved in a relationship which is absolutely irreducible. Thus

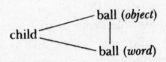

and also later in the development of the sentence-utterances, when the child couples not a thing and a sound but the two elements of the primitive sentence

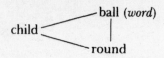

There are three elements involved in a triadic relationship which cannot be further reduced without destroying the relationship. One important feature of triadic phenomena should be noted first off. We are dealing, not with thoughts or subjective states, but with behavior and observables, with people, words and things, and what people do with words and things—a state of affairs which is surely cogenial to the behavioral scientist.

Now, as you must know, a great deal of effort has been expended by psychologists in trying to explain triadic behavior as a series of stimulus-response dyads. And while I am no judge of this vast literature, I will note only that an increasing number of theorists would agree with Noam Chomsky that the acquisition of language by the human species is a phenonemon for which the natural sciences, as we know them, do not presently have adequate models. Chomsky, I believe, goes too far and falls into the old Cartesian trap, the mind-body split, which to a behavioral scientist must seem like turning back the clock a hundred years.

But what has all this got to do with our original question, Is a Theory of Man Possible?, and with the chasm between the medical and psychotherapeutic disciplines, a chasm which even now is only bridged with some such tenuous and shaky term as "psychosomatic"?

I would suggest that if man is indeed unique among the species in crossing the symbols threshold, and if Charles Peirce is right in saying we can study this unique phenomenon as a relationship between observable elements, then surely a good place to look for a minimal consensus view of man is as a languaged creature, not man the mind-body composite, but Homo symbolificus, man the symbol-mongerer.

So I would like to spend the rest of this time with a few brief remarks about some consequences for behavioral science of the new semiotic or triadic theory, to suggest a few ways in which

Charles Peirce's semiotics may serve both as a fructifying and as a unifying concept in the diverse and often bewildering variety of approaches to the human psyche which we have encountered since Freud.

Let us consider, for example, some of the terms we are accustomed to using when we talk about that aspect of man we ordinarily label as mental or part of the psyche. The question is: Are these terms destined forever to be locked into the psyche? Do we settle permanently for the Cartesian split between body and mind? Or does semiotics give us a new way of looking at things?

What about the following terms which we are accustomed to using, both in psychotherapy and anytime we are talking about the human psyche, terms which we think we understand and consider meaningful but which are so difficult to bring under the purview of the scientific method—what about such terms as "the conscious" and "the unconscious," which we associate with Freud; "interpersonal relations," which we associate with Buber and Sullivan; "self-role-taking" and "inferiority feelings," which we associate with Adler; "authenticity," "inauthenticity," "being oneself" or "failing to be oneself," which we associate with the existentialist analysts? What about the communication breakdowns emphasized by transactional analysis? What about the sudden insight into the way things are arrived at often under conditions of emotional stress which the Gestalt therapists speak of? Are these concepts destined to remain the exclusive property of this or that particular school of psychotherapy? Or is it possible to approach anthropology or a general theory of man which offers some prospect of bestowing order and relation onto these diverse approaches?

I will only suggest a beginning.

Let us look at the general models of man, or men, persons, engaged in that uniquely human activity, indeed in that very act which makes him human: the transaction in which one person utters a symbol—a word—or draws a painting, whatever—and a second person receives the symbol and understands it—or perhaps misunderstands it—to be about something else, which both persons have experienced.

What we have is two triads pushed together with an interface between them—and there's the rub of it and also the joy of it: what happens across the interface.

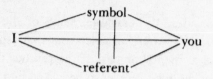

Notice that we are not talking about psyches—rather, we are talking about a special kind of creature, organism if you like, in interaction with other organisms and with the environment through the mediation of a special kind of stimulus or sign, the symbol.

If we approach this phenomenon either genetically, as something you discovered when you were about two years old, or phylogenetically, as something the species hit upon some forty thousand years ago, or phenomenologically, as something that is going on right now between us, certain interesting questions arise.

I will simply list a few.

Consciousness. Ordinarily, we think of consciousness as a state of the psyche, a more or less isolated awareness which we have trouble relating not only to other consciousnesses but to the very body within which it resides. But notice the etymology of the word, which, as in the case of so many words, is curiously revealing. "Conscious" means "knowing with." And "knowing with" is not a state of affairs but a relation, or rather two relations, the relation of knowing and the relation of with. Does this offer us a sort of clue for getting at consciousness as something besides a queer kind of ghost inhabiting a machine called the body? The phenomenologists offer us another clue. They say that consciousness is not simply a state—we are never simply conscious—rather we are always, when we are conscious, conscious of something. Consciousness is always intentional. It is always about something else. The semioticist would make a further suggestion: not only are we always conscious of something; we are also conscious of it as something we conceive under the symbol assigned to it. And, without the symbol, I suggest we would not be conscious of it at all. Helen

Keller was not really conscious of the water flowing over her hand until Miss Sullivan spelled its name in the other hand.

To return to the semiotic model, is not consciousness nothing more or less than the act or transaction by which I communicate with you or with myself a symbol, sentence, line of poetry, map, whatever, through which we both look at and perceive what the thing, the symbol, is about? The transaction can, of course, take place between myself and myself. I can debate with myself, hassle myself endlessly, and be so thoroughly conscious, knowing-with, that I can't go to sleep. When the dialogue stops, consciousness stops. Sleep ensues.

Also, the notion of the unconscious, as used by Freud, always bothered me. It seemed to be a region or zone of the psyche, the lower part of this ghost which inhabits the body. It was natural to think of the unconscious as having contents which under certain conditions emerged into consciousness like a creature of the ocean depths breaking water and leaping up into sunlight.

Yet I wonder if the unconscious is nothing more or less than what we have experienced, either in the world or within ourselves, but have not yet named or formulated or have not yet had it named or formulated for us by something else.

Are we not all, in fact, familiar with what has been called the Helen Keller phenomenon—wherein Helen rejoiced to have something named for her which she had in a sense known all along, the water: yet, in another sense, had not known. In a sense I say, because she knew it, the water, as an animal knows it, could respond to it, look for it when she got thirsty, but was not conscious of it until another person pointed it out and named it for her. And does it not still happen with us that when we are reading a great novel or a great poem or seeing a great play or film or even listening to music, that in the best parts we experience this same expansion of consciousness, this same sense of discovery, of affirmation, when the novelist writes of an experience we've had and only vaguely recognized but had not had it pointed out until this moment. The responses is an affirmation: "Aha! yes, that's it! Sure enough, that's the way it is! I never thought of it before but"—and so on.

The suggestion, then, is that the conscious and the unconscious are major variables in the relations of the semiotic structure—just as reinforcement and extinction are major variables in the stimulus-response dyad.

Another notion we may be familiar with from the existentialist analysts is the concept of world as opposed to an environment, *Welt* instead of *Unwelt*. But this is rather a vague and unsatisfactory distinction from the point of view of behavioral science—what do you mean by "world"?—yet a semiotic analysis provides an immediate clarification and empirical grounding. For once the symbol threshold is crossed, we all have a world whether we like it or not. Other organisms respond only to those stimuli in the environment which satisfy needs or threaten. A chicken has an environment but it does not have a world. It notices the shadow of a hawk and responds accordingly. But it pays no attention to a walnut or the shadow of a tree. But once Helen Keller knew the name of water, she had to know the name of everything else until the world was named for her. A two-year-old child goes about naming everything under the sun or asking its name. Men account for the world and its organism, willy-nilly correctly or incorrectly. But chickens have no myths. It is both the glory and the folly of man that the world he perceives is the occasion of all manner of wonder, discovery, and explanation as well as misperception and gross distortions.

Then there is the peculiar predicament of the human self, the "I" and the "you" and the "they" vis-à-vis the world.

If there is any one characteristic which sets psychiatry apart from other medical disciplines, it is surely this peculiar trait of its subject matter: that, unlike any other organism, man is subject to the wildest and most erratic fluctuations in his own perception of himself. Scripture says (and semiotics would agree) that man is born to trouble as the sparks fly upwards. Do not psychiatry and psychotherapy have for their very subject matter those manifold anxieties, depression, suspicions, self-hatred, feelings of inadequacy, and all the rest, which the human self falls uniquely prey to?

Semiotics would call attention to the strange position of the symbolizing self in the world which it discovers. In a word, the self can perceive, formulate, symbolize everything under the sun except itself. A self stands in the dead center of its universe, looking out. The paradox of consciousness is that the stranger we meet on the street and glance at for a second or two we see more clearly than we shall ever see ourselves. Hence the tortuous pilgrimage of the self in search of its own identity, a search which involves role-taking, ego states, growth, and self-testing which, of course, are the everyday business of psychotherapy.

The "you" or "thou" is, as you see, assigned a unique position in the semiotic model. In other words, the I-you or interpersonal relation is, accordingly, not merely a desirable state of affairs, as Buber would say, but is rather the very condition of being and knowing and feeling in a human way. It, this interpersonal relation, is a major variable in all semiotic transactions and its manifestations occur in a continuum running from the I-it through the I-you-they to the I-all-of-you.

The "they" in its turn can be understood as either participating in the interpersonal community or as being assigned a separate status as world object, along with shoes and ships and sealing wax.

Please note that once the symbol-mongering organism has a world, he must place himself in this world. He has no choice. He cannot not do it. If he refuses to make a choice, then he will experience himself placed in this world as one who has not made a choice. He is not like a dog or a cat who, when deprived of all stimuli, goes to sleep. Unlike an organism in an environment, a man in a world has the unique capacity for being delighted with the world and himself and his place in the world, or being bored with it, anxious about it, or depressed about it. He can exploit it, celebrate it, be a stranger in it, or be at home in it. He has, moreover, the perverse capacity for getting things backwards and upside down. He, of all creatures, is capable of feeling good during hurricanes and sad on ordinary Wednesday afternoons.

It would not be difficult, in fact, to make out the case that most of modern literature, the novel and poetry in particular, is nothing more or less than a calling attention to the remarkable fact that contemporary man feels strangely out of place in the very world he, more than any other man in history, has most successfully transformed for his own use. The hero or anti-hero of the contemporary novel is a man who finds himself stuck into a world without knowing how or why, or understanding his relation to it, and yet cannot escape his dilemma.

Then, is a theory of man possible?

By "theory" in this case, I, of course, do not mean a comprehensive anthropology, philosophy, or theology but rather a minimal coherent working model which can accommodate both a view of man—man as organism in an environment—which he is—and also those unique, triumphant, and perverse options—options for misery and joy—to which man seems particularly prone.

If I do not think much of man as organism in an environment or of man as body-plus-soul as an adequate model, it is not because I do not believe man is an organism or that man does not have a soul. It is rather that it doesn't do you or me much good as behavioral scientists to draw a picture of man as superchimp responding to signals, or as angel-beast, a strange composite of mind and stuff.

Freud's model makes the same mistake, I believe, as the older behaviorists. Both used dyadic models. The only change Freud made was to transfer the dyadic model from matter interacting with itself to psyche interacting with itself. If you will think about it, most of Freud's terminology is borrowed from the dyadic sciences and applied to psychic events: such terms as libidinal energy, repression, instincts, drives, aggression, dynamism, cathexis, and so on.

The upshot, of course, was that the Freudians and the behaviorists were both talking the same language but were sealed off from each other by the mind-body barrier. Unlike Alice's situation in *Through the Looking-Glass*, there was no way to step through the mirror in either direction. And so the argument between the behaviorists and Freud was never really joined and now is not even interesting.

But if we begin with what we know and can observe and point at, that man does indeed transact with his environment and with other men through the mediation of signs, but in a quite different way from other organisms, we can see a beginning. We can see a structure and a relationship between person and person, person and things, person and symbols, a system of transactions quite as open to observation by behavioral scientists as the responses of rats. Yet it is a system which, unlike other energy systems we are familiar with, has a whole new set of parameters and variables.

It is precisely the value of such a model that such realities as consciousness, the unconscious, community, loss of community, intersubjectivity, alienation, self, loss of self, authenticity, inauthenticity, and so on, can be articulated as parameters and variables of a single model rather than being assigned haphazardly to a mysterious entity called a psyche.

So here is the beginning of a theory of man as a semiotician might see him: Man is that creature who transacts with his fellow creatures and with the elements of his environment just as other organisms do but in a unique way, unique both in structure and in function, a way which, moreover, can be correlated both with his behavior as we observe it and with new anatomical structures in the cerebral cortex. To say so is only to suggest a minimal working model. As such, it opts neither for mechanism nor materialism nor theism, nor any of the perennial quarrels which have always vexed the larger question of man.

I can even visualize the hospital of the future in which the first signs the patient sees in the corridor do not read INTERNAL MEDICINE, SURGERY, OB-GYN, DERMATOLOGY, PSYCHIATRY UPSTAIRS, but rather two big signs just inside the front door, one pointing left, one right (I won't say which is which), but one reading DYADIC DISORDERS; the other, TRIADIC DISORDERS.

NAMING
AND BEING

2

What is naming? Is it an event which we can study as we study other events in natural history, such as solar eclipses, glandular secretions, nuclear fusion, stimulus-response sequences? Let us take a concrete example. A father tells his two-year-old child that *this*, pointing to a certain object, is a ball. The child understands him, and whenever his father speaks the word, the child looks for the ball and runs to get it. But this is not naming. The child's understanding is not qualitatively different from the understanding which a dog has of the word "ball"; it can be construed in terms of response conditioning, sound waves, neural impulses, brain patterns. It is, in other words, a sequence of happenings which takes place among material beings and is, in this respect, not utterly different from a solar eclipse, glandular secretion, or nuclear fusion.

But one day the father utters the word "ball" and his son suddenly understands that his father does not mean find the ball, or where is the ball, but, rather, this *is* a ball—the word "ball" *means* this round thing.

Something has happened. We may quarrel about the good and the bad of it—some saying with the Polish semanticists that what has happened is a major catastrophe for the human race, some saying with Helen Keller that what has happened is nothing less than the discovery of the world and the coming to oneself as a person—but, beyond any doubt, something has happened. During the next few weeks, the child will hold the ball and speak its name a thousand times to anyone who will listen, or to no one at all. In so doing, he experiences a joy which has nothing to do with the biological need-satisfactions which have determined all previous joys. What, then, has happened? Is the child launched upon a delusional state which will plague him the rest of his life, or has he hit upon the secret of knowing what the world is and of becoming a person in the world?

Whatever has happened, it is a scandal to modern philosophers of meaning. The semioticists are determined that meaning shall be a response, not utterly different from a solar eclipse or from dog salivation. But, having said this, they are left with the problem of accounting for man's often foolish behavior with symbols, and of dealing with the offensive little sentence "This is an oyster," for, clearly, as they never cease to tell us, *this* is not an oyster and a man cannot eat the word "oyster." It is for this reason that so many semioticists are bad-tempered—they are forced to be moralists and to scold man for his follies. One can easily imagine that astronomers would be bad-tempered, too, if, after discovering the laws of planetary motion, they discovered that solar eclipses refused to obey these laws and, in general, behaved perversely. But it would be a very poor astronomer who spent his time scolding the planets instead of trying to figure out why they behave as they do.

Name giving and naming are a scandal to the behaviorist and semanticist, because something unprecedented has taken place: naming is, in fact, utterly different from a solar eclipse or a conditioned response. If one tries to explain naming as a sequential happening among material existents—as a sound calling forth a thought or referential activity—one misses the point, or, as Mrs. Langer says, one leaves out the most essential feature of the material. A name does not call forth something, it *names* something.

But it does not help very much to say that a name names something. In leaving it at that, we only succeed in concealing, rather than clarifying, a most mysterious happening. What does take place when something is named? What is the meaning of the mysterious question, What is that? What is the meaning of the even more mysterious answer, "That is a ball"? Let us consider the situation immediately before and immediately after the act of naming. The elements are the same in each case. There are four of them: the father, the child, the ball, and the word "ball," which trembles in the air. What happens is clear enough in the simple case when the child understands the word "ball" as a signal and looks for the ball. The child's behavior is a sign-response sequence, strikingly similar to Mead's "conversation of gesture" involving two dogs, barks, and a bone. But then it dawns upon the child that the sound "ball" means the round thing. He holds the ball before him and utters the same sound, and now he, too, intends that this sound shall mean the ball. From this point forward, we may no longer use the causal-sequential frame of reference which had served so well for the understanding of every event in the universe from stellar phenomena to glandular secretions; henceforward, we must find some other frame of reference. What has changed in the situation? The four elements are still the same: the father, the child, the ball, the word "ball." And yet we know from the testimony of blind deaf-mutes as well as from the observation of normal maturation not only that something new has happened but that the event is probably the most portentous happening in the development of the person. Here, however, we encounter a difficulty; for trying to penetrate the act of naming is like trying to see a mirror while standing in front of it. Since symbolization is the very condition of our knowing anything, trying to get hold of it is like trying to get hold of the means by which we get hold of everything else. As a consequence, naming passes itself off as the most trivial of events: a thing is named, and what of it? What could be more transparent? Where is the mystery?

We begin to appreciate the mystery when we realize that the act of naming, or denotation, is generically without precedent in natural history. I mean this in the most radical sense possible. One may reply with a shrug that a glandular secretion or a conditioned response is likewise without precedent in the universe. But considered in the broadest frame of reference, glandular secretions and conditioned responses are the same sort of events as stellar explosions or nuclear fusions. There occurs an energy exchange mediated by structures, a sequential interaction which lends itself to formulation as a function of variables, $a = f(b)$. The state following a nuclear fusion is, thus, a function of the state before. A dog's response to the signal "ball" is a function of the stimulus and the electrocolloidal state of the dog's brain. But when one names a thing or understands from another that a thing is so named, the event can no longer be interpreted as a causal function.

Something has happened, to be sure, but it is not an interaction. It is something utterly different: an affirmation. Naming or symbolization may be defined as the affirmation of the thing as being what it is under the auspices of the symbol. When the child understands that by the word "ball" his father means the round thing, his understanding is of the nature of a yes-saying. Helen Keller's memorable revelation was the affirmation of the water as being what it is. But an affirmation requires two persons, the namer and the hearer. This is water, means that this is water *for you and for me*. Only a person may say yes, and he may say it only to another person. A dog may appear to say yes by acquiescing to a command, but its acquiescence is a reaction and not a yes-saying.

By the sign an organism is oriented to the world according to its needs of survival and reproduction. An animal takes notice only of things which are either dangerous or beneficial to it. That which is neither dangerous nor beneficial is passed over. But the child who learns that *this* is a ball will then wish to know what is *this here* and what is *that over there*. He will wish to know the name of the swallow in the sky, even though the swallow is nothing to him biologically. The swallow is ignored by the tiger, but the child must know what the swallow is. The scandal is, as Gabriel Marcel has said, that when I ask what is this strange flower, I am more satisfied to be given a name, even though the name may mean nothing, than to be given a scientific classification. If I see a strange bird, ask my bird-watcher friend what it is, and he tells me it is a blue-gray gnatcatcher, I am obscurely disappointed. I cannot help thinking that he is telling me something *about* the bird—that its color is blue-gray and that it catches gnats—when I really want to know is what it *is*. If he tells me it is a starling, I am satisfied. This is enough to make a semioticist lose his temper. He will tell me that I am only falling victim to primitive word-magic. There is something in what he says, as we shall see; yet it is possible that there is another reason for my satisfaction. It has to do with the new orientation which has come about as the result of naming. This orientation is no longer biological; it is ontological. It has to do with a new need—a need which no longer is an adaptive or reproductive need but the need to affirm the thing as being what it is for both of us. But how can a bird, a flower, be affirmed? It can be affirmed only by means of a name. As Allen Tate has pointed out, it was a general belief in the West until the seventeenth century that human beings do not know things directly, as do the angels, but only through the medium of something else: the symbol. In order that the strange bird be known and affirmed, a *pairing* is required: the laying of *symbol* alongside *thing*. This pairing is the source of the scandal, for it occurs by the use of the copula "is." This is monstrous when understood as a real identity, but the difficulty disappears when it is understood as an intentional relation of identity. Korzybski became angry when anyone picked up a pencil and said this is a pencil. Say anything at all about the pencil, he insisted, but never say it is a pencil. But unless you and I say it is a pencil, unless it "is" a pencil for both of us, we may not say anything about it at all.

Naming brings about a new orientation toward the world. Prior to naming things, the individual is an organism responding to his environment; he is never more nor less than what he is; he either flourishes or he does not flourish. A tiger is a tiger, no more, no less, whether he is a sick tiger or a flourishing tiger. But as soon as an individual becomes a name-giver or a hearer of a name, he no longer coincides with what he is biologically. Henceforth, he must exist either authentically or inauthentically. An organism exists in the biological scale of flourishing-not-flourishing; a person exists in the normative scale of authentic-inauthentic. The scales are not the same. A person may flourish biologically while, at the same time, living a desperately alienated and anonymous life, or a person may be sick biologically and, at the same time—perhaps even as a result of it—live authentically. In the joy of naming, one lives authentically. No matter whether I give a name to, or hear the name of, a strange bird; no matter whether I write or read a line of great poetry, form or understand a scientific hypothesis, I thereby exist authentically as a namer or a hearer, as an "I" or a "thou"—and in either case as a co-celebrant of what is. But when names no longer discover being but conceal it under the hardened symbol, when the world comes to be conceived as Alice's museum of name-things: shoes and ships and sealing wax—then I am bored. I exist as a nought in the center of the picture-book world of the *en soi*. A tiger neither celebrates being nor is he bored by it. Confronted by being which is biologically neutral, he goes to sleep. Since a person does not coincide with what he is, he may be either better or worse than a tiger.

An organism is oriented to the world according to its organismic needs, but a person is oriented to the world in the mode of truth-untruth. It is a mistake to speak of truth-untruth in connection with an organism and a sign. A duck may make an error about a sign and mistake a hunter's call for a duck's call. Yet, even if he is killed, until the moment of his death, he never ceases to be what he always was, an organism responding to a sign according to a conditioned brain pattern. But for a person the selfsame symbol which discloses being may be the means by which being is concealed and lost. The symbol "sparrow" is, at first, the means by which a creature is known and affirmed and by which you and I become its co-celebrants. Later, however, the same symbol may serve to conceal the creature until it finally becomes invisible. A sparrow becomes invisible in ordinary life because it disappears into its symbol. If one sees a movement in a tree and recognizes it and says it is "only a sparrow," one is disposing of the creature through its symbolic formulation. The sparrow is no longer available to me. Being is elusive; it tends to escape, leaving only a simulacrum of symbol. Only under the condition of ordeal may I recover the sparrow. If I am lying wounded or in exile or in prison and a sparrow builds his nest at my window, then I may see the sparrow. This is why new names must be found for being, as Heidegger thinks, or the old ones given new meaning, as Marcel thinks.

The fear of an organism is appropriate; it is no more nor is it less than is warranted by the sign which arouses fear. The measure of the fear and the visceral and muscular response to the fear are specifically determined by the character of the threat. But the anxiety which follows upon symbolization is ambiguous. The same anxiety may be destructive biologically—for it serves no biological function: one is afraid of nothing—and at the same time a summons to an authentic existence. It is for this reason that a physician and a metaphysician take opposite views of anxiety— Freud looking upon anxiety as a symptom of a disorder to be gotten rid of, Kierkegaard looking upon it as the discovery of the possibility of becoming a self.

*Anxiety may simply occur when something is encountered which can neither be ignored nor named. Anxiety may, thus, vary all the way from a slight uneasiness to terror in the face of the uncanny. A strange bird may cause a slight unrest until it is named; but the appearance of a three-masted trading schooner in place of the usual two-masted one may provoke terror among Melanesian islanders. In the everyday world, one is under the strongest compulsion to construe things one way or another—even things which are in fact unknown tend to be construed as things which are already known. Once Helen Keller knew what water was, she had to know what everything else was. After this total construction of one's world, it is only when something is radically different and resists interpretation in terms of the familiar symbols that one experiences the "uncanny"—that which is not yet known or symbolized.

By the same token, anxiety may also occur when one discovers that, of all the things in the world, oneself is the only being that cannot be symbolized. Everything else in the world tends to become ever more densely formulated by its name: *this* is a chair, *that* is a ball, *you* are Robert, *we* have democracy and freedom. But I myself escape every such attempt at formulation. A person who looks at a group picture looks for himself first: everyone else in the picture looks more or less as he knew they would—they are what they are; but he does not know what he is, and so he looks to see; and when he finds himself, he always experiences a slight pang: so that is who I am! But this formulation is ephemeral, and he will do the same thing with the next group picture. The being of the namer slips through the fingers of naming. If he tries to construe himself in the same mode by which he construes the rest of the world, he must necessarily construe himself as nothing, as Sartre's characters do. But this is not to say that I am nothing; this is only to say that I am that which I cannot name. I am rather a person, a namer and a hearer of names. Nor are you formulable under the auspices of a symbol. If I do conceive you as a something in the world rather than as a co-celebrant of the world, I fall from the I-thou to the I-it. Yet I am not able to dispose of you as finally as I dispose of shoes and ships and sealing wax. There remains your stare, which may not be symbolized. If I am determined to dispose of you by formulation, I had better not look at you.

Even in its most primitive form, naming is a kind of judgment. It is also a kind of primitive abstraction. It is an affirming of a thing to be one of a sort of things. But this sort is not usually what is meant by a concept. It is far less abstract—I take it to be roughly equivalent to Lotze's "first universal." This primitive abstraction contains the *Anlage* both of scientific abstraction and of poetical naming. When a tribesman utters a single word which means the-sun-shining-through-a-hole-in-the-clouds-in-a-certain-way, he is combining the offices of poet and scientist. His fellow tribesmen know what he means. We have no word for it because we have long since analyzed the situation into its component elements. But we need to have a word for it, and it is the office of the poet to give us a word. If he is a good poet and names something which we secretly and privately know but have not named, we rejoice at the naming and say, "Yes! I know what you mean!" Once again we are co-celebrants of being. This joy is as cognitive and as ontological as the joy of a hypothesis. It is a perversion of art to look upon science as the true naming and knowing and upon art as a traffic in emotions. Both science and art discover being, and neither may patronize the other.

> *Daffodils,*
> *That come before the swallow dares, and take*
> *The winds of March with beauty.*

This is a naming and a knowing and a truth-saying at least as important as a botanical classification.

If we must speak of a "need" in connection with human behavior, let us speak of it as Heidegger does: "The need is: to preserve the truth of Being no matter what may happen to man and everything that 'is.' Freed from all constraint, because born of the abyss of freedom, this sacrifice is the expense of our human being for the preservation of the truth of Being in respect of what-is. In sacrifice there is expressed that hidden *thanking* which alone does homage to the grace wherewith Being has endowed the nature of man, in order that he may take over in his relationship to being the guardianship of Being" (Martin Heidegger, *Existence and Being*).

1960

THE STATE
OF THE NOVEL:
DYING ART OR
NEW SCIENCE?

The novel is regularly said to be dying—and now it is said with perhaps more justification than at any other time. In fact, it is difficult now even to speak of the novel as a generic art form. If one uses as a criterion the familiar features of the traditional novel—plot, scene, characterization, action, denouement, development of character, and so on—it is hard to find a worthy example of the ancient art. Anything can and does pass for a novel now. A novel is what you call something that won't sell if you call it poems or short stories. Autobiography is novel. History is novel. Sociology is novel. Tirade is novel. I am not complaining. For the undeniable fact is that nonnovels which pass as novels now are usually better than novels which look like novels. *Love Story* and *Oliver's Story*, which look like novels—have characters, good people, bad people, love, action, and so forth—are not very good. In fact, the less said about them, the better. Céline's novel *Castle to Castle*, which has no nice people at all and resembles a novel less than it does a cobra striking repeatedly, one venomous assault after another, is memorable and somehow astringent. After reading it, one feels revolted perhaps but also purged. After reading *Love Story* and such memorable lines as "Love means never having to say you're sorry," the reader *needs* a purge. He certainly doesn't need an emetic. Maybe there are times when an honest hatred serves us better than love corrupted by sentimentality, meretriciousness, sententiousness, cuteness. Beckett's novels, where nothing much happens, people say very little, and what they say is usually misunderstood, are more honest, bracing, less depressing than eventful good-story Harold Robbins novels. In Joseph Heller's *Something Happened*, nothing happens, yet it is somehow more eventful than a Jacqueline Susann novel where everything happens. The last great conventional novel may have been *War and Peace* or perhaps *Middlemarch*. *Gone with the Wind* bears a certain resemblance to a great novel but what it really is is very good soap opera.

Here I am making a couple of assumptions which I shall not bother to defend, since they seem to me self-evident. One is that if we take the novel seriously, it follows that it is an art form just as a poem or a painting or a symphony is an art form. And if this is the case, it follows that while it is true that a novel should have an action, it does not suffice for it to be a "good story." That is to say, it is a good thing to tell a good story or to hear a good story, but it doesn't necessarily follow that a good story is good art. Good art tells some home truths about the way things are, the way we are, about the movement or lack of movement of the human heart. In great ages, when people understood each other and held a belief in common, great stories like the *Iliad* or *War and Peace* were also great art, because they affirmed the unspoken values which a people held in common and made it possible for a people to recognize themselves and to know who they are. But there are other times when people don't know who they are or where they are going. At such times storytelling can become a form of diversion, perhaps even a waste of time—like the prisoners facing execution Pascal talks about who spend their time crapshooting instead of trying to figure out how they got in such a fix and what is going to happen to them.

So my main assumption is that art is cognitive; that is, it discovers and knows and tells, tells the reader how things are, how we are, in a way that the reader can confirm with as much certitude as a scientist taking a pointer-reading.

A corollary to the proposition that art in general and the novel in particular are cognitive is that the stance of the novelist in the late twentieth century is also diagnostic. The implication is that something has gone wrong, which it certainly has, and that the usual experts cannot tell us what it is—and indeed that they may be part of the problem.

Something, it appears, has gone wrong with the Western world, and gone wrong in a sense far more radical than, say, the evils of industrial England which engaged Dickens. It did not take a diagnostician to locate the evils of the sweatshops of the nineteenth-century Midlands. But now it seems that whatever has gone wrong strikes to the heart and core of meaning itself, the very ways people see and understand themselves. What is called into question in novels *now* is the very enterprise of human life itself. Instead of writing about this or that social evil from a posture of consensus from which we agree to deplore social evils, it is now the consensus itself and the posture which are called into question. This state of affairs creates problems for the novelist. For in order to create a literature, whether of celebration or dissent, a certain shared universe of discourse is required. It is now these very shared assumptions which are called into question. Forty years ago Steinbeck had an easy job writing about the Okies and the dust bowl. It is a different matter now when the novelist confronts third-generation Okies in California who have won, who seem to have everything they want—and yet who seem ready any minute to slide physically and spiritually into the Pacific Ocean.

So the novelist today is less like the Tolstoy or Fielding or Jane Austen who set forth and celebrated a still intact society, than he is like a somewhat bemused psychiatrist gazing at a patient who in one sense lives in the best of all possible worlds and yet is suffering from a depression and anxiety which he doesn't understand.

There are similarities, I think, between these two branches of art and science; that is, novel-writing and psychiatry. There is also an intriguing difference between the points of view of the two professions. The issue between science and art is of perennial interest to me, since I started off in science in college, in medicine, was headed for psychiatry, and ended up writing novels—and so I hope it will also have general interest as an example of culture-crossing and perhaps as an occasion also of shedding some light on what the two cultures of art and science have to do with each other.

It is all the more intriguing in this case because at first sight it would appear that the two points of view are directly opposed. If the novelist is right, the psychiatrist is deceiving himself. If the psychiatrist is right, the novelist is crazy.

If the latter is the case, then novelists stand in need of psychiatrists—as in fact they often do. But it may also be the case that psychiatrists and other nonnovelists stand in need of novelists and that it is the novelist who is peculiarly equipped to locate such elusive phenomena and answer such odd questions as: What is pathological and what is "normal" in the last quarter of the twentieth century?

More often than not, however, novelists and psychiatrists find themselves either talking at cross-purposes or upstaging each other from carefully prepared vantage points. Some psychologists and psychiatrists profess to understand such things as creativity which I do not understand. Novelists, on the other hand, often find psychiatrists easy prey in their novels. The long-term goals which psychology erects, such large abstractions as emotional maturity, meaningful intersubjective relations, and so on, do invite a certain satirical treatment.

This is all in good fun. But what is important to notice is that the hero or anti-hero of the contemporary novel hardly qualifies under any of these conventional mental-health canons—emotional maturity, autonomy, and so forth. Indeed, he, and more recently she, is more often than not a solitary, disenchanted person who is radically estranged from his or her society, who has generally rejected the goals of his family and his peers, and whose encounters with other people, friendships and love affairs, are regularly attended by misunderstandings, misperceptions, breakdowns in communication, aggressions, and withdrawals, all occurring in a general climate of deflated meaning. People in novels meet, talk, make love, and go their separate ways without noticeable joy or sorrow. Indeed, the main emotion one encounters in contemporary fiction is a sense of unreality, a grayness and flatness, a diminished sense of significance. Relations between people take the form of silences, misunderstandings, impersonal sexual encounters.

If someone were to propose to the hero of modern fiction that he undergo psychotherapy to make his life more meaningful and to improve his interpersonal relations, one can imagine his response.

Now, of course, the issue can be settled very quickly in favor of psychology if we make the obvious inference—that the hero of the contemporary novel is the way he is because that's the way the novelist is, a difficult, unhappy, cut-off sort of person. Might it not indeed be the case that the novelist writes novels precisely because of his somber view of the world and his own difficulties with people? Like the poet in Allen Tate's definition, is he not a shaky man who steadies and affirms himself by the creative process?

To a degree, this diagnosis is probably correct. We are dealing here with several half-truths. Most novelists and those poets who have not yet suicided would probably agree—with an important reservation. The poet may admit to being a wounded man, yet point out that the wounded man often has the best view of the battle. The novelist or poet may in his own perverse way be a modern version of the Old Testament prophet who, like Hosea, may have a bad home life, yet who, nevertheless and despite himself, finds himself stuck with the unpleasant assignment of pointing out to his fellow citizens that something is wrong, that they are on the wrong track.

What I am suggesting is that art and science, in this case the novel and psychology, have different ways of approaching the truth and different truths to tell. Contradictions appear only when one discipline invades the territory of another.

But let me get down to cases. Perhaps one example from current fiction will suffice to convey the special flavor of a commonly encountered fictional view of the dislocation of modern American life.

In the novel *Something Happened*, Joseph Heller writes about Bob Slocum and his family. Slocum is a successful middle-aged executive who works in New York and lives in Connecticut. He is the current version of the John Marquand character a generation ago who suffered a kind of gentle disenchantment with life. But things seem to have gotten worse since. None of the Slocums is noticeably neurotic. On the contrary, they are a gifted, attractive, and intelligent lot, the best of an affluent, upwardly-mobile, upper-middle-class Northeast exurban society. But Bob Slocum is unhappy, his wife is unhappy, his son is unhappy, his daughter is unhappy. Everyone is afraid of at least one other person. When the family assembles at mealtime, the traditional social celebration of all past civilizations, the occasion is a disaster of misunderstandings, sarcasms, put-downs, and uproar. "Can't we get through one meal in peace?" somebody asks. No, they can't.

Bob's wife drinks. Bob chases office girls and prostitutes without enthusiasm. Yet he succeeds in his profession. Like Marquand's hero, he gets his promotion, buys a new house in Connecticut. This is how he feels about the new house:

> All of us live now—we are well off—in luxury . . . in a gorgeous two-story wood colonial house with white shutters on a choice country acre in Connecticut off a winding picturesque asphalt road called Peapod Lane—*and I hate it*. There are rose bushes, zinnias and chrysanthemums rooted about, and I hate them too. I have sycamores and chestnut trees in my glade and my glen, and pots of glue in my garage. I have an electric drill with sixteen attachments which I never use. Grass grows under my feet in back and in front, and flowers come into bloom when they're supposed to . . . Families with horses for pets do live nearby, and I hate them too, the families *and* the horses . . . I hate my neighbor and he hates me.

Something Happened is the title of Heller's novel. Something has happened all right. Actually, nothing much happens in the novel, but something must have happened before, something dreadful, but what is it? How did these good people get in such a fix? What happened? We are not sure, but whatever it was, it was not a single event in the usual sense of events in traditional novels, like the fatal wounding of Prince Andrei in *War and Peace*, or even a tragic historical event like America importing slaves from Africa. It is more like some aboriginal disaster, the Original Sin of the twentieth century. But where do we locate the disaster? What was the nature of the Fall? Has something dreadful happened to Bob Slocum or to the society in which he lives? or both?

Fictional examples could be multiplied. Indeed, the twentieth-century novel might be set forth as one or another aspect of disenchantment ranging from the gentle disillusion of the Marquand character to the derisive wise-acre disgust of Bob Slocum, with stopovers at the restiveness of the Hemingway expatriate, the metaphysical anxiety of the European existentialists, the apathy of Camus's Meursault, the rampaging gallows humor of a Portnoy.

Someone has in fact characterized the change in direction of the great body of poetry and fiction for the past hundred years as the Great Literary Secession, meaning that poets and novelists have, for whatever reason, registered a massive dissent from the modern proposition that, with the advance of science and technology and education, life gets better, too.

This issue, I would suppose, must sooner or later be confronted by anyone, scientist or artist or layman, interested in trying to figure out how things are and how to make life more tolerable both for oneself and for other people. Do we not indeed have the sense that the question grows daily more urgent? That there is a cumulative sense of crisis which allows us less and less room for temporizing? Something has happened, all right. But perhaps something worse is about to happen.

Perhaps the issue can be clarified by making it both more concrete and more hypothetical. Given the unhappiness of Bob Slocum, let us assume the added circumstance, admittedly unlikely in this case, that Bob Slocum has submitted himself to science to diagnose and correct his pathology. Since he is unhappy, he goes like many Americans to the expert of unhappiness to find out what is wrong. He goes to a psychiatrist. Now what kind of therapeutic goals do we envision for him? How would we like to see him change? Or would he like to change? Suppose we imagine his future in terms of the conventional abstractions used to define such goals—namely, that he become more creative, autonomous, productive, and so forth, that he become more integrated in the life of his community. These goals seem worthy and unexceptionable, but do we not have a sense of misgiving when we picture such a Bob Slocum in the future, no longer unhappy and derisive, but, as they say nowadays, being "into" this or that, into ceramics or folk-dancing, or working for the political party of his choice? And if we secretly like him better the way he is, how do we articulate and justify a preference for his unhappiness?

The possibility I want to raise is whether, from the novelist's point of view, there may be at least two kinds of distresses to which people fall prey.

One is a distress with which one can surely deal as straightforwardly as a surgeon dealing with abdominal pain. It, too, is pain pure and simple; that is, suffering without referent or redeeming qualities, anguish, sadness, conflict, terror which cripples and paralyzes. People hurt and come for relief to friends and experts who specialize in this kind of hurt, and friends and experts try to help them.

Such distress, in short, can be understood as a malfunction of the psyche which can be addressed from the traditional posture of the medical sciences, that of an observer who recognizes a class of disorders to which he applies a class of techniques.

But another kind of distress engages us, that is, us novelists. It is the ironic disaffection of Bob Slocum in *Something Happened*, the suicide of Quentin Compson in Faulkner's *The Sound and the Fury*, the loneliness of Ivan Karamazov, the anxiety of Roquentin in Sartre's novel, the flatness and banality experienced by J. Alfred Prufrock, the bemusement of Joan Didion's solitary heroine cruising the freeways of Los Angeles.

As different as are these fictional disorders, they share certain features in common. They are manifested by characters who are not only not portrayed as sick people but who rather are put forward by their creators, the novelists and poets, precisely because they are held to possess certain insights into the way things are, insights not yet shared or perhaps only dimly shared by most of their fellow denizens of the Western world. Yet it is these latter who by virtue of their freedom from symptoms, it would seem, would be judged by all the traditional criteria of mental health to be better off, happier, and healthier than the dislocated fictional hero.

It appears, indeed, that science and art are taking here directly opposed views, that what science regards as normal, art regards as somehow the failure or coming short of the *self*, and that what art regards as an appropriate response to the age we live in, science sees as antisocial or aberrant behavior.

Insights, I suggest, are what the novelist has in mind, insights into the way things are. But what things? And where? Certainly we are talking about a pathology. Something has happened, all right, something has gone wrong, but what? Is it a psychic disorder which can be diagnosed from a scientific, therapeutic stance? Or is it something else? Is it the final passing of the age of faith? Are we talking about a post-Christian malaise, the sense of disorientation which presumably always comes whenever the symbols and beliefs of one age are no longer taken seriously by people in a new age?

Clearly, we are talking about a species of alienation, the traditional subject matter of psychiatrists, the original alienists. But notice that the novelist is raising a Copernican issue and standing the question on its head. Who is alienated? And from what? And is one better off nowadays alienated or unalienated?

Toward the end of identifying what the novelist is up to, I would like to go a bit deeper into this matter of literary alienation, deeper than Heller's character, Bob Slocum, who, after all, might be put down as yet another projection of yet another novelist. American novelists in particular are by the very nature of their calling and their peculiar place or nonplace in the culture a perverse and dislocated lot. Bob Slocum, like Alexander Portnoy, can, after all, be read as a convenient satirical vehicle by means of which the novelist practices a kind of double-edged therapy, on the one hand flailing away at all those features of U.S. society he doesn't like, and on the other hand exposing and, he hopes, exorcising his own personal demons. And has a good time doing both. Both novels are very funny, funny enough to give the reader leave not to be too seriously challenged and engaged.

Other novels are not so easily disposed of. I'll choose one, a classic of sorts, though not necessarily the best, toward the end of shedding some light on what I consider the peculiar diagnostic role of the novel in this century.

I have in mind Sartre's *Nausea*. It is germane to our purpose, I think, not because it somewhat self-consciously sets forward certain of Sartre's philosophical theses, which do not directly concern us here, but as an onslaught on the "normal" or what is ordinarily taken for the normal. Unlike Sartre's later political novels, it is interesting because the attack is phenomenological, not political, an examination, that is, of the way things are.

What interests us about Roquentin, the protagonist of *Nausea*, in the present context is his conscious and deliberate alienation from those very aspects of French culture which by ordinary standards one would judge as eminently normal; for example, the apparently contented lives of the provincial bourgeoisie and the successful lives of the savants of the Academy of Science.

Roquentin is a historian. He lives a quiet life in the provincial city of Bouville, a routine existence consisting of research in the local library, solitary walks, eavesdropping on conversations between strangers, a mechanical sexual relation with the patron of a café.

"I live alone, entirely alone," Roquentin tells us. "I never speak to anyone, never. I receive nothing, I give nothing."

Yet he observes objects and people in the minutest detail, a scrap of newspaper in the gutter, people sitting in cafés, people strolling in the street, people who seem to fit into the world, who talk and listen to each other and give every appearance of understanding themselves and the world.

His favorite diversion is walking downtown on Sunday morning and watching whole families dressed in their Sunday best promenade and greet each other after Mass.

... a gentleman holding his wife by the arm, has just whispered a few words into her ear and has started to smile. She immediately wipes all expression from her chalky, cream-colored face and blindly takes a few steps. There is no mistaking these signs: they are going to greet somebody. Indeed, after a moment the gentleman throws his hand up. When his fingers reach his felt hat, they hesitate a second before coming down deliberately on the crown. While he slowly raises his hat, bowing his head a little to help its removal, his wife gives a little start then forces a young smile on her face. A bowing shadow passes them: but their twin smiles do not disappear immediately; they stay on their lips a few instants by a sort of magnetism. The lady and gentleman have regained their impassibility by the time they pass me, but a certain air of gaiety still lingers around their mouths.

Sartre's point seems to be the paradox that although the bourgeoisie seem happy and all together, there is nevertheless something wrong with them. Their lives are a kind of masquerade, an impersonation; they are not themselves. Sartre calls it bad faith. Roquentin with all his dislocation appears to know something they don't know—yet seems worse off for his knowledge, at first simply out of it, isolated, then at length overtaken by attacks of anxiety and nausea at what he takes to be a revelation of the true nature of things, a highly unpleasant glimpse into being itself.

It is important to notice that *Nausea* is no ordinary freethinking rationalistic-skeptical assault on the Catholic bourgeoisie. For Roquentin (and Sartre) has as little use for the opposition, the other triumphant sector of French society, the anticlerical members of the academy, famous doctors, generals, and politicians. Roquentin is equally repelled by the rational believer and the rational unbeliever like Renan.

Roquentin visits the Bouville museum where there are displayed a hundred and fifty portraits of the famous. He stops at the portrait of Dr. Parottin, member of the Academy of Science.

Now I stood before him and he was smiling at me. What intelligence and affability in his smile! His plump body rested leisurely in the hollow of a great leather armchair. This unpretentious wise man put people at their ease immediately . . .

It did not take long to guess the reason for his prestige: he was loved because he understood everything; you could tell him everything. He looked a little like Renan, all in all with more distinction.

Now, what are we to make of Sartre's and Roquentin's alienation? Can we lay it to the literary acrobatics of French intellectuals, who ever since Descartes are well known for their ability to hit on a single philosophical thesis and use it for a yardstick to measure the whole world? Or shall we trace it to the social malaise of the French between two great wars?

Or is Sartre saying something of value about the condition of Western man in the twentieth century, or perhaps about the human condition itself?

Or is Sartre's existentialism to be understood as only a way station in his transit from a bourgeois intellectual to a Marxist ideologue?

If Sartre is correct, then things have indeed been turned upside down. For in his novel the apparently well are sick and the apparently sick are on to the truth. But is the truth an unpleasant business we would do well to avoid? Roquentin thinks he knows something other people don't know, that he has made an unpleasant discovery which scarcely makes for happiness but allows him to *live* with an authenticity not attained by the happy bourgeoisie and the triumphant scientists. Anxiety, a sense of unreality, solitariness, loss of meaning, the very traits which we ordinarily think of as symptoms and signs of such-and-such a disorder are here set forth as appropriate responses to a revelation of the way things are and the way people really are.

If this is the case and things are indeed turned upside down, there is nothing much that psychiatrists could do about it—or would want to. It is hardly feasible for therapists to treat people who don't think they are sick, whether they are the happy bourgeoisie or the unhappy existentialist.

What I have in mind, however, is the intermediate case, someone located, as perhaps most of us are, between the intact bourgeoisie and the triumphant scientists on the one hand and the alienated hero of the novel on the other—a character who, let us say, falls somewhere between Roquentin and his existential despair and Bob Slocum and his comic disgust.

What, in short, are we to make of the widespread sense of malaise experienced by a great many people in these times and of the diametrically opposed views of this malaise taken by scientists and artists?

I'm afraid I cannot give a clear-cut answer to the question: Who is crazy, novelists or scientists? Rather will I content myself with a more modest yet, I think, significant goal. It is to return to my original assumption, that art is cognitive, as cognitive and affirmable in its own way as science, and that in the case of the current novel what it cognizes, discerns, knows, and tells is of a unique order which cannot be grasped by the scientific method. It is an elementary axiom that the truth which science tells about things and events is a general truth. The scientist is only interested in a molecule of sodium chloride or a supernova or an amoeba or even a patient insofar as it resembles other molecules, other supernova, other amoebae, and even other patients sharing the same disorder. But the peculiar fate of the human being is that he is stuck with the consciousness of himself as a self, as a unique individual, or at least with the possibility of becoming such a self. The paradox of the triumph of science and technology is that to the degree that a person perceives himself as an example of, a specimen of, this or that type of social creature or biological genotype, to precisely this same degree does he come short of being himself. The great gap in human knowledge to which science cannot address itself by the very nature of the scientific method is, to paraphrase Kierkegaard, nothing less than this: What it is like to be an individual, to be born, live, and die in the twentieth century. If we assume, consciously or unconsciously, that science can answer such questions, we will never even be able to ask the questions, let alone answer them. Who then can address himself to the question? The individual person, of course, who, while accepting the truth and beauty of science, retains his sovereignty over himself. But someone else also speaks to the same issue: it is, of course, the artist who finds himself in league with the individual, with his need to have himself confirmed in his predicament. It is the artist who at his best reverses the alienating process by the very act of seeing it clearly for what it is and naming it, and who in this same act establishes a kind of community. It is a paradoxical community whose members are both alone yet not alone, who strive to become themselves and discover that there are others who, however tentatively, have undertaken the same quest.

There is, I would think, a puzzle here for many American readers in the so-called novel of alienation. I know from experience that many young readers find themselves put off and perhaps with good reason by the somber view of life portrayed by so many novelists, both European and American, and I never argue with the reader who tells me that he is happy and that things are, after all, not so bad. But if the novelist is correct in his apparent dissent from the traditional American proposition and if it is true, as I suggest, that the contemporary novel at its best is cognitive and exploratory, in its own way as scientific as nuclear physics, perhaps some light can be shed on our confusion by taking note of the more familiar dilemmas of science in general and psychiatry in particular. We are all aware, I think, of the dangers of the passive consumership of technology, confronted as we are by the dazzling credentials of science. A certain loss of personal sovereignty occurs when a person comes to believe that his happiness depends on his exposure to this or that psychology or this or that group encounter or technique.

There is a similar danger attendant upon literature and art— what Kierkegaard might have called the perils of the aesthetic sphere. If it is true that the poet and novelist are in the vanguard in their foreboding that something has gone badly wrong and in their sketching out of the nature of the pathology, let the reader both rejoice and beware, rejoice that the good novelist has the skill to point out the specters which he, the reader, had been only dimly aware of, but beware in doing so of surrendering the slightest sovereignty over himself. If one happens to be a writer or a scientist and lucky enough occasionally to hit on the truth, or if one is a reader or a consumer and lucky enough to benefit from a great medical discovery or a novelistic breakthrough which excites him— well and good. Well and good, that is, as long as one never forgets that the living of one's life is not to be found in books, either the reading of them or the writing of them.

1977

NOVEL-WRITING IN AN APOCALYPTIC TIME

$\rightsquigarrow$

At first I thought of giving these remarks some such title as "The Vocation of the Novelist" or "The Place of the Novelist in American Life." But both of these sounded impossibly grandiose— entirely apart from the fact that I don't know what the vocation of the novelist is or the place of the novelist in American life. In fact, I'm not even sure he has a place.

Next I considered the title "The Vocation of the Southern Novelist." This sounded only a little less grandiose and more than a little dreary. The expression "the Southern novelist" has always depressed me, conjuring up as it does a creature both exotic and familiar and therefore boring, like a yak or llama in the zoo—this in a sense in which the expression Northeastern novelist or Missouri novelist does not.

There is nothing logically wrong with the noun-phrase "Southern novelist." It does no more than denote someone who has a connection with the South and writes novels. As such, I have no objection to it and indeed would not have it otherwise, since I cannot imagine writing what I write if I did not come from the South. Maybe I'd be a novelist if I came from Idaho, but I doubt it.

The trouble is, the expression "Southern novelist" connotes too powerfully in the public consciousness, so powerfully that the connotation tends to close off the class so that all instances of the class tend to get assigned to the class like a Disposall. You can imagine, for example, a non-Southerner browsing in a non-Southern bookstore, picking up an interesting-looking new novel and inquiring of the non-Southern clerk, who may say something like, "She's one of the best young Southern novelists," whereupon the non-Southern customer is apt to put it back in short order, thinking he knows all he wants to know about Southern novelists, including female Southern novelists—which is one reason why Southern novelists don't sell many books.

What I object to is the undue attribution of a particular sort of regionalism which the expression invites—regionalism in the bad parochial sense, not the good universal sense in which the best writers are all regionalists. Even William Faulkner is generally thought of as a Southern novelist. But Hemingway and Bellow are not thought of as Northern novelists. Cervantes is not thought of as an Andalusian novelist. Cézanne is not thought of as a Provence painter.

Therefore, I refuse to say anything about Southern novelists as such. So the proper title of these remarks should be something like "Some Disconnected Remarks about the Peculiar Activity of Novel-Writing," or rather "The Peculiar Activity of the Novel-Writing of One Person Living in the State of Louisiana during What May Well Be the Last Years of Western Civilization."

Not exactly a jazzy title. Not exactly a broad, universal, or uplifting subject.

But it can't be helped. The older I get, the less I seem to know, and the less edifying my writing is. When I was thirty, I thought I had things pretty well figured out—or at least I believed that those things which were not already explained by science were in principle explainable. When I was forty, I thought that what was not explainable by science—and there turned out to be a lot—could be explained by bringing God into it.

But now I have difficulty with the simplest questions, questions which I am sure graduate students have ready answers for.

Take American literature, for example. I do not have the faintest idea why there was a great literature in New England in the first half of the nineteenth century, growing out of a sour Puritanical money-grubbing society—and no comparable literature in the South at the same time, though we like to think we had the makings of just such a culture, a leisure class, close connections with Europe, Walter Scott, *The Edinburgh Review* and *The Spectator* on our bookshelves.

So I don't know why a successful mercantile society in Massachusetts produced a handful of great writers and a successful patrician agrarian society in South Carolina and Virginia did not. Nor do I know why a victorious North after the Civil War did not produce a great literature—while the South, not merely defeated but exploited like a colony for the next half century, then further impoverished by the Great Depression—why the South, just then of all times, should suddenly have produced the Fugitive poets, the New Criticism, and how it ever came to pass that a dandyish affected young man should have come home to an insignificant Mississippi town and written *The Sound and the Fury*—which is something like Jerome Kern writing *Show Boat* in Hollywood and going home to Brooklyn to write Beethoven's Third Symphony.

My inability to account for such things and many other things as well has to do with what I conceived to be the extremely limited vocation of the novelist, this novelist anyhow, in these times. The novelist, I have come to believe, is only good for one or two things these days—and they do not include being prophetic or making broad pronouncements about the decline of the West, the nature of evil, loneliness, God, and so forth. The embarrassment of the novelist is that after he masters his one or two tricks, does his little turn, some readers tend to ascribe this success to a deeper wisdom—whereas it is probably the very condition of his peculiar activity that he doesn't know anything else—which is to say that a person who asks a novelist anything about life and such, how to live it, is in a bad way, indeed.

No, what interests novelists in these peculiar times, or at least this novelist, and what they are mainly good for, is not such large subjects as God, man, and the world, but rather what he perceives as fault lines in the terrain, small clues that something strange is going on, a telltale sign here and there. Sign of what? A sign that things have gotten very queer without anyone seeming to notice it, that sane people seem to him a little crazy, and crazy people sometimes look knowledgeable—a little like the movie *The Body*

Snatchers, where everybody looks and acts normal, except that they are not—but no one notices, except the poor novelist, who has nothing better to do than to notice that people are not themselves yet feel obliged to act as if they were.

There have been times when societies were triumphant and became true cultures, when people, through their values and beliefs, knew who they were and were at one with themselves. And then maybe it was the function of poets to celebrate the triumph. The *Iliad*, the *Aeneid*, *The Divine Comedy*, *Henry V*, *War and Peace* were such celebrations.

Even in bad times, major writers had major roles—like Langland, Chaucer, Milton, Whitman. Because, bad as times were, there was still a consensus of sorts. Symbols signified. A people could be rallied, consoled, entertained, told stories to, or at least affirmed in their unhappiness. A dirge, a lament, even a jeremiad, implies an intact society.

But what to make of times such as these about which antonymous adjectives, best and worst, desperate and hopeful, signify equally? It is a peculiar century which sees the greatest advances in science and in the social betterment of man, yet which has been called by Raymond Aaron the century of terror. It is a time notable not so much for its series of world catastrophes, the millions who have been slaughtered, the Holocaust, but for the banality with which these atrocities are committed and taken note of.

In such peculiar times it is perhaps one function of the novelist to mention these peculiarities—like an obnoxious little boy calling attention to the Emperor's state of undress. In this case, the Emperor is the German doctor who loves Mozart best of all and plays in a quartet as a relaxation from his experiments in the death camps—or the decent middle-class Englishman who flies the lead Lancaster bomber which marks out an undefended Dresden for the firestorm. Both are following orders and both, if they are good Germans and Englishmen, love their dachshunds and corgis and detest cruelty to animals. Is it an accident that the century of terror is also the century of sentimentality? What the novelist notices is not how awful the happenings are but how peculiar it is that people don't seem to notice how awful the happenings are.

Technology advances. The media improves dramatically. Consider the difference between the poor black-and-white photographs of the bodies stacked like cordwood at Dachau and the superb color shots of the gaily dressed bodies at Jonestown. The numbers of innocent dead are huge but do not amaze: six million in Germany, fifteen million in the Ukraine are no more comprehensible than the billions and billions of light-years Carl Sagan talks about. One listens, looks, then tunes into a talk show where people get properly angry about potholes, labor unions, handguns, inflation. And, after all, what else can one do? It is the century of good times, instant media, large numbers, and telephotos of stacked corpses.

The times are actually crazier than this, because it is not as if this were simply another dreadful century like the fourteenth, the century of the Black Death—which everyone knew was a bad time. But what is one to make of a century which is not only the worst but also in some ways the best. Because it *is* in some ways the best. The advance of science and technology is little short of miraculous. It is the first time in history that a poor man, at least in the Northern Hemisphere, could free himself from a lifetime of grinding poverty, disease, and early death.

To add to the difficulties of the novelist in such peculiar times is the breakdown of the consensus, of a common language, a shared discourse denoting a common set of referents. Poets and novelists and nonpoets and nonnovelists don't seem to be living in the same world or talking about the same things.

Poets and novelists seemed to be possessed by a whole separate coven of witches, demons, terrors, and premonitions, of which the general population seems by and large oblivious. Either one is crazy and the other sane, or the former has gone crazy for reasons which the latter has not yet caught on to.

And, to tell you the truth, I am still not sure which is right: whether it is the poet and novelist who, like the man in Allen Tate's definition, is a shaky man trying to reassure himself in a generally sane world, or whether it is the population at large which is slowly going mad and the poet who has the sensibility or vulnerability—thin skin—to notice it.

Particularly striking is the contrast between apocalypse and well-being in the New South. How can a magazine like *Southern*

Living, whose message, if it has a message, is: Here is the good life in a good place—how can such a magazine, the most successful publication in the history of the South, be published in the century of terror? Is it because the South, or parts of the South, is in fact one of the last places where one can in fact live a civil life among civil folk—or is it just that in the Sunbelt the diversions of technology, restoration, climate, media, sports, and fun are more successful? Or is it both? What interests the latter-day novelist anyhow is that here is the proper locale for his own peculiar apocalypse—not the sociological horrors of the Old South, Tobacco Road, and the Snopeses, not even the falling apart of the New South cities, the street crimes and drugs—but the more elusive apocalypse of the country club, the quaint Vieux Carré, the five thousand happy Midwest tourists who visit a tastefully restored mansion on the River Road. I wouldn't dare write of the twentieth century as such—most writers, I believe, sense that these evils are too vast and too close to be portrayed in any aesthetic mode; in fact, my own hunch is that only a major theological vision like Dostoevsky's can accommodate such evils, that a truly demonic age is too much for writers of sociological realism. Therefore, I tend to agree with Vonnegut, who said that the only way to write about such vast atrocities is not to write about them. He lived through the firestorm at Dresden and was able to write a novel about it by not describing the firestorm.

But show me a couple, a man and wife, who have moved into the condo of their dreams on the Gulf Coast or fronting the Heritage golf course at Hilton Head to live the good life, except that the man is spending seven instead of six hours in front of his cable TV and has graduated from a six-pack to an eight-pack, and the woman is spending more and more time at Gloria Marshall's and reading Nancy Friday and Judith Krantz—and neither man nor wife has said a word to the other for days, let alone touched each other—and I'm on home grounds.

It is one thing to live in bad times where a common language is spoken, values and beliefs shared in common, like the fourteenth century, which had the Black Plague but also had Langland and Chaucer, one of whom wrote about how bad things were and the other told stories and cheered everybody up and both were understood. It is something else to live in a time of great good and evil which nobody understands, where there are many kinds of discourse each of which makes a kind of sense to its own community, but where the communities don't make sense to each other and none of them makes sense to the novelist, who feels more and more like the canary being taken down the mine shaft with a bunch of hearty joking sense-making miners while he, the canary, is already getting a whiff of something noxious and is staggering around his cage trying to warn the miners, but they can't understand him nor he them.

The deeper we get into the century, the more sense people make, but they are making different kinds of senses which don't compute with each other. Carl Sagan explains everything without God, from the most distant galaxies to our own individual nastiness, which is caused by our reptilian brains. Radio and TV preachers explain everything by God, man's happiness with God, man's unhappiness without God. Humanists explain everything by coming out for the freedom and dignity of the individual. One hundred million books have been written by psychotherapists on how to be creative and self-fulfilling. And here's this nice ordinary American who works hard all day and is watching his six hours of TV and his wife is reading *The National Enquirer* and is more likely to set store by astrology and psychics than by science or God. The slaughter and the terror of the century continues. And people are, by and large, nicer than ever.

It is a peculiar time, indeed, when a writer doesn't know who the enemy is, or, even worse, when he can't stand his friends. I mean, you have to envy a writer like Flannery O'Connor, who saw the enemy clearly, namely a certain sort of triumphant humanist, and who could discern the orthodox virtues of backwoods preachers and of assorted nuts and murderers. She knew where the devils were, but if she were beating the same devils now, she would find herself in some strange company, on the same side as Jerry Falwell and Jimmy Swaggart. Of course, just because Jimmy Swaggart believes in God doesn't mean that God does not exist. But it doesn't make life any easier for the novelist. Indeed, it is probably yet another sign of the general derangement of the times that a writer these days who happens to be a believer is more apt to feel at home with the hardheads, the unbelievers, rakes, drunks, skeptics, Darwinians, than with the Moral Majority. But here again: just because the Moral Majority comes out for morality doesn't mean that one should be immoral.

Mere anarchy is loosed upon the world, as the poet said. But just when you've decided you have no use for the Moral Majority, you hear them attacked by the likes of Bob Guccione, editor of *Penthouse*, and Sidney Sheldon, novelist of a certain sort, and you're not so sure. But what about the unbelieving novelist? He has his own troubles. If you feel obliged to take on the Establishment, capitalism, Christendom, to save the environment, to shoot down the bourgeoisie in the good old-fashioned rebel style of Jack London, Upton Sinclair, Hemingway, Ernest Thompson Seton, you may also find yourself with some strange bedfellows, assorted California flakes who are *into* this and that mind-altered states, saving snail darters, chanting mantras. My favorite bumper stickers are slightly deranged, not the ones like HONK IF YOU LOVE JESUS or NO NUKES or JANE FONDA YES! but rather NUKE JANE FONDA. My favorite is: GOAT ROPERS NEED LOVE TOO.

All this is to say only that the vocation of the fiction writer has no doubt always been a peculiar business and is now more peculiar than usual. A recent poll reported that about half of American college graduates are depressed, disliked their jobs and spouses, suffered identity crises, didn't know who they were or what they wanted to do. Come to think of it, this is also a good description of a novelist. No doubt there have been times when poets and novelists knew what they wanted to do, were the celebrants of the culture, the pointers-out who set forth meanings and goals. But it may be the very nature of the novelist now that he knows less, can do less than anybody else, and therefore is not fit to do anything much, except stand back and watch for cracks in the edifice.

Certainly, there are plenty of experts who seem to know everything in their fields. Carl Sagan seems to know everything about science. Jimmy Swaggart knows everything about God and salvation. Irene Kassorla knows everything about what nice girls do.

The trouble is that when you put together half a dozen experts

on religion, science, creativity, and sexuality, plus their lay followers, what you've got is a small deranged society.

To make matters worse, the novelist has to work with a
medium which, like everything else these days, is polluted. Words
are polluted. Plots are polluted. In the best movie of last year, a
disturbed young man played by Timothy Hutton consults a psychiatrist a couple of times, breaks down, hugs the psychiatrist, says
"I love you," and is cured. He also has a communication problem
with his father. They *both* break down, hug, cry, say "I love you."
All is well. Lines of communication are opened. Love is the answer.
Who is going to protect words like "love," guard against their
devaluation? One hopeful sign about the movie was that God was
not mentioned.

True, love does make the world go round. In fact, I believe
it does. The trouble is that when words get abused, cheapened,
exhausted, worn thin as poker chips, the novelist is losing his only
tools. Always in deep trouble, he is now in deeper trouble than
usual.

The great poets and novelists always wrote about the nature
of God and love, of man and woman. But how can even Dante
write about the love of God, the love of a man for a woman, if he
lives in a society in which God is the cheapest word of the media,
as profaned by radio preachers as by swearing. And "love?" Love
is the way sit-com plots and soap operas get resolved a hundred
times a week.

In such times as these, a time of pollution and corruption of
meaning, it is no wonder that the posture the novelist often finds
natural is that of derision, mockery, subversion, and assault—to
mock and subvert the words and symbols of the day in order that
new words come into being or that old words be freshly minted—
to assault the benumbed sensibility of the poor media consumer,
because anything other than assault and satire can only be understood as a confirmation of the current corrupted meanings of such
honorable old words as love, truth, beauty, brotherhood of man,
life, and so on. There may be times when the greatest service a
novelist can do his fellow man is to follow General Patton's
injunction: Attack, attack, attack. Attack the fake in the name of
the real.

So the novelist is entitled to a certain measure of sourness and disenchantment and opting-out. Nevertheless, he may find a degree of use in his very uselessness. If he doesn't qualify as a prophet these days, he may at least serve as a curious outsider and a watcher, a kind of monitor—something like those instruments they stick into the earth on each side of the San Andreas Fault. In those beautiful peaceful California valleys, everything seems absolutely normal, absolutely intact, except that the instrument regularly records that the earth has sheared another couple of inches.

Everybody knows more than the novelist, but what the novelist may be good for, despite his shakiness and fecklessness, or perhaps because of it, is to record what other people, absorbed as they are in their busy and useful lives, may not see—a certain upside-downness about modern life—that, for example, there is something deranged about normal people and that crazy people may be trying to tell us something.

If the novelist's business is, like that of all artists, to tell the truth, even when he is lying, that is, making up a story, he had better tell the truth no matter how odd it is, even if the truth is a kind of upside-downness. And if it is the novelist's business to look and see what is there for everyone to see but is nonetheless not seen, and if the novelist is by his very nature a hopeful man—he *has* to be hopeful or he would not bother to write at all—then sooner or later he must confront the great paradox of the twentieth century: that no other time has been more life-affirming in its pronouncements, self-fulfilling, creative, autonomous, and so on—and more death-dealing in its actions. It is the century of the love of death. I am not talking just about Verdun or the Holocaust or Dresden or Hiroshima. I am talking about a subtler form of death, a death in life, of people who seem to be living lives which are good by all sociological standards and yet who somehow seem more dead than alive. Whenever you have a hundred thousand psychotherapists talking about being life-affirming and a million books about life-enrichment, you can be sure there is a lot of death around.

Everyone admits the atrocities of the century, which we like to think of as horrifying, inexplicable, and occurring at a great remove from us. True, every century has its horrors, but what the novelist notices, peculiar fellow that he is, is that in these strange times people, himself included, seem to experience life most vividly, most immediately, remember places best, on the occasion of war, assassination, hurricanes, and other catastrophes. The real question is seldom asked. It is not: How do we prevent the final war? but: What do we do if we succeed? Can man get along without war?

Everyone remembers exactly where he was and what he was doing when Kennedy was shot—how places and things and people and even green leaves seemed to be endowed with a special vividness, a memorable weight. But what the novelist is interested in is the in-between times, the quality of ordinary Wednesday afternoons, which ought to be the best of times, but are, often as not, times when places, people, things, green leaves seem to be strangely diminished and devalued.

Could it be that this paradoxical diminishment of life in the midst of plenty, its impoverishment in the face of riches, is the peculiar vocation of the novelist to catch a glimpse of, by reason of his very dislocation, but also because none of the experts seem to recognize its existence, let alone explain it? There is something worse than being deprived of life: it is being deprived of life and not knowing it. The poet and the novelist cannot bestow life but they can point to instances of its loss, and then name and record them.

Perhaps the first inkling of this strange new diagnostic vocation of the novelist was hit upon by Faulkner in *The Sound and the Fury* and in the person of Quentin Compson. It is no accident, I think, that Quentin arrived at his final solution, not in Yoknapatawpha County, that postage stamp of a universe where most Faulkner scholars do their archaeology, in a Southern locale drenched in history and tragedy, in placidness, but rather in a nonplace, wandering around the back streets of a bland Boston suburb, almost as faceless and featureless a place as a set of map coordinates. Faulkner, as usual, knew what he was doing. If he had set Quentin's suicide in the South against a backdrop of Gothic decor dark with blood and tears, it would have been robbed of its meaning.

Quentin was a lover, but a lover of such strange loves as to burst the cheap simulacrum with which the word "love" has come to be invested. He loved his sister but he loved death more—who loved death above all, as Faulkner put it. Loved her and hated this life, life in place and history and clock time, which his father described as the mausoleum of all hope and desire. How, indeed, is one to live in this peculiar time and history and on ordinary Wednesday afternoons? So prophetic was Quentin's predicament that only now, some fifty years later, are we beginning to grasp the full ambiguity of it: that he was not merely suicidal and therefore sick, and that his love for Caddy was incestuous and therefore even sicker. But that he was also on to something. He could not bear to live in time and place and history, not in the clock time and the bland coordinates of a Northern exurb, and not in the dark, sustaining history of the South. Now it has become possible to wonder, as perhaps it was not possible fifty years ago, to what extent his suicide was his own peculiar response not merely to his own life and history but to this life and these times. That is to say, fifty years ago we might have been content in Quentin's case with, say, the diagnosis of a Boston psychiatrist: suicide following affective-depressive disorder—perhaps with some Southern genetic pathology. Now we wonder whether Faulkner was not telling us something else, maybe even better than he himself knew. Even the incest theme, Quentin's love for Caddy, looks less and less like sexual pathology than it does like a longing for a new start, a new order of things, perhaps even a new race of men begotten of Caddy, a new life. Is it possible that Quentin's strange vision of a new life in hell with Caddy is his own parallel version of Dilsey's redeemed life here and now, in this time and place, and in the Time Afterward, after her redemption?

But the novelist, unlike Quentin, must by virtue of his very calling be on the side of life. Otherwise, he would not go to the trouble of writing and put up with all its miseries and loneliness. But, before life can be affirmed for the novelist or his readers, death-in-life must be named. Naming death-in-life as Faulkner did with his character Quentin is a thousand times more life-affirming than all the life-affirming self-help books about me being okay and you being okay and everybody being okay when in fact everybody is not okay, but more than likely in deep trouble. Beware of people who think that everything is okay. My own secret belief is that Leo

Buscaglia, leading apostle of love and okayness, is in deep trouble and will soon require psychiatric help.

Faulkner may have been more prophetic than he knew in dislocating Quentin. If Quentin Compson's suicide was the failure or refusal to live in a place and in time and in history, it was at least a recognition of the problem—which I take to be better than many current solutions of the problem, that is, avoiding it: avoiding place by moving, avoiding time by filling it, avoiding history both past and present by dreams of the future.

But, to finish with this strange fellow we started with, the so-called Southern novelist. If there is such a place as the South and if it is as different from the rest of the country as it is said to be, and if the difference lies precisely in its peculiar sense of time and place and history, and if its literature for the past fifty years has been distinguished by this very sense—it's going to be interesting indeed to see what the next few years bring. Because the South has now been deprived of its chief claim to uniqueness and what some have seen as a wellspring of its literature; namely, defeat and a tragic sense of history. For the South is now victorious. It is not even called the South any longer but the Sunbelt, and the power shift and money shift is far advanced. Even the universities are gradually getting better off, while the Harvard endowment has dropped to almost a billion. Parts of the South are more literate and prosperous than New England in the early 1800s.

The prospect is a little frightening. For if the leadership falls to the South, that is to say, the Sunbelt, is there a culture here equal to the task? Or will it go by default to the Sunbelt Southwest, the Dallas–Vegas–L.A. axis? Have you noticed, come to think of it, that weathermen on national TV have started calling this region the Old Confederacy when they point to the weather map, as if it were a slightly embalmed region, a sort of expanded Williamsburg? But the point is: if there was an Old South, did it have time to develop a culture in the plenary sense of a coherent society in which values and beliefs merge to issue in a major literature and art? And if the virtues attributed to the Southern Renascence are valid, the virtues of rootedness in place and time, to what extent will these prove to be enduring virtues, serviceable over the years, and to what extent did these virtues depend on a standing pat and a looking back and a kind of *Schadenfreude*, a secret relishing and romanticizing of defeat and tragedy, virtues which won't be much use in a burgeoning Sunbelt of agribusiness, superdomes, condos, and high-rises.

Quentin Compson opted out of time and place, precisely because Faulkner knew all about time and place and what was wrong with old places drenched in time and new nowhere places out of time. The question for the future is whether in the victorious South there will be writers who can name death-in-life and affirm life even in victory and prosperity.

One sign that the South has won, after all, is that the Southern Literary Renascence seems to be over. Southern novelists nowadays are in as much trouble as novelists anywhere. I notice a certain tentativeness in young Southern fiction writers—as if they still had one foot in Faulkner country, in O'Connor country, in Welty country, but over there just beyond the interstate loom the gleaming high-rises of Atlanta. So which way to jump? I mean, how do you write about third-generation Snopeses who have moved to Memphis and joined an encounter group?

But because the South has won doesn't necessarily mean the end of the South and its literature. Just because we all may soon be able to live in tastefully restored shotgun cottages in New Orleans or carriage houses in Savannah or condos and villas on the golf course, or even in an A-frame on Grandfather Mountain and have cable TV, it doesn't mean the world has come to an end. Where there is life, there is—and so forth and so forth.

All joking aside, or rather some joking aside, assuming that we in the South have something unique, unique about its literature, unique about its way of living, which is of value and should be preserved; assuming also that the country as a whole is in deep trouble and this unique something about the South may be of some use, I can only suppose that the coming poets and novelists of the South will face an extraordinary challenge. The challenge will simply be *what to do* in the face of the peculiar nature of the economic victory of the Sunbelt and the ongoing Los Angelization of the Southern community. I am not at all certain that the present-day South is equal to it. One danger is that the Southern writer may himself, herself, become Los Angelized, Chicagoized, Connecticutized, that he may try to out-Didion Didion, out-Bellow Bellow, out-Cheever Cheever. Then he is sunk for sure. Because they can do it better, those things they do, their little and not so little numbers. I am assuming that by now he or she, the young Southern fiction writer, has finally gotten clear of the ever-lengthening shadow of Yoknapatawpha County, the vast mythic twilight, and will not try to go back—he can't go back—and will not try to become a neo-Agrarian.

The Southern novelist can't go back now, back to the wilderness, back to the small Alabama town in *To Kill a Mockingbird*. He'd better not even look back. Because if he does, he'll turn into something worse than Lot's wife—a bad novelist.

His real challenge, as it always is with the artist, is somehow to humanize the life around him, to formulate it for someone else, to render the interstates, to tell the truth, to show how life is lived, and therefore to affirm life, not only the lives of poor white people and poor black people in the Georgia countryside and in Mississippi towns and hamlets, in Faulkner country, in Welty country, but even life in a condo on a golf course.

1986

HOW TO BE AN
AMERICAN NOVELIST
IN SPITE OF BEING
SOUTHERN AND
CATHOLIC

❧

My title is only half serious. It is serious insofar as it speaks to a curious handicap in the marketplace. The simple empirical economic fact is that people don't tend to buy Southern novels or Catholic novels and especially not Southern Catholic novels. I recall my astonishment at being told that the salesmen at Farrar, Straus and Giroux, my publisher, wanted me to drop the subtitle of a novel I once wrote called *Love in the Ruins*, which was, *The Adventures of a Bad Catholic at a Time Near the End of the World*—the suggestion being that the word "Catholic," even "Bad Catholic," might put people off. Curious, I say, because both traditions, being a Southern writer and being a Catholic writer, are not dishonorable. Faulkner was not a bad writer. Neither were Dante or Cervantes. Flannery O'Connor united both traditions and is duly, albeit posthumously, celebrated. Yet the fact remains that, to this good day, American critics, that is to say non-Southern American critics, are still baffled by O'Connor and generally can't make head or tail of what she was about.

I am interested in examining the reasons for this double disability. I do not think the reasons ordinarily advanced are altogether credible. One hears, for example, that the Southern novel is too self-consciously Gothic, violent, grotesque to be identified with the reader's ordinary life. And, of course, there is Flannery's famous rebuttal that the Southern novelist can write about freaks because he, she, can still recognize one. Implied here is the theological issue that, ever since the beginnings of the so-called Southern Literary Renascence, theological concerns have informed Southern literature in a sense not comprehensible to the secularized mind of the non-Southern reader, who has lost his theological bearings and therefore has no standard by which he can determine who is a freak and who is not—and who himself is apt to be more freakish than he might realize.

Yet these familiar arguments do not seem to address the crude commercial reality of the bookstore, the mysterious fact that a serious and excellent novel can somehow get labeled Southern or Catholic in such a way as to put off the reader. The mystery lies in the fact that there is something more than ethnicity or regionalism involved. For example, the same prospective reader is evidently not put off by the ethnic Jewishness of, say, a Malamud or a Roth or a Bellow. Nor is it held against Updike and Cheever that they generally write about a very localized and atypical Northeast upper middle class.

Could it be simply that more Jews and more Northeasterners buy and read books than do Southerners and that they would rather read about themselves? Not necessarily, because a Styron can write about a young Southerner and a Holocaust survivor and be widely read. And, of course, there are Catholic writers who specialize in novels about papal intrigue, spies in the Vatican, the misdeeds of bishops, and sell very well.

Or could it be simply that many Americans don't like Southerners or Catholics? But, then, presumably many of these same Americans don't like Jews, either.

No, the reasons are more mysterious. I suspect they have to do with the curious phenomenon of labeling, which probably falls within the domain of semiotics, or the science of signs. Somehow, when a novel gets labeled as Southern or Catholic, the labeling entails a tighter and more inclusive semantic bonding than if the novel were described as, say, Midwestern or Protestant. This has little to do, I think, with ordinary prejudice, whether anti-Southern or anti-Catholic. What happens is that when a customer walks into a bookstore and inquires about a book and is told that it is a distinguished Southern novel, the novel tends to be automatically assigned to a certain category or pigeonhole where it is perceived as having certain exotic and recognizable properties, so much so that the reader almost feels that he already knows what it is about. What I would also like to suggest is that the Southern novelist may not be altogether blameless, that he or she can easily succumb to the temptation of the exotic, to past successes of Southern writers, ever since Cable and Mark Twain, at playing the old game of amazing Yankees. Even Faulkner, I suspect, yielded sometimes to the temptation of "writing Southern"; that is, of living up to a certain degree of exoticness expected of one—in much the same way that a Southerner might find himself talking more Southern on Fifth Avenue than he would dream of talking on Peachtree Street.

But before getting around to the Southern novelist, let me say a word about the general state of American letters. It is poor. In the first place, only about two percent of Americans regularly read books. Of this two percent, only a small fraction read serious novels. We're talking about a hundred thousand people at the most. Whereas sixty million people watched the episode in *Dallas* which solved the mystery of who shot J.R.

One diagnosis of this state of affairs by men of letters might run something like this: literacy in America has declined for a variety of reasons—bad schools, decay of the family, most of all, the six or seven hours of daily TV. This decline of literacy is accompanied by a rise in philistinism in America: a preference for the skillfully marketed and packaged product for the consumption of the mass man—the Top Ten on TV, NFL telecasts with the quite well-done Miller Lite and Mean Joe Green commercials— plus a few big commercial novels, whether the Harold Robbins novel in which sex figures second only to money, the Barbara Cartland novel in which sex becomes something called romance, or the Judy Blume novel in which teenagers are introduced to sex like Tarzan and Jane.

Other causes of philistinism are cited: the takeover of inde- pendent publishers by the conglomerates who are not interested in taking on a young promising novelist, losing money on him or her against the time when his promise might be fulfilled—like Hemingway or Faulkner.

These facts may be true enough. But it is not simple. There is another reason for the poor state of the American novel. It is the poor state of the American novel. The fact is that novels these days, even serious, so-called literary novels, are not very good. In fact, with a few honorable exceptions, they are atrocious; that is to say, ill conceived or badly written or both.

I recently had the depressing experience of serving as a judge in a national fiction contest and having to read some 250 novels. I won't pretend I read all of them. Sometimes it is enough to read one page or even one paragraph. These were, presumably, the best offerings of the publishers. My only conclusion is that, far from it being the case that it is all but impossible to get a first novel published these days, surely anybody can get a novel published. Either that or 250 authors have connections, are the girlfriends or boyfriends of editors.

Even serious writers, writers of established reputations, seem to be either repeating themselves without enthusiasm or getting hysterical or withdrawing into private sex fantasies. Political novelists, once full of energy and the good vinegar of protest in the 1960s, take to writing reveries about Marilyn Monroe.

I have a theory about the unhappiness of what I would call the American protest novelist; that is, the novelist, usually from the Northeast, sometimes the West Coast, with strong ideological, generally leftist, convictions. My theory is that he secretly envies Aleksandr Solzhenitsyn, despite the terrible ordeal which Solzhenitsyn suffered, despite his rightest sympathies. He envies the fact that a novelist can so irritate the state that the state will go to a great deal of trouble to get rid of him. Solzhenitsyn takes on the entire leadership of the Soviet Union, indicts it before the world, and gets away with it. There, imprisoned in the Gulag, is the indomitable novelist writing his novel in secret and on toilet paper; and here is the American novelist, free, uncensored, with his word processor and plenty of paper—and stuck on dead center, stalled out, paralyzed by freedom. Moreover, he, Solzhenitsyn, wins. He not only takes on the state, he beats it, turns his ordeal to good account, makes a metaphor of his imprisonment, and wins the Nobel Prize.

Compare the American protest novelist. He, too, takes on the whole establishment, attacks Nixon, Eisenhower, whoever, attacks American middle-class values. And what happens? Nothing. He waits in vain for the knock at the door, for the FBI to haul him off for questioning. He even watches Presidential news conferences, hoping to be denounced. Nobody denounces him. In fact, nobody pays much attention.

Worst of all, if the novel is a commercial success, it is bought by Hollywood. The poor radical protest writer becomes a rich radical protest writer. And surely the worst indignity of all: he is seduced by the enemy without the enemy's knowledge. He is like the wretched man in Dostoevsky's *Notes from the Underground* who swore to get even with his enemy by walking directly toward him on the sidewalk and forcing him to yield—and who at the last second yields himself, without the other even noticing. Whereupon he, the protest writer, is apt to become hysterical. I am thinking of two writers who evidently believed that if the attack could be made shrill enough, outlandish enough, atrocious enough, the Establishment would have to take notice. One writer wrote a play, *MacBird*, whose thesis was that Lyndon Johnson had conspired like Macbeth to have Kennedy killed. Another wrote a novel about the Rosenberg case in which Nixon makes love to Ethel Rosenberg and ends by being sodomized by Uncle Sam in Times Square.

Still, no one paid much attention, least of all the political establishment.

It is both the curse and the blessing of American novelists that no one has taken them seriously since Harriet Beecher Stowe. Can you imagine an American President saying to an American novelist these days, as Lincoln said to Harriet Beecher Stowe: "So you are the little lady who started the big war?"

It is a curse, because the American artist, like the American professor, comes to feel that he occupies a marginal and far from honorific place in the culture. Unlike the Herr Professor in Heidelberg, or Sartre or Camus in France, he seems increasingly irrelevant to the main concerns of society. It is a blessing, because the American novelist, dispensed against his will from effective ideological partisanship, has to come across on a bigger scale and in spite of his ideology. Sartre had a political following and was the worse for it. He wrote his best novel when he was sitting alone and bemused in a café in Le Havre. Dante and Dostoevsky were as narrowly partisan as they come, but *The Divine Comedy* and *The Possessed* succeeded in spite of their political vendettas.

The American novelist, that is to say, has in the end to fall back from politics to a statement about the human condition—or else write unseriously. Hence *Huckleberry Finn, Moby-Dick*, and *The Sound and the Fury*. Then he's taken seriously. A final remark about "Northern" novelists. They are often accused of writing not only overly politicized books but dirty books. The accusation is unjust. I don't know any serious writers who are pornographers; that is, who deliberately set out to titillate the reader, hoping he, the reader, will pass the word and more people will buy the book. Not that there are not plenty of pornographers, but I'm not interested in them. I am not interested in making a moral condemnation of pornography, because pornography involves a different set of stimuli from literature and therefore does not concern us here. No, the explicit and obligatory sex in so many novels, like the hysterical politics, is often a frantic and last-ditch attempt to get the attention of an increasingly listless readership. Like the hysterical political novel which is written from the fear that nobody is listening, the kinky-sex novel is often written from the fear of writing about real and age-old human relationships. There is this to be said about the current pornographic novel: it is generally less boring than the nonpornographic novel. I sometimes think novelists write about sex in order to avoid boring themselves to death. After all, sex is interesting, even to a solitary novelist. Especially to a solitary novelist. The most outlandish and atrocious protest novel is largely ignored. But so is the explicit-sex novel. Who is left to be shocked?—except a few PTA members and library boards here and there. So, like a drowning swimmer whose frantic gestures are ignored by the folks on the beach, the novelist resorts to even more bizarre exhibitions.

Take a recent example: *The World According to Garp*, much admired by some people. The crucial scene is an auto accident in which one person is killed and another person is castrated in an act of fellatio. This is no mean literary feat: to unite gratuitous violence, kinky sex, and bizarre tragicomedy in one scene.

The key word is gratuitous. Only if the action is sufficiently uncalled for and sufficiently bizarre can the novelist penetrate the benumbed senses of the reader and especially the critic. The novel, of which this is the climactic scene, was hailed as a fresh and original talent.

This fictive technique can be defended—like the Mississippi farmer who said that it takes a two-by-four to get the attention of a mule.

This is the main difference between the Northern novel and the Southern novel: where there is nothing to attack or defend, the novelist has only one recourse: he has to do stunts. And like a circus acrobat's, each stunt has to be more death-defying than the last. Which brings me to the present-day so-called Southern novel—which is, if possible, in even worse shape.

We hear a good deal about the Southern Literary Renascence. It's all true. There was such a thing and I don't have to tell you how remarkable it was. Within the space of twenty or thirty years there occurred a flowering of poetry, fiction, and criticism unprecedented since the New England of Hawthorne and Thoreau and Emerson. What we do not hear about and what is not generally noticed or remarked is that not only is the Southern Literary Renascence over and done with. The Great Literary Depression has set in.

This is to say only that, as far as I can tell, there are very few promising young novelists coming along. There are any number of festivals and seminars which celebrate the Southern Literary Renascence. But what nobody likes to talk about is that there are few if any writers under forty who could be called renascent.

Among the 250 or so novels I had the misfortune to have to read last year, Southern fiction was, with one or two exceptions, both scantier and more dispirited than the rest. It was as if the young Southern fiction writers were well enough aware of the great figures of the Renascence—Faulkner, Warren, Welty, O'Connor, and the rest—but were themselves at something of a loss. One certainly wanted to get out from under Faulkner, but where do you go from there? There were a few examples of what I would call the Tennessee–Texas School, recounting the picaresque adventures of country-music types, hell-raisin' drunk-in-the-whorehouse good ol' boys whose profoundest thoughts were about bad cops and bad preachers—a far cry from the Nashville poets of the 1920s and of a general literary quality just short of *Smokey and the Bandit*.

As for Southern women novelists, I seem to detect the emergence of a new genre. Unlike their Northern sisters who go in for heavy feminist accounts of the alienation of housewives in Teaneck, of anxiety and depression and suicide among Radcliffe grads, an increasing number of Southern women novelists are writing what I would call the Southern Belle Confessional Novel, or What Really Went on at Sweet Briar.

An interesting reversal of social roles is taking place. In past times women writers like George Eliot and George Sand might be noted for their unconventional sexual behavior but nevertheless wrote the standard fictive prose acceptable to a civil society. But there is now a new female Southern writer who does the opposite: who talks nice and writes dirty—just like Mary Lou down the street—because she is Mary Lou down the street.

The conventional wisdom is that the Southern writer had a literary advantage because he inhabited a region which had, as we have heard so often, a sense of place, of rootedness, of kinship, a tradition of storytelling, and perhaps, above all, a tragic sense of history. This was true enough and to a degree is still true.

The Southern asset was always the presence of tradition, both Christian and Greco-Roman, which was palpable enough so that even in its decadence there was something of substance to get hold of, to attack, the crumbling porticos, the gentry gone to seed like Faulkner's Compsons. And to defend: so that a Catholic writer like Flannery O'Connor could find herself nourished by the extravagant backwoods Protestant fundamentalism of Georgia.

What does the Northern novelist have to attack or defend? Republicans? A defunct liberalism? And when he attacks or defends, who cares? What does John Irving have to defend? Or attack? Circus bears? A dog with a cute name like Sorrow? A bear with the cute name State o'Maine who can drive a motorcycle? None of these are pornographers. Jerzy Kosinski writes dirty these days, not by design, but by default. He doesn't have anything else to write about. In some cases, dirty writing must be defended. Kosinski writing dirty is less boring than Kosinski writing clean. But even in the best of times, the Southern writer was at a certain disadvantage in the marketplace. His attraction was ever a certain exoticness, either Gothic violence or outlandish humor. But there was a price to be paid. The Southern novelist, from Cable on, is tempted to exploit the Northern reader's gullibility about Southern exoticness and to tell whoppers. But the game gets old in the end and Southern novels get labeled as such—so that if a new book is heralded as a "Southern novel in the best tradition," the book buyer is all too apt to pass it up because he has had enough of Southern novels in any tradition.

So the Southern novel became a victim of its own success. Its secret of success was that at first it was easy to captivate Yankees, whether by Cable's quaint Creoles or Caldwell's rednecks or Faulkner's broken-down gentry. I've always suspected that even Faulkner laid it on a bit thick—and knew that he did so—the thicker the better for innocent Yankee critics like Malcolm Cowley who are prepared to believe anything about Mississippi. But what to do now when the game has been played out and the old defeated and exotic South has turned overnight into the victorious and prosperous Sunbelt, and Atlanta and Dallas look more and more like New York. And Lafayette looks more and more like Houston.

So the aspiring novelist in the Sunbelt is apt to find himself at a loss.

Should he, sitting in his Atlanta or Houston high-rise, try to recapture his rural roots, when the chances are that he never saw a sharecropper's cabin or a cracker except when he was driving through southern Georgia on his way to Fort Lauderdale for the spring break?

Or should he try to catch up with Updike and Cheever and do a number on the Hilton Head crowd? But it's hard to beat Cheever and Updike on their own ground.

He doesn't know quite what to do and that may explain an article I read in a Texas journal which called attention to the embarrassing fact that there are no first-class writers of fiction in all of Texas. Think of it! The state which has the biggest and best of everything, which is probably on its way to being the richest state in the Union, furthermore has lavish cultural facilities, as they are called, good symphony orchestras, art museums, and so forth, yet not a single first-line novelist!

I'm not sure we in Louisiana have any reason to congratulate ourselves, since we are rapidly becoming Texasized. Just the other day I read about a local oil man who had made two billion dollars and boasted that he had never read a single novel. I wish I could be sure he had made a mistake.

Just as the celebrated virtues of locale and tradition can become a burden to the new Southern novelist, so can that other mainstay of Southern culture, its pervasive Christianity. It is still *there* in a sense in which it is not there in the rest of the country. It is part of the air we breathe. It may be there to nourish and inform as it has some writers. It may be there to oppress and therefore to be attacked and satirized, but it is there.

The South has been called a Jesus-haunted country. Even when the Southern writer was not a believer, he could not escape, would not want to escape this haunting presence. There are two things Southern writers have always been stuck with, blacks and Jesus. This obsession works both ways, for better and worse. In the best writers, believer or unbeliever, it works wonders. Dilsey, in Faulkner's *The Sound and the Fury*, goes to church on Easter Sunday and for this reason is the only whole living person in the household of ghostly Compsons.

Even Erskine Caldwell, out to profane, had to have something to profane. Try to imagine Caldwell's Jeeter Lester blaspheming in California. Who would care? How do you blaspheme in California? What does blasphemy signify in a counterculture?

Like Flannery O'Connor, I would defend the Christian culture of the South as, on the whole, a literary asset. From a Catholic perspective at least, Christianity is a belief inherently congenial to the vocation of the novelist in a way in which, say, Buddhism, Marxism, Freudianism, behaviorism, is not. To say so offends the conventional wisdom that dogma constrains the freedom of the artist. The word "dogma" of course has gotten to be a swear word and is used pejoratively. Whereas what it signifies, of course, is simply belief in the central Christian mysteries; for example, the

Incarnation. In this sense, dogma is a guarantee of the mystery of human existence and for the novelist, for this novelist anyhow, a warrant to explore the mystery. I've never met a believing artist who felt constrained by his belief, but I've met any number who believed in nothing but an abstract freedom and who were not only constrained but paralyzed by some internal inquisition of their own making.

The Christian ethos sustains the narrative enterprise in ways so familiar to us that they can be overlooked. It underwrites those very properties of the novel without which there is no novel: I am speaking of the mystery of human life, its sense of predicament, of something having gone wrong, of life as a wayfaring and a pilgrimage, of the density and linearity of time and the sacramental reality of things. The intervention of God in history through the Incarnation bestows a weight and value to the individual human narrative which is like money in the bank to the novelist. Original Sin is out of fashion, both with Christians and with Jews, let alone unbelievers. But any novelist who does not believe that his character finds himself in a predicament not entirely of his own making or of society's making is in trouble as a novelist. And any novelist who begins his novel with his character in a life predicament which is a profound mystery to which he devotes his entire life to unraveling, like Pascal's man in his cell—which is to say, every great novelist for the past three hundred years from Cervantes to Camus—is a closet Jew or Christian whether he likes it or not.

Another way of saying this is that I don't recall reading a good novel which was informed by a Marxist belief in an inexorable dialectic of history—and I've read plenty of bad ones—or a good novel informed by a preoccupation with the mechanisms of one's own psyche, or a good novel which was informed by a belief in the illusoriness of this here-and-now life in this here-and-now world. If the world is not real, why bother to write a novel about it or read a novel about it? And, for this reason, very few Buddhists, Californian or Asian, have.

Yet we are all familiar with a great literature going back at least as far as Dante informed by the tragedy and comedy of real people each embarked on a real pilgrimage for good and ill.

The Southern novel of a generation ago was so informed. So

is the current so-called Jewish novel, which, though apparently past its prime, is the liveliest of current American literary phenomena.

It has always seemed curious to me, by the way, that the Jewish experience, apparently such a rich source of literature in the Northeast and Midwest, has so far no comparable counterpart in the South. And yet the Southern Jewish experience is singularly rich, both in its own right and in its sensitivity to the complex social class and race mix which comprises the South. The Southern WASP, Catholic, and humanist traditions have found voices. The Southern woman novelist is, of course, preeminent. There are distinguished black voices. But the Southern Jewish voice, with a few exceptions, is yet to be heard. I don't quite know why. I make no claim to prophetic powers, yet I make bold to predict that the next Southern literary revival will be led by a Jewish mother, which is to say, a shrewd self-possessed woman with a sharp eye and a cunning retentive mind who sees the small follies and triumphs and tragedies around her and has her own secret method of rendering it, with an art all her own and yet not unrelated to Welty, O'Connor, and Porter. It may take a Southern Jewish voice to articulate the fact, increasingly evident, that the modern world is in the grip of demonic powers. Like Isaac Singer, she might speak of demons; unlike Singer, she might mean it. And, unlike Singer, she might be taken seriously.

It would be interesting, by the way, to compare the Southern and Jewish experience in the terms of the encounter of a strongly knit, beleaguered tradition emerging into the heady air of the American consensus, where, for a few years at least, it flares like a match struck in pure oxygen, before it flames out—that is, blends with the general cultural chemistry around it. The best of literary times for the South, strangely enough, were not the antebellum years of a leisure society which might have produced a Jane Austen or a Samuel Johnson and did not, did not even come close, but rather a time after years of defeat and humiliation when a few young Southerners entered the mainstream of American culture in a full consciousness of their own roots.

But if there are literary assets in the Christian view of man, there are also serious impediments in the current historical manifestation of Christendom. It has to do with the devaluation of the Christian vocabulary and the media inflation of its contents. The old words, God, grace, sin, redemption, which used to signify within a viable semiotic system, now tend to be either exhausted, worn slick as poker chips and signifying as little, or else are heard as the almost random noise of radio and TV preachers. The very word "Christian" is not good news to most readers.

Theoretically, one should prefer the good news of the Sunday-morning media sermons to the sex and violence of weekday TV. But after listening to what is called the Christian network for a couple of hours, it is a relief to get back to J.R. and Dallas.

The Christendom of the Old South with its grim roadside signs—PREPARE TO MEET ETERNITY —served the novelist's purposes better than Oral Roberts's cheerful announcement that Something Good Is Going to Happen to You. The Southern inkling was rather that something bad is going to happen to you, if it hasn't happened already.

The triumphant Christendom of the Sunbelt creates problems for the Southern novelist, whether he is believer or unbeliever. If he is an unbeliever, he may feel like attacking it, but really he hasn't the heart. It's like shooting fish in a barrel. Who needs another Elmer Gantry?

If he is a believer, he is in a different kind of trouble. He finds himself in bed with the wrong bedfellows. What makes it difficult for him is that they are proclaiming the same good news he believes in, using the same noble biblical words, speaking of the same treasure buried in a field, but somehow devaluing it. If these are the fellows who have found the treasure buried in a field, then what manner of treasure is it?

I hasten to say that his, the writer's, discomfort has nothing to do with the ancient Catholic–Protestant quarrel. Catholic or Protestant, he is equally unhappy.

He feels like Lancelot in search of the Holy Grail who finds himself at the end of his quest at a Tupperware party.

Is he being elitist? Perhaps. Does he dislike Jerry Falwell too easily and for the wrong reasons? Does he have the same ironic contempt that the cultivated Greek intellectuals had for St. Paul? Well, I don't really think so. But before he writes off the Moral

Majority, he had better consider the alternative, or one alternative. I once saw a debate between Jerry Falwell and Bob Guccione, editor of *Penthouse*, and had no trouble at all choosing between the Gospel According to Falwell and the Gospel According to Guccione.

At any rate, finding himself in the thriving Sunbelt informed as it is by a species of triumphant Christendom, with the highest percentage of churchgoers anywhere in the world except South Africa, the writer tends to fall silent. His natural inclination, Christian or not, is, like Søren Kierkegaard's, to attack Christendom. If he is a Christian, he must be at last as cunning and devious as Joyce advised—more cunning even than Joyce, for he is working with a prostituted vocabulary which must be either discarded or somehow miraculously rejuvenated. The stance which comes most naturally to him is not that of edification but rather that of challenge, offense, shock, attack, subversion. With the best of intentions, he subverts both the Christendom and the paganism of his culture and he does so cheerfully and in good heart, because as a creature of the culture he is subverting himself, first, last, and always.

So there, as I see it, is the present plight of the Southern novelist: both beneficiary and victim of the label "Southern" and, whether he likes it or not, the denizen of a clamorous Christian culture which he is in a sense stuck with, whether he is Christian, Jew or humanist.

So what is he to do? Let me make an assumption before I make a suggestion. The assumption is that he is still heir to a unique literary legacy, the same tradition which informed the Nashville poets and critics and the Deep South novelists of the 1920s and 1930s. His great advantage is that he can see the American scene from both the inside and the outside—inside because, living as he does in the resurgent Sunbelt, he is more American than ever; from the outside because he's still Southern whether he likes it or not, which is to say he can still see the American proposition from a tragic historical perspective. He knows in his bones that things can come to grief and probably will. And whether he is a believer or not, he is also more likely to know that man is tragically flawed and is born to trouble as the

sparks fly up. He is subject to his own version of Murphy's Law—
not that if something can go wrong, it will—but rather that
something has already gone wrong and is going to get worse
without the supervention of a mystery beyond the scope of a
sociological or a psychological novel.

So what should he do? His natural mission in this place and
these times is, if not search and destroy, then probe and challenge.
His greatest service is to attack, that is to say, satirize. Don't forget
that satire is not primarily destructive. It attacks one thing in order
to affirm another. It assaults the fake and the phony in the name
of the truth. It ridicules the inhuman in order to affirm the human.
Satire is always launched in the mode of hope.

What else to do in a Sunbelt South increasingly informed by
a flatulent Christendom and Yankee money-grubbing? For the
danger is that we are going to end up with the worst of both
worlds, the worst of Southern Christendom—that is, an inflated
media Christendom without the old Southern pieties—and the
worst of Northern materialism—a kind of mindless money-sports-
Vegas culture without stern secular saints like Thoreau, Emerson,
Melville, Hawthorne.

James McBride Dabbs, a wise man, once wrote that a great
culture is recognizable through its artists and its saints and not by
its GNP. And the South, he said, with all its promise, paradoxically
did not have time to develop a full-fledged culture. And why not?
Because, through bad luck, historical accident, and human weakness, it got diverted through most of its history by a single-minded
preoccupation, its great obsession with slavery and race—from
which it is only just now emerging. So it is no accident that in the
last century its heroes were military and political, its patron saint
a general, Robert E. Lee.

Although we in the South like to make much of the high
culture of antebellum plantation life, of our close ties to Europe,
the Grand Tour, college years abroad, of grand pianos imported
from France, of bookshelves full of sets of English novelists,
especially Walter Scott—and, later on, of an embattled period
following the Defeat—let's face it: it is difficult to name a single
world-class writer in the South until the 1920s, if we except the
early political writings of the Virginians and such marginal types

as Poe and Mark Twain. But little or nothing of literary value came from the mainstream of the culture itself. Why? Because of the Great Obsession. It is difficult for a man to write a great novel in a state of paranoia, or a great poem when most of his energies go to trying to convince himself and the world that black is white—or rather that black is black, that black is not beautiful but black is happy anyhow.

Only in the past generation has it become possible for Southern writers, white and black, to get out from under the terrible burden of race, either the defense of it or the condemnation of it.

Who are the culture heroes of the South now? Bear Bryant, Burt Reynolds, Kenny Rogers, and Hershel Walker. Now, no one would deny that these are admirable fellows. Recently, on the occasion of Bear Bryant's 315th football victory, Southern senators sponsored a vote of acclamation. It's fine for Bear Bryant so to be acclaimed. But I don't recall a similar vote when Faulkner won the Nobel Prize or Eudora Welty won the Gold Medal for American Literature.

This is probably as it should be. A writer worth his salt is probably better off in an adversarial relation with the U.S. Senate. I, for one, would get very nervous if my writings were acclaimed by the Louisiana legislature. Beware of the novelist who is on intimate terms with Presidents, bishops or Billy Graham, Dr. Spock or Madalyn Murray O'Hair.

What I am saying is that the artist, poet, or novelist is not necessarily at home in the South or the United States now—if he ever was—and that is as it should be. If in the best of times it is the artist's vocation to celebrate his culture—like Dante or Shakespeare or Tolstoy—in other times it may be his vocation to nag, to challenge, to be a thorn in the side, even a pain in the neck. But in so doing, and this is the point, he is not subverting, he is not the enemy of the people. He, she, if he is any good, is always speaking from his truest self to the reader and affirming himself in a way which the reader cannot fail to recognize. Even at his most satirical, he is not destructive, for the entire literary enterprise is mounted in hope—otherwise, he would not take the trouble to set pen to paper, for serious writing is no end of trouble and misery.

Above all, he is open to the mystery of his art. By this openness and this mystery, I am speaking of a necessary sensitivity to the hidden dimensions and energies of his characters and of the presence of the mystery which may always erupt in their lives and which, for want of a better word, we may call grace. Neither he nor his characters may know why certain things happen as they do. But unless such things do happen and unless he, the novelist, is open to them, he is forever doomed to a literary sociology and psychology, or to being politicized, and whether it is liberal or conservative politics, it doesn't matter: the writing is going to be bad. When I speak of "serious" writers, I am also speaking of comic writers. They are not mutually exclusive categories. What I am not talking about, will not even take the trouble to deal with, are the clones and prostitutes and pimps of current commercial writing. In the South, such writing often takes the form of Southern belles and good ol' boys who think they have to write like whores talk. Fanny Hill had certain skills, but writing was not one of them. And Southern good ol' boy poets and novelists who think that if you drink enough and chase enough students, somehow the great god Dionysus is going to inspire you. Unfortunately, Dionysus was not obliged to sit down at a typewriter, and it would have been just as well if some of these fellows hadn't either.

What is at issue is a very great opportunity. The American novel is, with a couple of honorable exceptions, demoralized. The young Southern artist, fiction writer, and poet are presently hanging fire. He doesn't know which way to jump. He knows he comes from a great tradition, but God help him if he tries to go back, back to Faulkner's Mississippi or O'Connor's Georgia. We've been there. God help him, too, if he tries to do a Cheever or an Updike number on a town like Lafayette.

I'm afraid he's on his own. His freedom and opportunities are so great that it scares him. He can't go back to sharecroppers' cabins and crumbling mansions haunted by Confederate ghosts. Yet he probably lives in a teeming Sunbelt community, with an ethnic mix, an amalgam of economic prosperity and spiritual dislocation which is the very stuff of fiction. Take this fellow, this Midwesterner transplanted to Louisiana who has made two billion dollars from oil leases and has never read a novel, who lives in an antebellum mansion in New Orleans and who is so absorbed in deal-making that he is a stranger to his friends and family. Maybe he can't use me, but I can sure use him.

Maybe it's hopeless. Maybe the artistic future of the victorious Sunbelt is less Nashville poetry and more Nashville sound, more *Smokey and the Bandit* in film, more Texas soap opera, and in literature, the latter-day adventures of would-be Scarlett O'Haras, or the Confessions of a Georgia Co-ed.

But I don't think it's hopeless. Writers turn up in the unlikeliest places—people who just decide to go their own way, tear up the book, make their own music. Two such names come immediately to mind: Beth Henley in Mississippi and John Kennedy Toole in Louisiana, whose writings are outrageous, funny, yet eminently serious.

The possibilities of the "Southern novel" are unlimited, unlimited in its ability both to re-create the South and to shape American literature, which God knows could use it.

The possibilities of failure and default are also unlimited.

Being no prophet, I decline to speculate, though, like a prophet, I tend to be pessimistic.

But we'll see.

1984

FROM FACTS
TO FICTION

❧

There follows the story, for whom it may interest, of how it came to pass that a physician turned writer and became a novelist. It is hardly a momentous or a typical story. But perhaps it is the nature of the beast that no writer finds his vocation typically. Nor can I imagine this account to be of any use to either would-be physicians or would-be writers. I would not recommend to young writers that they serve an apprenticeship in medicine or to physicians that they take up novel-writing.

But perhaps what value there is in my experience is to be found in the oddness of it, specifically in the circumstance that it is possible for a man to set out seriously with a scientific vocation, change in midstream to an artistic vocation, practice it quite as seriously, offer his wares in an open market, and, in a moderate degree, succeed. Perhaps the only moral to the story is that a serious writer, or any other artist for that matter, is a peculiar bird who has to find his own way in his own time and who had better be left alone to do so.

At any rate, it came to pass in my own life that I found myself left very much to my own devices, although it was not the sort of aloneness I had bargained for. What happened was that while I was working as a pathologist at Bellevue Hospital in New York, where my duties included the examination of the tissues of tuberculous patients, I contracted pulmonary tuberculosis and found myself flat on my back in a sanatorium in the Adirondack Mountains, faced with the prospect of a year or more of enforced inactivity.

The chronicle of such a misfortune—for misfortune it certainly seemed at the time—is perhaps best related in terms of its consequences for one's inner life, the area of the deepest convictions and the unspoken assumptions by which every man lives his life (and if a man thinks he has no such assumptions, they are all the stronger for not being recognized).

Though I am descended from a long line of lawyers, my own bent from the beginning had been toward science—and still is. It was the elegance and order and, yes, beauty of science which attracted me. It is not merely the truth of science that makes it beautiful, but its simplicity. That is to say, its constant movement is in the direction of ordering the endless variety and the seeming haphazardness of ordinary life by discovering underlying principles which as science progresses become ever fewer and more rigorously and exactly formulated—at least in the physical sciences.

At Columbia University's College of Physicians and Surgeons, I was particularly attracted by a pervasive attitude among some of my teachers. It can best be expressed by a phrase we students heard again and again: "the mechanism of disease." It struck me then, as now, as an idea of the most revolutionary simplicity and beauty; namely, that even the *dis*-order of *dis*-ease, which one generally takes to be the very disruption of order, could be approached and understood and treated according to scientific principles governing the response of the patient to the causative agents of disease. This response *was* the disease as the physician sees it! Of course, it was hardly a new idea, but, new or old, it was an exciting discovery for a young man who had always thought of disease as disorder to be set right somehow by the "art" of medicine.

Such, at any rate, was one reason I found myself in the pathology laboratory at Bellevue, where it seemed medicine came closest to being the science it should be and furthest from the arts and crafts of the bedside manner. Under the microscope, in the test tube, in the colorimeter, one could actually see the beautiful theater of disease and even measure the effect of treatment on the disease process. Then came the cataclysm, brought to pass appropriately enough by one of these elegant agents of disease, the same scarlet tubercle bacillus I used to see lying crisscrossed like Chinese characters in the sputum and lymphoid tissue of the patients at Bellevue. Now I was one of them.

What was the effect of cataclysm, the interruption of my chosen career, and the two years of physical inactivity which followed? An effect there was, it could hardly have been otherwise, but it was not, I hasten to say, any slackening of my allegiance to the rigor and discipline of the scientific method. The effect was rather a shift of ground, a broadening of perspective, a change of focus. What began to interest me was not so much a different question as a larger question, not the physiological and pathological processes within man's body but the problem of man himself, the nature and destiny of man; specifically and more immediately, the predicament of man in a modern technological society. I began to read, no longer Macleod's *Physiology* or Gay's *Bacteriology*, but the great Russian novelists, especially Dostoevsky; the modern French novelists, especially Camus; the existentialist philosophers, Jaspers (also a physician), Marcel, and Heidegger.

If the first great intellectual discovery of my life was the beauty of the scientific method, surely the second was the discovery of the singular predicament of man in the very world which has been transformed by this science. An extraordinary paradox became clear: that the more science progressed, and even as it benefited man, the less it said about what it is like to be a man living in the world. Every advance in science seemed to take us further from the concrete here-and-now in which we live. Did my eyes deceive me, or was there not a huge gap in the scientific view of the world (scientific in the root sense of the word "knowing")? If so, it was an oversight which everyone pretended not to notice or maybe didn't want to notice.

After twelve years of a scientific education, I felt somewhat like the Danish philosopher Søren Kierkegaard when he finished reading Hegel. Hegel, said Kierkegaard, explained everything under the sun, except one small detail: what it means to be a man living in the world who must die.

The long and short of it was that I decided to give up medicine and take up writing. In the next two years I wrote two novels which were returned with rejection slips or with pained notes which began, "Despite some occasional splendid passages, I am sorry to have to inform you—" etc. These were the years of the "splendid passages." My resources were dwindling; my health was uncertain; I sold a few articles for small sums—I even wrote a book about the philosophy of language which the publisher didn't even bother to return and I didn't ask for. As far as my novel-writing went, it began to seem that I should have stuck to pathology. But at least, I told myself, I could write "an occasional splendid passage."

Anyhow, I wrote a third novel, *The Moviegoer*, in something over a year. It was accepted by the first publisher to see it and won the National Book Award for Fiction in 1962. It sold fairly well in the hardcover edition and somewhere around half a million copies in paperback.

The moral here, I suppose, is that if a book is any good, it can find a publisher and an audience. At least I can testify to this in my own experience; a writer does not have to compromise himself or his talent to be published.

As far as the actual writing of *The Moviegoer* is concerned, and setting aside the matter of its merit, the question has been put to me: What happened? How did it happen that you can write two bad novels and then a third which is a great deal better? This is an interesting question, one which, however, I do not pretend to be able to answer. I can only report that something did happen and it happened all of a sudden. Other writers have reported a similar experience. It is not like learning a skill or a game at which, with practice, one gradually improves. One works hard all right, but what comes, comes all of a sudden and as a breakthrough. One hits on something. What happens is a period of unsuccessful effort during which one works very hard—and fails. There follows a period of discouragement. Then there comes a paradoxical moment of collapse-and-renewal in which one somehow breaks with the past and starts afresh. All past efforts are thrown into the wastebasket; all advice forgotten. The slate is wiped clean. It is almost as if the discouragement were necessary, that one has first to encounter despair before one is entitled to hope. Then a time comes when one takes a pencil and a fresh sheet of paper and begins. Begins, really for the first time.

One begins to write, not as one thinks he is supposed to write, and not even to write like the great models one admires, but rather to write as if he were the first man on earth ever to set pencil to paper.

To return to a scientific analogy: what comes to my mind when I think of a writer sitting down to create something new, however modest that creation, is not the picture of a man setting out to entertain or instruct or edify a reader. It is the picture, rather, of a scientist who has come to the dead end of a traditional hypothesis which no longer accounts for the data at hand. It is my belief that anyone writing serious fiction today is somewhat like the physicists around 1900 after the Michelson–Morley experiment and quantum data had overthrown Newtonian physics. That is to say, in modern literature it is man himself who is called into question and who must be defended, and it is the very nature of man which must be rediscovered and reexpressed in fresh language of a new poetry and fiction and theater.

John Barth said recently that now in the last third of the twentieth century it was no longer permissible to write nineteenth-century novels. I agree. When I sat down to write *The Moviegoer*, I was very much aware of discarding the conventional notions of a plot and a set of characters, discarded because the traditional concept of plot-and-character itself reflects a view of reality which has been called into question. Rather would I begin with a *man* who finds himself in a *world*, a very concrete man who is located in a very concrete place and time. Such a man might be represented as *coming to himself* in somewhat the same sense as Robinson Crusoe came to himself on his island after his shipwreck, with the same wonder and curiosity.

1966

PHYSICIAN AS NOVELIST

❧

O̲r, Why the Best Training for a Novelist in These Last Years of the Twentieth Century Is an Internship at Bellevue or Cook County Hospital, and How This Training Best Prepares Him for Diagnosing T. S. Eliot's *The Waste Land*. But let us speak of vocations. What one ends up doing with one's life is surely one of God's mysteries. And a good deal of luck, good luck and bad luck, is involved as well as, I firmly believe, God's providence. Who among us is doing what he, she, dreamed of doing when he, she, was eight, twelve, sixteen? Perhaps it is just as well we are not. At twelve I wanted to fly the Pacific because Lindbergh had flown the Atlantic.

I'd like to share with you some of the misfortunes, peculiar turns of fate, and finally the piece of luck or Divine Providence, as the case may be, by which I turned out doing what I am doing, something which had never occurred to me to do, not once in my wildest dreams, but which I like doing, not because I do it all that well but because I am incompetent doing anything else. Growing up, I was a reluctant attendant at Sunday school and a secret devotee of science, or what I took to be science. My favorite writer in my teens was H. G. Wells, who believed that all events in the cosmos, even human history, can be explained by natural science, and a rather crude science at that.

Actually, it is not a bad way to grow up in the twentieth century, an age that will certainly be known—if we survive—not only for its tragedies, millions dead from its great wars and the Holocaust, but for its spectacular scientific advances, from the study of subatomic particles to the exploration into the far reaches of the cosmos. The best of our time is marked by the truth and beauty of science as surely as the cathedral at Chartres is the high-water mark of the thirteenth century.

But what I wish to propose to you is this: that for a certain type of educated denizen of this age it is only through, first, the love of the scientific method and, second, its elevation and exhaustion as the ultimate method of knowing that he becomes open to other forms of knowing—sciencing in the root sense of the word—and accordingly, at least I think so, to a new kind of revival of Western humanism and the Judeo-Christian tradition—again, if we survive. A large order. And of course I am not suggesting that one cannot be raised a believing Presbyterian, Jew, or Catholic, or as an unbelieving humanist or simply as a passive consumer, and live happily ever after in one's faith or nonfaith without a second thought about the prevailing scientism of the age.

No, I am speaking of a rather more typical denizen of the age who believes, as part of the very air he breathes, that natural science has the truth, all the truth, and that the rest—religion, humanism, art—is icing on the cognitive cake; attractive icing, yes, but icing nonetheless, which is to say, noncognitive icing, emotional icing. Notice that I distinguish here between scientism as an all-pervading ideology and the scientific method as a valid means of investigating the mechanisms of phenomena. But please allow me, after the fashion of physicians, to relate a short history.

Here is a young man, a disciple and devotee of science, whose education has been thoroughly scientific, who settles on medicine as his vocation and chooses a medical school famous for its scientific approach to medicine as the study of the mechanism of disease.

Then, early on, his career is cut short by a serious, disabling, but nonfatal illness. What to do? In the end he returns to the South and changes professions, decides to become a writer—in the South at least, still an honorable profession. But how to go about it? The long and short of it: he writes two novels, one a bad imitation of Thomas Mann, the other a worse imitation of Thomas Wolfe—which is very bad indeed. But no luck. Some kind words from publishers, but no deal.

What to do now? To cut it even shorter: after much casting about and considerable depression if not despair, the thought finally occurred to this fellow—by luck or by providence—why not forget about other writers, however distinguished, and go your own way? What was there to lose? Wasn't this what Newton, Darwin, and Freud had done in science?

And so it came to pass that he wrote a short novel in which he created a character, an amiable but slightly bemused young man of a certain upper-class Southern background, and set him down in Gentilly, a middle-class district of New Orleans, in order to see what would happen to him. For he has given up on the usual verities—home, family, church, country—and instead elects a solitary existence of selling stocks and bonds to the local burghers, hiring a succession of lovely secretaries, and—going to the movies. He enjoys bad movies.

What happens to him is that in the very anxiety of his despair, cool as it is—indeed, as the very consequence of his despair—it occurs to him that a *search* is possible, a search altogether different from the scientific explorations mounted by scientists or by the most perceptive of psychoanalysts. So the novel, almost by accident, became a narrative of the search, the quest. And so the novel, again almost by accident—or was it accident?—landed squarely in the oldest tradition of Western letters: the pilgrim's search outside himself, rather than the guru's search within. All this happened to the novelist and his character without the slightest consciousness of a debt to St. Augustine or Dante. Indeed, the character creates within himself and within the confines of a single weekend in New Orleans a microcosm of the spiritual history of the West, from the Roman patrician reading his Greek philosophers to the thirteenth-century pilgrim who leaves home and takes to the road.

But, as a physician, perhaps I can give a more respectable analysis of this case history, after the fashion of professors in the amphitheater discussing a case after the patient has been wheeled out.

My point is that the stance of the physician is appropriate

here. For his stance is that of the diagnostician. A diagnostician is a person who stands toward another person in the relation of one who knows that something has gone wrong with the other. He, the physician-novelist, has a nose for pathology.

In his case, that of the physician-novelist, the pathology he discovers in his characters has afflicted the very society that surrounds him. It might be called scientism or, perhaps more accurately, what Whitehead called the "misplaced concrete." What he, Whitehead, had in mind was not the truth and beauty of the scientific method, but a certain abstractedness and disorientation that follows upon the elevation of science to an all-enveloping ideology. One looks at an amoeba and sees it as an example of, a specimen of, a biological class. Very good. One looks at a fellow human being and sees him, her, as a typical example of a certain sort of outgoing Midwesterner, or perhaps a recognizable specimen of a sardonic, backward-looking Southerner. Not so good. For what one is missing is precisely that which makes this specimen human, his uniqueness.

So what I have in mind here is the imperial decree of scientism (not of science) to discredit other ways of knowing.

In a word, a respectable epistemological word, what he, the novelist's character, discovers in his search is that there are other ways of knowing not only quite as valid as scientific propositions but of far more critical significance in one's personal life.

Thus, while he had admitted all along the universal validity of such sentences as "The square of the hypotenuse equals the sum of the square of the other two sides," or, "Water boils at one hundred degrees centigrade at sea level," now all at once he, the novelist's character, the pilgrim-searcher, is able to take note of other kinds of sentences that he had ignored before. Perhaps in his wanderings he encounters another person. The stranger has an unusual air about him. He is on to something. But he is not a guru who conveys to him some universal truths about the self and the cosmos. No; he, the stranger, is a news-bearer, and, of all things, news of an event in history. News? History? Hardly the stuff of empirically verifiable scientific sentences.

The stranger is not importunate. He is serious but almost

offhand in his manner, smiling. "I have something to tell you," he says to the pilgrim. "A piece of news. It is of great importance to you. Whether or not you choose to believe me is your affair."

Perhaps the pilgrim does not believe the stranger, as well he might not. Let me note here what is extremely important and the source of much confusion. The physician-novelist is not himself a news-bearer, and he is not in the business of writing edifying tales. He has other fish to fry. It is enough for him to have discovered and put his finger on the peculiar lesion of the age. Perhaps by this very act the abscess is lanced, the ear drained so that the patient, whatever else he might do, can at least hear. Nevertheless the physician, insofar as he is a novelist, is in the business of diagnosis, not therapy.

Like all artists, he is interested, not in edifying, but in discovering and pointing out and naming certain sectors of reality, both within oneself and outside oneself, which had gone unnoticed. Whereupon he, the novelist's character, is free, as only a man can be free, to act accordingly.

But—and I can hear the question despite my disavowals— what are you suggesting? Are you suggesting that one must be a believing Jew or Christian to write good novels? Certainly not— though one is tempted to make the case and indeed present the evidence that the Jewish novelist, secular or religious, has a certain advantage, what with his unique placement in a strictly linear time and history. By a "certain view of reality" I am speaking of the linearity of history, the density of things and events, the mystery and uniqueness of persons, a view that seems natural to us but is in fact the cultural heritage of Judeo-Christianity. Which is to say that I haven't read any good Buddhist novels lately. It is to say also that B. F. Skinner, who believed that all life is a matter of stimuli and responses, could not possibly write a good novel— though I believe in fact that he did try. It is to say that the novels of H. G. Wells could not possibly be otherwise than as bad as they are. And I have never read a Marxist novel without being over- whelmed by the thesis.

Finally, it also helps the novelist to have interned at Bellevue or at Cook County Hospital. For one develops a nose for pathology.

And it is only when one sees that something is wrong that one can diagnose it, point it out and name it, toward the end that the patient might at least have hope, and even in the end get well.

1989

HERMAN MELVILLE

✢

What does a present-day Southern writer make of Melville? Strangely enough, what first comes to mind is not the greatness of *Moby-Dick* or the strange, flawed originality of *Billy Budd*, but rather a certain chagrin and a sort of melancholy wonder.

What did it feel like, one wonders, to have written *Moby-Dick*, an experience which Melville called being broiled in hellfire, and which was surely a triumphant taking-on of hell and coming through? It was surely akin to the sense of triumph Dante felt emerging from his own inferno. But to write *Moby-Dick*, publish it, sell a few hundred copies, see it drop dead and go out of print, disappear apparently forever, and then to spend the last twenty years of one's life as a customs inspector on the New York docks, so obscure and forgotten that a British critic visiting America couldn't even find you—what did it feel like? And then, at the end, to write *Billy Budd*—again, as far as Melville was concerned, stillborn, unpublished, unread. What did *that* feel like? Was there a certain species of satisfaction in living the most ordinary life imaginable? Was it an exercise in obscurity like that of Bartleby the scrivener, riffling through the valises of rich folk returning from the Grand Tour, and then going home to humble quarters?

And where did Melville come from? A lapsed Calvinist from a middle-class New York family. My grandmother in Georgia might have said of the Melvilles, had she known them and been asked about them: "The Melvilles? Well, of course, you know, they were in trade." That meant that they didn't belong to the upper class of the professions—the doctors, lawyers, plantation owners, and people of leisure. It was the latter, presumably, who had the time and the wherewithal to write, read, cultivate the arts, and so forth. They had the libraries; and they often went to Europe for their education. But I confess to a certain chagrin. Why? Because there was not a single Melville—or anything close—in the entire antebellum South, from the Virginia Tidewater to the New Orleans Vieux Carré and the River Road. A huge country, with an extensive leisure class, close European connections, and plenty of Calvinists, lapsed and unlapsed. And plenty of people in trade. Why no Melville? The conventional wisdom has a ready answer: the slavery did you in.

Well, yes and no. The Greeks—Aeschylus and Sophocles, for instance—had slaves: it didn't do them in. But the South got stuck with slavery because it was profitable. While the Melvilles were in the dry-goods business and didn't stand to make a nickel on slaves, Southern writers, political and otherwise, were feeling guilty because they spent most of their time defending slavery. Now, defending slavery is a strange occupation and it takes a lot of energy. It's impossible to imagine, for example, a South Carolina writer in the 1850s thinking about whales, Rousseau, and Original Sin.

On the other hand, defending cannibals and making a case for an earthly paradise in the valley of the Typee is also a strange occupation for a writer. And being obsessed with the innocence of natural man is surely as pernicious an activity as defending slavery. But these flowerings of genius are mysterious affairs, and I'm not sure that even the critics know the answers. One might also ask: Where were the New England writers in the 1920s and 1930s, when the Nashville poets and the Mississippi novelists were getting on their way?

But there's something else afoot in Melville's case. It has to do with what the structuralists call intertextuality. Now, there is a lot of real goofiness in structuralist criticism. One can imagine a structuralist critique of *Moby-Dick* in the style of Lévi-Strauss: a table of binary opposites listing right whales in one column and wrong whales in another, and the right whales are the sperm whales and the wrong whales are wrongly called right whales. One could "deconstruct" Melville, too, discounting his authorial intention and putting forward the thesis that *Moby-Dick* is really about a homosexual relationship between Ishmael and Queequeg. It has been done, in fact, and it may or may not be true; but it's not really important because that's not what excited Melville and it's not what excites the reader.

But there is something interesting about the idea of Hawthorne as an intertext for Melville, or Melville as a countertext for Hawthorne, which is another way of saying that it is impossible to imagine Melville writing *Moby-Dick* without the somber figure of Hawthorne at his shoulder. The structuralists are right about intertextuality. But I believe it can be stated in ordinary language—without the jargon. There's a strange paradox about writing novels. It is simply this: there's no occupation in the universe that is lonelier and that at the same time depends more radically on a community, a commonwealth of other writers.

I needn't mention the half-dozen extraordinary writers and thinkers confined to a couple of small towns in Massachusetts. But there's a difference between the mediated loneliness of a writer like Melville, for whom Hawthorne stood close by (whether actually present or not), and the absolute loneliness of a Southern writer of the 1840s or 1850s. For all I know, there were dozens of potential Hawthornes and Melvilles and Thoreaus in the Virginias and Carolinas of the 1840s. But there's no such thing as a sovereign and underived text, except possibly for Faulkner, who came from God knows where.

Perhaps the South at that time was too big, too well off, the writers too scattered, too politicized, too full of hubris. Who needed to write? I like to imagine that what happened to literature in the South in the 1920s and 1930s was the same sort of thing that happened to New England a hundred years before. It's just that the post-Christianity and alienation of the Massachusetts writer took a hundred years to reach Mississippi.

Try to imagine Melville today writing in New York about his obsession with the natural depravity of man and blaming God for it. He would be referred to an analyst. It is hard to say who would be more certifiable at Yale or Harvard now—Melville, who believed in the depravity of man and blamed God for it, or Dostoevsky, who believed in the depravity of man and looked to God to save him from it.

The common denominator, I think, between Southern writing of this century and Northeastern writing of the last is a certain relation of the writer to a shared body of belief. I don't mean that a writer has to be informed by a belief like Dante's. But surely there's a certain dialectical relation to a shared belief that helps a writer, even if the relation is unbelief, as in the case of Euripides, who had no use for the gods and didn't lose any sleep over it, or Melville, who had no use for God but could never get over it.

The vocabulary remains intact; there is a common universe of discourse. It is shared by believer and scoffer, even when the scoffer is like Melville or Joyce and cannot relax in his unbelief. Take these factors, a shared belief or a shared warfare against belief, a major talent like Melville's, a community of one's peers, and a common universe of discourse, and you've got the makings of a major literature.

Moby-Dick was not only dedicated to Hawthorne, it was written at him. Written to the reader, yes, but always past Hawthorne, with an eye cocked for Hawthorne's approval at the very least. At the most, it was written to amaze Hawthorne, out-Hawthorne Hawthorne. Not only Man is depraved, but God, too. We know what Melville thought of Hawthorne. He ranked him with Shakespeare, but in a peculiar sense. By Melville's own admission, it was Hawthorne's great power of blackness that appealed to his Calvinist sense of innate depravity and Original Sin. We know how Melville felt after he wrote *Moby-Dick*, and he gave the book to Hawthorne. He said he had written a wicked book, broiled in hellfire, and that he felt fine, as spotless as a lamb, happy, content. Here he used an expression, a strange expression—he referred to the "ineffable sociabilities" he felt in himself.

Surely this is the key to the paradox—the ineffable sociability in writing. Intertextuality, if you please. As lonely as is the craft of writing, it is the most social of vocations. No matter what the writer may say, the work is always written to someone, for someone, against someone. The happiness comes from the ineffable sociabilities, when they succeed, when the writing works and somebody knows it.

But this still doesn't explain where *Moby-Dick* came from, and why Southern writers to this day are knocked out by it in a way they are not knocked out by Poe, Emerson, Thoreau, or even Hawthorne, and in a way Northern writers may not be. The Northern intellectual generally finds *Moby-Dick* comprehensible to the degree he can attach this or that symbol to it—hence the vague descriptions one is always reading about *Moby-Dick* being an allegory about evil.

Now, allegories are dull affairs. I've never read a readable one. And *Moby-Dick* is not dull. Melville had other fish to fry—if you will forgive the expression.

I like to imagine that *Moby-Dick* came to pass in the following way. Like many great works of literature, it was a consequence, not merely of great gifts, but also of great good luck. Perhaps one could even speak of providence or grace. But here is where the luck comes in. One sets out to make up a story, spin a yarn, probably for money. After all, that's how one makes one's living. Perhaps one has fought in a war, bummed around Europe, had six wives, signed up on a whaler out of Nantucket, jumped ship in the South Seas, lived with cannibals. One has become famous, writing about it. One has become a sort of Louis L'Amour of the South Seas, and gets in a few licks at the missionaries for good measure. So, what to do, the writer? You start another whaling yarn. Why not? But then something untoward, extraordinary happens. As the narrative unfolds, one becomes aware that in its very telling something else is being told, a ghostly narrative of great import told by a ghostly self, perhaps one's own shadow self.

This is not to say that at the beginning one might not have had some species of allegory in mind, especially when one has named the chief characters Ishmael and Ahab—the one after a biblical character kicked out into the desert with God's permission, the other after a bad king God had assured would end by having his blood licked by dogs. An allegory is a dreary business. What is not dreary is a narrative that unfolds not merely itself but oneself and others' selves. There's no straining for a symbol of truth. The narrative is the thing.

That is why *Moby-Dick* is so good and *The Confidence-Man* is so boring. The happiness of Melville in *Moby-Dick* is the happiness of the artist discovering, breaking through into the freedom of his art. Through no particular virtue of his own, he hit on a mother lode. The novel—the freedom of its form often paralyzing to the novelist—suddenly finds itself being shaped by a larger unity which cannot be violated. Everything works. One kills six birds with every stone. One can even write a treatise on cetology, which comes off as a kind of theology.

Objective correlatives are easy pickings, lying around like Sutter's gold nuggets. One describes as simple a thing as a wooden crutch, a wire-shaped piece of wood which holds a harpoon, and it turns into a theory of literature. One describes the try-pots, the hellish fire, and the heat amidships of the *Pequod* at full sail through the night, and it becomes one's very soul, both damned and freed.

The freedom and happiness of the artist is attested by his playfulness, his tricks, his malice, his underhandedness, his naughtiness, his hoodwinking the reader. So happy is the metaphorical distance between the novelist and his narrative that he's free to cover his tracks at will. Not only do I not have to strive to mean such-and-such, he seems to say, but I deny that I mean it. I might mean the opposite, because with the *Pequod* under full sail through the night with its try-pots blazing I don't have to worry about a thing. The great whale is as sportive as the *Pequod*; nothing can stop the one but the other. No wonder Melville told Hawthorne: I would sit down and dine with you and all the gods in old Rome's pantheon.

To the Southerner, then, here's the luck of Melville: that the novelist's terrible loneliness has somehow stumbled into the ineffable sociability Melville spoke of. Melville impresses Southern writers for the same reason Dostoevsky impresses Southerners. Neither was afraid to deal with ultimate questions. It may be that the South, which has been called a Christ-haunted place, is something like New England a hundred years ago.

Melville is Dostoevsky turned inside out. Both men saw the depravity of man. One saw it as the occasion of his salvation; the other blamed it on God. Melville is perhaps the lesser writer, not because one might disagree with his theology and philosophy, but because in the end both are perhaps incoherent.

Dostoevsky would never have put up with the Rousseauean nonsense that Melville swallowed hook, line, and sinker. In the end, Melville ends up with the eminently readable science fiction of *Billy Budd*, a queer mishmash of Schopenhauer and Rousseau. One hears that *Billy Budd* is about innocence and evil. It's both a lot better and a lot worse than that. The evil is the last vestige of Melville's Calvinism—man's depravity.

In Melville, the only believable part of Judeo-Christianity (as Schopenhauer put it)—the innocence—comes not from human nature but from outer space. Billy Budd is man before the Fall, man exempted from the Fall, a creature dragged in from some loony planet invented by Melville and Rousseau, who neither understands evil nor needs salvation from it. Dostoevsky would have laughed out loud. Billy Budd, in Dostoevsky's hands, would have turned out to be a child molester.

And therefore a good deal more believable. But Melville was not afraid to address such matters, and that's why he means so much to us.

1983

DIAGNOSING
THE MODERN
MALAISE

❧

From the first, I was emboldened to accept an invitation to speak here at Cornell during the Chekhov festival, not because I am a Chekhov scholar, but because of my admiration for him and a strong fellow feeling which has something to do with certain superficial resemblances between us. He was a physician and a writer of fiction. I was a physician and am a writer of fiction. We both had pulmonary tuberculosis. It also cheered me to learn from the Ukrainian writer Potapenko that Chekhov, like me, was not at all keen on doctoring and was always glad of an excuse to get away from it. He did a bad job with his own illness, never took it seriously even when he was dying of it.

There the resemblances seem to stop. Chekhov never wrote a novel. I never wrote a short story or play and don't intend to. One reason is that, after reading a Chekhov play or short story, one tends to be intimidated.

But as I thought about it and began to read further into Chekhov, it occurred to me that there were other concerns which I shared with him, concerns which it seems appropriate to speak of now because they are of even greater moment to us than in the nineteenth century.

Again I find myself coming back to his medical training. And, accordingly, I hope it won't sound presumptuous to say that his great genius, it seems to me, brought a certain set of mind from medicine to literature which served well in his case and in my case has been indispensable. I refer to the diagnostic stance which comes so naturally to the physician—diagnostic at the outset, and in the end, one hopes, therapeutic.

Part of the natural equipment of the doctor is a nose for pathology. Something is wrong. What is it? What is the nature of the illness? Where is the lesion? Is it acute or chronic, treatable or fatal? Can we understand it? Does the disease have a name or is it something new?

Accordingly, I shall use as my point of departure, not the conventional view of Chekhov as a masterful portrayer of life as it is, of people with all their faults and foibles, without judgment or ideology. I think rather of a less well-known Chekhov, Chekhov the literary clinician, the pathologist of the strange spiritual malady of the modern age; the Chekhov, in short, of those remarkable stories "A Dreary Story" and "Ward Number Six." What is wrong with Nikolai Stepanovitch in "A Dreary Story"? An eminently successful physician, scientist, professor, he has accomplished all he set out to accomplish. He placed his faith in Science and Science served him well. All academic honors are his and he is acclaimed throughout Russia. But what happens? Instead of enjoying his triumph, it turns to ashes in his mouth. The story ends with him alone in a hotel room in Kharkov, unable to love anyone, himself included, unable to see the slightest value or meaning in life.

Although Chekhov would, if he were here, be outraged or pretend to be outraged at the suggestion that his story might be about anything so grandiose as the spiritual plight of Western man or the loss of meaning in the modern world—for he had a healthy contempt for didactic writing and an almost fanatic vocation to show people the way they are. Yet how like the contemporary antihero of the so-called existentialist novel is Nikolai Stepanovitch— who, if he were translated into the here-and-now, would be a Nobel Prize laureate at Cornell who chucks it all and finds himself alone and bemused in a Holiday Inn in Dallas.

In his story "Ward Number Six," the psychiatrist finds himself a patient in a mental hospital. This switch pleases me particularly. In fact, I have carried the paradox one step further in a recent novel and raised it to a general principle that the so-called normal world is so crazy that only a patient in a mental hospital can recover a degree of perspective and stability.

At any rate, what interests me in this connection is the extraordinary apposition in Chekhov of a scrupulous respect for life and reality in the concrete, a distaste for ideology, a refusal to bend fact to thesis, this on the one hand, and, on the other, his recurring diagnostic approach to the ills of the modern world—which, after all, entails a certain degree of abstraction and generalizing and sciencing. In his story "A Case History," Korolyov, who seems to be Chekhov's mouthpiece, judges social problems from the point of view of the doctor accustomed to making accurate diagnoses of chronic ailments.

The point is that now, almost a hundred years later, I would propose to you that this literary-diagnostic method which Chekhov used sporadically is even more appropriate to the fictional enterprise of the late twentieth century, more appropriate than in other times, say Shakespeare's England or even Chekhov's Russia. In other times, the sense of wholeness and well-being of society, or at least much of educated society, outweighed the suspicion that something had gone very wrong, indeed. To the degree that a society has been overtaken by a sense of malaise rather than exuberance, by fragmentation rather than wholeness, the vocation of the artist, whether novelist, poet, playwright, filmmaker, can perhaps be said to come that much closer to that of the diagnostician rather than the artist's celebration of life in a triumphant age.

Something is indeed wrong, and one of the tasks of the serious novelist is, if not to isolate the bacillus under the microscope, at least to give the sickness a name, to render the unspeakable speakable. Not to overwork the comparison, the artist's work in such times is surely not that of the pathologist whose subject matter is a corpse and whose question is not "What is wrong?" but "What did the patient die of?" For I take it as going without saying that the entire enterprise of literature is like that of a physician undertaken in hope. Otherwise, why would we be here? Why bother to read, write, teach, study, if the patient is already dead?—for, in this case, the patient is the culture itself.

Such terms as diagnosis and pathology are of course used analogically here, but I am using the word "science" deliberately and unequivocally in its original and broad sense of discovery and knowing rather than its current and narrow sense of the isolation of secondary causes in natural phenomena. For, if I believe anything, it is that the primary business of literature and art is cognitive, a kind of finding out and knowing and telling, both in good times and bad, a celebration of the way things are when they are right, and a diagnostic enterprise when they are wrong. The pleasures of literature, the emotional gratification of reader and writer, follow upon and are secondary to the knowing.

Accordingly, if there has been any one thing I have wanted to leave with students, it is my conviction of the high seriousness, indeed the critical importance, of the profession of letters in this age, whether teaching, writing, scholarship, criticism, or, indeed, reading. In fact, as I shall presently suggest, the cognitive role of literature at the present time, its success or failure, may be more critical than the combined efforts of NASA, Cal Tech, and MIT.

The strategy of the novel in the late twentieth century is surely different from the fiction of the past two hundred years. Literature in earlier times might be understood as an attempt to dramatize conflicts and resolutions, articulate and confirm values in a society where there already existed a consensus about the meaning of life and the world and man's place in it. Given such a consensus, a corpus of meanings held in common, it was possible for a novelist or playwright or poet to create a fictive world within which the behavior of the characters could be understood, approved, disapproved, and the reader accordingly entertained, edified, and, in the case of great literature, his very self and his world confirmed and illumined by the work of the novelist.

In short, any literature requires as the very condition of its life a certain consensus, an already existing intersubjective community within which both novelists and readers can traffic in words and symbols, myths and beliefs, which mean approximately the same thing for both writer and reader.

Now, I think it fair to begin with the assumption, which seems fairly obvious, that, as the poet said, the center is not holding, that the consensus, while it might not have disappeared, is at least seriously called into question. The question which concerns us here, of course, is whether the deterioration of the consensus is so far advanced that the novel is no longer viable. Indeed, to judge from a good many contemporary novels, films, and plays, it often appears that the only consensus possible is a documentation of the fragmentation itself. The genre of meaningless has in fact become the chic property, not only of the café existentialist, but even of Hollywood. I would like to think that such is not the case. Rather do I believe that the vocation of the novelist is as valid as it ever was, but that it has become different, more difficult, more challenging—and more critical in its importance.

Let me specify briefly what appears to be the nature of the change in the community in which we find ourselves and the correspondingly changed posture of the novelist.

To state the matter as plainly as possible, I would echo a writer like Guardini who says simply that the modern world has ended, the world, that is, of the past two or three hundred years, which we think of as having been informed by the optimism of the scientific revolution, rational humanism, and that Western cultural entity which until this century it has been more or less accurate to describe as Christendom. I am not telling you anything you don't already know when I say that the optimism of this age began to crumble with the onset of the catastrophies of the twentieth century. If one had to set a date of the beginning of the end of the modern world, 1914 would be as good as any, because it was then that Western man, the beneficiary of precisely this scientific revolution and Christian ethic, began with great skill and energy to destroy himself.

Christendom began to crumble, perhaps most noticeably under the onslaught of a Christian, Søren Kierkegaard, in the last century. Again I am not telling you anything new when I suggest that the Christian notion of man as a wayfarer in search of his salvation no longer informs Western culture. In its place, what most of us seem to be seeking are such familiar goals as maturity, creativity, autonomy, rewarding interpersonal relations, and so forth.

To speak of the decay of Christendom is to say nothing of the ultimate truth of Christianity, but only to call attention to a cultural phenomenon and the symbols with which it was conveyed. What concerns us here is that, from the perspective of the novelist, literary attempts to revive traditional expressions of Christendom are seldom undertaken anymore. Even when they were, it was often with the sense of a nostalgic revival of a way of life, or else undertaken with the skill of a great novelist in portraying a belief which he did not necessarily subscribe to. I am thinking in particular of the Southern Agrarians and of Faulkner's Dilsey. But most contemporary novelists have moved on into a world of rootless and isolated consciousnesses for whom not even the memory and the nostalgia exist. As Lewis Simpson put it: "The covenant with memory and history has been abrogated in favor of the existential self."

But before speaking of the kind of novel which becomes possible in such an age, the "post-modern" or "post-Christian" as it is often called, I should like briefly to characterize the age itself, or one or two traits of it, from the point of view of the novelist. For the latter is, like his predecessors, seeking some remnant of a common ground where he can gain sufficient footing so that he can see and tell and where he hopes there will be others, other writers, other readers, who share, if not a consensus, a common belief of myth, at least a sense of predicament shared in common.

Toward this end, it seems fair to describe the times not merely in conventional terms as a world which has been transformed by technology both for good and evil, the evil being, of course, the very real ugliness of much of the transformation and the very real depersonalization of many people living in such a world.

What is not so self-evident yet of far greater import to the novelist is the more subtle yet more radical transformation of the very consciousness of Western man in an entirely unexpected way by the scientific and technological worldview. I am not talking about the mechanization and homogenization and dehumanization one hears about so often—though I would not quarrel with these descriptions. We are all familiar with an entire literature about the ennui of life in suburbia and the split-level nightmare. Yet this literature itself is generally even more boring than the life it portrays. Aside from the worth or lack of it in such novels, I cannot escape the suspicion of a degree of bad faith both in the novelist and in his characters, that, in short, for all their complaints, neither of them would dream of changing places with the nineteenth-century housewife or the low-paid nineteenth-century novelist.

No, the real pathology lies elsewhere, not in the station wagon or the all-electric kitchen, which are, after all, very good things to have—but rather in the quality of the consciousness of the novelist and his characters. I can only characterize this consciousness by such terms as impoverishment and deprivation and by the paradoxical language of the so-called existentialists, terms like loss of community, loss of meaning, inauthenticity, and so on—paradoxical because such deprivations occur in the face of strenuous efforts toward better consumership, more communication, a multiplication of communities, finding "more meaningful relationships," "creativity," and so on.

The deprivation I speak of is both more radical and more difficult to define. But I'll try.

Every age, we know, is informed by a particular belief or myth or worldview shared in common by the denizens of the age. Thirteenth-century Europe was certainly informed by Catholic Christianity, seventeenth-century New England by Puritan Christianity, present-day Thailand by Mahayana Buddhism. But we miss the point if we say that the Western world and the life of Western man has simply been transformed by scientific technology. This is true enough, but what has also happened is that the consciousness of Western man, the layman in particular, has been transformed by a curious misapprehension of the scientific method. One is tempted to use the theological term "idolatry." This misapprehension, which is not the fault of science, but rather the inevitable consequence of the victory of the scientific worldview accompanied as it is by all the dazzling credentials of scientific progress. It, the misapprehension, takes the form, I believe, of a radical and paradoxical loss of sovereignty by the layman and of a radical impoverishment of human relations—paradoxical, I say, because it occurs in the very face of his technological mastery of the world and his richness as a consumer of the world's goods.

Like Nikolai Stepanovitch in "A Dreary Story," the moment of our victory in science seems to be attended by a strange sense of loss and impoverishment. In certain areas, such a surrender of sovereignty is not disabling. When something goes wrong in our technological environment, if something needs fixing, whether it is one's car or one's intestinal tract, we have reason to believe that "they" can fix it, "they" being the appropriate specialist. Our expectations are not unreasonable. Very few of us have the time or inclination to master carburetor repair or the physiology of the GI tract. But what happens when one feels in the deepest sense possible that something has gone wrong with one's very self? When one experiences the common complaint of the age, the loss of meaning, purposelessness, loss of identity, of values, and so on? Here again, I am the last person to suggest that psychiatrists do not have an important role; indeed, an increasingly important role. The problem I am speaking of is only too well known to psychiatrists. What I do suggest is that a radical loss of sovereignty has occurred when a person comes to believe that his very self is also the appropriate domain of "them"; that is, the appropriate experts of the self. A typical case of such a surrender of sovereignty is the patient who is delighted when he can present his psychiatrist or analyst with a symptom or dream which fits the prevailing theory—or when he performs well in an encounter group. The patient is, in effect, saying, "I may be sick but how happy I am when I can present my doctor with a sickness or a symptom or a dream which is recognized as a classical example of such-and-such a neurosis: I am an authentic neurotic!"

But what has all this to do with the state of the novel? Strangely enough, it is this very misapprehension of the scientific method, its elevation to an all-encompassing world view, which breaks new ground for the novelist and indeed opens the possibility of a new and critical role for the novelist of the future.

Let me oversimplify this misapprehension and state it as briefly as possible. What I am about to say is no secret to the scientist, is in fact a commonplace, but it is not generally known by laymen. The secret is simply this: the scientist, in practicing the scientific method, cannot utter a single word about an individual thing or creature insofar as it is an individual but only insofar as it resembles other individuals. This limitation holds true whether the individual is a molecule of NaCl or an amoeba or a human being. There is nothing new or startling about this and nothing a scientist would disagree with. We all remember taking science courses where one was confronted with a *sample of* sodium chloride or a *specimen of* a dogfish to dissect. Such studies reveal the properties shared by all sodium chloride and by all dogfish. We have no particular interest in this particular pinch of salt or this particular dogfish.

But perhaps we are a bit startled when we are told that this same limitation applies to psychiatry. In the words of Harry Stack Sullivan, perhaps the greatest American psychiatrist: To the degree that I am a psychiatrist, to this same degree I am not interested in you as an individual but only in you and your symptoms insofar as they resemble other individuals and other symptoms.

Again, what has this to do with the novel? Perhaps I can state the connection best by describing my own discovery. As a person educated in science, as an admirer of the elegance and truth of the scientific method, and at the same time as a medical student undergoing psychoanalysis with the intention of going into psychiatry, it dawned on me that no science or scientist, not even Freud, could address a single word to me as an individual but only as an example of such-and-such a Southern type or neurotic type or whatever. All very well and good, you say, but so what? But you see, there is a Catch-22 here. The catch is that each of us is, always and inescapably, an individual. Unlike a dogfish, we are stuck with ourselves and have somehow to live out the rest of the day being more or less ourselves. And to the degree that we allow ourselves to perceive ourselves as a type of, example of, instance of, such-and-such a class of Homo sapiens—even the most creative Homo sapiens imaginable—to this same degree do we come short of being ourselves.

As to the novel, I can only speak in terms of the discovery which led me to take up novel-writing, a vocation for which I was otherwise singularly unqualified. For, of course, a novelist should be well educated in the humanities, in literature, and if he is a Southern novelist, I am told that he is supposed to be saturated by the Southern tradition of folklore, yarns, storytelling, family histories, and such. If you want to be another Faulkner, you have to spend a good deal of time hunkered down on courthouse lawns listening to old-timers talk about the way things were. I qualify under none of these canons, having been born and raised in

Birmingham, Alabama, in a new house on a new golf course. The only stories I ever heard were jokes in the locker room.

What did at last dawn on me as a medical student and intern, a practitioner, I thought, of the scientific method, was that there was a huge gap in the scientific view of the world. This sector of the world about which science could not utter a single word was nothing less than this: what it is like to be an individual living in the United States in the twentieth century.

This discovery had all the force of a revelation, at least for me, brought up, as perhaps most of us are, in the tradition of John Dewey and William James, the proposition of American pragmatism that science deals with truth and art deals with diversion, play, entertainment; anyhow, some form of emotional gratification.

But what are we to make of a man who is committed in the most radical sense to the proposition that truth is attainable by science and that emotional gratification is attainable by interacting with one's environment and at the highest level by the enjoyment of art? It seems that everything is settled for him. But something is wrong. He has settled everything except what it is to live as an individual. He still has to get through an ordinary Wednesday afternoon. Such a man is something like the young man Kierkegaard described who was given the task of keeping busy all day and finished the task at noon. What does this man do with the rest of the day? the rest of his life?

But my question and my discovery was this: if there is such a gap in the scientific view of the world, e.g., what it is to be an individual living in the United States in 1985, and if the scientist cannot address himself to this reality, who can? My discovery, of course, was that the novelist can, and most particularly the novelist. Oddly enough, it was the reading of two nineteenth-century writers, Kierkegaard and Dostoevsky, who convinced me that *only* the writer, the existentialist philosopher, or the novelist can explore this gap with all the passion and seriousness and expectation of discovery of, say, an Einstein who had discovered that Newtonian physics no longer works.

But before saying any more about the novel as a serious

instrument for the exploration of reality, a cognitive instrument, let me take notice of what I take to be two traits of nineteenth-century life which are peculiarly open to novelistic treatment and are also the consequence of an all-encompassing scientific-technological worldview.

One is the isolation, loneliness, and alienation of modern man as reflected in the protagonists of so many current novels, plays, and films. This alienation can be traced to a degree, I think, to this very surrender, albeit unconscious, of valid forms of human activity to scientists, technologists, and specialists.

The other trait is the spectacular emphasis on explicit sexual behavior in novels and films.

It is not difficult to show that one has a good deal to do with the other.

The upshot of these two trends is often a novel or a film about a man or woman who, though isolated in the midst of two hundred million Americans and rendered, so to speak, incommunicado, embarks on a series of sexual encounters which at the end leave the individual much as we found him or her, still isolated, still surrounded, so to speak, by a cocoon of silence.

This depiction of explicit sexuality is beset by all kinds of ambiguities. On the one hand, one can say fairly I think, and I for one believe, that there is such a thing as pornography and that there are a large number of bad writers and bad filmmakers who make a lot of money by writing novels and making movies designed to excite sexually the viewer and reader. I will say no more about pornography than that I think it has nothing to do with literature. And although I deplore pornography, the real difficulty is both more radical and has more serious consequences.

The real pathology is not so much a moral decline, which is a symptom, not a primary phenomenon, but rather an ontological impoverishment; that is, a severe limitation or crippling of the very life of twentieth-century man. If this is the case and if this crippling and impoverishment manifests itself often in sexual behavior, the latter becomes the proper domain of the serious novelist.

What has happened, I think, is that, with the ongoing impoverishment of human relations by a misapprehension of the scientific ethos which pervades the Western world, it inevitably came to pass that for many people, readers and writers, genital sexuality came to be seen as the only, the "real," the basic form of human intercourse. It is a matter of what we come to see as real. By either reading or misreading Freud, we, the laymen and lay women, have come to believe that most forms of human relations and human achievement are surrogates of, sublimations of, and therefore at some time remove from the "real" relation and the "real" energy, which is genital and libidinal.

Take a film like *Last Tango in Paris*—which I happen not to think a very good movie. But I do not think it pornographic, either. In this film two people who remain strangers throughout perform a series of sexual operations on each other, mostly in dead silence, and in the end one kills the other. Two things happen, an impersonal sex and a dispassionate violence. Perhaps these are the only two things that can happen. A case might be made that, given a certain urban environment and an educated class of laymen alienated from each other and from themselves, only two real options remain, genital sex and violence, and perhaps the realest of all, death.

Sex, violence, and death are real enough, but is anything else real? And if not, is the work of the novelist and filmmaker simply the documentation and cataloguing of this impoverishment of the real in contemporary life?

I suggest an alternative for the novelist which is perhaps more radical, at least more venturesome and challenging than a mere documentation of isolation, depersonalized sex, and violence. If there is no such alternative, then we should have quit with Kafka, who limited human activity to a few moves to and fro in a dark burrow, an occasional encounter with another creature in the dark where one gropes, touches, feels, perhaps copulates, perhaps does not, then goes his own blind way. Or with Beckett, whose people, buried up to their necks in refuse, crack a few stale jokes to pass the time.

What I suggest is that there lies at hand for the artist, especially the novelist, an instrument for exploring the darkness of Kafka's burrow or Marlon Brando's unfurnished apartment or Beckett's wasteland, an instrument in every sense as scientific and as cognitive as, say, Galileo's telescope or Wilson's cloud chamber. Indeed, this may be the only instrument we have for exploring the great gap in our knowing, knowing ourselves and how it stands between ourselves and others.

This instrument is, of course, art in general and literature in particular.

The cognitive exploratory dimension of art has always been present, but its discovering power is often masked in a stable society united by an ethos and belief held in common. When people already know who they are, their literature celebrates and affirms the already existing relationships and hierarchies of society. One thinks of Shakespeare's affirmation of the monarchy, of what constitutes a good king and a bad king and the people's relation to each.

But what is the function of literature in a period like this, a time when one era has ended and the new era has not yet come into being; that is to say, has not yet articulated itself, does not even know its name?

One important function of fiction in such a time, at least as I see it, is exploratory. If Fielding's *Tom Jones* is a celebration of life in eighteenth-century England, the fiction of our time is more like Robinson Crusoe, who has been shipwrecked on a desert island—with important differences. This island is even stranger than Crusoe's. For one thing, it is overpopulated; yet many of its inhabitants feel as lonely as Crusoe. For another thing, Crusoe saw himself as an intact member of European Christendom, and even a desert island as a tissue of meaningful signs. Such-and-such an animal track spelled danger. Such-and-such a fruit meant *eat me*. He knew what to do. But the castaway of the twentieth-century novel does not know who he is, where he came from, what to do, and the signs on his island are ambiguous. If he does encounter another human on the island, a man Friday, he has trouble communicating with him or her. Certainly, if two post-modern men met on an island today, like Crusoe and Friday, neither would dream of trying to convert the other—for conversion implies there is something to be converted from and converted to. Perhaps some sort of sexual encounter is possible, perhaps a joint scientific venture; certainly, murder is possible. But what else?

Then what is the task of serious fiction in an age when both the Judeo-Christian consensus and rational humanism have broken down? I suggest that it is more than the documentation of the loneliness and the varieties of sexual encounters of so much modern fiction. I suggest that it is nothing less than an exploration of the options of such a man. That is, a man who not only is in Crusoe's predicament, a castaway of sorts, but who is also acutely aware of his predicament. What did Crusoe do? He looked around. He explored the island. He scanned the horizon. He looked for signs from across the seas. He combed the beach—for what? Perhaps for bottles with messages in them. No doubt, he also launched bottles with messages in them. But what kind of messages? That is the question.

The contemporary novelist, in other words, must be an epistemologist of sorts. He must know how to send messages and decipher them. The messages may come not in bottles but rather in the halting and muted dialogue between strangers, between lovers and friends. One speaks; the other tries to fathom his meaning—or indeed to determine if the message has any meaning.

Compare recent fiction with the community taken for granted in the traditional novel; for example, the reception described at the beginning of *War and Peace* where Anna Pavlovna and her guests discuss the Napoleonic Wars. Conversation occurs, looks are exchanged, all perfectly understood in a community of shared meanings and assumptions about the nature of things. Even quarrels require sufficient common ground to be recognized as quarrels. People in Beckett's novels and plays don't quarrel.

To change the island image, the community of discourse in the current novel might be likened to two prisoners who find themselves in adjoining cells as a consequence of some vague Kafka-like offense. Communication is possible by tapping against the intervening wall. Do they speak the same language? These quasi-conversations or nonconversations might be found in novels and plays from Kafka to Sartre to Beckett to Pinter to Joseph McElroy.

If this view sounds gloomy, allow me to express a kind of perverse hope and preference. I don't know whether this is a symptom of my own neurosis or whether it says something about the way things are. In a word, I'd rather be a prisoner in a cell tapping messages to a fellow prisoner in the twentieth century than be a guest at Anna Pavlovna's reception in Moscow in 1805. The challenge now is both more critical and more exciting than the defeat of Napoleon. For the challenge now is nothing less than the exploration of a new world and the re-creation or rediscovery of language and meanings. The Psalmist said sing a new song. And, for a fact, the old ones are pretty well worn out.

But to get back to my thesis, the diagnostic and cognitive role of modern fiction. When one age ends and the traditional cultural symbols no longer work, man is exposed in all his nakedness, which is uncomfortable for man but revealing for those of us who want to take a good look at him; which is to say, at ourselves. And I take it for granted that, by the very nature of things and how things are known, it lies within the province of art—literature in particular, and not the natural sciences—to undertake this exploration.

It is at this point that modern fiction cannot help but approach a kind of anthropology, a view of man abstracted from this or that culture—for that is indeed where he finds himself today, shucked like an oyster and beheld in all his nakedness and, I might add, uniqueness. Chekhov, being both a scientist and a superb artist, knew this better than most: that, with the method of science, one beholds what is generally true about individuals, but art beholds what is uniquely true.

It is no accident, moreover, that so much of modern fiction has converged with a movement of European philosophy and that the same name, the much overworked term, existentialist, has been applied to both. For both approaches—say, Kierkegaard's in philosophy and Dostoevsky's in fiction—share a view in common, that of man, not mankind, but a particular man who finds himself in some fashion isolated from the world and society around him, a society which in both the philosophy and the fiction is viewed as more or less absurd, if not moribund. This man, then, is viewed as alienated from his culture, not as an abstraction, not as specimen Homo sapiens alienatus pinned like a dogfish to a dissecting board, but rather as an individual set down in a time and a place and a predicament. The subject of the novel may be outside his culture, but his predicament is no less concrete and acute than that of Prince Andrei Bolkonsky in the Battle of Borodino. He may be sitting alone in a café listening to the conversation of the bourgeoisie in Bouville, or she may be spinning around the interstates or holed up with a stranger in a motel like a character in a Joan Didion novel.

In any case, what is being explored and set forth in this kind of serious novel is not primarily the hypocrisy of the bourgeoisie or the wasteland of New Orleans but the fundamental predicament of the character himself or herself. Accordingly, what is being explored or should be explored is not only the nature of the human predicament but the possibility or nonpossibility of a search for signs and meanings. Depending on the conviction of the writer, the signs may be found to be ambiguous or meaningless—or perhaps a faint message comes through, a tapping on the wall heard and deciphered and replied to.

The point is that fiction of all things can be used as an instrument of exploration and discovery; in short, of sciencing. To illustrate what I mean, I would like to conclude by giving a single example of fiction as a cognitive instrument for exploring an unknown terrain. The example is taken from a novel I wrote, not because I think all that highly of it, but because it illustrates the method I have in mind.

This is the story of a confused young man, a Southerner afflicted with recurring amnesia, a sense of disorientation, and assorted other complaints, who finds himself living at the YMCA in New York, where he has spent several years and all his money in intensive psychoanalysis. One day he decides he has had enough of the analysis, rises from the couch, and bids his analyst farewell. Now, instead of exploring his own psyche, he sets forth on an actual journey, returns to the South and his point of origin. It is there, he feels, that there is some dread secret to be discovered, something that happened, something he can't quite remember because he can't bear to remember.

After a series of adventures, he finds himself at last standing in front of his father's house in a small Mississippi town, the house of his childhood. It is night. He watches the house from the darkness of the great oaks. It was there, he remembers, that his father used to walk up and down, listening to Brahms, reciting "Dover Beach," his favorite poem, or talking about the decline of morals and manners in the modern world. He, the father, has just won a victory over the Ku Klux Klan, yet he seems even sadder than usual.

Suddenly he, the son, remembers his father's suicide, that on just such a night, in this very place, under these very oaks, after listening to Brahms and reciting "Dover Beach," his father had bade him farewell, gone into the house, and shot himself.

Then, was his father right in his despair? The son stood in the dark under the trees looking at the house and thought about it. Is there nothing, or is there something? Is there a sign? At this point he does what might seem to be an insignificant thing. He is standing under a huge water oak, the same place where his father used to stand. Like Kafka's creature in its dark burrow, he can't see much, but his hand remembers something. It remembers the iron hitching post next to the tree. It remembers that the bark of the tree had grown around the little iron horsehead atop the post. His hand explores.

Again his hand went forth, knowing where it was, though he could not see, and touched the tiny iron horsehead of the hitching post, traced the cold metal down to the place where the oak had grown around it in an elephant lip. His fingertips touched the warm finny whispering bark.

Wait. While his fingers explored the juncture of iron and bark, his eyes narrowed as if he caught a glimmer of light on the cold iron skull. *Wait.* I think he was wrong and that he was looking in the wrong place. No, not he but the times. The times were wrong and one looked in the wrong place. It wasn't even his fault because that was the way he was and the way the times were, and there was no other place a man could look. It was the worst of times, a time of fake beauty and fake victory. *Wait.* He had missed it! It was not in the Brahms that one looked and not in the old and sad poetry but—he wrung out his ear—but here, under your nose, here in the very curiousness and drollness and extraness of the iron and bark that—he shook his head—that—

He breaks off. He feels he's on to something, a clue or sign, but it slips away from him.

I chose this passage because of its resemblance to the famous scene in Sartre's *Nausea*—in fact, it was written as a kind of counterstatement—where Roquentin is sitting in a park in Bouville and experiences a similar revelation as he gazes at the roots and bark of a chestnut tree. Sartre intended the scene to be a glimpse into the very nature of the being of things, and a very unpleasant revelation it is, described by Sartre by such adjectives as obscene, bloated, viscous, naked, de trop, and so on.

Will Barrett, too, sees something in the bark, the same extraness as he calls it, gratuitousness, but for him it is an intimation, a clue to further discovery. And it is not something bad he sees but something good. In terms of traditional metaphysics, he has caught a glimpse of the goodness and gratuitousness of created being. He had that sense we all have occasionally of being on to something important.

As it turned out, he missed it. That was as close as he ever came.

The point is that, in a new age when things and people are devalued, when meanings break down, it lies within the province of the novelist to start the search afresh, like Robinson Crusoe on his island. Tree bark may seem a humble place to start. But one must start somewhere. The novelist or poet in the future might be able to go further, to discover, or rediscover, not only how it is with tree bark but how it is with man himself, who he is, and how it is between him and other men.

1985

EUDORA WELTY
IN JACKSON

❧

What is most valuable about Eudora Welty is not that she is one of the best living short-story writers. (It was startling that when I tried to think of anybody else as good, two women and one man came to mind, all three Southerners: Katherine Anne Porter, Caroline Gordon, and Peter Taylor.) Nor is it that she is a woman of letters in the old sense, versatile and many-voiced in her fiction and as distinguished in criticism. No, what is valuable is that she has done it in a place. That is to say, she has lived all her life in a place and written there and the writing bears more than an accidental relation to the place. Being a writer in a place is not the same as being a banker in a place. But it is not as different as it is generally put forward as being.

It is of more than passing interest that Eudora Welty has always lived in Jackson and that the experience has been better than endurable. This must be the case, because if it hadn't been, she'd have left. Although I do not know Eudora Welty, I like to imagine that she lives very tolerably in Jackson. At least, she said once that she was to be found "underfoot in Jackson." What does such an association between a writer and a town portend? It portends more, I would hope, than such-and-such a trend or characteristic of "Southern literature."

For Eudora Welty to be alive and well in Jackson should be a matter of considerable interest to other American writers. The interest derives from the coming need of the fiction writer, the self-professed alien, to come to some terms with a community, to send out emissaries, to strike an entente. The question is: How can a writer live in a place without either succumbing to angelism and haunting it like a ghost or being "on," playing himself or somebody else and watching to see how it comes out? The answer is that it is at least theoretically possible to live as one imagines Eudora Welty lives in Jackson, practice letters—differently from a banker banking but not altogether differently—and sustain a relation with one's town and fellow townsmen which is as complex as you please, even ambivalent, but in the end life-giving. It is a secret relationship but not necessarily exploitative. One thinks of Kierkegaard living in Copenhagen and taking great pride in making an appearance on the street every hour, so that he would be thought an idler. But it is impossible to imagine Kierkegaard without Copenhagen. Town and writer sustain each other in secret ways. Deceits may be practiced. But one is in a bad way without the other.

The time is coming when the American novelist will tire of his angelism—of which obsessive genital sexuality is the most urgent symptom, the reaching out for the flesh which has been shucked—will wonder how to get back into a body, live in a place, at a street address. Eudora Welty will be a valuable clue.

1969

FOREWORD TO

A CONFEDERACY

OF DUNCES

❦

Perhaps the best way to introduce this novel—which on my third reading of it astounds me even more than the first—is to tell of my first encounter with it. While I was teaching at Loyola in 1976 I began to get telephone calls from a lady unknown to me. What she proposed was preposterous. It was not that she had written a couple of chapters of a novel and wanted to get into my class. It was that her son, who was dead, had written an entire novel during the early sixties, a big novel, and she wanted me to read it. Why would I want to do that? I asked her. Because it is a great novel, she said.

Over the years I have become very good at getting out of things I don't want to do. And if ever there was something I didn't want to do, this was surely it: to deal with the mother of a dead novelist and, worst of all, to have to read a manuscript that she said was *great*, and that, as it turned out, was a badly smeared, scarcely readable carbon.

But the lady was persistent, and it somehow came to pass that she stood in my office, handing me the hefty manuscript. There was no getting out of it; only one hope remained—that I could read a few pages and that they would be bad enough for me, in good conscience, to read no farther. Usually I can do just that. Indeed, the first paragraph often suffices. My only fear was that this one might not be bad enough, or might be just good enough, so that I would have to keep reading.

In this case, I read on. And on. First with the sinking feeling that it was not bad enough to quit, then with a prickle of interest, then a growing excitement, and finally an incredulity: surely it was not possible that it was so good. I shall resist the temptation to say what first made me gape, grin, laugh out loud, shake my head in wonderment. Better let the reader make the discovery on his own.

Here, at any rate, is Ignatius Reilly, without progenitor in any literature I know of—slob extraordinary, a mad Oliver Hardy, a fat Don Quixote, a perverse Thomas Aquinas rolled into one—who is in violent revolt against the entire modern age, lying in his flannel nightshirt in a back bedroom on Constantinople Street in New Orleans, who between gigantic seizures of flatulence and eructations is filling dozens of Big Chief tablets with invective.

His mother thinks he needs to go to work. He does, in a succession of jobs. Each job rapidly escalates into a lunatic adventure, a full-blown disaster; yet each has, like Don Quixote's, its own eerie logic.

His girlfriend, Myrna Minkoff of the Bronx, thinks he needs sex. What happens between Myrna and Ignatius is like no other boy-meets-girl story in my experience.

By no means a lesser virtue of John Kennedy Toole's novel is his rendering of the particularities of New Orleans, its back streets, its out-of-the-way neighborhoods, its odd speech, its ethnic whites—and one black in whom Toole has achieved the near-impossible, a superb comic character of immense wit and resourcefulness without the least trace of Rastus minstrelsy.

But Toole's greatest achievement is Ignatius Reilly himself, intellectual, ideologue, deadbeat, goof-off, glutton, who should repel the reader with his gargantuan bloats, his thunderous contempt and one-man war against everybody—Freud, homosexuals, heterosexuals, Protestants, and the assorted excesses of modern times. Imagine an Aquinas gone to pot, transported to New Orleans, from whence he makes a wild foray through the swamps to LSU at Baton Rouge, where his lumber jacket is stolen in the faculty men's room where he is seated, overcome by mammoth gastrointestinal problems. His pyloric valve periodically closes in response to the lack of a "proper geometry and theology" in the modern world.

I hesitate to use the word "comedy"—though comedy it is—because that implies simply a funny book, and this novel is a great deal more than that. A great rumbling farce of Falstaffian dimensions would better describe it; *commedia* would be closer to it.

It is also sad. One never quite knows where the sadness comes from—from the tragedy at the heart of Ignatius's great gaseous rages and lunatic adventures or the tragedy attending the book itself.

The tragedy of the book is the tragedy of the author—his suicide in 1969 at the age of thirty-two. Another tragedy is the body of work we have been denied.

It is a great pity that John Kennedy Toole is not alive and well and writing. But he is not, and there is nothing we can do about it but make sure that this gargantuan tumultuous human tragicomedy is at least made available to a world of readers.

1980

REDISCOVERING

A CANTICLE FOR

LEIBOWITZ

❧

This book, *A Canticle for Leibowitz*, is recommended, but not without certain qualifications. That is to say, I would not want my recorded enthusiasm for it and the fact that I have read it several times to be taken as a conventional literary ploy to call attention to an underrated work of literature. Thus, I am not setting up as a Malcolm Cowley rehabilitating a neglected Faulkner. For the fact is, the peculiar merit of this novel is traceable to virtues which are both subliterary and transliterary. For one thing, it is science fiction—parts of it appeared in the *Magazine of Fantasy and Science Fiction*, which I take to be a high-class sci-fi pulp—and its prose, while competent, is not distinguished. So it is not as "good" as, say, Katherine Mansfield. Yet it is of more moment than Katherine Mansfield. It is also of more moment than the better-known sci-fi futuristic novels, *1984* and *Brave New World*.

Another reason for not recommending it is that it is not for every reader. Walter M. Miller, Jr.'s *A Canticle for Leibowitz* is like a cipher, a coded message, a book in a strange language. From experience I have learned that passing the book along to a friend is like handing *The New York Times* to a fellow passenger on the Orient Express: either he will get it altogether or he altogether won't.

Like a cipher, the book has a secret. But, unlike a cipher, the secret can't be told. Telling it ruins it. But it is not like "giving away" a mystery by telling the outcome. The case is more difficult.

A good indication of the peculiar nature of the secret is that the book cannot be reviewed. For either the reviewer doesn't get it or, if he does, he can't tell. My first inkling of this odd state of affairs occurred when I read a review of *Canticle* after receiving a review copy. I had read the book with the first of the pricklings of excitement I was to feel on successive readings. But I could not write the review. Why? Because when I tried to track down the source of the neck-pricklings, my neck stopped prickling. Then I read the review, which was written by a smart man, a critic. It dawned on me that the reviewer had *missed* it, missed the whole book, just as one might read a commonplace sentence which contains a cipher and get the sentence but miss the cipher.

To say that the book is a cipher and that some readers have the code and some do not makes it sound like a gnosis, something like Madame Blavatsky's *Secret Doctrine*, which only an elect lay claim to understanding. But it's not that, either.

Rather has the mystery to do with conflicting anthropologies; that is, views of man, the way man is. Everyone has an anthropology. There is no not having one. If a man says he does not, all he is saying is that his anthropology is implicit, a set of assumptions which he has not thought to call into question.

One might even speak of a consensus anthropology which is implicit in the culture itself, part of the air we breathe. There is such a thing and it is something of a mishmash and does not necessarily make sense. It might be called the Western democratic-technological humanist view of man as higher organism invested in certain traditional trappings of a more or less nominal Judeo-Christianity. One still hears, and no one makes much objection to it, that "man is made in the image of God." Even more often, one hears such expressions as "the freedom and sacredness of the individual." This anthropology is familiar enough. It is in fact the standard intellectual baggage of most of us. Most of the time, it doesn't matter that this anthropology is a mishmash, *disjecta membra*. Do you really mean that God made man in His image? Well, hm, it is a manner of speaking. If He didn't and man is in fact an organism in an environment with certain needs and drives which he satisfies from the environment, then what do you mean by talking about "the freedom and sacredness of the individual"? What is so sacred about the life of one individual, especially if he is hungry, sick, suffering, useless? Well, hm, we are speaking of "values"; we mean that man has a sacred right and is free to choose his own life or, failing that, a creative death. And suppose he is incompetent to do so, may we choose it for him? Well—

So it goes. At the end of an age and the beginning of another, at a time when ages overlap, views of man also overlap and such mishmashes are commonplace. We get used to a double vision of man, like watching a ghost on TV.

Or, put mathematically, different ages locate man by different coordinates. In a period of overlap, he might be located by more than one set of coordinates. Culture being what it is, even the most incoherent anthropology seems "natural," just because it is part of the air we breathe. The incoherence is revealed—and the reader experiences either incomprehension or eerie neck-pricklings— only when one set of coordinates is challenged by the other: Look, it is either this way or that way, but it can't be both ways.

The anthropology in *A Canticle for Leibowitz* is both radical and overt. Accordingly, the reader is either uncomprehending, or vaguely discomfited—or he experiences eerie neck-pricklings.

The time is *ca.* A.D. 2600. The place is Arizona perhaps, or where Arizona was. Brother Francis Gerard is making his Lenten fast in the desert. Far away, on the broken interstate, a stranger appears, a pilgrim. Brother Francis, unused to strangers, hides and waits for him in the rubble of some ancient buildings left over from the holocaust of the twentieth century. Brother Francis belongs to the Albertian Order of Leibowitz, whose abbey is close by. The stranger approaches, speaks to the novice, writes two Hebrew letters on a rock, and goes his way. The rocks cave in and Brother Francis falls into an ancient fallout shelter. There he finds an old toolbox and a memo: "Pound pastrami, can kraut, six bagels—bring home." He also finds a circuit design with the signature I. E. Leibowitz.

Could it be a relic of the Blessed Leibowitz, founder of the order? And who was the old pilgrim who wrote the two letters, which read from right to left, ZL?

So opens *Canticle* and already the reader, if he is going to, shall have experienced the first of his agreeable-eerie pricklings. It is a cross-vibration. These good vibes come two directions.

First, Miller has hit on the correct mise-en-scène for the apocalyptic futuristic novel. The setting is the desert. An old civilization lies in ruins. There is silence. Much time has passed and is passing. The survivor is alone. There is a secret longing in the reader either for the greening of America, vines sprouting on Forty-second Street, or for the falling into desert ruins of such cities as Phoenix. Phoenix should revert to the lizards.

Such is the ordinary stuff of good end-of-world novels, a sense of sweeping away, of a few survivors, of a beginning again. Here is the authentic oxymoronic flavor of pleasurable catastrophe. Shibah destroys, but good things come of it.

But the neck-pricklings, the really remarkable vibes, come from another direction in *Canticle* and set it apart from every other novel in the genre.

For the good vibes here are *Jewish*. The coordinates of the novel are radically Jewish-Christian. That is to say, the time line, the x coordinate, the abscissa runs from left to right, from past to future. But the time line is crossed by a y axis, the ordinate. What is the y axis? It is Something That Happened or Something That Will Happen on the time line of such a nature that all points on the time line are read with reference to the happening, as before or after, minus or plus. The Jewish coordinates are identical with the Christian save only where y crosses x.

To apply Jewish-Christian coordinates to a sci-fi novel is almost a contradiction in terms. Because all other sci-fi novels, even the best, *1984* and *Brave New World*, are written on a single coordinate, the time line. There is a Jew in *Brave New World*, Bernard Solomon, but his Jewishness is accidental. He could as easily have been a Presbyterian or a Sikh.

In all other sci-fi fiction, the abscissa extends infinitely in either direction and is not crossed by a y axis. When a starship lands on a strange planet and intelligent beings are encountered, one's questions have to do with the other's location on the time line. Have you split the atom yet? Can you dematerialize? What is the stage of evolution of your political system?

For Jewish coordinates (I say Jewish because for our purposes it doesn't matter whether the coordinates are Jewish or Christian, since both have an intersecting y axis, and, after all, the Jews had it first) to be applied to the sci-fi genre is a radical challenge of one set of coordinates by another. It is either absurd—and some reviewers found it so—or it is pleasantly dislocating, setting up neck-pricklings. It is something like traveling to a habitable planet of Alpha Centauri and finding on the first rock: "Kilroy was here." Or it is like turning on a TV soap opera and finding that the chief character is Abraham.

In *Canticle*, the great Fire Deluge fell upon the earth in the ancient twentieth century and the maimed and misbegotten survivors were so enraged by the scientists who encompassed their destruction that they set in motion the Simplification: the complete destruction of technology, books, and whatever. An order of monks was founded to save what they could of the ancient twentieth-century civilization and they did, as they did in another Dark Age. They became "bookleggers" who either rescued books from the bonfires of the Simplification or committed them to memory. If a booklegger was caught, he was strung up on the spot. So, indeed, was Blessed Leibowitz martyred. Here, for one thing, was an alliance which baffled some reviewers: Jews, Catholic monks, and atomic scientists.

So passed the years and the Abbey of the Albertian Order of Leibowitz kept its little horde of precious documents out in the desert. In one of his best strategies, Miller shows how it is that keeping a few books is not enough to save a culture. When one age dies, its symbols lose their referents and become incomprehensible. The nicest touch of all: the monks copy blueprints, illuminating them with gold leaf, scrolls, and cherubs, filling in most of the space with ink "—even though the task of spreading blue ink around tiny white letters was particularly tedious."

At length, in another six hundred years, the thirst for knowledge revives and the new savants (from Texarkana Empire!) come to visit the abbey to see what can be salvaged from the wisdom of the ancients.

Miller uses this new renaissance adroitly to dramatize the

perennial conflict, not between science and religion, but between the new adherents of x axis, the single time line, and the keepers of the old coordinates. The hotshot physicist addresses the monks on the subject of the new science.

> After some discussion of the phenomenon of refraction, he paused, then said apologetically: "I hope none of this offends anybody's religious beliefs," and looked around quizzically. Seeing that their faces remained curious and bland, he continued for a time, then invited questions from the congregation.
>
> "Do you mind a question from the platform?" asked the abbot.
>
> "Not at all," said the scholar . . .
>
> "I was wondering what there is about the refrangible property of light that you thought might be offensive to religion?"
>
> "Well—" The thon paused uncomfortably. "Monsignor Apollo, whom you know, grew quite heated on the subject. He said that light could not possibly have been refrangible before the Flood, because the rainbow was supposedly—"
>
> The room burst into roaring laughter, drowning the rest of the remark.

But the abbot has a sinking feeling about the thon. My God, he asks, are we destined to repeat the same cycle of renaissance, triumph, cataclysm?

The peculiar virtue of the novel lies in the successful marriage of a subliterary pop form with a subject matter of transliterary import. Literature, in one sense of the word, is simply leapfrogged. Katherine Mansfield is bypassed.

Canticle is an agreeable battle of coordinates. The eerie neck-pricklings derive from the circumstance that the uni-axis time line of futuristic fiction has never been challenged before and so has become one of those unquestioned assumptions which form us far more firmly than any conscious philosophy. Miller lays the old coordinates over the uni-axis—like one of those clear plastic overlays in mathematics texts—and the reader experiences a slight shiver, or annoyance, or nothing at all.

When Miller's starship, which leaves the earth in the second holocaust, reaches Alpha Centauri and discovers intelligent beings there, most of the astronauts will ask the strangers the usual uni-axis time line questions: What is the state of your agriculture? Have you split the atom yet? What about your jurisprudence? Etc.

But at least one of the astronauts will be a fellow like Walter Miller and he will ask a different set of questions—questions which, oddly enough, the strangers may understand better than his fellow astronauts. "How is it with you? Did something go wrong? Was there a disaster? If so, where do you presently stand in relation to a rectification of the disaster? Are you at a Time Before? Or a Time After? Has there been a Happening? Do you expect one?"

When he finishes *Canticle*, the reader can ask himself one question and the answer will tell whether he got the book or missed it. Who is Rachel? What is she?

1971

THE MOVIE
MAGAZINE:
A LOW "SLICK"

❧

The magazine phase of America's own kaleidescope of literature has divided itself by a natural evolution into two classes. They are, as their writers and publishers have so aptly dubbed them, "pulps" and "slicks." This general classification naturally omits such magazines as *Harper's* and *The Atlantic Monthly*, which, though their interiors are of a refined pulpy nature, represent the other extreme in magazine literature. Published largely by Street and Smith, the "pulps" differ little either in dimension or content, concern the activities of every imaginable sort of adventurer, and exist solely to provide amusement for persons incapable of understanding more pretentious literature. "Slicks," however, are characterized by no such uniformity, their only common trait being the glossy quality of their pages. In appearance they range from the angular *Popular Mechanics* to the sprawling *Saturday Evening Post*, in content from *Contract Bridge* to *Popular Aviation*, with more general type magazines, such as *Liberty*, in between, in price from five to fifty cents, and in literary value from A to Z. Somewhere near the bottom in literary value, near the top in popularity, appears that highly specialized yet numerously represented species of "slick," the movie magazines.

Movie magazines represent a unique class of specialty "slicks." Unlike other arts and sciences, the movie industry enjoys so many devotees that a large number of magazines may be supported.

The constant appearance of new magazines in the competitive field and the sustained existence of the most inferior publication indicate a large, easily satisfied patronage.

It is in the quality and nature of its readers that the movie magazines differ so curiously from other "slicks" dealing with particular subjects. Readers of *Contract Bridge* undoubtedly constitute the intelligent minority of bridge players. But the percent of moviegoers who read movie magazines certainly do not represent the intelligent minority interested in moviemaking as a fine art. The reader of *Scientific American* is in a small way an explorer in the field of science. But the steady reader of *Silver Screen* knows very little about the production of movies and cares less. *She*, for *he* is outnumbered three to one, is incapable of distinguishing a projector from an extra; yet she buys her copy or copies of Hollywood magazines and reads them till they fall apart. She is to be found only in America and is possessed with a neurotic curiosity which demands knowledge of every intimate detail of her idol's life. She does not know acting from arm waving, yet she writes countless letters of praise and criticism to both actor and magazine. She is not satisfied with seeing a Hollywood actor perform; she must know his love life and his spinach recipe. Careful research has unearthed as possible steady movie-magazine readers lovelorn old maids, high-school boys and girls, romantic working girls, and fanatical movie-scrapbook keepers. College students may be included as a possible type, but their motives in reading are entirely healthy and transient.

The emotional unbalance of these types is admirably exploited by the movie magazines. The romantic yearnings of the female class and the hero worship and sex consciousness of the males are granted blissful satisfaction. The first movie magazine so successfully met the demands of its readers that its formula has been retained to the present day. There have been only slight changes in the methods of formula application, and with the exception of two quite different and almost independent movie publications, the comic movie magazine and the fiction movie magazine, the growth of this magazine has been a profuse but unprogressive multiplication.

The usual motion-picture magazine, typified by such publications as *Hollywood, Movie Mirror*, and *Screenland*, follows well-defined conventions in its makeup. All are products of a program providing for various departments which, though they studiously masquerade under many titles, differ but little in content. The ever-present gossip column may be called Hollywood Keyhole by *Screenland* and Movie Detective by *Silver Screen*, but both contain the inevitable alternating light-and-dark print paragraphs parading the idiosyncrasies and domestic infelicities of the stars. Equally institutional are the interviews and features, the confidential editorial comment, the letter boxes, and the movie reviews.

Scores of movie magazines appear monthly, and in each copy these prescribed departments follow each other in relentless succession, varying little in content or arrangement. This sameness is undoubtedly due to the method of production. A few large publishing companies such as MacFadden, Fawcett, and Street and Smith publish the large majority of the numerous magazines, so numerous that the ingenuity of the title-makers appears now to be completely exhausted. Each house is responsible for several magazines and each group seems to be turned out by one huge staff. Such conditions prohibit originality and necessitate the production of a practically mechanized article.

The only variety provided for by formula and mode of production is that of time and circumstance. Time passes and circumstances change, to the great delight of the movie-magazine readers. They can perceive the difference between a 1929 *Silver Screen* and a 1935 *Picture-Play*; they know that Ruth Chatterton got her first divorce in the former and that Bing Crosby's wife had twins in the latter. But, to the casual observer, one is precisely like another. He is equally agreeable to reading an old magazine as he is to a new one, for he desires only to look at the pictures and read the fan letters, which, if anything, improve with age.

The bulk of the screen magazine is composed of interviews and feature articles. These two departments differ in name and form only; for, although the "interviews" claim to be authentic and contain quoted matter in the first person, great doubt has arisen in the minds of American fans as to whether a Hollywood star was ever interviewed.

Every movie interview and feature embodies one or all of three motives: to reconcile the peculiarities and weaknesses of a movie star to the ideal held by the fans, to trace the star from his honky-tonk days to his Hollywood pinnacle, and to give the world the star's philosophy of life. The first device is unadulterated hooey, the second is a dramatized rise-to-fame yarn with a small element of truth, and the third is a stock series of common-sense platitudes which apparently guide the lives of all the stars. Strangely enough, many articles give a star's advice for a successful married life, the premise supposedly being that practice makes perfect.

All features and interviews are prefaced by bold-print explanatory paragraphs summing up the article's contents. Typical as an explanatory paragraph is this heading to a feature in a recent *Screenbook*: "Bob Montgomery is one of the few who have zoomed swiftly and suddenly to stardom and kept his perspective." Desultory inspection of screen magazines will prove this "few" to be practically all of Hollywood. It is, evidently, unwritten law among interviewers to invest all stars with a naïve modesty and to disavow all rumors to the contrary. This excerpt from last month's *Hollywood* illustrates the general nature of "disavowers": "Has Janet Gaynor changed? Is she different off the screen? You have read that Janet Gaynor has gone difficult, a genteel word for high-hat. Is it only a legend, a myth?" And like thousands of its predecessors, it turned out to be a malicious myth.

The life-story type of article appears under titles like these: "When I Had a Dime between Me and the Breadline," "Franchot Tone Once Did Not Have an Easy Time Eating Three Meals a Day." More specific are these episodic experiences from the life history of a star: "John Boles Once Served as a Spy in the World War," "Fredric March's Diary in the South Seas," "Victor McGlaglen Once Fought Jack Johnson."

Articles dealing with screen villains invariably aver that the villain is in real life a generous and sweet person far removed from the evil character he portrays. C. Henry Gordon, the lamp-headed gentleman who looks like Hitler in a convex mirror, is "not at all like the villain he plays," according to *Silver Screen*. And, with the feature writer, it does not go without saying that Bette Davis, in real life, is nothing like the slut of *Bordertown* and *Of*

Human Bondage. Her genuine sweetness of character must be reestablished by claiming that she sends money to a second cousin in Shanghai.

In their well-meant intention to salve over inconsistencies in the lives of movie stars with their bland ballyhoo, feature writers are liable to commit ridiculous contradictions in the course of time. A few years ago, when the tough hero came into vogue, one magazine wrote, "James Cagney is mean to everybody. He even threw a grapefruit at his butler for not putting sugar on it." Last month the same magazine ran a feature beginning: "Despite his rough exterior James Cagney is one of the most refined personalities in Hollywood." Such inconsistencies can only lead one to believe that ballyhoo is the byword and that the interviewer of "Clark Gable at Home" no more saw Clark than the feature writer of "Clark Gable Bear Hunting."

Probably somewhat responsible for that impulse which prompts even the mature and intelligent to pick up a movie magazine and glance through its contents is that most diverting department, the letter box. In this section of the movie magazine are to be found the soul utterances of a curious people. The most inferior magazine contains the most diverting letter box; for the gushing extravagance of the letters combine with the earnest manner with which they are set forth by the magazine to produce a delightful conglomeration of incredibly bad taste. *Photoplay*, however, specializes in scintillating constructive criticism, a principle which this fan letter doubtless embodies in a burst of originality: "An idea has occurred to me. I think the private life of the screen stars are [*sic!*] their own business, not the public's." Another *Photoplay* fan relates an experience which the college student should find helpful: "I used to feel tired and blue whenever I had a test facing me the next day at college, until I finally went to a movie the night before one. The next day I made the highest mark I have ever made. No more do I dread test days."

The best fan letters are awarded cash prizes, ranging usually from $1 to $25. Many letters go unrewarded, and after comparing these with the prize-winning letters, we still find it impossible to conjecture what the judges consider prize-winning material. It is indeed a pity that all letters cannot receive $10, as did this one, written by a sixteen-year-old Mae West admirer: "I just saw *Belle of the Nineties* and I enjoyed it immensely, but it is a shame they had to cut out so many good scenes. In spite of that I saw the picture twice."

The sentiments of the University of North Carolina are succinctly expressed by this $10 letter which begins: "Janet Gaynor's sugar-coated sweetness is beginning to cause nausea."

A typical prize-winning letter of praise is this restrained message from a Black Water, Kansas, maid: "I will just say that Bing is just the handsomest, dearest, sweetest, most charming actor I have ever laid my eyes on." Why this letter should win $5 while letters like the following go unrewarded will forever remain a mystery: "Any doctor will tell you that Garbo's grunting and fluttering of the eye-lids denote a bilious condition."

The prosaic thirties have contributed little poetry to the letter boxes of motion-picture magazines, but ten years ago as much space was devoted to poems as to letters. In an old copy of *Film Favorites* is to be found this choice bit:

> *Some like Barrymore*
> *But I like Gary more.*

Certainly, Ogden Nash must have been a movie-magazine fan.

Movie magazines often draw from a stock repertory of "special features" in an attempt to break the monotony of the prescribed makeup. These "special features" are calculated to awaken interest by their personal application or opportunity for personal gain. A common species of "special features" is the prize contest, which, since it must be cinematic, appears usually in the form of a page full of unnamed star pictures, with cash prizes offered him who can identify them. *Picture-Play* introduced a variation when it presented in a recent edition back-view "stills" of several popular movie actors. *Screenland*, last month, ran a series of cartoons each of which embodied the title of a famous movie. *Covered Wagon*, for example, was represented by a fat lady sitting atop a baby carriage.

Appearing only occasionally now are the once very popular

contests, the winners of which got a free ticket to Hollywood and a promised contract from one of the studios. These contests with their irresistible terms have been obliterated by the justified and highly publicized accusations brought against them. Since lurid pictures of a Hollywood overflowing with starving contest winners were conjured up in American minds, the Hollywood contests have lost caste. The only current contests comparable to the old sensations are occasional offers of magazines to reproduce the best pictures submitted and to send them for approval to the casting directors of several studios.

Another variety of "special feature" which is constantly employed occurs in the form of fashion hints, beauty advice, and cooking secrets of the stars, typified by such recent *Screenbook* "scoops" as "What Sue Morris feeds Chester for Sunday night supper," "Lili Damita's new spring frock," "Ginger Rogers's facial work-out."

Probably the most characteristic and revealing of the magazine institutions is the movie-review department. Although the reviews are supposed to be competent guides to current movies, their comments sound remarkably like the advertising previews of the movies themselves. It is difficult to conjecture whether the unflagging praise which is heaped on most of the movies is due to some great fidelity felt by the movie magazines toward their mother art or to substantial sums paid the magazines for advertising by the studios. Whatever may be the case, all movies are accorded ratings from fair on up, whether by stars, checks and double-checks, or thermometers with the 100 degree mark representing perfect. The reviewers' vocabulary includes such qualifying epithets as "interesting," "thrilling," "exciting," "entertaining," and "sweet." Their rare judgment is illustrated by the high mark awarded *Gridiron Flash*, which was said to be a "fair picture of college life." Chapel Hill moviegoers will recall that the same picture nearly caused the destruction of the local theater.

With the growth of the motion-picture magazine industry from the unnoticed appearance of a few copies twenty years ago to the regular vomiting of prodigious quantities and varieties of magazines which it amounts to today, certain outgrowths and divisions have occurred. In pre-Depression days the price of all movie magazines was fixed at twenty-five cents. But 1929 brought an end to this utopian, several hundred percent profit, existence, and with the general fall in prices all the magazines except *Photoplay* promptly dropped to ten or fifteen cents.

Among the large group of movie magazines, class distinctions have arisen, dictated by the three price divisions, ten, fifteen, and twenty-five cents. The great majority of the magazines, such as *Silver Screen, Screen Play, Movie Mirror, Hollywood,* and *Screenbook,* lie in the cheapest classes; some few like *Picture-Play* belong to the intermediate group; while only one, *Photoplay,* continues to maintain its pre-Depression price of twenty-five cents.

Although all movie-magazine readers agree that *Picture-Play* is a better magazine than *Silver Screen,* the five-cent price distinction in the lower classes is difficult to account for. In dimension, content, and quality of paper, no difference is noticeable between *Picture-Play* and the dime magazines. Unless the two prices are arbitrary actions of the publishing companies involving no real difference in quality, practically the only justification of the nickel difference is the slightly more lurid appearance of the covers of the fifteen-cent magazines, the more sensational nature of their interviews, and their superior skill in blotting out double chins and affixing eyelashes in the photographs of the stars.

But in the case of the aristocrat of the large family, class distinction is immediately visible. *Photoplay* justifies its subtitle, "The Aristocrat of the Motion Picture Magazines," by presenting a higher grade of photography and a greater variety in arrangement. Its photographic technique is predominately *Vanity Fair*esque. In the profile view of Clark Gable, for instance, bold shadows are made use of to obscure the oddly foreshortened ear which appears so disconcertingly in cheaper magazines. The makeup formula is disregarded to the extent of including some fiction and occasionally a Montgomery Flagg drawing—anything to provide variety and to elevate itself above the bourgeoisie, whose attempts at originality are illustrated by *Screenbook*'s crossword puzzle superimposed on the broad face of Joan Crawford. But, despite all these demonstrations, *Photoplay* hardly escapes the fundamental hooey which stamps all members of its species. Its editorial comment and interviews are just as ridiculous as the rest and often more so because of their pretentiousness.

Besides this large class and its internal class distinctions, there exist two outgrowing types of motion-picture magazines, the comic movie magazine and the fiction movie magazine, of which the most popular are *Film Fun* and *Screen Romance*, respectively. Neither of these two types attempts to give intimate glimpses in a screen star's life. Both rather adopt the attractions of other common and more general "slicks."

Film Fun is a combination of a sex magazine and a comic magazine, saturated with a Hollywood atmosphere. "Stills" are shown with feeble jests printed below them; full-length photographs of scantily dressed chorus girls are reproduced with dismally punned epigrams appending. The ninety percent nudity of *Film Fun* is responsible for its popularity in university towns, or perhaps it is the magnificent wit that college students can't resist.

Screen Romance and its imitators combine with considerable subtlety the short-story magazine with the glamour of Hollywood. The plots of recent movies are given in short fictional form, illustrated with "stills" from the movie version. The prose of *Screen Romance* is the slushy idiom of its noncinematic brother "slicks," *True Story* and *True Romance*, and is tirelessly applied to all movie themes, irrespective of the type of plot. Its stereotyped, sex-conscious style undoubtedly suits a large number of movies, but when it is applied to *David Copperfield* and *The Little Minister*, the effect is odd, to say the least.

Movie magazines, with their interviews, letters, and reviews, will go down in history as an eloquent manifestation of a particularly crude Americanism. That the situation is peculiarly American is demonstrated by the amazement and chagrin of foreign actors, who, upon entering this country, find that they are required not only to perform before a camera but to stage a continuous three-ring circus. Many return to their native Hollywoods, but some conform to these peculiar demands and obediently live strange and abnormal lives which occasion endless speculation from the delighted fans. Among the most successful conformists is Garbo, who has conspired with her press agents so cunningly that most Americans consider her one of the world's major mysteries.

The *raison d'être* of the movie magazine is the abnormal curiosity of its readers about the private life of the movie stars. It has no justifiable existence, for none of the large group of magazines offers intelligent criticism or information pertaining to the movie world. The "yes" reviews can hardly pass for criticism, nor can the Hollywood news items claim to be informative. The inquisitive moviegoer, who is naturally interested in the gigantic art of moviemaking, can find intelligent magazine comment only in the movie reviews of noncinematic periodicals. If the relatively small theatrical and literary worlds can support such magazines as *The Stage* and *The Saturday Review of Literature*, which have successfully disregarded the sex life of actors and authors, a similar periodical can certainly be supported by the movie industry.

Naturally, the average moviegoer is not the intellectual equal of the theatergoer or the reader of first-class books, but he is certainly far superior to the movie-magazine fan. Unfortunately, however, the latter type has been mobilized by movie magazines into a loud, influential voice, booming effectually at Hollywood. This class of moviegoer has deluged Hollywood with letters of approval and disapproval and has undoubtedly been partly responsible for the unsatisfactory condition of the movies. The more valuable comments of higher-class movie devotees number far less than the notorious "fan letters" and lack the influential publicity of the movie magazines.

The appearance of an increasing number of good movies and the mounting discontent against the poor majority indicate shifting trends in the fan public. A few years ago Jean Harlow kept America in a constant turmoil, while a picture like *Disraeli* was a box-office failure. Today, even Mae West productions are abdicating in favor of such films as *David Copperfield, The Gay Divorcée*, and *The Little Minister*. Such improvement indicates either the cultural advance of movie fans or the adoption of a militant attitude by an intelligent, brave minority. Whatever may be the case, good movies have proven to be profitable undertakings. The necessity of a superior movie magazine, offering an intelligent appraisal of the Hollywood scene, is becoming increasingly apparent. And with its advent one may hope for a decline in popularity of that masquerading "pulp," the current movie magazine, and a corresponding conservation of large quantities of paper and ink.

1935

ACCEPTING
THE NATIONAL
BOOK AWARD FOR
THE MOVIEGOER

❧

You, the judges, have made it difficult for me. You must know that the main source of creative energy of a Southern writer is a well-nourished rancor against Yankees. His natural writing posture is that of a man drawing a bead on Yankee culture. Then something like this happens and spoils everything. It takes all the heart out of a Southerner to be treated so well. Why, a fellow is liable to go back home and not write another word for the next ten years. It has happened, you know.

Nevertheless, I wish to thank—and thank from the bottom of my heart—the judges, Miss Jean Stafford, Mr. Herbert Gold, and Mr. Lewis Gannett; the sponsors, the American Book Publishers Council, the American Booksellers Association, and the Book Manufacturers Institute. And, by your leave, I cannot let this opportunity pass without thanking two other people and two other institutions: my agent, Miss Elizabeth Otis, and my editor, Mr. Stanley Kauffmann, who contributed far beyond the call of duty and ten percent—in fact, I'd just as soon not say how much they did help me—the house of Knopf for their usual beautiful job of bookmaking, and finally my wife, for reasons known to her.

Somewhere in the novel the main character, Jack Bolling, talks about his aunt, who has diagnosed his difficulties as the symptoms of a previous incarnation. I have something of the same feeling now. Because the last time I was in New York (not counting one weekend) was twenty years ago and the occasion was so different that it is hard to believe it belongs to the same lifetime. I was employed as an intern at Bellevue Hospital, assigned to the morgue to do autopsies. The medical staff would assemble and go over a case and make their best guess as to the cause of death. Then it was my job to stand up with a trayful of organs, lungs, liver, spleen, and such, taken from the poor fellow, and give them the answers.

Yet, though these two occasions seem to belong to different incarnations, perhaps they are not unrelated. Providence works in strange ways.

Now, I'm not recommending that novelists of the future serve their apprenticeships in the Bellevue morgue, and I'm not saying that our culture is dying and all that remains is to cut out the organs and see at last what was wrong. And certainly I'm not saying that I have the answers in the way a Bellevue pathologist has the answers on a tray before him.

Nor do I claim any such pretensions for *The Moviegoer*, for when all is said and done, a novel is only a story, and, unlike pathology, a story is supposed first, last, and always to give pleasure to the reader. If it fails of this, it fails of everything.

But since it seems appropriate to say a word about *The Moviegoer*, it is perhaps not too farfetched to compare it in one respect with the science of pathology. Its posture is the posture of the pathologist with his suspicion that something is wrong. There is time for me to say only this: that the pathology in this case has to do with the loss of individuality and the loss of identity at the very time when words like the "dignity of the individual" and "self-realization" are being heard more frequently than ever. Yet the patient is not mortally ill. On the contrary, it speaks well for the national health that pathologists of one sort and another are tolerated and even encouraged.

In short, the book attempts a modest restatement of the Judeo-Christian notion that man is more than an organism in an environment, more than an integrated personality, more even than a mature and creative individual, as the phrase goes. He is a wayfarer and a pilgrim.

I doubt that I succeeded, but I thank you for what you have done.

CONCERNING

LOVE IN THE RUINS

❧

I want to thank the Publishers' Publicity Association [of the 1971 NBA Award] for inviting me to talk. I am happy to be here, although, to tell you the truth, I don't feel much like talking about this novel, which is to be published this spring by Farrar, Straus and Giroux. This is the case probably because of a writer's natural reluctance to say something about a book which presumably has already said what the writer wants to say, no more nor less. But this leaves me in the peculiar situation of talking about a book which you haven't read and which I don't feel like talking about.

One trouble is, no matter what I say about the novel, it will be misleading. For example, if I describe it as a futuristic satire set in the United States somewhere around 1983, the statement would be accurate. Yet it would be misleading. Because, inevitably, you would connect it with Orwell's *1984* or perhaps with Huxley's *Brave New World*. Whereas the fact is, it is not in the least like either.

Orwell and Huxley were writing political satire. They were concerned with certain totalitarian trends in society, Orwell with Big Brother Stalinism, Huxley with a scientifically manipulated anthill state. Their arguments were well taken, so much so that they rank as truisms now, and are accepted by everybody, even by some Soviet writers.

What I was concerned with in this novel is something else

altogether. What interested me is what can happen in a free society in which Orwell and Huxley have carried the day. Everybody agrees with Orwell and Huxley, yet something has gone wrong. For this novel deals, not with the takeover of a society by tyrants or computers or whatever, but rather with the increasing malaise and finally the falling apart of a society which remains, on the surface at least, democratic and pluralistic.

One thing that happens is that words change their meanings. The good old words remain the same, but the meanings begin to slip. In 1983, you see, we will still be using words like "freedom," the "dignity of the individual," the "quality of life," and so on. But the meanings will have slipped. Right now, in 1971, the meanings have already begun to slip, in my opinion. It is the job of the satirist, as I see it, to detect slips and then to exaggerate them so that they become noticeable.

Let me hasten to say that I am not setting up as a prophet. A prophet aims to be right. A novelist prophesizes in order to be wrong. A novelist likes to think he can issue warnings and influence people. This is probably not the case.

I thought of using as a motto for the novel Yeats's line about the center not holding. For indeed, in the novel, the center does not hold. But even to say this is misleading. It suggests a political satire which attacks right and left and comes down on the side of moderate Republicans and Democrats. I had a different center in mind.

Actually, the novel is only incidentally about politics. It is really about the pursuit of happiness. The locale is a subdivision called Paradise Estates. Everyone there has pursued happiness and generally succeeded in being happy. Yet something is wrong. As one character says, we were all happy but our hearts broke with happiness. Liberals begin to develop anxiety. Conservatives begin to contract high blood pressure and large bowel complaints.

It is true that an almost total polarization does occur: between left and right, white and black, young and old; between Los Angeles and San Francisco, between Chicago and Cicero. But there is also a split within the person, a split between the person's self, a ghostly self which abstracts from the world and has identity crises, and the person's body, which has needs, in this case mostly sexual.

So the novel is satirical, but I wish to assure you that in its satire it does not discriminate on grounds of race, creed, or national origin. What I mean is, there is a little something here to offend everybody: liberal, conservative; white, black; hawk, dove; Catholic, Protestant, Jew, heathen; the English, the Irish, Swedes, Ohioans, to mention only a few. Yet I trust it is not ill-humored, and that only those will be offended who deserve to be.

Really, though, I was not concerned primarily with ideological polarization. What seemed more important to me are certain elements of self-hatred and self-destructiveness which have sur- faced in American life, elements common to both left and right. This accounts for the apocalyptic themes of the book: love in the ruins, end of the world, a few people surviving, vines sprouting in the masonry, etc. For I sense a curious ambivalence in people's attitude toward such things. The prospect of catastrophe has its attractions. I have the same ambivalence myself. For example, there is something attractive about the idea of Forty-second Street falling into ruins and being covered by Virginia creeper.

So, when people talk about the greening of America, you have to remember that the greening can take place only where the masonry crumbles. I only wanted to call things by their right names. I mean to say, it is all very well for some young people and a few aging gurus to attack science and technology and to go live in the ruins, in love and peace, and to touch each other. On the other hand, it is not a small thing, either, to turn your back on two thousand years of rational thinking and hard work and science and art and the Judeo-Christian tradition. I am not arguing. Very well, one turns one's back. I only wanted to explore some of the consequences. What happens in the novel is that the hero finds himself living in a ruined greening Howard Johnson motel with three girls. One of the girls is a Presbyterian.

What I really wanted to do, I guess, was call a bluff. For it has often seemed to me that much of the violence and alienation of today can be traced to a secret and paradoxical conviction that America is immovable and indestructible. Hence the acts of desperation. Blowing up a building is, after all, a nutty thing to do. The fact is that America is not immovable and indestructible.

Just now, of course, the violence has abated. We are experiencing what has been described as a period of eerie tranquillity. People seem to be thinking things over. In fact, if I had to describe this novel, I would call it an entertainment for Americans who are thinking things over in a period of eerie tranquillity.

But the novel is not saying: Don't rock the boat, cool it, be moderate, vote moderate Republican or Democrat. No, it rocks the boat. In fact, it swamps the boat. What I wanted to investigate was how the boat might actually go under at the very time everybody is talking about the dignity of the individual and the quality of life. I wanted also to investigate the best hope of the survivors.

But rather than talk about the novel and mislead you, I prefer to close these remarks by mentioning two features of my own background which may account for the peculiarities, if not the virtues, of this novel.

One is that my original vocation was medicine and that for this reason my literary concerns are perhaps more diagnostic and therapeutic than they otherwise would be. The fact is, I can't resist the impulse to thump the patient and try to figure out what's wrong with him. This medical habit has its literary dangers. It could make for moralizing, telling people what to do, and for heavy-handed satire. I hope it doesn't.

The other thing is the circumstance that I come from the Deep South. I mention this only to call your attention to a remarkable event that has occurred in the last year or two, which has the most far-reaching consequences, and which has gone all but unnoticed. It is the fact that for the first time in a hundred and fifty years the South is off the hook and once again free to help save the Union. It's not that the South has got rid of its ancient stigma and is out of trouble. It's rather that the rest of the country is now also stigmatized and is in even deeper trouble.

So, if the novel has any messages, one might be this: Don't give up, New York, California, Chicago, Philadelphia! Louisiana is with you. Georgia is on your side.

THE COMING CRISIS
IN PSYCHIATRY

A new theme is being heard in American psychiatry. At the present time it is taken to be little more than another variation on the Freudian motif—as such, in fact, is it advertised by Erich Fromm (*The Sane Society*, 1955), who has given it the name "humanistic psychoanalysis." The possibility I should like to explore is whether this new insight, if it is valid, does not require a radical recasting of the concept of man for the social sciences. What makes the matter worthy of attention is the fact that the issue has been raised, not by the old enemies of Sigmund Freud and his teachings, but within the profession. Someone has remarked that, great as has been the impact of Freud on psychiatry, it has been even greater in the fringe areas of the social sciences, in popular science, and in the arts. If you are looking for pure Freudian doctrine, you are more likely to hear it nowadays from the social worker in Des Moines or the sophomore psychology student than from the analyst, who is more apt to be eclectic. As in the history of so many seminal ideas, at the very moment it is conquering in the provinces, it is being called in question at its source and center.

The issue is simply this: Is psychiatry a biological science in which man is treated as an organism with instinctive drives and needs not utterly or qualitatively different from those of other organisms? Or is psychiatry a humanistic discipline which must take account of man as possessing a unique destiny by which he is oriented in a wholly different direction?

It is hardly necessary to add that the issue has arisen among psychiatrists—as indeed it is proper that it should arise—not because of any idea of making concessions to religious points of view, but from the necessity of accounting for the human "data."

There is, moreover, a note of urgency about the crisis which would not obtain, say, in a science like geology. The sciences of man do not operate in a vacuum.

The question, then, is no longer whether the social sciences, given sufficient time (as they like to say), may succeed in applying the biological method to man, but whether the very attempt to do so has not in fact worsened man's predicament in the world. The pursuit of physics does not change the physical world; it is all the same to most subatomic particles whether there is or is not a science of physics. But if Western man's sense of homelessness and loss of community is in part due to the fact that he feels himself a stranger to the method and data of his sciences, and especially to himself construed as a datum, then the issue is no longer academic.

It is increasingly noticeable that American psychiatry has almost nothing to say about the great themes that have engaged the existential critics of modern society from Søren Kierkegaard to Gabriel Marcel. The very men whose business is mental health have been silent about the sickness of modern man, his emotional impoverishment, his sense of homelessness in the midst of the very world which he, more than the men of any other time, has made over for his own happiness. Would anyone seriously contend that these themes are peculiar to postwar Europe and have no bearing on American life?

The suspicion is beginning to arise that American psychiatry with its predominantly functional orientation—its root concepts of drives and counterdrives, field forces, cultural criteria—is silent because, given its basic concept of man, it is *unable* to take account of the predicament of modern man. Fromm speaks of a "pathology of normalcy," maintaining that a man who meets every biological and cultural norm may nevertheless be desperately alienated from himself. This kind of suggestion cannot fail to be offensive to most

American social scientists, for the simple reason that, however much they may wish to, they have no criterion for evaluating illness except as a deviation from a biological norm.

Fromm's diagnosis is startling, indeed. Though he attempts to associate his views with psychoanalytic theory and to smooth over the differences, it becomes clear that what he proposes is not merely a variation of but is in many ways the exact reverse of what would be forthcoming under the method of analysis. Who is mentally healthy? What about the man or woman who lives, say, in the Park Forest development near Chicago, who has a good sexual relation with his or her partner, who feels secure, who is socially adjusted, who has many acquaintances, who consumes all manner of goods and services, participates in "cultural activities," enjoys "recreational facilities," who is never lonely? Here is how one of them talks, according to Fromm:

> I never feel lonely, even when Jim's away. You know friends are nearby, because at night you hear the neighbors through the walls.

Marriages which might break up otherwise are saved, depressed moods are kept from becoming worse, by talking, talking, talking. "It's wonderful," says one young wife.

> You find yourself discussing all your problems with your neighbors—things that back in South Dakota we would have kept to ourselves.

Who is mentally healthy? Surely these happy suburbanites, who have few symptoms, who succeed most of the time in escaping boredom and guilt and anxiety. No, says Fromm. These people are desperately alienated from themselves. They are in fact without selves. They experience themselves as things, as commodities, or as nothing. They are—though Fromm does not use these words— in the position of the man in the Gospel who would gain the whole world and lose his soul.

What about the symptoms of guilt and anxiety when they do appear? In the traditional analytic view, of course, guilt and anxiety are just that—symptoms. That is to say, they are evidences of "dis-ease," the resultant of a tensional imbalance in the unconscious. In Freud's words, they are the outcome of an "interplay of forces," instinctive forces versus repressive forces.

It was perfectly natural that in the nineteenth and the early twentieth centuries the biological method of medical science should have been taken over by the psychiatrist, and that a mental symptom should have been looked upon as evidence of a process which the patient knew nothing about and which the scientist has made it his business to learn something about. Certain chest pains are a symptom of a cardiac disorder which the sufferer has no way of identifying unless he has studied the subject. In a similar way, guilt and anxiety were regarded as overt signs of covert psychic disorder, signs whose meanings could be fathomed only by the use of special techniques, such as psychoanalysis.

Not necessarily so, says Fromm. Though he does not rule out the unconscious origin of neuroses, he makes it clear that the guilt and anxiety of the alienated man of the Western world are wholly *appropriate* reactions: a sense of guilt for the man who feels his life running through his hands like sand; of anxiety for the man who confronts himself and discovers—nothing. This is the age of anxiety because it is the age of the loss of self.

Let us oversimplify for a moment and put the question as concretely as possible. What shall we make of two individuals, suburbanite A, who is tranquilized in his never-ending consumption of goods, services, entertainment, and human intercourse; suburbanite B, who feels himself an alien in Park Forest, who knows not who he is and is afraid? We have no choice under the biological method but to consider A "normal" and B "pathological." To suggest that both are lost to themselves, and that the difference is that B knows it and A does not, is to imply a criterion of human existence which is quite foreign to the adaptive criteria of biology.

The Freudian analyst, confronted with the symptoms of estrangement, anxiety, and guilt, has no choice but to proceed by formula: Now, let's see if we can find out what has gone wrong and get rid of it. A man walks into a psychiatrist's office suffering from acute "free-floating" anxiety. It turns out that his life is otherwise unremarkable, that he has satisfied every biological and cultural "need," that he has nothing to fear. Any high-school student, in such a case, can tell you that his anxiety is a symptom of a disorder of the unconscious originating in infancy. Certainly, the student will aver, his anxiety has no basis in his present life.

The suggestion now comes (from Fromm, and especially from the existentialists) that it may have everything to do with his present life. In the case of the anonymous consumer who is lost to himself, lost to the possibility of existing as an individual human being in a true community of other human beings, the anxiety may be quite the reverse of a symptom. It may be the call of the self to the self, in Kierkegaard's words: the discovery of the possibility of freedom to become a self.

This is strange talk from an analyst. (It is perhaps stranger still that Fromm should try to link up his diagnosis with Marxian economic theory and make no mention of the existentialists.) What is being called in question is nothing less than the fundamental concepts of psychiatry. Responsible social scientists are suggesting for the first time that human existence must be evaluated by standards quite different from those which the analyst abstracts from his "data." The existential criteria apply to analyst and data alike. Fromm suggests, for example, that the brilliant American psychiatrist Harry Stack Sullivan was himself alienated, because he looked upon the lack of self in American life as a normal state of affairs.

Why does the biological method fail to comprehend man? Perhaps it is because the scientist will invariably allow a double standard: one for his data, one for himself. Freud, for instance, tried to derive all human activity from various expressions of libidinal energy; but what account can Freud give of his own lifelong quest for the truth? How an "interaction of forces" can be sublimated into a search for truth is never explained.

Carl Gustav Jung quite frankly declares that as a scientist he has no interest in the truth value of his patients' beliefs; his only concern is the discovery of the workings of the psyche, the requirements for mental well-being, whatever they may be. Thus, Jung approves of the Catholic dogma of the Assumption, not because it is true, but because it happens to validate the "anima archetype." Yet Jung himself is, one presumes, searching for the truth. What account can he give, in terms of his theory, of his own lifelong project? It would be easy to list others like Freud and Jung, but common to all is the posture of the spectator questioning his data in search of the *real*, the *hidden* motivations behind the various illusory goals by which man deceives himself.

Fromm implies that scientists, too, share our common humanity and can fall victim to the "pathology of normalcy" as easily as the next man.

The next question is inevitable. If Fromm's "normative humanism" does not derive its norms from biological categories, then where do they come from? Is there a goal of human living beyond that of adjustment to society and consumption of its goods? If there is such a goal, does this mean that psychiatry is dependent upon religion for its orientation? What justification, from a purely psychiatric point of view, can be offered for an abandonment of the biological method?

II

The question now being raised in psychiatry is whether there is not a "true estate" of being human, and whether the objective-biological concept of human life not only fails to apprehend it but may actually worsen man's predicament in the world. It may seem farfetched to cite Freud and Jung and others as practitioners of the biological method; but both of them have a double standard under which "instinct mechanics" or "myth-mongering" is attributed to the patient while truth seeking is supposed to be peculiar to the doctor.

Erich Fromm's "normative humanism" frankly implies that there are norms other than the biological and the cultural. Viktor E. Frankl's "medical ministry" is an attempt, not to probe the unconscious, but to correct the conscious worldview of the patient. Leslie Farber writes in a recent issue of *Psychiatry* that we are becoming uneasily aware that objective scientific knowledge is "the wrong viewpoint, the wrong terminology and the wrong kind of knowledge—ever to explain the human being."

The radical departure of these new points of view lies in their tacit recognition of a standard of human existence wholly different from that by which we judge the flora of Australia or the ape population of the Congo. It means that there is being proposed as the central criterion of man's well-being the very thing most detested by the biological method: a value scale of rightness, authenticity; in short, a concept of human nature and what is proper to it.

An empirical scientist might reasonably ask at this point: By what right do you drag in the very value judgments which we have spent the last three hundred years getting rid of? Next you'll be suggesting that we go back to Aristotle's physics and say that the apple falls to the ground because it is seeking its rightful place.

That is a good question. One does not lightly go beyond the objective method, which has proved so fruitful at the inorganic and lower organic levels. No one is suggesting, of course, that the biological method is not valid as far as it goes. What is being suggested is that a man who has satisfied every biological and cultural need that can be abstracted by the scientific method may nevertheless be desperately alienated from himself—that, in other words, there are goals beyond the biological. There is no use pretending that "humanistic psychoanalysis" can be viewed as a variety of Freudian theory. This is not just another Freudian "heresy." This is apostasy.

What possible scientific justification can be offered for the proposal by responsible social scientists that the objective method of the sciences is inadequate for treating man *as man*?

The answer can only be that there are certain human needs quite impervious to the biological approach. As Fromm puts it, there are no physiological substrata to the needs of relatedness and transcendence. In the language of the existentialists, there are certain traits of human existence which are utterly different from the traits of the world; and not only does the existing self fail to understand itself by objective science, but in so doing it falls into an unauthentic existence.

This brings us close to the Scholastic view that, while human beings share certain characteristics with other creatures, they are capable of higher perfections peculiar to themselves. But however one chooses to say it, it is a far cry indeed from the usual language of American sociology and psychology.

The new theme, then, is the inkling that it is possible, entirely apart from religious convictions, to speak of the sickness of Western man. We all know perfectly well that the man who lives out his life as a consumer, a sexual partner, an "other-directed" executive; who avoids boredom and anxiety by consuming tons of newsprint, miles of movie film, years of TV time; that such a man has somehow betrayed his destiny as a human being.

What Fromm is saying was perhaps said more plainly by Pascal three hundred years ago when he spoke of the man who comes into this world knowing not whence he came nor whither he will go when he dies but only that he will for certain die, and who spends his life as though he were not the center of the supreme mystery but rather diverting himself (and, we might add, adjusting himself). Such a man, said Pascal, is worse than a fool.

What does it mean to say that a man may become alienated, fall prey to everydayness, become unauthentic? Fromm provides us with a close analysis of the pathology of Western man, the "marketing personality" who regards himself as a commodity, who consumes goods, not to use them, but to *have* them.

Central to Fromm's analysis is the thesis of alienation, "that man does not experience himself as the active bearer of his own powers and richness, but as an impoverished 'thing.' " He gives to alienation a Marxist reading, attributing it to the capitalistic mode of production, in which man's productivity becomes a commodity through its money value.

The existentialists, it is hardly necessary to add, view man's plight not as the by-product of a particular economic system but rather as the perennial condition of human existence, a condition necessarily entailed by man's freedom. It is indeed hardly credible that the alienation of Western man is due to capitalism, as Fromm suggests, or that tinkering with economics will cure the disease. However serious the situation of the mass man of the West, it seems hopeful in comparison with that of the Soviet consumer.

There is surely a much larger problem, as Henri Bergson and José Ortega y Gasset and Gabriel Marcel have seen it, of man's increased *responsibility* in the technical age. He is free to use his inventions in a human way or to "fall prey to them," as the existentialists put it.

Fromm revives the biblical idea of idolatry. A new car is a

great good, but it brings with it the threat that it can alienate the possessor. The danger in owning a new car is not that in it we may run over somebody: what is far more likely to happen is that we may fall prey to our possession, that we will look upon it, not as a means of getting from place to place, but as a sort of fetish object to be acquired for its own sake. But, after offering us an exciting glimpse of man's freedom, freedom to live authentically, freedom to fall prey to idolatry, Fromm then disappoints us by proposing economic formulae by way of solution. After excoriating the sin of abstraction for two hundred pages, he falls victim to the greatest abstraction of all: man conceived as Homo economicus.

If it does not suffice to construe man as an organism responding to its environment by maintaining itself, adapting itself and reproducing itself, how, then, shall we conceive him? In what new frame of reference? This is not an academic question. Anxiety—according to Sullivan, the chief subject matter of psychiatry—is, under one frame of reference, a symptom to be gotten rid of; under the other, it may be a summons to authentic existence, to be heeded at any cost. Clearly, it is a matter of some importance to know which it is.

Moreover, the ultimate role of psychiatry itself is very much at issue. Should psychiatry supplant religion and set itself up as a sort of secular priesthood? Should it give way to religion? Or if, as most would undoubtedly agree, each has its proper domain, then where is the line to be drawn between the "medical ministry" and the religious ministry? The lines are fluid indeed at present, but it is a hopeful sign that men on both sides now appear to recognize that there *are* lines to be drawn and legitimate areas of cooperation marked out.

One or two questions suggest themselves in connection with Fromm's "normative humanism." His picture of the alienated consumer is quite vivid. But what about the other end of the scale? What is the opposite of alienation? What is the goal of mental health?

Mental health, in the humanistic sense, is characterized by the ability to love and create, by the emergence from the incestuous ties to family and nature, by a sense of identity based on one's experience of self as the subject and agent of one's powers, by the grasp of reality inside and outside ourselves, that is, by the development of objectivity and reason.

If biological standards no longer suffice, then our criterion of mental health must derive from the unique traits of human existence. These are, according to Fromm, creativity, productivity, and love, which go to make up the "productive orientation," instead of the "marketing orientation."

There is something curiously vague about Fromm's normative goals as compared with his concrete picture of man's plight. The goal of life is to "live productively," he says. This sounds very much like the mental-hygiene recommendations of the Overstreets—that the goal of life is to achieve "emotional maturity"; that the secret of Socrates, Jesus, and Buddha was that they achieved emotional maturity.

Now, this may even be true in a weird, abstractive fashion—although to characterize Him who said "I am the way" as a psychologist of emotional maturity is, to say the least, a strange description. But what of the alienated man of the twentieth century who reads this vast library of popular mental hygiene and dutifully sets out in quest of "emotional maturity," "productive orientation," "cultural integration," and suchlike? To the degree that a man stakes everything on a goal isolated by the scientific method, to this same degree is he destined to despair.

Somewhere there has occurred a fatal misplacement of the real. To hold out to a man lost in the abyss of anxiety and anonymity the solution of a "productive orientation" is like telling a man who has fallen into a pit that the answer to his troubles is a pitless orientation.

What has gone wrong? A clue is perhaps to be found in Fromm's ambiguous treatment of transcendence. If there is any one feature which all existentialists agree upon as an inveterate trait of human existence, it is transcendence. Some, like Gabriel Marcel, may regard it as the true motion of man toward God; others, like Jean-Paul Sartre, may regard it as an absurd striving, the "useless passion." But, atheistic or theistic, they would all agree that transcendence is the one distinguishing mark of human existence. In Friedrich Nietzsche's words, man is he who must surpass himself.

To Fromm, transcendence means creativity, and creativity means biological reproduction. Man transcends himself by creating life (or by destroying life), things which other creatures do, to be sure, but only man does them in perfect awareness. This is, to say the least, a curious sort of transcendence. It is hard to see how the trait can be so secularized and flattened without losing its meaning. What Fromm wants is that transcendence should not be transcendent.

We learn soon enough where the rub is. Where even the atheistic existentialists would be candid enough to admit man's incurable God-directedness, Fromm seeks to secularize. This, he says, is what transcendence *should* be. Biological prejudice seems to be getting the better of an empirical insight. Someone has said that the besetting sin of the objective social scientist is his reformer's zeal: having shown how society works and has to work, he always appends a last chapter on how to change all this.

It remains only to remark how Fromm's theoretical commitments limit and specify his "normative humanism." He lays it down as an axiom that monotheism, like totemism, is a stage in cultural evolution, and is even now being superseded. Then, having ruled transcendent being out of court, he concludes that the worship of God is itself idolatry and alienation.

If one were to suggest, as Martin Heidegger does, that modern man's loss is his loss of being, that his homelessness is a homelessness from being, Fromm would probably reply that such metaphysical notions are also being superseded by cultural evolution. One can't help thinking of what Marcel, in describing the spirit of the age, calls "ontophobia," the dislike of being.

It is not necessary at this point to adduce the serious objections which anthropologists currently raise to the dogma of cultural evolution. But I shall point out an inconsistency. Fromm makes a great point of man's emergence from animal nature into freedom, of man as being the one creature who is capable of living authentically or of falling into idolatry and alienation. But once we have come into this new condition—in which living according to the biological standards of adaptation is cited as a lapse into an *unauthentic* existence—how can we possibly judge human existence by evolutionary criteria? Once we have transcended animal nature, as Fromm describes it, and discovered goals beyond the biological, by what right do we apply biological yardsticks to these superbiological goals?

It does not seem to be asking too much to require social science to be "open" in its theoretical commitments, or, as Christopher Dawson would say, to be more empirical and less religious. If there is such a thing as transcendence in man's nature, it would seem to be the proper function of psychiatry to take due note of it, not to change it according to some theoretical bias.

God is absent, said Johann Christian Hölderlin; God is dead, said Nietzsche. This means one of two things. Either we have outgrown monotheism, and good riddance; or modern man is estranged from being, from his own being, from the being of other creatures in the world, from transcendent being. He has lost something—what, he does not know; he knows only that he is sick unto death with the loss of it.

1957

THE CULTURE
CRITICS

❧

Things look bad all right. The future is as black as can be, so black that people either have to talk about it all the time or else not at all, and who can blame them? A good deal has been said about the people who don't talk about it at all, who take one look at the bad news on the front page and turn to Ann Landers and the puzzles. Psychiatrists, in fact, have a word for it: selective inattention. But not much has been said about the people who do talk about it.

Some of those who talk about it are wise and responsible men, who are as worried as the rest of us but who know we'll never get out of the fix we're in unless somebody does some serious figuring. But there is also abroad in the land a spirit of what might be called the *Weltschmerz* of the Cocktail Party. Those possessed by it sound as scared as we are, scareder, but they are betrayed by a telltale gleam in the eye and moistness of the lip. They just got in from Washington, where they have a friend who sits three chairs behind Max Taylor at the meetings of the Joint Chiefs. "I happened to see Jack right after the meeting and I said, 'Good Lord, man, what's the matter with you? Your face is as white as a sheet.' All Jack would say was: 'I can't tell you, but I can say this much: I'm frightened.' " There are the tremblers, and there are the professional gravediggers of the West. Western civilization might have had its virtues in the past, but now, in their eyes, the jig is up.

Thomas Griffith is one of the wise and responsible men. His *The Waist-High Culture* sounds at first like one more indictment of American culture. These indictments must be pleasant to write, and they make pretty good reading, too—many of the charges are true, and anyhow it is always salutary to see Hollywood and Madison Avenue and the exurbs get a well-executed comeuppance. The weaknesses of these books lie not so much in what is said, however, as in what is not said. The indictment is, to a degree, true. But if it occurs to the reader to ask: In whose name are you making the indictment? Now that you have annihilated suburbia, what do you propose in its place? the answers are noticeably muted. Riesman's analysis of the other-directed man may be offered as a piece of objective sociology which steers clear of norms, but certainly no other-directed man would want to remain other-directed after reading *The Lonely Crowd*.

If it is not "good" to be tradition-directed, inner-directed, or other-directed, what is the "good" category? Who is the fourth man? He is, of course, the mature man. The fact is, however, that the mature man of Riesman and Fromm and the Overstreets is a somewhat shadowy fellow himself. We don't, to tell the truth, hear too much about him.

The trouble is that popular sociology is open to an occupational temptation. The objective posture of the social scientist is apt to be turned into a superior vantage point from which negative judgments are pronounced upon society in the guise of objective observations. In Vance Packard's latest book (*The Status Seekers*), for example, there are many fascinating items about the growing status-consciousness of Americans, the rather frightening lengths to which people will go to have the right address and the right antiques in their homes. Such phenomena as these and the social credentials of Northeastern executives (being white, Anglo-Saxon, and Episcopalian) are sociological facts. It is all too easy, however, for the cruising social critic to take the final step back and see all human motivations as a rat race of status-seeking and backbiting. In the heady atmosphere of social science, even the most universally accepted social norms become suspect. When Vance Packard observes that, among Air Force personnel, SAC pilots have achieved high status and that, among churchgoers, a madame of a house of prostitution is awarded a low status, it looks as if sociology has exposed yet another piece of monkey business. Yet it would be more straightforward either to assent to society's estimate of the SAC pilot and the madame or else take exception to it, rather than to relegate all of society's values to a vaguely disreputable limbo of ordinary people who act in an ordinary way as against those of us who are privileged to understand them.

But if olympianism is a defect of much of social-indictment literature, it is not a fault of *The Waist-High Culture*. Griffith is an acute social critic and is as aware as anyone of the tendencies toward banality and the second-rate in much of American life. But if he sees the well-advertised faults of suburbia and the executive suite, he has a second sight which gives the book its peculiar value. He sees people, and he never forgets that what must in the last analysis be confronted is not a trend or a social class but a particular fellow living in a particular house and finding himself in a particular concrete predicament.

It is no doubt legitimate, for sociological purposes, to speak of a member of the upper middle class who has his house done over in Early Federal, with decorator Picassos as status symbols. But let us not forget that this same class member may have saved a comrade's life in battle, suffers from sinusitis, has a sick wife, and works like a dog to pay his debts. He cannot really be understood by a sociology of motivations but only by a larger view of man which takes account of what a man is capable of and what he can fall prey to. There is not really such a thing as a consumer or a public or a mass man except only as they exist as constructs in the minds of sociologists, ad men, and opinion-pollsters.

The Waist-High Culture never succumbs to the passion for the abstract (perhaps it is Griffith's reporter's training which saves him; he is now foreign news editor of *Time*). He has heard the indictment often enough and does some pretty expert indicting himself, but he confesses to "a nagging doubt about the validity of the indictment." The American people are a vital people, he reminds us, and they are no more satisfied with the stuff that flows into their living rooms than are their critics. The suburbanite may in a sense have been seduced by the pleasures of the middle class, but it would be nearer the truth to describe his predicament as one of blighted intentions, the satiety and discontent of which follow seduction. "If guilty, they are not guilty as charged, and are at least entitled to the old frontier verdict: 'Guilty, but not so dern awful guilty.' "

The American intellectual does not escape the indictment— or rather it is his escape which is charged against him. But if his performance has been a sorry one, it is only the other side of the same coin of mediocrity. The rest of us are disappointing in our docility before mass culture, and the intellectual is hardly more helpful in his self-promotion to an elite. It is the hardest thing in the world to see the intellectual in any other framework than the class lines he himself has drawn: us free creative individuals versus you slobs, or us normal red-blooded Americans versus you crummy eggheads.

In his book, Packard succumbs a bit to the temptation and polishes off the intellectuals with some diverting remarks about status-seeking eggheads in Upper Bohemia. Griffith gives them a rough time, too, but he does so from the sense of loss of the intellectual's contribution and what he sees as the latter's self-imposed isolation from the community.

The alternative to isolation is not necessarily togetherness. In any case, what is so distressing about isolation and togetherness is the impoverishment of both, the sense of needless loss which cannot but come over one when he considers either the alienated intellectual or the stratified commuter. If any one theme runs through these quite different social critiques, it is the *poverty* of the classes, not only the down-and-outers, and indeed not so much the blue-collars, but the middles and uppers, both upper country club and upper Bohemia. It is the remarkable discrepancy between the opportunities at hand and the felt meagerness of life as it is lived. The status-seeker is such a poor man and so unnecessarily so. But he is no poorer than the jackdaw of the salons who is "up" on everything and in love with nothing, who knows what Edmund Wilson thinks of the Dead Sea Scrolls but has never read St. John's Gospel (apologies to Griffith).

Griffith began to have his nagging doubts when he heard for perhaps the hundredth time what he calls the European Speech. It took place in the Piazza San Marco. His cultivated European friend extended a hand to the cathedral and the campanile and began to go on about how beautiful and restful it was, how we Europeans move among beautiful things and have time to enjoy art and music. But in America—the hurrying and the scurrying. Where are you going? Why do you bustle so? Yes, it is true: the American must always nod. "Our hurry *was* mad, our newness was often slapdash, and here was great beauty." Yet there is something wrong with the European Speech. The two things don't really go together: the leisureliness of the café life and the building of St. Mark's Cathedral. The cathedral had been built by ambitious and bustling men, not by café sitters. It would be easy enough to launch a counterattack on cultivated Europeans as a race of museum keepers, café philosophers, and America haters, but Griffith does not do this. He likes and admires them, for one thing. Nor is he much interested in their rather superficial charge of hustle-bustle. He is concerned to make a far more serious self-accusation.

The sobering fact is, and this is no European or Hamiltonian saying so, that there has occurred a decline in the quality of American life: "—never in the history of the world has there been such a proliferation of the second-rate." The decline, moreover, has occurred in direct proportion to the extension of the suffrage. In 1971, when the electorate amounted to less than five percent of the American people, the *Federalist Papers* were written in the form, not of a treatise in political science, but of pamphlets to sell the Constitution to the public. Men were described therein as universally venal, ambitious, vindictive, and rapacious. The *Federalist* authors had some very clear-eyed and hardheaded notions about the weaknesses of human nature and the attendant dangers to the republican form of government. But now the first rule of politicking and pamphleteering is to flatter the little man—though this very phrase expresses a contempt and cynicism which the *Federalist* authors would never have subscribed to. Attack malefactors of great wealth or bleeding-heart liberals, but don't lay a finger on the voter, especially not the independent voter who despises politics and breaks away from his TV once every four years to vote for a man—because he looks sincere on TV. It is this very flattery which the *Federalist* authors warned against.

Yet it is still possible to prescribe democratic therapy for democratic failings. Certainly the answer is not a restriction of suffrage. We may defend quality, says Griffith, but we will never defend privilege. The fact is that the great issue is still in doubt: democracy has by no means proved that it provides a hospitable soil for quality in politics, science, or art. What makes the stakes so high is that it could so provide for quality and in a fashion never dreamed of by the aristocratic patrons—or it could fail so utterly as to justify the famous remark in *The Third Man* about what six hundred years of democracy produced in Switzerland: the cuckoo clock.

Griffith's book might be said to present, not the solution, but the dilemma of the educated American—assuming that the latter is something more than a "social unit," that he is also a man who is to a degree aware of his own predicament. Both Griffith's and Packard's books are valuable pathologies of the American sickness. Yet one can't avoid the impression that Packard thinks he is treating a skin disease and is very sure of his diagnosis, while Griffith knows that the sickness is a lot deeper and a lot obscurer. Packard's diagnosis is status-seeking and class-stratification, and in the last chapter he prescribes his cure: we ought to cut it out. A $12,000-a-year white Protestant junior executive living in a development of $12,000-a-year white Protestant junior executives ought to get to know Jews and Negroes, poets and milkmen. It would make for a more interesting life. Sure it would, and it would be a good thing, all in all. But the question is whether or not this new intergroup group would not and does not habitually fall prey to its own strain of the virus: not status-seeking and social stratification maybe, but a compulsive other-directedness and an antic nonconformity which may conceal a spiritual wasteland more desolate than Levittown. The trouble goes deeper than one's choice of friends or cars. It is, as Griffith knows very well, a religious dilemma in that ultimate goals are involved. To say so is by no means to prescribe religious conversion as a social technique. For "religion" is itself apt to be conceived in terms specified by the very worldview for which it is prescribed as a cure.

The predicament is evident enough. It is more or less generally recognized, even by sociologists, that, despite unprecedented cultural and material advantages, the lives of a great many people in

America and the West (not to mention the Communist countries), often the very people in a position to enjoy the fruits of Western culture and prosperity, have sunk to unprecedented depths of paltriness and banality. Psychologists have described a new syndrome, "destination sickness," a disillusionment exemplified by the Marquand character who realizes his ultimate goal and finds waiting for him the station wagon and the country club. And the dilemma is felt as such. The victim knows he is victimized. He is aware of the blight of his intentions. He is aware, moreover, of the fecklessness of the usual prescriptions. Griffith must know in his heart of hearts that there is no use in calling for a recovery of "clarity of purpose" or a return to the vigor and integrity of the *Federalist* authors, no more use than Packard's naïve injunction to stop status-seeking and social-stratifying.

Griffith is more acutely aware than Packard of our cultural dependence on the Judeo-Christian ethos. "Even those of us who live with no faith live on its accumulated moral capital," he writes. And certainly those of us who profess to live with faith are the more at fault for our failure to demonstrate a necessary connection between faith and the good life. Much of the so-called religious revival in American life looks uncomfortably like the very status-seeking and hard sell so acutely diagnosed by both Packard and Griffith.

Nevertheless, a final remark is in order. As Griffith has decided, after much reflection, that there is something wrong with the European Speech, we might, after much listening, append another nagging doubt. There is something wrong with the Ethical Secularist's Speech. As Griffith observes, the latter usually considers himself to be as commendably motivated as those with faith, and often is. To these good folk, who live so securely on the accumulated capital of the Christian faith, the core of faith itself is apt to appear as an anomaly, easily dispensable and in fact dispensed with one or two standard objections. It seems pertinent here to raise a question, not about the objections, but about the posture from which the objections are mounted. The point is that, even though the objections be answered, nothing is really changed for the objector. All that business about God, the Jews, Christ, the Church seems no less dispensable—queer—whether it is true or not. Yet our ethical friend who is aware of the sickness might do well to consider the possibility that the dislocation of his times is related to this very incapacity to attach significance to the sacramental and historical-incarnational nature of Christianity. Instead of chewing over the same old objections, that is, he should consider the more pressing problem: how is it that even if these things were all true, could be proved, it would make no difference to me?

For what is being assaulted today in the literature of alienation is this nice old secular height from which he mounts his objections. But as the assault goes on, the questions which occur to us begin to change. It no longer seems so appropriate to ask: Why do people do these things—seek status symbols and the miserable pleasures of the middle? as it is to ask: Why should they not do such things, or anything else?

And when, inevitably, the question of religion is raised, it should be remembered that the relation of Christianity to Western culture and one's own culture is much too radical to be settled by one's fancied aversion to this particular dogma or that particular churchgoer. Indeed, such a good man—better than we, we admit first off, since this matter of comparative worth seems to bother him—might sooner or later come to see that, culturally speaking, our posture is something like the cat in the cartoon who ran off the cliff and found himself standing up in the air. Maybe he can get back to earth by backing up; on the other hand, he might be in for a radical change of perspective.

1959

THE FATEFUL RIFT: THE SAN ANDREAS FAULT IN THE MODERN MIND

❧

In these brief remarks I wish to offer two propositions for your consideration. One is that our view of the world, which we get consciously or unconsciously from modern science, is radically incoherent. A corollary of this proposition is that modern science is itself radically incoherent, not when it seeks to understand things and subhuman organisms and the cosmos itself, but when it seeks to understand man, not man's physiology or neurology or his bloodstream, but man *qua* man, man when he is peculiarly human. In short, the sciences of man are incoherent.

I hasten to reassure you that I am not here to attack the social sciences in the name of the humanities. It may be true that science teaches nothing about living a life, or as Kierkegaard would say, they, the sciences, have not one word to say about what it is to be born a man or woman, to live, and to die. It may be true, but it doesn't do much good to keep saying it. It may be true, too, that the social sciences are themselves disordered, with each claiming to be primary and to explain all the others, but it is not very interesting to keep saying so.

The second proposition is that the source of the incoherence lies within science itself, as it is presently practiced, and that the solution of the difficulty is not to be found in something extra-scientific, not in the humanities or in religion, but within science itself. When I say science, I mean science in the root sense of the word, as the discovery and knowing of something which can be demonstrated and verified within a community.

What I am raising here is not the standard humanistic objection to science, that it is too impersonal, detached, abstracted, and that accordingly it does not meet human needs, does not take into account such human experience as emotions, art, faith, and so on. Such objections may or may not be justified, but even if they are, they leave the status quo ante unchanged, science as regnant over the entire domain of facts and truth, with religion and suchlike in charge of hopes and feelings and anything else they wish to claim. Perhaps scientists' sovereignty can be disputed, but my purpose here is not to challenge science in the name of humanism. Scientists are used to and understandably unimpressed by such challenges. No, my purpose is rather to challenge science, as it is presently practiced by some scientists, in the name of science.

Surely there is nothing wrong with a humanist, even a novelist, who is getting paid by the National Endowment for the Humanities, taking a look at his colleagues across the fence, scientists getting paid by the National Science Foundation, and saying to them in the friendliest way, "Look, fellows, it's none of my business, but hasn't something gone awry over there that you might want to fix?"

We novelists would surely be grateful if scientists demonstrated that the reason novels are increasingly incoherent these days is because novelists are suffering from a rare encephalitis, and even offered to cure them.

My proposal to scientists is far more modest. That is to say, I am not setting up either as physician or as the small boy noticing the naked Emperor. It is more like whispering to a friend at a party that he'd do well to fix his fly.

For it can be shown, I think, that in certain areas science, as it is presently practiced, fails on its own terms, not in its ruling out traditional humanistic concerns as "unscientific" or "metaphysical" or "nonfactual," but in certain areas fails rather in the confusion and incoherence of its own theories and models. This occurs, I think it can be shown, in the present-day sciences of man.

There is nothing new in what I am proposing. I wish it was my discovery. But it was pointed out a hundred years ago by an

American scientist and philosopher whom most people never heard of and who has been ignored by scientists ever since—until recently.

I wish to present this man's discovery to you, albeit in the briefest terms, which the limitations of time require, not merely to show what light it sheds on the incoherence of science and of our own view of the world, but for its promise of contributing to a new and more coherent anthropology; that is, a theory of man.

The puzzling thing is that the incoherence is both known and unknown, as familiar on the one hand as a member of one's own family, and as little remarked. It is like a long-standing family embarrassment, like Uncle Louie, who, it is true, is a little strange but has been that way so long that it is not so much a case of covering up as having got used to it. We don't talk about Uncle Louie. The understanding is that that is the way things are and nothing can be done about it.

The embarrassment occurs, as I say, when the natural sciences, so spectacularly successful in addressing the rest of the cosmos, address man himself. I am speaking of such sciences as psychology, psychiatry, linguistics, developmental anthropology, sociology.

Something odd happens. It is not merely, as the excuse sometimes runs, that the subject matter, man, is complex and difficult. So is the cosmos complex and difficult. But in the case of the cosmos there is the sense that the areas of ignorance are being steadily eroded by the advance of science. In the case of the sciences of man, however, the incoherence is chronic and seems to be intractable.

Take a familiar example, psychology, Psych 101, the college survey course we all took. Here's what one studies or at least hears about—and I mention only those items most familiar to sophomores: neurones, signals, synapses, transmitter substance, central nervous system, brain, mind, personality, self, consciousness, and later such items as ego, superego, archetypes. We all remember, but what about it?

What is remarkable—to a Martian visitor or a college freshman who doesn't know any better—is that there seem to be two sorts of things, very dissimilar things, named in the list. The words early in the list refer to things and events which can be seen or measured, like neurones, which are cells one can see through a microscope, or signals, which are transmissions of electrical energy, which one can measure, along a nerve fiber. The later words, like "self," "ego," "consciousness," refer to items which cannot be seen as things or measured as energy exchanges. They can only be described by some such words as "mental" or "mind."

Here again, I'm not telling you anything you don't already know, and here again you might ask, so what? For is it not a commonplace and in fact the very nature of the beast that in psychology we deal with "mental" and "physical" entities, with mind and matter? And I will not quarrel with however you wish to define matter, as stuff or things or electrons and protons in motion. And is it not also the nature of science, the assumption that goes without saying, that yes, the gap may be there, but yes, the gap is being closed or is in principle closable?

But is it not also the nature of the beast, something that we all know in our heart of hearts, that no, the gap is not being closed, and, further, that no, the gap is not in principle closable—that is, not by the present regnant principles? How, even in principle, can mind be connected up with matter?

In fact, in speaking of the "mental" and the "physical," of the psyche and the brain, and with however much hope and sophistication we wish to phrase it, are we not admitting that we are still hung up on the horns of the ancient dualism of Descartes, however much we wish to believe we had gotten past it? Descartes, if you recall, divided all reality between the *res cogitans*, the mind, and the *res extensa*, matter. God alone, literally, knew what one had to do with the other.

Could it be true, by the way, what Tocqueville said of Americans years ago: that Americans are natural-born Cartesians without having read a word of Descartes?

But in natural science we do not like to admit that we are still split by a three-hundred-year-old dualism. Nor should it be the case.

Might we not, in fact, reasonably expect that the appropriate scientists, psychologists in this case, can tell us what one has to do with the other, or how to get from one to the other, from "matter" to "mind"? If they are not going full steam ahead on bridging this peculiar gap, they must at least have some inkling.

As a matter of fact, as far as I can tell, they are not and do not. In Psych 101, the problem of the ancient dualism is usually dismissed in a sentence or two—like Reagan dismissing the national debt. Or the solution is not sought but declared found. Here are some samples:

Mind is a property of the organization of neurones, their circuitry and the neurotransmitters between them.

Or: The relation of brain to mind is analogous to that of computer to its software.

Or: Both brain (and its mind) and computer are information processors.

Or: The only difference between us and the Apple computer is complexity.

But here's the best statement I've come across of such awkward things as mind and consciousness. It is from a textbook, *Physiology of Behavior* by Neil R. Carlson. "What can a physiological psychologist say about human self-awareness? We know that it is altered by changes in the structure or chemistry of the brain. We conclude that consciousness is a physiological function, just like behavior."

These statements are something less useful than truisms. To say that mind is a property or function of the organization of the brain is like saying that Raphael's *Orléans Madonna* is a property of paint and color.

These uneasy little sentences can be read in two ways. Either they are saying this: Everybody knows that Cartesian dualism is insurmountable, so the best we can do is a quick semantic fix of the mind/body problem by writing a "brain" sentence and a "mind" sentence, like hopping back and forth through Alice's looking-glass. Or we can treat it as a pseudo-problem, a matter of bad semantics, ignore it, and go about our business.

I refer to this gap in scientific knowledge as an incoherence, from the Latin *in-cohaerere*, a not-sticking-together. By this word I mean that we are not talking about an ordinary area of ignorance which is being steadily eroded by advancing knowledge—like the tremendous advances in cosmology or in the physics of subatomic particles. No, this gap is incoherent and intractable, at least from the present posture of natural science. That is to say, no amount of effort by "brain" scientists and "mind" scientists can even narrow the gap. It is not like tunneling under a river from both sides and meeting in the middle. It is more like ships passing in the night.

Can anyone imagine how a psychology of the psyche, like Freud's or Jung's, however advanced, can ever make contact with a Skinnerian psychology of neurones, however modified and elaborated it is, for example, by some such refinement as Gestalt and "cognitive" psychology?

There are similar incoherences in other sciences of man. Sociology and cultural anthropology have to do with groups and cultures, with people; this is to say, human organisms. But sociology deals with such things as self, roles; anthropology with such things as sorcery, rites. But how do you get from organism to roles and rites?

Linguistics is about the sounds people make. Many organisms make sounds to attract attention in courtship, to scare off predators, to signal to other creatures the finding of food, to call their young, and so on. So do human organisms. But they, human organisms, also make sounds which form sentences which tell the truth about things, lie, or don't make any sense at all. How did this come to pass?

I can draw you a picture of an organism responding to a stimulus. Can you draw me a picture of an organism asserting a sentence?

Even the great scientist Darwin, who connected up everything else, had trouble when he came to this peculiar activity.

Here's how Darwin went about it. The mental act, Darwin claimed, is essentially of the same nature in an animal as it is in man. How does he know this? He writes: "When I say to my terrier, in an eager voice (and I have made the trial many times), 'Hi, hi, where is it?' she at once takes it as a sign that something is to be hunted, and generally first looks quickly all around, and then rushes into the nearest thicket, to scent for any game, but finding nothing, she looks up into any neighboring tree for a squirrel. Now do these actions not clearly show that she had in her mind a general idea or concept that some animal is to be discovered and hunted?"

This is a charming account, and it is not necessary to comment on it except to note that later scientists would probably smile and shrug, but some of them might add: "Well, maybe not dogs, but what about dolphins or chimps?"

Both Darwin and Freud were great men, maestros of the organism and the psyche, made huge contributions, but nowadays no one would claim that either had bridged the gap. Darwin addressed himself to one side of it in his study of the origin of species through the struggle of spontaneous variations. Freud treated a very different though hardly less savage struggle, the warfare between the id and superego. Darwin and Freud were true revolutionaries and were accordingly accused by their enemies of being too radical. When in truth, as it now appears, they were not radical enough. For neither can account for his own activity by his own theory. For how does Darwin account for the "variation" which is his own species and its peculiar behavior—in his case, sitting in his study in Kent and writing the truth as he saw it about evolution? And if Freud's psyche is like ours, a dynamism of contending forces, how did it ever arrive at the truth about psyches, including his own?

Freud, in fact, did exempt himself and his truth-telling from the sexual dynamics of other human psyches.

Perhaps the oddest thing about these incoherences is that we do not find them odd. We do not find it odd to jump from the *natural* science of the biology of creatures to a *formal* science of the utterances of this particular creature without knowing how we got there. We do not find it odd that there is only one science of chemistry and neurology but at last count more than six hundred different schools of psychotherapy, and growing. We accept the explanation that, after all, the mind is vastly more complicated than a molecule of sodium chloride or even a nerve cell. That may be true, but it doesn't explain why the physical sciences are converging whereas the psychic "sciences" are diverging; that is, getting nuttier.

In what follows, I wish to call your attention to the work of an American scientist who, I believe, laid the groundwork for a coherent science of man, and did so a hundred years ago. Most people never heard of him. But they will.

II

The man I speak of is Charles Sanders Peirce, scientist, logician (he gave us symbolic logic), philosopher, and founding father of semiotics, the science of signs, a discipline in high fashion these days. He was a difficult, eccentric man. One of his peculiar accomplishments was that he could write down a question which was bothering him with one hand and with the other simultaneously write the answer.

Although I speak here of Charles Peirce's "discovery," it was not altogether original with him, stemming as it did from the realism of the medieval Scholastics. By realism he meant that there is a real world and that it is possible in a degree to know it and to talk about it and be understood. Not only are material things and events real. So are the ideas and words by which we think and talk about them. As Peirce put it, "there are Real things out there whose characters are independent of our opinion of them." Although this may seem a commonplace to us, just ordinary common sense, this connection between things and words and knowledge has been under attack for three hundred years—by Descartes, who split off mind from matter, and by the English nominalists, who even now split off words and ideas from things. One made knowledge unexplainable. The other made it impossible. And this is to say nothing of the European materialism and idealism of Peirce's time, the first of which set out to explain everything by the doctrine of matter in motion, the other by various immersions in Kantian subjectivity, such as Hegelian idealism. One put everything in one box, the box of things, the other in the mind box, with no accounting of how to get from one to the other.

Fortunately, modern scientists have taken none of these still regnant philosophies seriously—whether nominalism, materialism, or idealism. If they had, there would have been no Newton or Einstein or Darwin. For if the world is not real, or if it cannot be known, why bother with science?

Despite bad philosophies, science—the physical and biological sciences—has advanced spectacularly. Yet, as we have seen, they, the scientists, are still trapped in the ancient dualism and still can't explain what the mind box has to do with the thing box—much to the detriment and confusion of the social sciences.

The great contribution of Charles Peirce was that he was a rigorous scientific realist and that he preserved the truth, as he saw it, of philosophical realism from Aristotle to the seventeenth century, salvaged it from the medieval language of the Scholastics, which is now all but incomprehensible to us, and recast it in terms familiar to scientists, to the most simpleminded empiricist, and even to us laymen. It, Peirce's realism, cannot now be escaped or fobbed off as Scholastic mumbo jumbo.

Peirce saw that the one way to get at it, the great modern rift between mind and matter, was the only place where they intersect, language. Language is both words and meanings. It is impossible to imagine language without both.

In a word, he said, and unlike the abstruse propositions of the Scholastics—like Being is Essence and Existence—it is as easily demonstrated as two plus two equals four; he said that there are two kinds of natural events in the world. These two kinds of events have different parameters and variables. Trying to pretend there is only one kind of event leads to all the present misery which afflicts the social sciences. And even more important, at least for us laymen, it brings a certain cast of mind, "scientism," which misplaces reality and creates vast mischief and confusion when we try to understand ourselves.

Peirce said: "There is not one but two kinds of natural events in the world." One he called dyadic, the other triadic. Dyadic events are the familiar subject matter of the physical and biological sciences: A interacting with B; A, B, C, D interacting with each other. Peirce called it a "mutual action between two things." It can apply to molecules interacting with other molecules, a billiard ball hitting another billiard ball, one galaxy colliding with another galaxy, an organism responding to a stimulus. Even an event as complex as Pavlov's conditioned dog salivating at the sound of a bell can be understood as a "complexus of dyads"—the sound waves from the bell, the stimulation of the dog's auditory receptors, the electrical impulses in the efferent nerves, the firing of the altered synapses in the brain, the electrical impulses in the efferent nerves to the salivary glands, and so on—the whole understandable as a sequence of dyadic events. The entire event, complex as it is, can be represented quite adequately by a simple drawing which shows structures (dog, neurones, axones, glandular cells) and arrows connecting them (energy exchanges, sound waves, electrical impulses). Such is the dyadic model.

Such events, indeed, are the familiar subject matter of the natural sciences, from physics and chemistry to biology and to Psych 101.

But there is another kind of event, quite as real, quite as natural a phenomenon, quite as observable, which cannot be so understood; that is, cannot be construed by the dyadic model. It is language. The simplest example I can think of—and it is anything but simple—is the child's early acquisition of language, an eighteen-month-old suddenly learning that things have names. What happens here is the same sort of thing that happens when a lecturer utters a complex sentence about the poetics of T. S. Eliot.

What happens when the child suddenly grasps that the strange little sound "cat," an explosion of air between tongue and palate followed by a bleat of the larynx followed by a stop of tongue against teeth, *means* this cat, not only this cat but all cats? And means it in a very special way: does not mean: look over there for cat, watch out for cat, want cat, go get cat—but: That is a cat. Naming is a new event. And, of course, soon after this naming "sentence" appear other primitive sentences: *There cat. Cat all gone. Where cat?*

As Peirce put it, this event cannot be explained by a dyadic model, however complex. Words like "cat" he called symbols, from the Greek *symballein*, to throw together, because the child puts the two together, the word and the thing. A triadic model is required. For even though many of the familiar dyadic events are implicated, the heart of the matter is a throwing together, one entity throwing together two others; in this case, *cat* the creature and *cat* the sound image.

This event is a piece of behavior, true enough, but any behavioristic reading of it as a sequence of dyads will miss the essence of it.

He, Peirce, was particularly interested in using the dyadic-triadic distinction to understand communication by a discipline which he called semiotics, the science of signs. He distinguished between an index and a symbol. A low barometer is, for a human, a sign, an index, of rain. The word "ball" is, for my dog, an index to go fetch the ball. But if I say the word "ball" to you, you will receive it as a symbol; that is, look at me with puzzlement and the suspicion that sure enough he's gone over the hill, and perhaps say, "Ball? What about it?" The difference between the two, variously and confusedly called index and symbol, sign and symbol, signal and sign, was perhaps most dramatically illustrated by Helen Keller's famous account: her first understanding of words spelled in her hand, like "cup," "door," "water," to mean go fetch cup, open door, I want water. Then the memorable moment in the pump house when it dawned on her that the word "water" spelled in one hand *meant* the water running over the other. It was nothing less than the beginning of her life as a person.

The triadic event, as Peirce would say, always involves meaning, and meaning of a special sort. The copula "is," spoken or implied, is nothing less than the tiny triadic lever that moves the entire world into the reach of our peculiar species.

This strange capacity seems to be unique in Homo sapiens. And even though there is nothing unscientific about assigning a "species-specific" trait to this or that species, if the evidence warrants, many scientists, including Darwin, find this uniqueness offensive. We are all familiar with the heroic attempts in recent years by psychologists and primatologists to teach language to primates other than Homo sapiens, particularly chimpanzees, using ASL, the sign language of the deaf, the premise being that the only reason chimps don't speak is that their vocal apparatus does not permit speech. The most famous chimp was Washoe, whom the Gardners claimed to have taught language; that is, the ability not only to understand and "utter" "words," the common nouns of language, but to form these words into sentences. But we are also familiar with the discrediting of these claims, mainly due to the work of Herbert Terrace. Terrace adopted a chimp, which he named Nim Chimsky, with every expectation of teaching Nim language as one would a human infant. What he learned was that Nim, though undoubtedly as smart as Washoe, was not really using language. What Nim and Washoe were really doing was responding to small cues by the trainer to do this or that, the appropriate behavior rewarded by a banana or whatever. The trainers were, doubtlessly, not acting in bad faith. What Washoe and Nim Chimsky were exhibiting, however, was not the language behavior of the human two-year-old but the classical reinforced response of the behaviorists. As Peirce would say, both Washoe's and Nim's "language" can be understood as a "complexus of dyads."

One can draw a picture with things (matter) and arrows (energy) connecting them, setting forth the behavior both of the chimp Washoe and the pre-language human infant with its responses to sights and sounds, its crying for mama and milk. But one cannot draw such a picture of an eighteen-month-old human who looks at mama, points to cat, and says "Da cat."

One would suppose that the appropriate scientist, the developmental psychologist, the psycholinguist, whoever, would zero in on this, the transformation of the responding organism into the languaged human. For it is undoubtedly the most extraordinary natural phenomenon in all of biological behavior, if not in the entire cosmos, and yet the most commonplace of events, one that occurs every day under our noses.

Unfortunately, such is not the case. What one finds in the scientific literature is something like this: a huge amount of information about the infant as organism, its needs and drives, its behavior and physiology. But when it begins to speak, what? What is thought to happen? What one finds are very careful studies of the *structure* of the earliest utterances and their development, the rules by which an eighteen-month-old will say "That a my coat," but not "A that my coat." *Rules, grammar, linguistic structure* are what we find, the same formal approach which issues later in the splendid disciplines of structural linguistics and even in "deconstructionism."

We go from biology (dyadic science) to grammar (triadic science) without anybody seeming to notice anything strange. Such *belle indifférence* can only have come to pass either because the scientist has not noticed that he has jumped the chasm or because he has noticed but is at a loss for words.

In sum, the scientists of man have little or nothing to say about jumping from the science of neurology, as Freud did, to a science of the psyche, whether Freudian and Jungian or what; or jumping from the natural science of biology to the formal science of grammar and structure.

Neither we nor the scientists seem to notice anything remarkable about this leap. Suffice it to say that such behavior in any other human would be regarded as strange, if not schizoid. It is as if we lived in a California house straddling the San Andreas Fault, a crack very narrow but deep, which has, however, become as familiar as an old shoe. After all, you can get used to anything. We can hop back and forth, feed ourselves and the dyadic dog on one side, or sit on the other, read Joseph Campbell or write a triadic paper, and never give it a second thought. Once in a while we might look down into the chasm, become alarmed, and take up a New Age religion like Gaia.

On one side are the dyadic sciences from atomic physics to academic psychology with its behaviorism and the various refinements and elaborations thereof. And on the other are the "mental" psychologies with such entities as consciousness, the unconscious, dreams, egos, ids, archetypes, and such.

I trust, incidentally, that when I speak of dyadic phenomena as descriptive of "matter" in motion, it will be understood that I am using the word "matter" to mean whatever you please—as long as it is also understood that such phenomena, at least at the biological level, are not challenged by so-called chaos science or the indeterminancy of particle physics, however vagarious and mystical the behavior of some particles and however chaotic some turbulences. Which is to say: Even though it has been tried, it is surely a silly business to extrapolate from the indeterminacy of subatomic particles to such things as the freedom of the will. At the statistical level, large numbers of atoms behave lawfully. Boyle's Law still obtains. If the will is free, it is no thanks to Heisenberg. As for chaos theory, it has been well described, not as a repudiation of Newtonian determinism, but as its enrichment.

Accordingly, like Charles Peirce, I insist on the qualitative and irreducible difference between dyadic and triadic phenomena. It is easily demonstrated. Take sociology, which concerns itself with the group behavior of human organisms. Now, we have a familiar scientific model for a dyadic science like the physiology of organisms. Though the phenomena may be very complex, I can draw you a picture of what is going on when there are transactions across a cell membrane. All I have to do is draw a line for the membrane and arrows going across it both ways. But sociologists are very fond of talking about such things as role-taking. Can you draw me a picture of role-taking? Who, what, takes the role? The human organism? How does an organism take a role? By becoming a person? How does an organism get to be a person?

Strangely enough, or perhaps not so strangely, a "mental" discipline like Freudian psychology lends itself very well to the Peircean dyadic model once one accepts the immateriality of the entities. One can very easily make a diagram showing things like ego, super ego, the unconscious, and using arrows to represent drives, repression, sublimation, and such—even though one recognizes that the whole drama takes place on the far side of the chasm from such "real" things as organisms, neurones, stimuli, responses. Valuable though Freudian psychology might be, it must nevertheless be understood as a transposition of dyadic theory to the realm of mental entities, with no account of how it got there.

But if scientists, both "physical" scientists and "mental" scientists, can operate comfortably on both sides of the Cartesian split, what happens when the serious scientist is obliged to look straight down at the dysjunction? That is to say, what is one to make of language, that apparently unique property of man, considered not as a formal structure but as a natural phenomenon? Where did it come from? What to make of it in anatomical, physiological, and evolutionary terms? The chasm must make one dizzy. Not many psychologists or neuro-anatomists want to look down. Norman Gesschwind is one who has. He points out that there are recently evolved structures in the human brain which have to do with speech and understanding speech, such as the inferior parietal lobule which receives information from the "primary sensory projection systems"; that is, the cerebral cortex which registers seeing and feeling water and hearing the word "water." These are described as "association areas." But Charles Peirce would call such associations dyadic events, as he would "information processing systems" like a computer. A computer, in fact, is the perfect dyadic machine.

What do biologists and anthropologists make of the emergence of language in the evolutionary scheme? The advantages of language in the process of natural selection are obvious. Julian Jaynes would go further and say that "the language of men was involved with only one hemisphere in order to leave the other free for the language of gods." Maybe, but setting aside for the moment "the language of gods," what goes on with the language of men? Jaynes doesn't say.

This is what Richard Leakey, the anthropologist, says, describing what happens in a human (not a chimp) when a human uses a word as a symbol, in naming or in a sentence: "Speech is controlled by a certain structure of the brain, located in the outer cerebral cortex. Wernicke's area of the brain pulls out appropriate words from the brain's filing system. The angular gyrus . . . selects the appropriate word."

Pulls out? Selects? These are transitive verbs with subjects and objects. The words are the objects. What is the subject? Draw me a picture of Wernicke's area pulling out a word or the angular gyrus selecting a word. Is there any way to understand this, other than supposing a tiny little person, a homunculus, doing the pulling and selecting?

Then, there is what is called the speech-act theory of Austin, Searle, and others, promising because it is the actual utterances of sentences which are studied. Thus, Austin distinguishes between sentences which say something and sentences which do something. The sentence "I married her" is one kind of speech act, an assertion about an event. "I do" uttered during the marriage is another kind, part of the performance of the ceremony itself. The classes of speech-act behavior have multiplied amid ongoing debate. But once again the Emperor's little boy becomes curious. "Speech-acts?" he asks. "What do you mean by acts? You never use the word 'acts' in describing the behavior of other creatures." An act entails an actor, an agent which initiates the act. Draw me a picture of a speech-act. Where, what, is the actor?

Such are a few of the manifold discomforts of the natural scientist who finds himself astride the Cartesian chasm, one foot planted in dyadic territory, the other in triadic. What happens is, he very quickly chooses one side or the other.

But how does Charles Sanders Peirce help us here? Are we any better off with Peirce's thirdness, his triadic theory, than we were with Descartes's *res cogitans* and *res extensa*?

Let me first say that I do not have the competence to speculate on the brain structures which may be implicated in triadic behavior. Nor would I wish to if I had the competence. Such a project is too uncomfortably close to Descartes's search for the seat of the soul, which I believe he located in the pineal gland.

No, what is important to note about the triadic event is that it is there for all to see, that in fact it occurs hundreds of times daily—whenever we talk or listen to somebody talking—that its elements are open to inspection to everyone, including natural scientists, and that it cannot be reduced to a complexus of dyadic events. The chattering of an entire population of rhesus monkeys is so reducible. But the single utterance of a two-year-old child who points and says "that a flower" cannot be so understood— even though millions of dyadic events also occur: light waves, excitation of nerve endings, electrical impulses in neurones, muscle contractions, and so on.

So what? one well might ask. Which is to say: Admitting that there is such a thing as an irreducible triadic event in language behavior, are there any considerable consequences for our anthropology in the strict sense of the word, the view of man that comes as second nature to the educated denizen of modern society?

There are indeed, and they, the consequences, are startling indeed.

For once one concedes the reality of the triadic event, one is brought face to face with the nature of its elements. A child points to a flower and says "flower." One element of the event is the flower as perceived by sight and registered by the brain: blue, five-petaled, of a certain shape; and the spoken word "flower," a Gestalt of a peculiar little sequence of sounds of larynx vibrations, escape of air between lips and teeth, and so on. But what is the entity at the apex of the triangle, that which links the other two? Peirce, a difficult, often obscure writer, called it by various names, interpretant, interpreter, judge. I have used the term "coupler" as a minimal designation of that which couples name and thing, subject and predicate, links them by the relation which we mean by the peculiar little word "is." It, the linking entity, was also called by Peirce "mind" and even "soul."

Here is the embarrassment, and it cannot be gotten round, so it might as well be said right out: *By whatever name one chooses to call it—interpretant, interpreter, coupler, whatever—it, the third element, is not material.*

It is as real as a cabbage or a king or a neurone, but it is not material. No material structure of neurones, however complex, and however intimately it may be related to the triadic event, can itself assert anything. If you think it can, please draw me a picture of an assertion.

A material substance cannot name or assert a proposition.

The initiator of a speech act is an act-or, that is, an agent. The agent is not material.

Peirce's insistence on both the reality and the nonmateriality of the third element—whatever one chooses to call it, interpretant, mind, coupler—is of critical importance to natural science because its claim to reality is grounded not on this or that theology or metaphysic but on empirical observation and the necessities of scientific logic.

Compare the rigor and clarity of Peirce's semiotic approach to the ancient mind/body problem to current conventional thinking about such matters. We know the sort of answer the psychologist or neurologist gives when we ask him what the mind is: that it is a property of brain circuitry and so on.

We now know, at least an increasing number of people are beginning to know, that a different sort of reality lies at the heart of all uniquely human activity—speaking, listening, understanding, thinking, looking at a work of art—namely, Charles Peirce's triadicity. It cannot be gotten round and must sooner or later be confronted by natural science, for it is indeed a natural phenomenon. Indeed, it may well turn out that consciousness itself is not a "thing," an entity, but an act, the triadic act by which we recognize reality through its symbolic vehicle.

In any case, it will be a matter of interest, if not of amusement, to see how scientists of the future, with their strong empiricist and materialistic traditions, come to grips with this nonmaterial, nonmeasurable entity. For sooner or later it must be confronted. There is no alternative if we wish to progress beyond the present incoherence of the social sciences and if we believe that man's unique behavior of language and symbol-mongering falls within the purview of natural science, which clearly it does. In any case, Peirce's little triad cannot be ignored as such traditional notions as "mind," "soul," "ideas" have been ignored.

III

But, and finally, what are the consequences of Charles Peirce's discovery that precisely that which is distinctive in human behavior, language, art, thought itself, is not accounted for, is not accounted for by the standard scientific paradigm which has been sovereign for three hundred years, that indeed, science as we know it cannot utter a single word about what it is to be born a human individual, to live, and to die?

There is one consequence which is good news indeed for us humanists. It is quite simply that these "sentences" of art, poetry, and the novel ought to be taken very seriously indeed since these are the cognitive, scientific, if you will, statements that we have about what it is to be human. The humanities, in a word, are not the minstrels of the age whose only role is to promise R&R to tired technicians and consumers after work. Rather are the humanities the elder brother of the sciences, who sees how the new scientist got his tail in a crack when he takes on the human subject as object and who even shows him the shape of a new science.

What to say about him, then, this strange new creature who *symballeins*, throws words and names together to form sentences?

To begin with, what to call it, this entity which *symballeins*, throws together word and thing? As we have seen, Peirce used a number of words: interpreter, interpretant, asserter, mind, "I," ego, even soul. They may or may not be semantically accurate, but for the educated denizen of this age they suffer certain semantic impairments. "Interpretant" is too ambiguous, even for Peirce scholars. "Soul" carries too much furniture from the religious attic. "Ego" has a different malodor, smelling as it does of the old Cartesian split.

Then don't name it, for the present, but talk about it, like

Lowell Thomas coming upon a strange creature in his travels, in this case a sure-enough beast in the jungle.

There are certain minimal things one can say about it, this coupler, this apex of Peirce's triangle. For one thing, it is *there*. It is located in time and space, but not as an organism. It has a different set of parameters and variables. For another, it is peculiarly and intimately involved with others of its kind, so that, unlike the solitary biological organism, it is impossible to imagine it functioning without the other, another. All solitary organisms have instinctive responses. But Helen Keller had to receive the symbol "water" from Miss Sullivan before she became *aware* of the water. Peirce's triad is social by its very nature. As he put it, "every assertion requires a speaker and a listener." The triadic creature is nothing if not social. Indeed, he can be understood as a construct of his relations with others.

Here's another trait. It, this strange new creature, not only has an environment, as do all creatures. It has a *world*. Its world is the totality of that which is named. This is different from its environment. An environment has gaps. There are no gaps in a world. Nectar is part of the environment of a bee. Cabbages and kings and Buicks are not. There are no gaps in the world of this new creature, because the gaps are called that, *gaps*, or *the unknown*, or *out there*, or *don't know*.

For this creature, moreover, words, symbols, and the things symbolized are subject to *norms*, something new in the world. They can be fresh and grow stale. Words can tell the truth or lie. Lying is something new in the cosmos.

There is time now to do no more than call attention to the intriguing and, I think, quite felicitous way in which the properties of this strange triadic creature as arrived at by a scientist and logician one hundred years ago flow directly into the rather spectacular portrait of man by some well-known twentieth-century philosophers who came at the same subject, Homo symbolificus, from the wholly different direction of European phenomenology. Such may be the shape of the science of man to come.

I will mention only a couple.

There is Heidegger, who uses the word "*Dasein*" to describe him, the human creature, a being there. The *Dasein*, moreover, inhabits not only an *Umwelt*, an environment, but a *Welt*, a world.

Most important, this *Dasein*, unlike an organism, exists on a normative axis. It can live "authentically" or "unauthentically." It is capable of *Verstehen*, true understanding, and *Rede*, authentic speech, which can deteriorate into *Neugier*, idle curiosity, and *Gerede*, gossip.

Gabriel Marcel and Martin Buber speak of the human being as radically dependent upon others, as an "I-thou" which can deteriorate into an "I-it." Marcel describes the being of a human as a being-in-a-situation. Sartre is less optimistic. His human being is *le pour-soi*, the solitary consciousness existing in a dead world of things, *l'en-soi*. As for the other, Marcel's person, Buber's thou, Peirce's listener, Sartre says only, "*L'enfer, c'est les autres*." Hell is other people. Finally, the *Dasein*, which has undergone a "fall," a *Verfallen* into an unauthentic existence, can recover itself, live authentically, become a seeker and wayfarer, what Marcel calls Homo viator.

The modern psychologist and social scientist cannot, of course, make head or tail of such existentialist traits as "a falling into unauthenticity" or a sentence like this of Marcel's: "It may be of my essence to be able to be not what I am." He, the scientist, generally regards such notions as fanciful or novelistic or "existentialist." But perhaps he, the scientist, lacks an appropriate scientific model. At any rate, it is possible that he, the modern scientist of man, will be obliged to take account of these fanciful notions, not by the existentialists, but by their old hardheaded compatriot, Charles Peirce.

Here is a prophecy. All humanists, even novelists, are entitled to make prophecies. Here is the prophecy: The behavioral scientist of the future will be able to make sense of the following sort of sentence which presently makes no sense to him whatever: *There is a difference between the being-in-the-world of the scientist and the being-in-the-world of the layman.*

And lastly, with this new anthropology in hand, Peirce's triadic creature with its named world, Heidegger's *Dasein* suffering a

Verfallen, a fall, Gabriel Marcel's Homo viator, man as pilgrim, one might even explore its openness to such traditional Judeo-Christian notions as man falling prey to the worldliness of the world, and man as pilgrim seeking his salvation.

But that's a different story.

Three

MORALITY AND

RELIGION

CULTURE,
THE CHURCH, AND
EVANGELIZATION

❦

When one considers U.S. culture from the perspective of evangelization, certain impediments, as well as opportunities, come immediately to mind. The impediments are more or less obvious and might indeed be attributed to most if not all modern Western industrialized societies. The impediments are worth mentioning because, paradoxically, it is in their very presence and practice, in their very negativity, that there is to be found certain unique opportunities for evangelization in a modern culture. But, first, allow me to state a few obvious things about U.S. culture. It is necessary to do so because, having stated the obvious, I should like to draw your attention to another feature of American culture which, though not unknown, has certain far-reaching and less obvious consequences.

The obvious features of this culture are, of course, its size and diversity, its tremendous ethnic variegations, its almost boundless religious pluralism. These are a commonplace, true enough, but a commonplace in which we take considerable pride. Yet in the very face of these manifold diversities there is at work a force, extraordinarily powerful but not necessarily beneficent, which makes for a uniformity of sorts. I am speaking, of course, of the mass media, television in particular. Americans, I have read, watch five or six hours of television a day—their children even more—

and by and large the same television. There are at present only four major networks.

Who can calculate the effect of such an extraordinary influence? To my knowledge, no one, no social psychologist, no information theorist, has the slightest notion of the impact upon the human psyche of such a massive input of images and words. We used to read about the cultural revolution wrought by the invention of printing. And revolution it was. But if books, written and read by a few educated people, turned the world upside down, how to calculate the effect of watching images on a small screen six hours a day, day after day, year after year, on the human mind, especially the mind of a growing child? One is familiar with certain obvious and superficial answers: that television does influence the consumer's behavior in the marketplace, makes some people drink more Coca-Cola, fly TWA, vote Democratic or Republican, and so on. But such answers hardly address what is surely the radical effect on the psyche itself of daily time spent on media and messages approximating the hours devoted to working and sleeping. Surely, there has not occurred in all of man's history an event of greater moment both for good and for ill, an event whose import is only barely beginning to be understood.

But we were speaking of the impediments and opportunities in the evangelization of a modern culture for which television has great potentiality as impediment and opportunity. The impediments? They are familiar enough, have been cited by any number of social critics. They include such social pathologies as the breakdown of the family unit, the increase in drug abuse and teenage pregnancies, the alarming rise in the incidence of depression and suicide among the young, and—what is almost a commonplace—an all-pervasive consumerism.

And one might add, at least from the Christian perspective, the ever-increasing secularization of society, especially of large segments of the more educated members of society. In this matter of secularization, I would insist on a distinction, a distinction which is surely all-important from the point of view of the evangelization of a culture. It is a distinction which must be kept in mind in the use of such terms as "secularization" and "scientific humanism."

The distinction which must be kept in mind is that between science and what can only be called "scientism." It is one thing, in other words, to speak of the magnificent achievements of natural science and the technology derived therefrom—science, with which, it goes without saying, the Church not only has no quarrel but which it must surely applaud—because the Church is ever on the side of truth and the search for truth, and also because of the obvious benefits conferred on man by science and technology in such areas as the treatment of disease and the improvement of the material standards of life.

Scientism is something else altogether. It needs to be mentioned in this context because it can be considered only as an ideology, a kind of quasi-religion—not as a valid method of investigation and theorizing which comprises science proper—a cast of mind all the more pervasive for not being recognized as such and, accordingly, one of the most potent forces which inform, almost automatically and unconsciously, the minds of most denizens of modern industrial societies like the United States.

Science, natural science, let us agree, is primarily a method, a method of arriving at truths of a certain order about natural phenomena. Neither it nor its practitioners ever claimed anything more for it. Scientism, however, is a certain cast of mind characteristic of laymen and consumers of popular science and scientific technology, laymen who may be educated but who are at a remove from the method and practice of science. Scientism is characterized less by the practice of a method of discovery and knowing than by what can only be called a surrender of sovereignty and a willingness to believe almost as a matter of course that the scientific method by virtue of its spectacular triumphs and the near magic of its technology can be extrapolated to a quasi-religious all-construing worldview.

To state the matter plainly: To the layman, the ordinary denizen of a modern technological society, it seems only natural that, in the face of the mysteries of life which confront him, the mysteries of nature, his own health, indeed of his very self and his existence, and the secret of his being—nothing seems more natural to him than that *they* know the answers. *They*, of course, are the scientists, the experts, the professors, the technologists of whatever field. And *their* fields of expertise are taken to include one's very self.

The impediments, then, to the evangelization of a modern secular society seem clear enough. They comprise mainly the secularization of the educated class and the loss of sovereignty by the layman to those whom he perceives an entire assemblage of experts privy to knowledge of every sector of reality—including himself.

The ongoing secularization of the universities—not necessarily a bad thing—often falls prey to a scientism, a misreading of and extrapolation from the scientific method, of a very different sort. It is of the order of what the philosopher Alfred North Whitehead once called the "misplacement of reality." Which is to say that, as a consequence mainly of the dazzling credentials of scientific theory, there is a temptation to assign a greater significance, even a "higher" reality, to statements of general theory rather than the statements of the particular events from which the theory was drawn. Thus, a sentence reporting an anomaly in an orbit of Mercury is quite naturally assigned to a "lower" order of significance than is Einstein's Special Theory, of which it is, let us say, an instance.

It is hardly surprising, then, that the evangel, the Gospel report of a single historical event—even though this event may be read by Christians as the single most important occurrence, the very watershed, of all history—should be seen by a certain set of the academic mind as exemplary; that is, as an instance of such-and-such recurring human proclivity for attributing divine manifestations to particular historical events.

It is indeed difficult to imagine a less hospitable environment for the Christian evangel than this very set of the academic mind, whether scientific, literary, or historical, to whom it comes as second nature, and no doubt with good cause, to see all singulars, whether the appearances of Halley's comet, or this novel or that play, or such-and-such a political revolution, as exemplary—that is, as examples of this cyclical movement of history or that expression of certain cultural influences which comprised the

Elizabethan literary renascence—or as an excellent demonstration of Newton's classical gravitational theory.

Thus, while it is all very well to speak of the Gospel, of Jesus Christ, and of the Church as a sign and a contradiction, a scandal and a stumbling block to the wise—and no doubt it is that—there is no need to make matters worse by countenancing a bad epistemology; that is, a theory of sentences which awards degrees of significance and value in direct proportion to the level of abstraction.

The opportunities for evangelization arise, paradoxically enough, from those very cultural traits which seem to oppose the evangel—the secularism, if you will, of modern societies, especially American—the consumerism, the scientism, the so-called secular humanism. No, not precisely from the secularization itself, but from its having run its course, from its exhaustion. To paraphrase David Riesman and José Ortega y Gasset, there is no lonelier crowd than the mass man, the anonymous consumer who has exhausted the roster of "need-satisfactions," as the expression goes, whether the latter be the consumption of the manifold goods of a sophisticated consumer society or the services of the four hundred or so different schools of psychotherapy.

But there is this to be said for "secular humanism"—it is not neutral.

Blow hot or blow cold, as the Gospel puts it, because we know what happens to those who blow lukewarm. In the present context, this injunction might, I think, be translated into the following cultural terms: Given two societies—one which is nominally and perhaps superficially Christian, say that of Victorian England or nineteenth-century Austria; another, a thoroughly secularized United States in the year 2000, when, let us suppose, the gurus of the psyche and the hucksters of the marketplace have had it their way, the Bible and prayers eliminated from all schools and universities, the Church ignored in the media save for an occasional rerun of a sentimental priest-movie like Bing Crosby's *Going My Way*—given these two cultures, I should judge that the latter, not the former, would be the more receptive to a serious Catholic evangelization and renewal.

It goes without saying, of course, that certain elementary human rights and political freedoms must be presupposed. The spiritual ground in the Soviet Union may be fertile indeed for evangelization, but not as long as the wall is still up, the air waves jammed, the presses closed, the gates locked. The news, after all, requires a news-bearer.

The openness of a modern society to evangelization and the omnipresence of television as the dominant medium raise both interesting possibilities and some cautionary questions in the matter of the relationship of the Church and culture. Clearly, if the average American and, for all I know, the average European watches six hours of television daily, what better medium can be imagined for the Church than television, which can transmit not only the words of the evangel but the entire panoply of the liturgy of the Church in all the splendor of its imagery, music, and rites?

Yet certain reservations come immediately to mind—and I am not speaking of the obvious unacceptability of viewing Mass on television as a substitute for assisting at Mass. I speak rather of certain special circumstances which obtain in the present-day culture of the media, at least in the United States, and especially in radio and television. Indeed, it is not too much to say that television and radio as religious media have been all but appropriated by a certain sort of preacher—not, by and large, ministers of the mainline Protestant churches, but rather various individuals, "TV personalities," who put themselves forward as evangelists, preachers of the Gospel, ministers of the Holy Spirit, and so on. Some dozen or so of these TV evangelists have achieved a species of stardom, acquired a great many followers, and have enjoyed great success in combining both a fundamentalist evangelical message and an appeal for money.

Some of these media evangelists have, unfortunately, been overtaken by public scandal of one sort and another. And though others are undoubtedly persons of good character, the general tone of the "religious program" has come to be perceived as comprising elements of showmanship, emotionalism, fundamentalism, and commercialism in such degree as to render them suspect to many, no doubt most, educated people.

I mention this well-known state of affairs only to raise an

intriguing question, the question, in a word, of the place of the Catholic Church in a society which seems to be increasingly polarized between a more or less educated class, certainly numbered in the millions, who are more or less informed by secular and scientistic values, and a clearly less educated class, at least as large, who might well express themselves as opposed not only to what they perceive as "atheistic science" and the "godless universities" but also, and quite as strongly, to the "rites and superstitions" of older Christian churches, and most specifically the Catholic Church.

Given the fact that the Catholic Church is the largest single religious body in the United States, some forty or fifty million communicants, and given the fact that it is now thoroughly "Americanized" (if that is the word)—that is to say, that it is no longer the immigrant Church of years ago, a composite, that is, of ethnic minorities—it is surely a matter of no little concern to identify the role of the Church in the rather singular mix which comprises U.S. culture today. To put it bluntly, what is the role of the Church in a society increasingly polarized, as described above, by the powerful forces of secularism, scientism, and consumerism, on the one hand, and, on the other, the gathering reaction to the fundamentalist sects so prominent in the media? More specifically, given the Church's love of and respect for the truth, including the truths of natural science, how does it proceed in such a society to discharge its commission from the Lord to carry the good news of the Gospel to the ends of the earth? In a word, to evangelize the pluralistic culture in which it finds itself? Surely the Church does not discharge this commission by adopting a fortress mentality, as it did earlier, and no doubt understandably, what with the dominant and hostile Protestant culture in which it found itself, and, as it might be tempted to do now, to erect barricades against what well might be perceived as an increasingly disordered if not pagan society.

To return to the impediments and the opportunities: the latter were never greater. It is, paradoxically, the very all-pervasiveness of the secularist-scientist ethic which creates its own opportunity. As Kierkegaard said of the science of his day, mostly Hegelianism, and given the impulse to extrapolate from a method of investigating a certain order of truth to an all-construing quasi-religious worldview—this scientism, said Kierkegaard, explains everything under the sun except what it is to be a man, to live, and to die. Nor do the manifold delights of consumerism and six hours of TV a day change this state of affairs. Indeed, it is in the very face of this massive consumption of goods and this diversion by entertainment, either despite it or because of it, that psychiatrists, not priests but psychiatrists, have remarked the ominous increase in the incidence of depression and suicide—to say nothing of the recourse to drugs. In a word, the consumer of mass culture is lonely, not only lonely, but spiritually impoverished.

I shall not presume to say more about the impediments and opportunities for the evangelization of a modern culture, except a final word about the special and indeed unique case of television. By the very virtue of its technique, its instant transmission of word and image, its near-total access to the entire population of a modern society, it would be difficult surely to imagine a more perfect instrument through which the Church can teach, inform, indeed evangelize.

Yet, by and large, at least in the United States, the Church does not. I am not prepared to say whether it should or should not, what with the bad odor of TV evangelism in general, as mentioned earlier.

What I cannot help but remember, however, is the effectiveness of a Catholic pioneer in TV evangelism. I am thinking of the telecasts of Monsignor Fulton Sheen some thirty or so years ago, a program which had an extraordinary following, both among Catholic and among non-Catholic viewers, and an extraordinary influence, I happen to know, upon the latter. Whether such use of this medium is advisable today—and whether such a communicator is available—is not for me to say. It is enough for now to call attention to this extraordinary medium—its inestimable influence on the lives of 250 million Americans—and the Church's neglect of it.

A final personal word, if you will permit me. As a convert to the Church and, accordingly, as one who is familiar with the point of view of a rather typical denizen of the secular culture of the United States, I can address one aspect of the matter of the evangelization of a culture of which born Catholics—that is, those who have, so to speak, never seen the Church from the outside—may not be sufficiently aware. It is, or was for me, the very steadfastness of the Church, which is perhaps its most noticeable mark, a steadfastness which is, of course, a scandal and contradiction to some and a sign to others, as grace permits. To me at one time it was, I admit, a bit of both. Depending on which, the contradiction or the sign, the Church is seen variously in a culture as reactionary, hidebound, medieval, and the like—or it is viewed for what it is, as Peter's Rock guarding the sacred deposit of the faith amid the tumultuous crosscurrents of culture and history.

One cannot fail to be aware of the manifold calls for change, from both within and without the Church, a change or modification of this or that doctrine, this or that discipline. I have no intention of addressing any of the current matters at issue, of which I am sure you are more knowledgeable than I. The Church can indeed change, has changed, might now or in the future change in its encounter with a particular culture, my own included. But I need not warn you, I am sure, of the dangers of overacculturation. We know what happened to some of the mainline Protestant denominations who are attuned to the opinion polls, so to speak, and trim their sails accordingly as the winds of culture shift. Instead of serving as the yeast which leavens the cultural lump, they tend to disappear into the culture.

By remaining faithful to its original commission, by serving its people with love, especially the poor, the lonely, and the dispossessed, and by not surrendering its doctrinal steadfastness, sometimes even the very contradiction of culture by which it serves as a sign, surely the Church serves culture best.

WHY ARE YOU
A CATHOLIC?

ᘒ

This assignment and the question above (which is sometimes asked in the same context) arouse in me, I'll admit, certain misgivings. One reason, the first that comes to mind, is that the prospect of giving one's "testament," saying it straight out, puts me in mind of an old radio program on which people, mostly show-business types as I recall, uttered their resounding credos, which ended with a sonorous Ed Murrow flourish: *This—I Believe*.

Another reason for reticence is that novelists are a devious lot to begin with, disinclined to say anything straight out, especially about themselves, since their stock-in-trade is indirection, if not guile, coming at things and people from the side so to speak, especially the blind side, the better to get at them. If anybody says anything straight out, it is apt to be one of their characters, a character, moreover, for which they have not much use.

But since one is obliged by ordinary civility to give a response, the temptation is to utter a couple of sentences to get it over with, and let it go at that. Such as: I am a Catholic, or, if you like, a Roman Catholic, a convert to the Catholic faith. The reason I am a Catholic is that I believe that what the Catholic Church proposes is true.

I'd as soon let it go at that and go about my business. The Catholic faith is, to say the least, very important to me, but I have not the least desire to convert anyone or engage in an apologetic or polemic or a "defense of the Faith." But a civil question is entitled to a civil answer and this answer, while true enough, can be taken to be uncivil, even peremptory. And it hardly answers the question.

One justifies the laconicness as a reaction to the current fashion of confessional autobiographies written not only by show-biz types and writers and politicians but by respectable folk as well, confessions which contain not only every sort of sonorous *This—I Believe* but every conceivable sexual misadventure as well. The sincerity and the prodigality of the confessions seem to be understood to be virtues.

There is also a native reticence at work here. It has to do with the disinclination of Americans to discuss religion and sex in the company of their peers.

When the subject of religion does arise, at least in the South, the occasion is often an uncivil one, a challenge or a provocation, or even an insult. It happens once in a while, for example, that one finds oneself in a group of educated persons, one of whom, an educated person of a certain sort, may venture some such offhand remark as

> Of course, the Roman Catholic Church is not only a foreign power but a fascist power.

Or, when in a group of less educated persons, perhaps in a small-town barbershop, one of whom, let us say an ex-member of the Ku Klux Klan—who are not bad fellows actually, at least hereabouts, except when it comes to blacks, Jews, and Catholics—when one of them comes out with something like

> The Catholic Church is a piece of shit

then one feels entitled to a polite rebuttal in both cases, in the one with something like "Well, hold on, let us examine the terms, power, foreign, fascist—" and so on, and in the case of the other, responding in the same tone of casual barbershop bonhomie with, say, "Truthfully, Lester, you're something of a shit yourself, even for white trash—" without in either case disrupting, necessarily, the general amiability.

Yet another reason for reticence in matters religious has to do with the infirmity of language itself. Language is a living organism and, as such, is subject to certain organic ailments. In this case it is the exhaustion and decrepitude of words themselves, an infirmity which has nothing to do with the truth or falsity of the sentences they form. The words of religion tend to wear out and get stored in the attic. The word "religion" itself has a certain unction about it, to say nothing of "born again," "salvation," "Jesus," even though it is begging the question to assume therefore that these words do not have valid referents. And it doesn't help that when religious words are used publicly, at least Christian words, they are often expropriated by some of the worst rogues around, the TV preachers.

So decrepit and so abused is the language of the Judeo-Christian religions that it takes an effort to salvage them, the very words, from the husks and barnacles of meaning which have encrusted them over the centuries. Or else words can become slick as coins worn thin by usage and so devalued. One of the tasks of the saint is to renew language, to sing a new song. The novelist, no saint, has a humbler task. He must use every ounce of skill, cunning, humor, even irony, to deliver religion from the merely edifying.

In these peculiar times, the word "sin" has been devalued to mean everything from slightly naughty excess (my sin was loving you) to such serious lapses as "emotional unfulfillment," the stunting of one's "growth as a person," and the loss of "intersubjective communication." The worse sin of all, according to a book I read about one's growth as a person, is the "failure of creativity."

One reason the poet and novelist these days have a hankering for apocalypse, the end of the old world and the beginning of the new, is surely their sense that only then can language be renewed, by destroying the old and starting over. Things fall apart but words regain their value. A boy sees an ordinary shell on the beach, picks it up as if it were a jewel he had found, recognizes it, names it. Now the name does not conceal the shell but celebrates it.

Nevertheless, however decrepit the language and however one may wish to observe the amenities and avoid offending one's fellow Americans, sometimes the question which is the title of this article is asked more or less directly.

When it is asked just so, straight out, just so:

"Why are you a Catholic?"

I usually reply,

"What else is there?"

I justify this smart-mouthed answer when I sense that the question is, as it usually is, a smart-mouthed question.

In my experience, the question is usually asked by two or three sorts of people. One knows quite well what is meant by all three.

One sort is perhaps a family acquaintance or friend of a friend or long-ago schoolmate or distant kin, most likely a Presbyterian lady. There is a certain type of Southern Presbyterian lady, especially Georgian, who doesn't mince words.

What she means is: how in the world can you, a Southerner like me, one of us, of a certain class and background which encompasses the stark chastity of a Presbyterian Church or the understated elegance of an Episcopal Church (but not a Baptist or Methodist Church), a Southern Christian gentleman, that is to say—how can you become one of *them*, meaning that odd-looking baroque building down the street (the wrong end of the street) with those statues (Jesus pointing to his heart, which has apparently been exposed by open-heart surgery)—meaning those Irish, Germans, Poles, Italians, Cajuns, Hispanics, Syrians, and God knows who else—though God knows they're fine people and I love them all—but I mean there's a difference between a simple encounter with God in a plain place with one's own kind without all that business of red candles and beads and priest in a box—I mean, how can you?

The second questioner is a scientific type, not just any scientist, but the sort who for certain reasons has elected a blunt manner, which he takes to be allowed by friendship and by his scientific mien—perhaps a psychiatrist friend, with their way of fixing the patient with a direct look which seeks to disarm by its friendly directness, takes charming leave to cut through the dross of small

talk and asks the smiling direct question: "Why *are* you a Catholic?"
But there's a question behind the question: I mean, for God's sake,
religion is all very well, humans in any culture have a need for
emotional bonding, community, and even atonement—in the sense
of at-one-ment—I myself am a Unitarian Universalist, with some
interesting input of Zen lately—but I mean, as if it were not
strange enough to elect one of those patriarchal religions which
require a Father God outside the cosmos, not only that but that
he, this Jewish Big Daddy, elected out of the entire cosmos to
enter the history of an insignificant tribe on an insignificant planet,
it and no other, a belief for which, as you well know, there is not
the slightest scientific evidence—not only that, but of the several
hundred Jewish–Christian religions, you pick the most florid and
vulgar of the lot—why *that*?

Yet another sort could be a New Age type, an amorphous
group ranging from California loonies like Shirley MacLaine to
the classier Joseph Campbell who, as wildly different as they are,
share a common stance toward all credos: that they are to be
judged, not by their truth or falsity, sense or nonsense, but by
their mythical liveliness. Here the question is not challenging but
congratulatory, not: "Why are you a Catholic?" but "So you are a
Catholic? How odd and interesting!"

Episcopalians are too polite and gentlemanly to ask the question—and are somewhat inhibited, besides, by their own claim on
the word "Catholic."

Jews, whatever they may think of the Catholic Church, are
too intuitive to ask the question, having, as they do, a sense of a
commonality here which comes of being an exotic minority, which
is to say: Never mind what I think of your religion or you of mine;
we've both got enough trouble at least to leave each other alone.

So the question remains: "Why are you a Catholic?"

Asked from curiosity alone, it is a civil question and deserves
a civil answer.

Accordingly, I will answer here in a cursory, somewhat technical, and almost perfunctory manner which, as unsatisfactory as
it may be, will at least avoid the usual apologetic and polemic. For
the traditional defense of the Catholic claim, however valid it may
be, is generally unavailing for reasons both of the infirmity of

language and the inattentiveness of the age. Accordingly, it is probably a waste of time.

My answer to the question, then, has more to do with science and history, science in its root sense of knowing, truth-seeking; history in the sense that, while what is true is true, it may be that one seeks different truths in different ages.

The following statements I take to be commonplaces. Technically speaking, they are for my purposes axioms. If they are not perceived as such, as self-evident, there is no use arguing about them, let alone the conclusions which follow from them.

Here they are:

The old modern age has ended. We live in a post-modern as well as a post-Christian age which as yet has no name.

It is post-Christian in the sense that people no longer understand themselves, as they understood themselves for some fifteen hundred years, as ensouled creatures under God, born to trouble, and whose salvation depends upon the entrance of God into history as Jesus Christ.

It is post-modern because the Age of Enlightenment with its vision of man as a rational creature, naturally good and part of the cosmos, which itself is understandable by natural science—this age has also ended. It ended with the catastrophes of the twentieth century.

The present age is demented. It is possessed by a sense of dislocation, a loss of personal identity, an alternating sentimentality and rage which, in an individual patient, could be characterized as dementia.

As the century draws to a close, it does not yet have a name, but it can be described.

It is the most scientifically advanced, savage, democratic, inhuman, sentimental, murderous century in human history.

I will give it a name which at least describes what it does. I would call it the age of the theorist-consumer. All denizens of the age tend to be one or the other or both.

Darwin, Newton, and Freud were theorists. They pursued truth more or less successfully by theory—from which, however, they themselves were exempt. You will look in vain in Darwin's *Origin of the Species* for an explanation of Darwin's behavior in writing *Origin of the Species*. Marx and Stalin, Nietzsche and Hitler were also theorists. When theory is applied, not to matter or beasts, but to man, the consequence is that millions of men can be eliminated without compunction or even much interest. Survivors of both Hitler's Holocaust and Stalin's terror reported that their oppressors were not "horrible" or "diabolical" but seemed, on the contrary, quite ordinary, even bored by their actions, as if it were all in a day's work.

The denizens of the present age are both sentimental and bored. Last year the Russians and the Americans united to save three stranded whales and the world applauded. It seemed a good thing to do and the boredom lifted for a while. This was not true, unfortunately, of the million Sudanese who died of starvation the same year.

Americans are the nicest, most generous, and sentimental people on earth. Yet Americans have killed more unborn children than any nation in history.

Now euthanasia is beginning.

Don't forget that the Germans used to be the friendliest, most sentimental people on earth. But euthanasia was instituted, not by the Nazis, but by the friendly democratic Germans of the Weimar Republic. The Weimar Republic was followed by the Nazis.

It is not "horrible" that over a million unborn children were killed in America last year. For one thing, one does not see many people horrified. It is not horrible, because in an age of theory and consumption it is appropriate that actions be carried out as the applications of theory and the needs of consumption require.

Theory supersedes political antinomies like "conservative" versus "liberal," Fascist versus Communist, right versus left.

Accordingly, it should not be surprising that present-day liberals favor abortion, just as the Nazis did years ago. The only difference is that the Nazis favored it for theoretical reasons (eugenics, racial purity), while present-day liberals favor it for consumer needs (unwanted, inconvenient).

Nor should it be surprising that for the same reasons liberals not only favor abortion but are now beginning to favor euthanasia, as the Nazis did.

Liberals understandably see no contradiction and should not be blamed for favoring abortion and euthanasia on the one hand and the "sacredness of the individual," care for the poor, the homeless and oppressed, on the other. Because it is one thing for a liberal editor to see the poor and the homeless on his way to work in his own city and another to read a medical statistic in his own paper about one million abortions. A liberal may act from his own consumer needs (guilt, sentimentality) and the Nazis may act from theory (eugenics, racial purity), but both are consistent in an age of theory and consumption.

The Nazis did not come out of nowhere.

It may be quite true what Mother Teresa said—if a mother can kill her unborn child, then I can kill you and you can kill me—but it is not necessarily horrifying.

America is probably the last and best hope of the world, not because it is not in the same trouble—indeed, the trouble may even be worse due to the excessive consumption in the marketplace and the excessive theorizing in academe—but because, with all the trouble, it preserves a certain innocence and freedom.

This is the age of theory and consumption, yet not everyone is satisfied by theorizing and consuming.

The common mark of the theorist and the consumer is that neither knows who he is or what he wants outside of theorizing and consuming.

This is so because the theorist is not encompassed by his theory. One's self is always a leftover from one's theory.

For even if one becomes passionately convinced of Freudian theory or Marxist theory at three o'clock of a Wednesday afternoon, what does one do with oneself at four o'clock?

The consumer, who thought he knew what he wanted—the consumption of the goods and services of scientific theory—is not in fact satisfied, even when the services offered are such techniques as "personal growth," "emotional maturity," "consciousness-raising," and suchlike.

The face of the denizen of the present age who has come to the end of theory and consumption and "personal growth" is the face of sadness and anxiety.

Such a denizen can become so frustrated, bored, and enraged that he resorts to violence, violence upon himself (drugs, suicide) or upon others (murder, war).

Or such a denizen may discover that he is open to a search for signs, some sign other than theorizing or consumption.

There are only two signs in the post-modern age which cannot be encompassed by theory.

One sign is one's self. No matter how powerful the theory, whether psychological or political, one's self is always a leftover. Indeed, the self may be defined as that portion of the person which cannot be encompassed by theory, not even a theory of the self. This is so because, even if one agrees with the theory, what does one do then? Accordingly, the self finds itself ever more conspicuously without a place in the modern world, which is perfectly understood by theorizing. The face of the self in the very age which was itself designed for the self's understanding of all things and to please the self through the consumption of goods and services—the face of the self is the face of fear and sadness, because it does not know who it is or where it belongs.

The only other sign in the world which cannot be encompassed by theory is the Jews, their unique history, their suffering and achievements, what they started (both Judaism and Christianity), and their presence in the here-and-now.

The Jews are a stumbling block to theory. They cannot be subsumed under any social or political theory. Even Arnold Toynbee, whose theory of history encompassed all other people, looked foolish when he tried to encompass the Jews. The Jews are both a sign and a stumbling block. That is why they are hated by theorists like Hitler and Stalin. The Jews cannot be gotten around.

The great paradox of the Western world is that even though it was in the Judeo-Christian West that modern science arose and flourished, it is Judeo-Christianity which the present-day scientific set of mind finds the most offensive among the world's religions.

Judaism is offensive because it claims that God entered into a covenant with a single tribe, with it and no other.

Christianity is doubly offensive because it claims not only this but also that God became one man, He and no other.

One cannot imagine any statement more offensive to the

present-day scientific set of mind. Accordingly, Hinduism and Buddhism, which have no scientific tradition but whose claims are limited to the self, its existence or nonexistence, which are far less offensive to the present-day scientific set of mind, are in fact quite compatible.

The paradox can be resolved in only two ways.

One is that both the Jewish and the Christian claims are untrue, are in fact nonsense, and that the scientific mind-set is correct.

The other is that the scientific method is correct as far as it goes, but the theoretical mind-set, which assigns significance to single things and events only insofar as they are exemplars of theory or items for consumption, is in fact an inflation of a method of knowing and is unwarranted.

Now that I have been invited to think of it, the reasons for my conversion to the Catholic Church, this side of grace, can be described as Roman, Arthurian, Semitic, and semiotic.

Semitic? Arthurian? This is funny, because what could be more un-Jewish than the chivalric legend of Arthur? And who could be more un-English than the Old Testament Jews?

Or are they? Or could it in fact have been otherwise? My first hero and the hero of the South for a hundred years was Richard I of *Ivanhoe*, who with his English knights in the First Crusade stormed the gates of Acre to rescue the holy places from the Infidel. But, earlier than that, there was the Roman Emperor Marcus Aurelius. If one wished to depict the beau ideal of the South, it would not be the crucified Christ but rather the stoic knight at parade rest, both hands folded on the hilt of his broadsword, his face as grave and impassive as the Emperor's. In the South, of course, he came to be, not the Emperor or Richard, but R. E. Lee, the two in one.

Bad though much of Southern romanticism may be, with Christianity and Judaism and Roman valor seen through the eyes of Sir Walter Scott, how could it have been otherwise with me? After all, the pagans converted by St. Paul did not cease to be what they were. One does not cease to be Roman, Arthurian, Alabamian. One did, however, begin to realize a few things. The holy places which Richard rescued, and whether he thought about it or not, were, after all, Jewish, and he probably did not think about it, because his crusaders killed Jews every which way on the way to the Holy Land. Yet Scott succeeded in romanticizing even the Jews in *Ivanhoe*. But did the European knight with his broadsword at Mont-St.-Michel make any sense without the crucified Jew above him? A modern Pope said it: "Whatever else we are, we are first of all spiritual Semites." Salvation, the Lord said, comes from the Jews.

In a word, thanks to the Jews, one can emerge from the enchanted mists of the mythical past, the Roman and Arthurian and Confederate past, lovely as it is. For, whatever else the Jews are, they are not mythical. Myths are stories which did not happen. But the Jews were there then and are here now.

Semitic? Semiotic? Jews and the science of signs? Yes, because in this age of the lost self, lost in the desert of theory and consumption, nothing of significance remains but signs. And only two signs are of significance in a world where all theoretical cats are gray. One is oneself and the other is the Jews. But for the self that finds itself lost in the desert of theory and consumption, there is nothing to do but set out as a pilgrim in the desert in search of a sign. In this desert, that of theory and consumption, there remains only one sign, the Jews. By "the Jews" I mean not only Israel, the exclusive people of God, but the worldwide *ecclesia* instituted by one of them, God-become-man, a Jew.

It is for this reason that the present age is better than Christendom. In the old Christendom, everyone was a Christian and hardly anyone thought twice about it. But in the present age the survivor of theory and consumption becomes a wayfarer in the desert, like St. Anthony; which is to say, open to signs.

I do not feel obliged to set forth the particular religious reasons for my choosing among the Jewish-Christian religions. There are times when it is better not to name God. One reason is that most of the denizens of the present age are too intoxicated by the theories and goods of the age to be aware of the catastrophe already upon us.

How and why I chose the Catholic Church—this side of grace, which leaves one unclear about who does the choosing—from among the Judeo-Christian religions, Judaism, Protestantism, the

Catholic Church, pertains to old family quarrels among these faiths and as such is not of much interest, I would suppose, to the denizens of this age. As for them, the other members of the family, the Jews and the Protestants, they are already all too familiar with the Catholic claim for me to have to repeat it here. It would be a waste of their time and mine. Anyhow, I do not have the authority to bear good news or to proclaim a teaching.

1990

A "CRANKY NOVELIST" REFLECTS ON THE CHURCH

❧

Let me express my pleasure at being at St. Joseph College Seminary and congratulate you for successfully completing your college seminary years. I envy you your four years in a Benedictine community. There is my own satisfaction in having a Benedictine abbey near the small Southern town where I live. I've heard more than one diocesan priest say affectionately that their four years at St. Ben's were among the happiest in their lives.

My understanding is that you are bound for a major seminary, perhaps at Notre Dame, and, one hopes, for Holy Orders. As a Catholic layman, I can only wish you well, for your own sake and for our sake, and express the hope, for good and selfish reasons, that it works out. We need you. I notice there are not many of you. We are all familiar with the famous shortage of vocations. The statistics are dire. The last numbers I saw were that the average age of a Catholic priest in the United States is presently fifty-six and that at the present rate of vocations it will be seventy-three in the year 2000.

This is all the more critical in view of the concomitant steady increase in the Catholic laity. There has been much talk, especially in the secular press, about the bare ruined choirs and the imminent dissolution of the Church, an end which has been regularly predicted for 1,900 years. A recent article in *Newsweek* spoke of worried bishops and even offered some suggestions for relaxing the standards of the priesthood, standards of education, the rule of celibacy, ordaining women, and so on. Since everyone is free with his expert opinion, let me put in my own two-cents worth. My own feeling is that the diagnosis is not all that difficult. One doesn't have to look beyond the values of a society which is ever more consumer-oriented, ever more inclined to view man as an immanent organism in an environment; therefore, a view of man which is in subtle ways not so much hostile but rather indifferent to Christ's radical injunction to his first priests: To follow me, go your way carrying neither purse nor scrip nor shoes. Hostility is no stranger to the Church; she often thrives under it: witness Poland. But there is a species of bland indifference which is all but invincible. The diagnosis, I say, is not hard to come by, but the solution is more difficult. I make bold to suggest one dimension of it. My own impression, from talking to some of you and your generation, is that the *one* place where the answer is not to be found is in the relaxation of the standards of the priesthood. It seems to me that with the best of you it is exactly the other way around, that far from it being the case that you might have been attracted by this or that fringe benefit—like the college graduates you used to hear about who, when they were interviewed by General Motors or Dupont, would first off inquire about the retirement plan. The best of your generation—perhaps of any generation—want something else. Aside from the supernatural dimension of your vocation—that it is God and not the fringe benefits who calls one and whose summons must be dealt with by each man in his own way—my impression is that your generation is less and less impressed by the easy pitch and more and more exhilarated by the singular challenge.

The very smallness of your number puts me in mind of a rather commonplace military metaphor. It is the recruiting policy of the Marine Corps. I notice that at the very time that the Army, Navy, and Air Force are advertising this or that benefit, good base pay, educational opportunities, the glamour of world travel, early retirement, the Marine Corps says in effect: "We're only the best, you are free to apply, you probably won't make it, there are not many of us and it's a tough life, but if you think you're good enough we'll take a look at you."

If this sounds like I'm comparing you to an elite corps, a chosen few, it's because I am.

Surely it is the high calling, the challenge, the very difficulties to be surmounted which attract one. There are also the peculiar difficulties and the challenge of a vocation in a world which never needed it more, yet which in a strange and unprecedented way is incapacitated, has ears and cannot hear, is both blind and unheeding.

But let me just say a word about some unnecessary difficulties, some areas where we laymen and lay women may have been at fault and have added inadvertently to the rigors of a vocation which, Lord knows, is difficult enough. I am speaking in particular of the vocation of the parish priest. In my book he is one of the heroes of this age. There is one positive good which may come to pass from the present crisis in vocations and the coming scarcity of priests, and it is this: the time may come when we, the Catholic laity, may come to value the very person we have taken for granted all these years. What we took and take for granted is the parish priest. Father was always there, is there, and is expected to be there, something like CLECO and Ma Bell. So natural did it seem that Father was always there that we took it as a matter of course when he was an extraordinarily good and faithful pastor and we were accordingly quick to criticize him when we detected a human failing.

We Catholics have a way of taking things for granted, the very sort of things which other people find extraordinary. I'll give you one example. The other day I happened to read a short review of a book in a magazine. The book was a new edition of the Rule of St. Benedict, published to celebrate the sesquimillenium of the saint's birth. Do you know what a sesquimillenium is? I had to look it up. It is 1,500 years. Now, that is remarkable. What struck me as even more remarkable is that no one seemed to find this remarkable. Yet every day we hear about this or that anniversary celebration: five hundred years since Luther's birth, two hundred years since Goethe's birth, seventy-five years since the Wright brothers' flight, a stamp commemorating James Audubon or Joe Louis. This is all very well. But here is a man who was born 1,500 years ago, who lived in a critical, disorderly time with certain resemblances to our own, who devised a rule for living in a community, a practical, moderate, yet holy rule which apparently is quite as useful now as it was 1,500 years ago. *1,500 years*. I call that remarkable. Yet very few people seem to find it remarkable— very few Catholics. Maybe the Benedictines do, but they don't say much about it, and the Jesuits practically nothing.

And so a favorite recreation among some is either to take the parish priest for granted or to complain about him. Father did so-and-so. Father is always asking for money. The roof of the church is leaking; why doesn't he get it fixed? Why is Father always asking for money? Father's sermon was too long. Father didn't give a sermon. Father read a letter from the Archbishop instead of giving a sermon. Father read a letter from the Archbishop and *then* gave a sermon. Father so-and-so in the next parish has a better sense of humor, so we go over there. Or: Do you know what that priest said to me when I told him I wanted to get my girlfriend fitted with an IUD? And so on.

I have written a couple of science-fiction novels about the future. But one doesn't have to be a prophet to guess what may happen if the present trend continues. Instead of Father always being there at the rectory to answer this or that complaint, the time may come when Father shows up once a month to say Mass, perform baptisms, and hear confessions—or maybe arrives in a jeep once a year, as he does in some parishes in South America. Then we may be as happy to see Father as is a Brazilian Indian.

The point is that the time may come when the Catholic Church and the Catholic people, both priests and laymen, will have become a remnant, a saving remnant, and that will be both bad news and good news. The bad news is that the familiar comfort of the parish in which the Church was taken to be more or less co-extensive with the society in which we lived is probably going or gone. The good news is that in becoming a minority in all countries, a remnant, the Church also becomes a world church in the true sense, bound to no culture, not even to the West of the old Christendom, by no means triumphant but rather a pilgrim church witnessing to a world in travail and yet a world to which it will appear ever stranger and more outlandish. It, the Church, will be seen increasingly as what it was in the beginning, a saving remnant, a sign of contradiction, a stumbling block, a transcultural phenomenon, a pilgrim church.

There is no more Christendom and it may be just as well. Thus, it may very well come to pass that you, graduates of St. Joseph's, if you should become parish priests, will be practicing your ministry in a world very different from the one we grew up in. You are less apt to be seen as a familiar artifact of the culture, a recognizable familiar figure, like the priest in movies who dresses like a priest—"Here's the padre"—"Hi, Father"—says things priests say, and is treated with a kind of unseeing deference.

This is not to say that Father Mike, in order to break out of the old cultural tableaux in which he felt perceived as a static figure, must necessarily shed his Roman collar for a T-shirt and designer jeans in order to appear as a man among men—or that Sister Scholastica has to shed both her name and her habit (in which I always thought she looked great, to tell you the truth) for a J. C. Penney pants suit in which she does not look so great, and takes back her old name of Debbie or Carol Jean, which I always thought she did well to get rid of.

There was a great deal to be said for the traditional role of the Church in which it *was* more or less co-extensive with the culture in which it found itself. One might have lived, for example, in the thirteenth century in a Catholic culture in which the culture itself was informed by the sacramental order of the Church. Or perhaps in Puritan New England or Irish-Catholic Boston, where one's church was as familiar and all-pervasive as the furniture of one's house. And even as a minority church, as a tiny beleaguered community, which the Catholic Church was and still is in much of the South, it was as a miniature culture that it survived, a small besieged enclave in which Father said such-and-such, Sister said so-and-so, and, besieged or not, it was the Catholic-ethnic culture which made one feel comfortable and at home, redolent as it was with incense and candlewax and all the vivid parochial particulars. It was beloved for the same reason it was detested. When a Catholic writer rebels against his faith and his past, as he seems so often compelled to do nowadays, it is really the whole cultural complex he is kicking out.

It is to be hoped, by the way, that American Catholic novelists and playwrights will someday achieve sufficient maturity that they can put their heritage to some better use than ridiculing their own tradition: noting some unfortunate nun who gave him a whack, probably deserved, in the third grade, some weary priest who bruised his feelings in the confessional. No more of that, says a certain sort of writer, and walks out of the Church forever, a free spirit he thinks now, except that it turns out he is not free after all and that he can only get steamed up by doing the same old number on the priest and sisters back at St. Aloysius.

I look forward to the time when the Catholic writer comes of age, as American Jewish writers have come of age in the last generation, and produces a comparable literature of affection and celebration.

I suspect that these writers are rebelling not against God and the Church, the priest, and the nun, the man and woman who have given up his and her life to serve God and the people of God—but rather against the cultural furniture of their own past, the wax-and-varnish smell of St. Aloysius's, Father Mike's peculiarities, Sister Scholastica's bad temper, under the romantic delusion that only if one can escape the particularities and constraints of the past can one breathe the pure air of art and freedom, when in truth what the truly Catholic writer knows, a writer like Flannery O'Connor, that it is only through the particularities of place, time, and history—even when it is, as the poet Gerard Hopkins said, "seared with trade; bleared, smeared with toil; / And wears man's smudge and shares man's smell"—it is only then that the writer achieves his art and all of us achieve humanity.

What is happening, I think, is that the Church is emerging from the stable, perhaps somewhat closeted community of the past into the dangerous and exciting atmosphere of a world community, a global village in which the Church and her people are no longer an exotic enclave but very much a voice among world voices, exciting because the Catholic presence is felt and the Catholic good news is heard and evaluated in its own right and not merely as a pleasant, quaint cultural item like that kindly old movie priest, Father Pat O'Brien, or the swallows at Capistrano.

Radical changes are occurring in the world into which you are graduating and which you may find yourself serving as a priest.

It is like no other world in Western historical experience, both in its opportunities and in its perils. Of course, it is now a commonplace that the Church itself is shaken by unprecedented internal stresses. Given any social or political issues, whether it be the arms race or liberation theology in Latin America, the Church finds itself badly divided. But is this such a bad thing, a falling apart of the happy consensus of older, safer times, or is it a sign of the maturity of the Church emerging into the clamor of the marketplace, however seriously disordered it is? And here, surely, is the most difficult challenge of all: to proclaim the Good News in a world whose values seem increasingly indifferent to the very meaning of the Good News. It is a strange world indeed, a world which is, on the one hand, more eroticized than ancient Rome, and yet a world in which the Good News is proclaimed more loudly and frequently than ever before by TV evangelists and the new fundamentalists. There occurs a kind of devaluation of language, a cheapening of the very vocabulary of salvation, as a consequence of which the ever-fresh, ever-joyful meaning of the Gospel comes across as the dreariest TV commercial. How to proclaim the Good News in a society which never needed it more but in which language itself has been subverted? Salvation comes from hearing, according to Scripture, but what is the bearer of the Good News to do when the hearing becomes as overloaded as the circuits of an $80 TV set?

Your task is very simple. As the Lord said: "All you have to do when you go out among the wolves is to be wise as serpents and gentle as doves." But the wolves these days are of a very different order from the ravening wolves of former times or the totalitarian persecutors of the present day. They are of a far subtler sort and perhaps more dangerous than the ravening species.

There are, as I see it, three enemies of the Good News in American society, wolves in sheep's clothing, for they are not overtly hostile, and yet the upshot is an indifference more subversive than hostility. They are the new idols of society.

The first is a consumership mentality, a bland but nonetheless tenacious addiction to the diversions of the media and the manifold goods and services of a technological society. It is difficult to see how the man, woman, or child who watches TV eight hours a day, in which the good triumphs every half hour on sitcoms, cops, and hospital shows, can be open to the Good News.

Another idol, even more subtle in guise, is the growing fascination with what can only be called the occult, the magical. Though it often masquerades under the honorable title of science, it is in fact anti-scientific. It hungers after any new curiosity or puzzle or mysterious phenomenon but is altogether indifferent to the vast mystery of life itself and the human condition. Sustained by an insatiable appetite for the superficially mysterious, it mistakes religion for its own credulity toward such things as astrology, the Bermuda triangle, UFOs, reincarnation, this or that self-appointed guru with mystical powers. I can remember when the traditional foes used to be science versus religion—which never made sense to me, because both lay claim to a certain order of truth, and truth can never be contradictory. But one does not have to be a seer to see what is happening before our eyes: a loss of interest in science in favor of pseudo-science. One happy outcome of this turn of events may well be a new alliance of science and religion such as existed in medieval times against the old and the new Gnosticism which periodically threatens the openness and catholicity of both science and Christianity with its appeal to the occult and mystical powers of the elite few.

And here in the South particularly, you will encounter a third force, not quite enemy perhaps, who ought in fact to be reckoned friend and ally but in these peculiar times may not be. So confused indeed are the battle lines these days that one can almost envy the Catholics in Communist countries where the enemy is plain to see and to rally against. I am speaking of some of our co-religionists and co-believers in Jesus Christ our Lord, not our brothers the mainline Protestants, but the new fundamentalists. They need to be mentioned because, here in the South at least, it is they who utter the name of the Lord loudest and most often, who are most evident both in media and in marketplace, whose schools are proliferating at a rate exceeding both public and parochial schools. In my opinion, they do a disservice by cheapening the vocabulary of Christianity and pandering to a crude emotionalism divorced from reason. I know that St. Paul said that the Gospel was a stumbling block to the wise, but it does not follow that in order to save the faith it is necessary to believe that the universe was created six thousand years ago. And it is not necessary, to save the integrity of man's soul and its likeness to God, to believe that God could not have created man's body through an evolution from lower species.

The crisis of the Church and the crisis of our youth often manifests itself in young Catholics rebelling against what they perceive as the dryness and ritual prayers of the Church and turning to the emotional appeal of the new evangelicals. Catholics have a lesson to learn here, I am sure, but I give myself permission to indulge my own prejudice—as a cranky novelist I can do this— and to say that the young person who turns his back on the apostolic Catholic faith with its two-thousand-year-old synthesis of faith and knowledge, art and science, with the sacramental presence of God Himself on the altar, to take up with some guru or Bible-thumper who has no use for sacrament or reason, this young person has in fact sold his birthright for a mess of pottage—or, as some wag put it, a pot of message. But, very well, let us leave off the criticism and recognize our own failings.

Some of us older Catholics, I know, take pleasure from the very things many young people find missing: the very understatement of emotion in the quiet corporate worship, and, above all, the ancient, enduring liturgical form of the Mass.

And, of course, at the opposite extreme from the young Pentecostal, with whom I have no quarrel, there is the older parishioner—and I know several—who are convinced that most of the troubles not merely of the Church but of the entire modern world can be traced to the abandonment of the Latin Mass after Vatican II. These are the types, God bless them, who look straight ahead during Mass, glowering, and put their hands in their pockets during the handshaking. Actually, we're not quite as bad as Auberon Waugh, Evelyn Waugh's son, who was so outraged at what he saw as the barbarous liturgy and the atrocious English renderings of the Mass that he departed for the Anglican communion, only to find the *Book of Common Prayer* so butchered by revisions that he came back, still disgruntled, to the Catholic Church as the lesser of evils.

To tell you the truth, despite all the cries of havoc, I don't find things all that bad. I have mentioned a few well-known difficulties and contretemps only to illustrate the general thesis that the cultural manifestation of the Church often gets confused with its historical and apostolic mission. Being human, which is to say creatures of a particular culture, we don't like changes. So, having taken note of what is commonly called the crisis of the Church, let me make a final personal observation: that if one judged only from the media, the national press, or network news, one would conclude that the Church is washed up, hopelessly divided politically, the Holy Father hopelessly behind the times. Yet one goes to Mass on any ordinary Sunday and there they are, the Catholic people, more than ever, at five, six, seven Masses a day. And there is the priest still, thank God, holding aloft the body of Christ. And let the Holy Father, this marvelous man, appear anywhere and there occurs all over the world a tumult not of despair and division but of rejoicing and hope, and not merely among Catholics.

That is why it is such a pleasure to see you here. I don't know how many of you will become parish priests. But I know how welcome you will be. I have mentioned the challenge only to emphasize the opportunities. The opportunity is simply this: that never in history has modern man been in greater need of you, has been more confused about his identity and the meaning of his life. Never has there been such loneliness in the midst of crowds, never such hunger in the face of satiation. Never has there been a more fertile ground for the seed and the harvest the Lord spoke of. All that is needed is a bearer of the Good News who speaks it with such authenticity that it can penetrate the most exhausted hearing, revive the most jaded language. With you lies the future and the hope. You and the Church you serve may be only a remnant, but it will be a saving remnant.

I salute you and congratulate you. God bless you.

1983

THE FAILURE
AND THE HOPE

❧

Those of us in the South who call ourselves Christians have come face-to-face with the most critical and paradoxical moment in our history. The crisis is the Negro revolution. The paradox lies in this: that the hope for the future—and both the hope and the promise, in my opinion, and for reasons which shall follow, were never greater—requires as its condition of fulfillment the strictest honesty in assessing the dimensions of our failure.

What lies at issue is whether or not the South will bring to bear its particular tradition and its particular virtues to humanize a national revolution which is in the main secular and which is going to be accomplished willy-nilly with or without the Christian contribution—or whether it will yield the field by default.

The failure of the Christian in the South has been both calamitous and unremarkable. And perhaps that is the worst of it: that no one finds the failure remarkable, not we who ought to know better, not the victims of our indifference who confess the same Christ, and not even the world who witnessed our failure. No one was surprised. The world which said many years ago, "See how the Christians love one another," would presumably have been surprised if these earlier Christians had violated each other or turned their backs upon the violation. Now as then, the children of the world are wiser than the children of light: they witnessed the failure we concealed from ourselves and found it not in the least remarkable.

The world, in fact, does not think badly of us. It holds us, generally speaking, to be good, an asset to the community. The sickness of Christendom may lie in fact in this: that we are judged by the world, and even to a degree have come to judge ourselves, as but one of a number of "groups" or institutions which have a "good" impact on society. One thinks of those panel programs and seminars on educational TV which set out to explore the means of combating juvenile delinquency, crime in the streets, drug addiction, and so on. Someone on the panel usually gets around to listing the forces for good in the community which can be enlisted in the battle. There is the home, the schools, the labor unions, the business community; and there are the churches . . .

And in the matter of racial injustice, the churches are treated with the same respectful impartiality. The media approvingly report the news that such-and-such a bishop has integrated the parochial schools or that this or that minister has joined a bi-racial committee, in much the same tone with which they report that IBM has set up its own Fair-Employment Practices Committee. The bad behavior of Christians is not treated as any worse or more scandalizing than bad behavior anywhere else. When God is invoked by the Klan and the Citizens' Councils, when ministers open the meeting with a prayer; when white Catholics in Louisiana get in fistfights with Negro Catholics on the church steps, nobody cries shame. The world does not laugh, and in fact is not even pleased. Because, as everyone knows, churches are, generally speaking, on the list of good institutions and do in fact make valuable contributions to the community—along with the home, the school, the media . . .

Christians in the South should, of all people, know better. Or perhaps it is more accurate to say that, if they don't know better, then Christendom is indeed sick unto death. But in their heart of hearts they do know better. Because the South, more so than the rest of the country, is still Christ-haunted, to use an expression of Flannery O'Connor's. Whatever the faults of the South, it is perhaps the only section of the United States where the public and secular consciousness is still to a degree informed by theological habits of thought, the old notions of sin, of heaven and hell, of God's providence, however abused and shopworn these notions may be. Flannery O'Connor, a Catholic novelist, counted it her great good fortune to have been born and raised and to work in the Protestant South. In the Catholic novel, she claimed, "the center of meaning will be Christ and the center of destruction will be the devil." The South has always known this, even when its morality was mainly concerned with sex and alcohol, to the exclusion of ordinary human cruelty. And the Southerner is apt to inherit, almost despite himself, a theological turn of mind. More likely than not, he has grown up in a place drenched in tragedy and memory and to have known firsthand a rich and complex world of human relationships which are marked by a special grace and a special cruelty and guilt.

Our region, I submit, is to a larger degree informed by theological habits of thought than is the rest of the country. And those of us who are professing Christians have better reason than most to understand the theological basis and consequences of our actions and less excuse to fall victim to the sociological heresy which sees the Church as but one among several "good" institutions which can be used to engineer a democratic society.

It is all the more shameful, then, that the failure is precisely a theological failure. How much more tolerable would have been our position if it had fallen out otherwise, if we could have said to the secular liberals of the Northern cities: Yes, it is true that we differ radically from you in our view of the nature of man and the end of man, that we have reservations about your goal of constructing the city of God here and now; further, we don't like some of the things you tolerate in your perfect city. But we applaud your attack on the perennial evils of poverty, inhumanity, and disease, and we, too, believe that men can be reconciled here and now but that they can be reconciled only through the meditation of God and the love of men for God's sake. We strive for the same goals; we say only that you deceive yourself in imagining that you can achieve these goals without God.

But we can't even say that. The defect has occurred on the grounds of our own choosing. The failure has been a failure of love, a violation of that very Mystical Body of Christ which we have made our special property at the risk of scandalizing the world by our foolishness. A scandal has occurred right enough, but it has not been the scandal intended by the Gospels. The failure, that is to say, has occurred within the very order of *sin* which we have taken so seriously and the world so lightly. Where we have failed worst is not in the sphere of community action wherein little store is set by theological values. Churches indeed have not done at all badly in discharging their sociological functions, combating juvenile delinquency and broken homes and alcoholism. The failure has been rather the continuing and unreflecting cruelty of Christians toward the Negro, the Negro considered not as beloved household pet ("Cruelty? No! Why, I would do anything for Uncle Ned and he for me!") but as member of the same Mystical Body, freed and dignified by the same covenant which frees and dignifies us. The sin has been the sin of omission, specifically the Great Southern Sin of Silence. During the past ten years, the first ten years of the Negro revolution, a good deal was heard about the "good" people of the South, comprising the vast majority, who deplored the violence and who any day would make themselves felt. But these good people are yet to be heard from. If every Christian era has its besetting sin— the medieval Church its inquisitional cruelty, eighteenth-century Anglicanism its Laodiceanism—the twentieth-century Christian South might well be remembered by its own peculiar mark: *silence*.

The default of the white Southern Christian was revealed in its proper ironic perspective by the civil-rights movement itself. When the good people of the South did not come forward when they were needed, their burden was shouldered by, of all people, the liberal humanist, who, like the man St. Paul speaks of in his Epistle to the Ephesians, is stranger to every covenant, with no promise to hope for, the world about him and no God—but who nevertheless was his brother's keeper. In the deep South of the 1960s, the men who nursed the sick, bound his wounds, taught the ignorant, fed the hungry, went to jail with the imprisoned, were not the Christians of Birmingham or Bogalusa but, more likely than not, the young CORE professionals or COFO volunteers, Sarah Lawrence sociology majors, agnostic Jewish social workers like Mickey Schwerner, Camus existentialists, and the like.

It is possible for a Southerner to criticize his region in the harshest possible terms, not because he thinks the South is worse than the rest of the country and can only be saved by the Berkeley–Cambridge axis, but for the exactly opposite reason: that, in spite of her failures, he suspects that it may very likely fall to the destiny of the South to save the country from the Berkeley–Cambridge axis. If this should prove the case, it is not simply because cities like Los Angeles and New York are exhibiting an almost total paralysis and fecklessness when confronted with Watts and Harlem, while at the same time Atlanta and Greenville are doing comparatively better. (Truthfully, I think the South is "doing better" for an odd mixture of Southern and Northern reasons, none of which have much to do with Christianity; for example, Southern good humor and social grace, plus a sharp Yankee eye for the dollar and the "public image.") No, the criticism is leveled and the game is worth the candle because, at least in one Southerner's opinion, the ultimate basis for racial reconciliation must be theological rather than legal and sociological, and that in the South, perhaps more than in any other region, the civil and secular consciousness is still sufficiently informed by a theological tradition to provide a sanction for racial reconciliation. (By contrast, the Catholic Church in other parts of the country also provides a powerful sanction but it is a purely religious sanction and not necessarily reflected in the habitual attitudes of civil bodies such as legislatures and school boards.) The South can, that is, if she wants to. She can just as easily choose the opposite course, like Protestant South Africa.

The thesis that it may fall to the South to save the Union, just as it fell to the North one hundred years ago, might appear not merely paradoxical but in the highest degree fanciful. Yet there are, I believe, good and sufficient reasons for entertaining special hopes for the future, not the least of which is the coming into being of peculiarly Southern groups of Christian churchmen. Like Israel, the South is still killing God's messengers, men like James Reeb, Jonathan Daniels, and Richard Morrisroe, but at least she is killing them and not ignoring them, or worse, conferring upon them lukewarm Civitan honors. And now she may have new prophets.

There are also historical reasons which are largely negative and have to do with the failure of other "good" traditions, traditions which, noble though they might have been and still are, do not perhaps possess the interior resources of renewal, which seems to be the perennial and saving gift of Christianity. These failures have cleared the ideological air as it has not been cleared since the first slave came ashore in Virginia. In the failure of old alternatives, future choices become plainer.

The traditions in question and their respective historical difficulties are: (1) the collapse of the old-style "good" white man in the South and the dramatic disintegration of his alliance with the Negro; and (2) the ongoing demoralization of the secular urban-suburban middle-class society, the very culture from which so many of the civil-rights activists derive.

The thesis of this article, for which there is not room to lay the proper ground, let alone defend, is that the major ideological source of racial moderation in the South has not been Christian at all but Stoic, that this tradition has now collapsed, that in spite of its nobility (or perhaps because of its nobility) it possessed fatal weaknesses and therefore served as a distracting and confusing alternative to racism, and finally that its collapse has confronted Christians with a crucial test, the outcome of which will be unequivocal triumph or unequivocal disaster. The chips, that is to say, are down and it is time they were.

The degree of reconciliation achieved under this noble and mainly non-Christian ethic was more considerable than is generally realized. As a result of the old "fusion principle," as it was known, the Negro in the Deep South enjoyed more civil rights in the period immediately following Reconstruction than at any time afterwards—until the last few months. Restaurants and trains were not segregated. Congressman Catchings of Mississippi, one of the noblest of the Old Redeemers, reported that there were more Negro officeholders in his district than in the entire North. This alliance, it is important to note, was struck between the Negro and the white conservative against the poor whites and the Radical Republicans. It has been this same white conservative leadership which in many parts of the South exerted a more or less consciously moderate racial influence even after it was politically overwhelmed by the latter-day Populist-racists, Vardaman, Heflin, Bilbo, and their followers. The old alliance with the Negro was in part politically motivated. But it also had a strong moral basis. It is the contention here that this morality was paternalistic and Stoic in character and that it derived little or none of its energies from Christian theology. Even in those instances where the best Southern leaders were, like Robert E. Lee, professing Christians, James McBride Dabbs has shown that there was a strong Stoic component in their character formation. Perhaps the most distinguishing mark, and, as it turned out, the greatest weakness of the Stoic morality, was its exclusively personal character and its consequent indifference to the social and political commonweal. The Stoic took as his model, either consciously or unconsciously, the Emperor Marcus Aurelius, who wrote in his *Meditations*: "Every moment think steadily, as a Roman and a man, to do what thou hast in hand with perfect and simple dignity and a feeling of affection and freedom and justice." Such a moral ideal, lofty as it is, has largely to do with the housekeeping of one's interior castle, specifically the maintenance of its order and the brightness of one's personal honor. In the light of such a code, the doctrine of the Mystical Body of Christ wherein each of us is a member, one of another, and no one is inviolate in the precincts of his soul, must remain incomprehensible.

But it was they, the Stoics, who lived by their lights and we who did not. The best of them kept the old broadsword virtues, while the Christians, by and large, egregiously sinned against their own commandments, through commission and omission—in the latter case, through an impoverished morality restricted largely to rules for the use of sex and alcohol. It was the Christians in the South who supplied the main ideological support for slavery. It is the Christians now who still underwrite segregation with Levitical quotations and Ham-Shem sociology. Nor is it enough to say that Christ was no social reformer and that St. Paul wasn't worried about freeing slaves. Where the Southern Christian failed was on his own ground, in his own performance in the face of here-and-now cruelty and suffering and inhumanity.

Even when the Christian did come to the aid of the afflicted and abused Negro, he often did so for Stoic reasons, with the old benevolence and the sense of personal bond toward Uncle Ned and Aunt Jemima, but without that larger and more mysterious charity which at one and the same time binds men close and sets them free, one of another, and does not keep books on gratitude.

Most of us have known the old tradition firsthand and recall it with affection and admiration. I remember in the most vivid way long conversations with my Uncle Will about the plantation system. At that time—in the 1930s—the sharecropper system was coming under heavy attack from "Northern liberals." As a planter, my uncle felt that the attacks were unjust. He believed that the sharecropper system was an outgrowth of a natural partnership between the Confederate veterans, who had nothing left but the land, and the Negroes, who had nothing but their labor. No doubt, he was right. To justify its use in modern times, he cited his own experience and that of his friends, who dealt with their tenants more than honorably, serving also as father and friend. To behave with dishonor was to these men a detestable thing, but to mistreat a Negro was unthinkable, precisely because the Negro was helpless. But other men, a great many other men, were not so scrupulous. And the Negro remained helpless, precisely because he had no entity in the public order of things, and neither law nor religion felt constrained to underwrite such an entity.

We may speak now of the old tradition without fear of patronizing it, because it was it and not the Christian tradition which fleshed out some of the noblest men this country has produced. We may go even further. As Dabbs wrote in his remarkable book, *Who Speaks for the South?*, the final evidence that there was something wrong with the South as a society, that in the last analysis it was not a great society, was that it produced neither saints nor great artists.

Stoic excellence, in short, was not enough. Its code had little relevance in the social and political order. For not only was there the tendency to wash one's hands of prevailing social evils; there was ever the temptation to *Schadenfreude*, the peculiar sin of the Stoic, a grim sort of pleasure to be taken in the very deterioration of society, the crashing of the world about one's ears. Southern literature is full of direful, eschatological—and pleasurable—reports of the decline and fall of both the South and the United States.

Though it was defeated politically around 1890, the Stoic tradition has persisted until recently. Nearly everyone in the South has known someone like Atticus Finch in *To Kill a Mockingbird*, with his quite Attic sense of decency (and his correspondingly low regard for Christianity) and his courage before the lynch mob. It is, however, this very Stoic tradition which has finally collapsed as a significant influence in the Southern community. The old conservative often became the new conservative, that is, a segregationist and "states' righter." The force for moderation is now more likely to be the businessman—the "power structure"—the mayor, the manager of the new IBM center or the NASA complex, who wants no part of the KKK or the Citizens' Councils, though for reasons which have nothing to do with Christ or with Marcus Aurelius.

The ideological vacuum created by the failure of the gentle tradition has been filled not by Christians but by other elements, the moderate business community and the secular reformer. The Christian clergy has been increasingly active, but the inertness of cultural Christendom is well known. Is it possible that this well-known lag between clergy and laity can be traced to still-viable Stoic elements in Christendom considered as a cultural artifact which one inherits more or less passively as he inherits language and custom?

There is not much doubt about the existence of such a lag. An increasingly familiar fact of life in the Southern parish, Protestant and Catholic, has come to be the tension between the "radical" new minister or priest and his "conservative" flock. There are the usual grumblings about brainwashing in the seminary. But is this lag to be understood in purely sociopolitical terms of liberal versus conservative? I think not, because this particular bias has proved quite as refractory to pulpit appeals as to political appeals. I suspect that a good deal of the offense taken can be laid to a fundamental Stoic offense to any demand for public appeal and political morality. There is still the old reflex which somehow rules the preacher out of bounds when he talks about social morality as well as sexual morality. The very man who will get up at all hours to get Ol' Jim out of jail, and even risk his life to protect Ol' Jim from the lynch mob, is also outraged when Jim's sons demand better schools and better police—not come hat in hand, but demand them as ordinary rights of a citizen. And, of course, the fact is that many of the old-style "good" people, both Christian and Stoic, have now turned against the Negro because of what they deem his "insolence." "If the Negro had not become aggressive," a good Christian man told me the other day, "I'd still be on his side. It is these demonstrations, his *demanding* rights of me, which changed my attitude." Of *me*? Here is the heart of the matter certainly: it is where the rights are deemed to come from which causes the offense.

Such a response can be traced, I believe, to an antique Southern preoccupation, not with theology as a rule of social intercourse, but with *manners*. By manners I do not refer in this context to that courtesy which one Christian awards another by virtue of the infinite value he assigns to the other's person, but rather to manners understood as a primary concern with an intercourse of gesture, a minuet of overture and response. It is an economy of gesture which, in its accounting of debits and credits, of generosity given and gratitude expected, of face and loss of face, is almost Oriental. (Note also the similarities of the classic Stoic tradition with certain Oriental moral philosophies.) A great part of the social intercourse between whites and Negroes in the South, I daresay, was founded on a complex and meticulously observed protocol of manners. And it came to pass that an extraordinary social fabric was woven between black and white, using these very elements and in the face of the most trying circumstances. Nor is this to say that this Southern tradition of manners is irrelevant to the problems of the day. It would be a great pity indeed if the ordinary everyday good manners of Southerners, black and white, should be overturned in the present revolution.

But the American Negro in 1965 may reply that the social graces of his ancestors in Alabama didn't in the end do him or them much good. It is his present "bad manners" which now offend his old ally—though, in all honesty, I must admit that the opposite seems the case: the continued "good manners" of the Southern Negro are nothing short of amazing. The point is, of course, that in a society based largely on an intercourse of manners even the mildest public and political action taken to redress grievances is apt to be received as a code infraction and hence "bad manners."

The old alliance failed through a fatal weakness which now stands revealed. It was based primarily on personal relationships and never really possessed the interior resources, political or religious, through which the integrity of the Negro's person could be guaranteed in its own right.

What is the lesson? The lesson is surely that, at the very time the old order has collapsed and new social forces are beginning to stir the South from its long sleep, the Christian laity is still responding with old cultural reflexes to a new and somewhat unmannered order of things. Surely also, the remedy is theological, not merely preaching a gospel of reconciliation, but teaching: setting forth, that is, what is the case as well as what ought to be. What is the case is that the Christian porch is no longer habitable, that pleasant site of cultural Christendom neither quite inside the church nor altogether in the street, from which one had the best of both, church on Sundays and at baptism and marriage and death, and the rest of the time lived in the sunny Old Stoa of natural grace and good manners. It doesn't work now.

The Negro in the South has a new ally. He is not the old-style gentleman or Stoic or quasi-Christian, but rather the liberal humanist who is, more likely than not, frankly post-Christian in his beliefs. The clergy has been active in the civil-rights movement, sometimes heroically so, but the impetus has not in the main been theological—except among black Southern Christians, but even in this case to a decreasing degree, especially among the younger Negroes. Among the volunteers of the Mississippi Summer Project of 1964, it was the exception rather than the rule to come across anyone who had come to Mississippi to implement Christian principles, even though the project was sponsored by the National Council of Churches. It was rarer still to find a Southern Christian layman. And yet they were on the whole an earnest and admirable young group.

Here is a point of view, not at all atypical, expressed by one of the volunteers:

> Along with my CORE class I teach a religion class at one every afternoon and a class on non-violence at four-fifteen . . . In religion they are being confronted for the first time with people they respect who do not believe in God and with people who do believe in God but who do not take the Bible literally. It's a challenging class because I have no desire to destroy their belief, whether Roman Catholic or Baptist, but I want them to look at things critically and to learn to separate fact from myth in all areas, not just religion.

There is no reason to doubt this statement—that this young person does not wish Baptists and Catholics to lose their faith—though a good deal could be written about the assumptions and begged questions behind the statement. What is noteworthy perhaps is a lack of seriousness, a certain casualness with which the perennially mooted religious questions are assumed to be disposed of. The old animus against the Christian proposition has been replaced by a shrug. Here, at any rate, is the new "good" man, a person of unquestionable good will and earnestness who explicitly disavows orthodox Christian belief. She places her confidence, not on the old verities, but on "facts" (that is to say, observable and replicable phenomena) and on social techniques.

This secularization of the civil-rights movement has been largely misunderstood in the South. The failure of Southern Christendom has not only been theological—a default in the duty of reconciliation—but prophetic in its blindness both to what happened and to what is to come. Confronted by a revolutionary and to a large degree non-Christian movement and obfuscated by his own Stoic reading of race relations—"We have nothing but love for our Negroes and they for us" etc.—the Southern Christian has all too often made the unhappy mistake of labeling the civil-rights movement as Communist, immoral, un-American, and so on. Apparently there are a few Communists involved, and apparently there has been some sexual misbehavior, but this is not an occasion for rejoicing. The reason the Christian racist goes to such lengths to discredit the new allies of the Negro and is so pleased when they uncover sexual sin is not hard to discover. For the bitterest pill for him to swallow is the fact, hardly to be contested and which in his heart he does not contest, that the Negro revolution is mainly justified, mainly peaceful (from the side of the Negroes), and mainly American. For to admit this hard reality would entail *pari passu* a confession of his own failure.

How stands the Christian then vis-à-vis the challenge of the new-style "good" man? Better off than before, I think, and less compromised than he was in his relation to the old-style Stoic quasi-Christian gentleman.

The present hope is to be found, paradoxically, as it is often the case with Christian hope, in the very extremity of the failure. The old Christian porch, that is to say, is becoming increasingly uninhabitable by moderately serious persons, which is to say our best young people. It is surely not too much to say that if Southern Christendom does not soon demonstrate the relevance of its theology to the single great burning social issue in American life, it runs the risk of becoming ever more what it in fact to a degree already is, the pleasant Sunday lodge of conservative Southern businessmen which offends no one and which no one takes seriously.

The larger hope and opportunity of the Christian Gospel lies, of course, in the terrible dilemma of the new "good" man himself, the denizen, we might call him, of the victorious technological-democratic society. A great deal has been written about him and his twentieth-century sickness. Suffice it here to say only what he has said about himself: that the very urban and middle-class society from which have come so many of the earnest young revolutionaries is itself marked by the malaise and anomie and other symptoms of the new sickness. There is nothing new in this. Indeed, preachers speak every Sunday about the emptiness of modern man and the One who can fill the emptiness. And they are right. But God help us here in the South (or in Chicago or Los Angeles) if we imagine that reconciliation is not our business here and now and that all we have to do is convert the Communists and bring Christ to the "empty modern man." Because these latter are not going to be listening. The fruits, by which they had every right to know us, were too meager.

1965

A VIEW OF
ABORTION, WITH
SOMETHING TO
OFFEND EVERYBODY

❧

I feel like saying something about this abortion issue. My credentials as an expert on the subject: none. I am an M.D. and a novelist. I will speak only as a novelist. If I give an opinion as an M.D., it wouldn't interest anybody, since, for one thing, any number of doctors have given opinions and who cares about another.

The only obvious credential of a novelist has to do with his trade. He trafficks in words and meanings. So the chronic misuse of words, especially the fobbing off of rhetoric for information, gets on his nerves. Another possible credential of a novelist peculiar to these times is that he is perhaps more sensitive to the atrocities of the age than most. People get desensitized. Who wants to go about his business being reminded of the six million dead in the Holocaust, the fifteen million in the Ukraine? Atrocities become banal. But a twentieth-century novelist should be a nag, an advertiser, a collector, a proclaimer of banal atrocities.

True legalized abortion—a million and a half fetuses flushed down the Disposall every year in this country—is yet another banal atrocity in a century where atrocities have become commonplace. This statement will probably offend one side in this already superheated debate, so I hasten in the interests of fairness and truth to offend the other side. What else can you do when some of your allies give you as big a pain as your opponents? I notice this about many so-called pro-lifers. They seem pro-life only on this one perfervid and politicized issue. The Reagan Administration, for example, professes to be anti-abortion but has just recently decided in the interests of business that it is proper for infant-formula manufacturers to continue their hard sell in the Third World despite thousands of deaths from bottle feeding. And Senator Jesse Helms and the Moral Majority, who profess a reverence for unborn life, don't seem to care much about born life: poor women who don't get abortions have their babies and can't feed them.

Nothing new here, of course. What I am writing this for is to call attention to a particularly egregious example of doublespeak that the abortionists—"pro-choicers," that is—seem to have hit on in the current rhetorical war.

Now, I don't know whether the human-life bill is good legislation or not. But as a novelist I can recognize meretricious use of language, disingenuousness, and a con job when I hear it.

The current con, perpetrated by some jurists, some editorial writers, and some doctors, is that since there is no agreement about the beginning of human life, it is therefore a private religious or philosophical decision and therefore the state and the courts can do nothing about it. This is a con. I will not presume to speculate who is conning whom and for what purpose. But I do submit that religion, philosophy, and private opinion have nothing to do with this issue. I further submit that it is a commonplace of modern biology, known to every high-school student and no doubt to you the reader as well, that the life of every individual organism, human or not, begins when the chromosomes of the sperm fuse with the chromosomes of the ovum to form a new DNA complex that thenceforth directs the ontogenesis of the organism.

Such vexed subjects as the soul, God, and the nature of man are not at issue. What we are talking about and what nobody I know would deny is the clear continuum that exists in the life of every individual from the moment of fertilization of a single cell.

There is a wonderful irony here. It is this: the onset of individual life is not a dogma of the Church but a fact of science. How much more convenient if we lived in the thirteenth century, when no one knew anything about microbiology and arguments about the onset of life were legitimate. Compared to a modern textbook of embryology, Thomas Aquinas sounds like an American Civil Liberties Union member. Nowadays it is not some misguided ecclesiastics who are trying to suppress an embarrassing scientific fact. It is the secular juridical-journalistic establishment.

Please indulge the novelist if he thinks in novelistic terms. Picture the scene. A Galileo trial in reverse. The Supreme Court is cross-examining a high-school biology teacher and admonishing him that of course it is only his personal opinion that the fertilized human ovum is an individual human life. He is enjoined not to teach his private beliefs at a public school. Like Galileo he caves in, submits, but in turning away is heard to murmur, *"But it's still alive!"*

To pro-abortionists: According to the opinion polls, it looks as if you may get your way. But you're not going to have it both ways. You're going to be told what you're doing.

1981

FOREWORD TO
THE NEW CATHOLICS

᳗

How to write about conversion if it is true that faith is an unmerited gift from God? How to describe, let alone explain it, if this is the case? When it comes to grace, I get writer's block. How to write about other people's conversions when one hardly understands one's own? What one does, of course, is write about the causes other than God's grace, the "proximate," the "material," the "psychological" causes.

One can write about conversion two ways. One way is to put the best possible face on it, recount a respectable intellectual odyssey. Such as: Well, my tradition was scientific. I thought science explained the cosmos—until one day I read what Kierkegaard said about Hegelianism, the science of his day: that Hegel explained everything in the universe except what it is to be an individual, to be born, to live, and to die. And for me this "explanation" would be true enough, I suppose. But then there is this. When I was in college, I lived in the attic of a fraternity house with four other guys. God, religion, was the furthest thing from our minds and talk—from mine, at least. Except for one of us, a fellow who got up every morning at the crack of dawn and went to Mass. He said nothing about it and seemed otherwise normal.

Does anyone suppose that one had nothing to do with the other? That is, thinking about Kierkegaard's dilemma and remembering my roommate's strange behavior—this among a thousand other things one notices or remembers, which, if they don't "cause" it, at least enter into it, at least make room for this most mysterious turning in one's life.

Here follows a motley crew of converts with whom I felt immediately at home, as motley (in the old, best sense of the word) as Chaucer's pilgrims.

Reading these seventeen very personal accounts, one finds oneself casting about for reasons for the variety, so many different kinds of people coming from so many different directions. One reason, of course, is the tumultuous pluralism of this huge country. Our materialism and consumerism are so commonplace that we are apt to forget the other term of the paradox: that we are the most religious of countries, more so than India, a vaster maelstrom of contending creeds and cults, not merely the hundreds of Protestant sects, the mainline Protestant churches, the Catholic Church, the varieties of Judaism, but also the new wave from the East, Far and Near, with more varieties of Buddhism, imported and homegrown, than are to be found in Tibet.

But there's another reason. It is not merely the catholicity of these Catholic-to-be pilgrims, coming as they do from every walk of life but also from every other sort of pilgrimage. These folk may be Rome-bound, but they've been most other places as well— Canterbury (C. of E.), Vienna (Freud), Albany (Seventh-Day Adventists), Down South fundamentalism, Up North New England parsonages, Harvard and Smith and Yale skepticism, "Jewish atheism" (as one writer described it), also "Orthodox Reformed Freudianism," Marxism–Leninism, Buddhism, rock music, the earthly love of men for and by women. Augustine always made more sense to me about this last than Freud; that is, the translation from the love of women (or men) to God. "Repression" and "sublimation" surely say more about Freud's dislike of women than about his quarrel with God.

No, it is not merely the exotic provenances of these pilgrims that dazzle the reader, but the inkling that it is the very catholicity of the Thing, the old-new Jewish–Christian Thing, the one holy Catholic apostolic and Roman Thing that, come at from so many directions, looks so different at the beginning and finally so much the same. Sure enough, all roads seem to lead to, and so forth.

Here they certainly do. She is the object of the pilgrimage and there She is, blemishes and all. Or, as one convert puts it here: What else do you expect anything this enormous and this old to be than, at times, something of a horror show?

Some themes recur. More than one pilgrim finds himself standing at a strange rectory door, wondering how he got there, never having said two words to a priest—and here I have to smile, remembering how it felt and also hoping that he, she, would not run into some exhausted, unhappy, and otherwise messed-up human. They didn't. In one case, the housekeeper answered the door, matter-of-factly shook her feather duster toward the parlor: "In there." That helps. "Well, here I am," one fellow said abruptly to the bemused priest. "What do I have to do?"

An interesting Anglican current runs here. In no case is the tone polemical. Rather, there is a lasting affection for the lovely Anglican things, for the *Book of Common Prayer*, for dear England herself—and a sadness at her cutting off the magisterium. One pictures this pilgrim as he turns away from the spires soaring above empty cathedrals in the gracious countryside, and takes the road to downtown, bustling St. Agnes's, where, lovely or not, the Lord is housed.

Books and reading figure here as largely as one might expect, and the writers one would expect, from Aquinas to Merton. But guess who turns up most often? C. S. Lewis!—who, if he didn't make it all the way, certainly handed along a goodly crew.

Sometimes it is the very prosaicness of the reading that catches the eye. One woman—and she is my fellow traveler, because I did the same thing—read St. Augustine's *The City of God*, was duly impressed, and then read *Father Smith Instructs Jackson*, no masterpiece to be sure but maybe all the better for the humble prose.

I can still see the grayish paperback, probably picked up from that rack at the back of the church, with the good Father Smith on the cover and Jackson—*Jackson!*—an earnest young man with a 1920s Harold Lloyd sort of haircut, head cocked attentively, listening. There was some good news here.

And there is good news in these remarkable stories.

1987

IF I HAD
FIVE MINUTES
WITH THE POPE

❧

Not that you need my advice, Your Holiness, but since I've been asked, here's a word or two—on the occasion of your visit to New Orleans.

1. Do not suppress the Society of Jesus at this time. While it may be true that the Jesuits as a body no longer seem to enlist themselves in the defense of the primacy of the Holy Apostolic See as they have done traditionally since Loyola and Xavier, it does not necessarily follow that most American Jesuits are working for a schism in the U.S. Catholic Church. Most, I think, are not.

2. Don't worry about a schism in the American hierarchy. While it may be true that a few U.S. bishops are as wimpy and gutless as the English hierarchy in the early sixteenth century and would probably follow an excommunicated adulterous king rather than lose their sinecures and heads, most, I think, like Bishop John Fisher, would not. For one thing, we don't have a king. For another, where would they go?

3. Don't worry about scientists. They pursue truth, from which the Church has nothing to fear. They become a matter of concern only when they begin mucking around with human life with their high technology; e.g., *in vitro* fertilization, wherein surplus fertilized ova are either discarded or frozen or experimented with—in the name of improving the "quality of life" of mankind. Such behavior bespeaks a certain confusion about the value of an individual

human life. Scientists tend to be smart about things and dumb about people.

My suggestion is that not you but the proper civil authorities deal with egregious offenders within constitutional constraints and according to established legal principles; viz., the punishment fitting the crime. For example, if a scientist is detected treating unborn human beings in such a manner—creatures that he probably calls zygotes—I suggest that the scientist's own genetic material be examined by impartial fellow scientists and that the scientist himself be accordingly discarded, experimented with, or frozen.

4. Don't suppress "liberation theologians"—who, after all, have their hearts in the right place in wanting to liberate the wretched of the earth from the bonds of poverty and oppression—but do disarm them, so they won't go around shooting people, a practice that may be condoned by Marxist–Leninists but that most theologians would agree is contrary to Catholic belief.

5. Don't bother about certain proud and fashionable unorthodox theologians in our Catholic universities. Academic freedom is important—remember the ruckuses in the University of Paris in the thirteenth century? It all comes out in the wash. Fact is, some of these popular dissenters strike me as showboaters out to curry favor with students—we all know the type—or sell their books. Some of them are worth listening to. Others will be remembered about as long as minor movie stars; e.g., John Travolta.

6. Do what you've been doing; that is, visiting ordinary orthodox Catholics around the world, concentrating on the poor of the Third World. Perhaps it is no accident that your seminaries in the latter are bursting at the seams while there is this well-known "dearth of vocations" in our enlightened and affluent society.

Don't worry about the present "dearth of vocations" among our young people. The Western world, both capitalist and Communist, is so corrupt and boring that sooner or later young people will get sick of it and look for something better. All it takes is a couple of high-livers, like Francis of Assisi, a real dude, and Clare, a rich teenage groupie, to turn it around, to actually put into practice the living truth of the Church's teachings, of the Gospel—indeed, of your own words.

You speak from the heart, Your Holiness, and down here in

Louisiana we understand you. We may not know much about such things as "the importance of the affirmation of social structures and empowerment rather than conversion," but we understand you.

Welcome to New Orleans, Your Holiness.

1987

AN UNPUBLISHED
LETTER TO THE *TIMES*

⚜

January 22, 1988

The Editor
The New York Times
229 West 43rd Street
New York, N.Y. 10036
Dear Sir:

The fifteenth anniversary of the Roe *v.* Wade decision of the Supreme Court seems as good an occasion as any to call attention to an aspect of the abortion issue which is generally overlooked.

The battle lines between the "pro-life" and the "pro-choice" advocates are so fixed, the arguments so well known, indeed so often repeated, that it hardly seems worth the time to enter the controversy on the present terms. Thus, while it may indeed be argued that in terms of Judeo-Christian values individual human life is sacred and may not be destroyed, and while it is also true that modern medical evidence shows ever more clearly that there is no qualitative difference between an unborn human infant and a born human infant, the argument is persuasive only to those who accept such values and such evidence. Absent these latter, one can at least understand the familiar arguments for a "woman's rights over her own body," including "the products of conception."

The issue, then, seems presently frozen between the "religious" and the "secular" positions, with the latter apparently prevailing in the opinion polls and the media.

Rather than enter the fray with one or another argument, which, whether true or not, seems to be unavailing, I should like to call attention to certain social and historical consequences which may be less well known—call the attention, that is, of certain well-known and honorable institutions such as *The New York Times*, the United States Supreme Court, the American Civil Liberties Union, the National Organization of Women, and suchlike who, while distinguished in their defense of human rights, may not accept the premise of the sacred provenance of human life.

In a word, certain consequences, perhaps unforeseen, follow upon the acceptance of the principle of the destruction of human life for what may appear to be the most admirable social reasons.

One does not have to look back very far in history for an example of such consequences. Take democratic Germany in the 1920s. Perhaps the most influential book published in German in the first quarter of this century was entitled *The Justification of the Destruction of Life Devoid of Value*. Its co-authors were the distinguished jurist Karl Binding and the prominent psychiatrist Alfred Hoche. Neither Binding nor Hoche had ever heard of Hitler or the Nazis. Nor, in all likelihood, did Hitler ever read the book. He didn't have to.

The point is that the ideas expressed in the book and the policies advocated were the product not of Nazi ideology but rather of the best minds of the pre-Nazi Weimar Republic—physicians, social scientists, jurists, and the like, who with the best secular intentions wished to improve the lot, socially and genetically, of the German people—by getting rid of the unfit and the unwanted.

It is hardly necessary to say what use the Nazis made of these ideas.

I would not wish to be understood as implying that the respected American institutions I have named are similar to corresponding pre-Nazi institutions.

But I do suggest that once the line is crossed, once the principle gains acceptance—juridically, medically, socially—innocent human life can be destroyed for whatever reason, for the most admirable socioeconomic, medical, or social reasons—then it does not take a prophet to predict what will happen next, or if not next, then sooner or later. At any rate, a warning is in order. Depending on the disposition of the majority and the opinion polls—now in favor of allowing women to get rid of unborn and unwanted babies—it is not difficult to imagine an electorate or a court ten years, fifty years from now, who would favor getting rid of useless old people, retarded children, anti-social blacks, illegal Hispanics, gypsies, Jews . . .

Why not?—if that is what is wanted by the majority, the polled opinion, the polity of the time.

Sincerely yours,
Walker Percy

[*Postscript: This letter did not appear in the* Times. *Nor was it acknowledged. On February 15, Dr. Percy wrote again.*]

I am sorry that you have evidently not seen fit to publish my letter of January 22 in your Letters-to-Editor section.

I should have thought that you would want to publish it, since it addresses what is a very controversial issue these days—even though the letter may run counter to your editorial policy. You are not known for suppressing dissent.

In the unlikely circumstance that you somehow did not receive the letter, I would be glad to furnish you with a copy.

The purpose of this letter is to establish for the record that you did in fact receive the first letter. For, if I do not receive an answer to this letter, it is fair to assume that you did.

[*Dr. Percy received no reply.*]

ANOTHER MESSAGE
IN THE BOTTLE

I feel a little wary about talking to teachers. This has to do with my lifetime respect for and fear of teachers, but also with a more recent and hard-won respect for your profession. Hard-won, I say, because I tried it myself a couple of times in recent years—not full-time like you, but in a small way, teaching a couple of classes in such subjects as creative writing and the contemporary novel. What I learned was that it is very hard work, much harder than I'm used to. Writing novels is much easier. I did learn something from the experience. It was that I couldn't teach and write at the same time. For me, at least, the two activities seen to draw from the same source of energy. Which is to say that I never cease to admire and be amazed at those of you who somehow manage to do both. And especially those of you who, like my daughter, teach full-time at a parochial school, run a household, and a family, and still manage to travel to New Orleans at night to take graduate courses. Myself, I'd rather make up a story.

There is another advantage to my profession, and that is that you are your own boss. You are free to write or say anything you please and the worst thing that can happen to you is that people won't buy your books. And since writers are, accordingly, an independent, even smart-aleck lot, and since I am no exception, and since in the past I have written not only novels but also nonfiction books and articles about other people's specialties when

I do not always know what I'm talking about, like philosophy, theology, semiotics, politics—I don't mind at all giving you my own theory of education.

I proposed it once before, with a noticeable lack of response from educators. But I'll tell you, anyhow. It comes from semiotics, or a theory of signs. In the human use of signs, which includes words and sentences of course, the theory goes that words which may in the beginning convey information with a sense of excitement—like Helen Keller first learning the word "water" spelled into her hand by her teacher Miss Sullivan—that these same words can become overused to the point of exhaustion, so that, instead of transmitting information, they block it. Instead of being attended by the excitement of discovery as in the so-called Helen Keller phenomenon, they are attended by boredom. This reverse phenomenon—which the German philosopher Heidegger has given the name *Alltäglichkeit*, or everydayness, and which I have called the ordinary-Wednesday-two-o'clock-in-the-afternoon phenomenon, which I would suppose you are familiar with—this phenomenon, by whatever name you call it, can, of course, be extended to most human activities, including one's job, which, humans being what they are, nearly always involves the use of signs, words, sentences, memos, computer symbols, telephone conversations, whatever. These activities, repeated day after day, tend to get worn out. And the sign-user gets worn out. This is true of writing and most professions, and I'm sure of teaching as well. Isn't it? You teach math the same time every day to the same students year after year and you get into a math rut. Or an English rut or a biology rut, it doesn't matter. Whether one is teacher or student, one gets fed up with teaching and being taught the same Shakespearean sonnets at eleven o'clock of a Tuesday—or looking at the same frog or dogfish laid out on the dissecting board in biology class.

Accordingly, this is what I proposed. It was meant for the college level, but it applies equally well at the secondary-school level. I pass it along to you free of charge as sound semiotic theory for revolutionizing education. I proposed that in an English literature class, the teacher, after going over a Shakespeare sonnet or a Longfellow lyric and observing the familiar symptoms of

Alltäglichkeit, everydayness, both in oneself and in the class—the drooping of eyelids, the gaze out the window, the teacher saying the right words but thinking about her plans for the evening or his salary—I propose that this English teacher pass out frogs or dogfish to the English class, put the dissecting board right on top of the poem—then comes the initial shock—then I can promise you that you'll get their attention. Then you say something like: "Well, what have we got here! A sonnet? No. A frog? Right. Now we've got thirty minutes left. Why don't we just poke around and see what we can see—girls can use their bobby pins, boys their Swiss Army knives—just look at that little emerald-green sac right here under the liver, that's the gall bladder, you know." Some will start poking around with real curiosity.

While in biology class, where the little corpses of frogs and dogfish have gotten pretty tattered and smelly over the weeks, what the biology teacher does is stand by the open window and look at the first April green and the first warm sunshine of the year. You open your book and say something like: "Okay, we've got a few minutes. Forget the dogfish. Just listen to this," and you read

> *Shall I compare thee to a summer's day?*
> *Thou art more lovely and more temperate:*
> *Rough winds do shake the darling buds of May,*
> *And summer's lease hath all too short a date . . .*

Now the point is that if you love this poem and if you're tired of dogfish, and if all of you have run into Wednesday-afternoon exhaustion of signs—a well-known semiotic phenomenon—they'll get it! They'll get both your excitement and the beauty of the poem.

I call this method "education by noncontextual shock." In this case, the message in the bottle is this: Yes, it is true, we are cast away on an island and pretty fed up with the island routine, the familiar signs, reading the few books we have, dissecting the few fish we've caught—when all of a sudden there's a bottle washed up on the beach and in it is a message, which begins: "Shall I compare thee to a summer's day?" Technically, this is called the defeat of the devolution or exhaustion of the sign by a shift of context—which sounds complicated but which is actually so simple that every child—and especially Helen Keller—knows all about it. Because all you have to do to awaken the wonder of a child—or Helen Keller, or a great scientist like Einstein—is to stop him/her and say, "Wait, let me show you something, take a look at this"—etc.

Now, I am willing to admit that you may have certain problems with the curriculum and the school board in putting my dogfish-sonnet theory into practice—and I know of only a couple of places it's been tried—but feel free.

Very well, so this is probably impractical pedagogy. The point is, of course, that something magical can happen between teacher and student, as you know better than I. I'm sure it's like writing: once in a while something good happens and makes it all worthwhile. Even if you're not a teacher, you can look back and remember such magic moments when you were a student. Strangely enough it is high-school teachers, not college or medical-school professors, whom I remember best. Maybe that is the age, secondary school or even primary, when you're most apt to be turned on, feel the spark jump, as it did between Helen Keller and Miss Sullivan. I remember taking plane geometry from Miss Shell in high school. Now, plane geometry does not exactly sound like the world's most exciting experience. But I'm telling you it was like a revelation when Miss Shell, who was about so high, drew a right-angle triangle on the blackboard and proved geometrically step by beautiful logical step that—let me think, it's been a while—the square of the hypotenuse equals the sum of the squares of the other two sides—isn't that it?

And then there is the biology teacher whose name I can't remember, who was also the football coach, I think. But coach or not, he got over to the class, or at least to me, the amazing idea that the organism—whether it was a frog or dogfish or the amoeba we looked at through the microscope—has this extraordinary property such that, no matter what happens on the outside, no matter how violent the changes in its environment, it has this extraordinarily complex mechanism by which it keeps its internal environment the same, in an almost perfectly steady state. Astounding! Or, as the kids would say, "Neat."

This brings me to my second message in a bottle—and surely the more important. Imagine a class of students and a teacher shipwrecked on an island—an island once populated, with buildings, schools, libraries intact, but now depopulated, perhaps by the neutron bomb. These castaways are the last survivors. Suppose, before the bomb, I had the privilege of launching one bottle with one message in it which would be certain to wash up on the beach of the island and be discovered by the castaways. What message would I send you? Let me say first that I agree with the great philosopher Kierkegaard about such messages. He said that, of course, the most important message would be the good news of our salvation to those who had not heard it but that he, not being an apostle, did not have the authority to deliver the good news. Neither do I. And we can further stipulate that the shipwrecked class we are talking about is the sophomore class of St. Scholastica Academy, so presumably they may already have heard the good news.

So what would my message in the bottle be? It would be very simple. One word, in fact. *Read!* Read: this word is really intended for the students, because it is a secret the teacher probably already knows. The message would be expanded to say something like this: "If you do not learn to read, that is, read with pleasure, that is, make the breakthrough into the delight of reading—you are going to miss out." And I don't mean you are going to miss out on books or being bookish. No, I mean that, no matter what you go into—law, medicine, computer science, housewifing, househusbanding, engineering, whatever—you are going to miss out, you are not going to be first-class unless you've made this breakthrough. You are going to miss out, not only on your profession, but on the great treasure of your heritage, which is nothing less than Western civilization.

This is no secret, of course; it is, in fact, a commonplace. But the reason I mention it is that I see so many kids growing up, strung out on seven hours of TV a day, who not only can't read but look on reading as some sort of boring assignment, a dreary chore. "Please," they'll say, "can I get back to Thundercats or Scooby Doo?"

That's my message. If you don't make the breakthrough into reading, you're not going to make the breakthrough into anything else. And no sooner do I stick it, the message, in the bottle and launch it in the ocean than I know right away what the hang-up is going to be when a student finds it on the island and reads it. "Oh boy, I've heard that before. He's talking about *literature*. Great Books and all that. Yeah yeah, I know all about that. Sure they're great, but frankly there is no way I am going to sit down and read Homer or *Macbeth*. And frankly," the student goes on to say, "I don't believe the teacher will, either."

Of course, he's right. I misspent my youth reading over a hundred Tom Swift and, at least, two hundred Rover Boy books. They were not exactly great books. The Rover Boys were all great guys. The bad guy was Dan Baxter. I can only remember one passage from the million or so words. It went like this:

" 'Throw down these rocks, Dan Baxter!' It was Tom, the fun-loving Rover boy."

Not exactly great literature.

The point, of course, is reading with pleasure. Later you can get to the great stuff, which, surprisingly enough, is even better and more fun than the Rover Boys.

Here again, it usually takes a teacher, somebody to turn you on—unless you happen to be some sort of reclusive genius like Marcel Proust, who apparently read everything without anyone's assistance. Or William Faulkner, also self-educated.

In my case, it was my father who read aloud to me. Reading aloud to a child—there is much to be said for it.

It is strange how vividly one remembers certain scenes from childhood. What I am thinking of is the experience of being read aloud to. Reading aloud. I am not sure we sufficiently understand or appreciate this experience both as a unique sort of communication between two people and as a shared flight of the imagination—two imaginations.

What I remember in every concrete detail was my father reading aloud to me Kipling's *Jungle Book* and Robert Louis Stevenson's *Treasure Island*. I was perhaps eight or nine. Yet I not only can remember exactly where we were, he sitting in a red-leather brass-studded chair by the fire, I standing alongside in my pajamas. One scene I remember particularly vividly. In *Treasure Island*, Jim Hawkins falls into a big apple barrel and takes a nap. He is awakened by a conversation a few inches away. Long John Silver is planning a mutiny. The boy listens in horror. Then John Silver reaches in for an apple . . .

What happens here is that the flight of the imagination, the mind's own conjuring up of the boy, of oneself as Jim Hawkins, shrinks away from Long John Silver's hand as the hand reaches into the dark apple barrel—that this re-creation of the imagination is a thousand times more vivid, more real, more present, than the war of the Gobots on the TV screen.

But more than that. Reading, first the reading aloud, then later simply reading, is not, as one might think, a private, reclusive sort of behavior, but a social transaction, if—and it's a big *IF*, if the literature is good. If the book is good and even if one is reading to oneself, what is happening is a very special sort of social event, a communication between writer and reader, involving what I call a "tetrad"; that is, not only two persons but an exchange of symbols between them and an exchange of referents—that is, what the symbols are about, what they conjure up.

There are two sorts of such out-of-body experiences in reading—which I am sure you are familiar with. One is ordinary good entertainment—call it inscape, if you will—in which you identify with a character and experience vicariously his or her adventures—like me as Jim Hawkins in the apple barrel. Such adventures can be literature of a very high order, such as Don Quixote or Huckleberry Finn, or low, such as Perry Mason detective novels, which are harmless enough, or Rambo movies, or any TV soap opera, which are less harmless.

The other literary experience is of the highest order—and I don't mean highest in the somewhat off-putting honorific sense of capital L, as in Literature of the Great Books—though they may be that, too—but highest in the amount of pleasure they give. This holds as equally true for drama and poetry as it does for fiction. What happens in each is that the reader is affirmed in his deepest and most inward experience. Another way of saying this is that that which seems most individual about oneself, the quirky unspoken part of one's experience, even the unspeakable, is suddenly illumined as part of the universal human experience. The exciting paradox of literature is that it is in one's own unique individuality that one is most human.

The best thing that can happen to a writer is to get a letter from a reader—usually a woman: women, let's admit it, are better readers; that is, more sensitive and observant than men. The letter is often about a section of a novel that one as a writer had the most doubts about, let's say because it seemed difficult, obscure, even idiosyncratic. But the reader says: "Yes! That's how it is! I didn't know anyone had ever felt that way!" and so on.

Of course, for my money, the story's the thing—narrativity, if we want to use the fancier word of the critics. This makes me old-fashioned in the view of some critics and some practitioners of the so-called anti-novel who'd rather put anything in a novel than a story of something happening to someone. This is not to say that they don't have a point, if they are mounting a conscious revolt against the mindless sequence of happenings which make up most so-called novels. They may also have a point if they are saying that much of what happens in modern life is so senseless that the only way to write about it is to write the Novel of the Absurd in which either nothing happens or the events which do happen don't make much sense or have much connection with each other. In these times, one must grant a degree of validity to this aesthetic of the anti-novel.

Another way of saying this is that both the reader is in a bad way and the novel is in a bad way if the reader's life is so meaningless that he or she has to confer a spurious meaning on his life by reading a novel by, say, somebody like Jackie Collins or Sidney Sheldon, which diverts him or her by a sequence of lively but meaningless events. This sort of reading may be better than drinking Bourbon or taking cocaine, but there are certain similarities: for example, one feels worse not better when it's over.

No, the novel is at its best when the story bears some relation of truth to one's own story, or, as one critic put it, true narrativity is nothing less than the movement of one's very self. T. S. Eliot had a fancy word for it: the objective correlative. By which he meant that, believe it or not, the adventures of Ulysses three thousand years ago, the fighting, the loving, the leaving, the journey, the arrival, are recognizable as the journey of one's most inward self. Same is true of the modern Ulysses of James Joyce. Or of Huckleberry Finn, floating down the Mississippi, with a new adventure around the bend. Or of Quentin Compson's unhappy adventures in Faulkner's *The Sound and the Fury*. Or of Haze Motes's weird crusade in Flannery O'Connor's *Wise Blood*. And it is not true of Jackie Collins or Sidney Sheldon or *Dynasty* or *Days of Our Lives*, which, if one is depressed, may offer an escape from the depression for thirty minutes, then leaves one more depressed than ever. This is not to put down *Days of Our Lives*, which I have watched off and on for thirty years with the sound off, but as a kind of conscious exercise in mild depravity, something like keeping a case of athlete's foot for thirty years in order to enjoy the scratching. I'm the first to admit there's something to be said for the pleasures of scratching an itch.

But here we're talking about literature.

So the message in the bottle to students marooned on an island which has been nuked by the neutron bomb, which leaves the library intact but which has killed off all TV personnel, scrambled all satellite transmissions of *As the World Turns* and *The Donahue Show*, killed the staff of Cinema Six, the movie theater, which still advertises *Black Widow*, *Rambo III*, *Mannequin*, *Bedroom Window*, *Call Girl*, and *Beast of the Black Lagoon*. So there's nothing left on the island but a library full of books. What to do—after exploring the island?

I'll give you the extreme case—and, unfortunately, I didn't make it up. I think it was Aldous Huxley. I think his character was the last survivor on a devastated earth. He's left his cave and is wandering through the ruins, picks up a tattered book, which happens to be Shakespeare's *The Tempest*. He reads it! With astonishment and delight! Now, honestly, who among us would go to the library on our day off, sign out a copy of *The Tempest*, take it home, turn off the tube, which is showing the Super Bowl, and read it? Read *The Tempest*? Would you? Do you think I would?

Am I suggesting that reading is a lost art and that the bomb has to fall in order that the few survivors might discover it, for lack of anything better to do? Well, not quite. But something of the sort is going on. Great Books are somewhat inaccessible. So, failing them, it is the task of living writers to do better than Jackie Collins, to be as diverting, if you can't do as well as Shakespeare or Faulkner.

Let's say that the castaways are marooned for years, with no TV and nothing but a big deserted library of a million books. For lack of anything better to do, they read. They read for years. Some books they like very much. Some they can't stand. But what's the verdict over the years? Which books are the favorites, and why? Certainly, after ten years, there will be a kind of consensus of what's bad and what's good. But will any standards emerge by which the castaways decide which is bad and which is good?

Here, of course, we get into all sorts of difficulties; that is, when we start talking about what's good and bad in literature and why, what's great and what's mediocre, what's moral and what's immoral, what's trash and what's enduring.

For example, a good many of the castaways might find themselves reading Louis L'Amour, dozens, hundreds of Louis L'Amour novels—for months. Now, there's nothing wrong with Louis L'Amour. He's a very skilled craftsman at what he does, which is to construct highly entertaining and diverting stories.

But after ten years a strange thing happens. The Louis L'Amour fan may find that after he's read all the books he does not go back and reread Louis L'Amour. But he does go back and reread, say, *Catcher in the Rye* or *Huckleberry Finn*. Why is that?

Here's another puzzlement. Let's say that he or she, as she explores the library, comes on a shelf in the fiction wing labeled "Christian Novels." What is the reader apt to do, whether he is a Christian or not? Keep moving, of course.

Why is that? What is the big turnoff about a label like Christian Novel? Let us admit that the reader's instincts in passing up this shelf are probably quite sound. Because he knows what he's probably in for. What he's in for in too many cases are books which set out to be "uplifting," "edifying," "moral." Now, what's wrong with being uplifting, edifying, moral? Nothing, if the uplift comes from the writer's art and not from his need to preach. As Flannery O'Connor used to say, show me fifty ladies who want to read uplifting books and what you've got is a book club.

Chaucer's *Canterbury Tales* and Dante's *Inferno* and O'Connor's *Wise Blood* are great Christian books, but not because the authors set out to be uplifting.

Why is it that Flaubert's *Madame Bovary*, which caused a great scandal when it was published, is a more truly Christian novel than, say, *The Big Fisherman*, which is about St. Peter and not only was edifying but also made a lot of money?

And what about pornography? We would all agree that pornography is bad, but on what grounds? There are those who say it isn't. And, let's face it, a certain number of the castaways would spend a good deal of time in the dirty-book section of the library. And if we can agree that pornography is bad, does it follow that descriptions of explicit sexual behavior are also bad? And if not, why not?

In a word, after ten years on the island, does any sort of standard begin to emerge by which the castaways can agree about what's bad and what's good?

Well, first, there will soon be a sort of agreement about pornography, what makes a book pornographic or, at least, different from other books.

It will soon become obvious to nearly everyone on the island that pornography is different from other writings, that it sets out to do something other books don't do. If other novels set out to entertain, or tell about how things are, create characters and adventures with which the reader can identify, pornography is doing something quite different. It sets out quite deliberately to stimulate the reader sexually. There is something with which Christians and non-Christians, scientists and English teachers, can agree. It is no great mystery. Pornography, which is a transaction in signs, is not really different from Pavlov's dog salivating at the sound of a bell which he has learned "means" the approach of food.

So, without getting into the vexed question of censorship or even of moral theology, I am content here to say that, whatever pornography is, it is not literature, not even bad literature. It is something else. To put it in semiotic terms, literature has to do with me writing words about something which you read with understanding and the pleasure, I hope, of affirming it. Pornography has to do with my using words as stimuli to elicit certain responses from you. Literature is an "I-you" transaction in which symbols are used to transmit truths of a sort. Pornography is an "I-it" transaction in which you become an "it," an organism manipulated by stimuli.

It is not necessary, I'm sure, to tell you who becomes the It in this transaction. It is the woman, of course, all women, who are degraded in their very persons by being used as objects.

Then, what is allowed? I don't mean allowed by censors. I mean allowed by the serious writer and the serious reader. What about explicit sex? Explicit violence?—there is also, of course, such a thing as a pornography of violence. The only rule I follow is that anything is allowed that serves the artistic purpose of the novel. The biblical *Song of Songs* is not pornographic, because the lover's description of the beloved serves the purpose of the writer.

But here the writer must be careful and know what he's doing. Because, if he's a serious writer, what he is worried about is not using "dirty words" or shocking the reader—after all, Flannery O'Connor used shock as her favorite literary device—no, what he is worried about is distracting the reader from the real purpose of the novel. If I have a certain truth or artistic form to convey in a novel, and if I write a scene which is so explicitly sexual or so explicitly violent that the reader is distracted, either by stimulation, that is, by sexual titillation, or by loathing and disgust, then I have lost him or her and have failed as a novelist.

This rule, for me, holds true whether we're speaking of the novel as high art, high comedy, or high entertainment. Thus, it will not do in *Huckleberry Finn* if Huck goes ashore for raunchy sexual encounters or Rambo-like violence, because such side trips distract from the main theme that works—Huck afloat on the raft on the Mississippi and, therefore, oneself afloat, on the way, on the road, spinning along in a zone of pure possibility, between states so to speak, on the way finally out West, lighting out for the territory, the perfect symbol for a new life of freedom.

So it is a delicate business, writing novels these days, if one is a serious writer—which, of course, includes being a comic writer—and not out for the skin trade, the *Playboy* voyeurs of certain best-sellers, which, admittedly, can be lucrative. One is going to lose some readers, overstimulate some, turn off others—like my aunt in Georgia, an old-style Presbyterian, who used, to say to me: "Walker, why do you have to use those terrible words? Why can't you write high-minded books like your Uncle Will?"—meaning William Alexander Percy, who was, in fact, more a high-minded writer than I.

What we're approaching is a kind of general criterion for telling good books from bad books, what makes good books good and bad books bad. The first rule of thumb, of course, is pleasure. A good book gives the reader pleasure, the sort of deep, abiding pleasure he likes to come back to. If a writer does not give pleasure, he'd better take up another line of work—unless he's writing textbooks, which are not supposed to give pleasure—but even here, as you know better than I, a really good textbook can be a delight.

But what is a good writer up to when he's writing a book that will give the reader pleasure? First of all, he's telling the truth. Bad books always lie. They lie most of all about the human condition, so that one never recognizes oneself, the deepest part of oneself, in a bad book. And even when a bad book gives its own sort of pleasure, either a pastime of diversion and adventurism, or the titillation of voyeurism, it leaves a sour taste in the mouth, like a hangover from bad Bourbon.

The truth of the novelist is a special kind of truth. What kind of truth? It is a truth more like good carpentry than like good reporting. Or, as the Scholastics used to say, art is a virtue of the practical intellect. It is in the sphere of making, not reasoning, not reporting. A good novel is like a good table. The parts have to fit; it has to work, that is, sit foursquare and at the right level. And it has to please. Its truth lies in the way it looks, feels, hefts—the touch and the grain of the thing. Its morality follows from the form and the excellence of the thing. That is to say, its morality comes from within, follows naturally from its making and is not imposed from without. It does not preach.

Let me say a final word about the relationship between the

art of the novel and Christianity, the Catholic faith in particular, at least as I see it. It might appear from what I have said—that art is in the sphere of making something—that novel-writing is pure craftsmanship and has nothing to do with religion. Indeed, mightn't Christianity even be a handicap to the writer, considering the number of bad so-called Christian novels that have been written? It can be argued that the most beautiful vases in the world were made by Greek pagans and Japanese Buddhists.

Here I can only give my own conviction. It is that there is a special kinship between the novel as an art form and Christianity as an ethos, Catholicism in particular. It is no accident, I think, that the novel is a creature of the Christian West and is virtually nonexistent in the Buddhist, Taoist, and Brahmin East, to say nothing of Marxist countries.

It is the narrativity and commonplaceness of the novel which is unique. Something is happening in ordinary time to ordinary people, not to epic heroes in mythic time.

It is no coincidence that in the very part of the world where novels have been written and read, the presiding ethos, the central overriding belief, is that the salient truth of life is not the teaching of a great philosopher or the enlightenment of a great sage. It was, rather, the belief that something had happened, an actual Event in historic time. Certainly, no one disagrees that the one great difference of Christianity is its claim—outrageous claim, many would say—that God actually entered historic time, first through his covenant with the Jews and then through the Incarnation.

Certainly, there is nothing new about this. What concerns us here is the peculiar relevance of this belief for novel-writing. I could also speak of its relevance to other art forms—drama and poetry, for example—and to the genesis of science.

But what kind of truth is a serious writer after when he sets out to give lasting pleasure?

It is truth of a special sort.

It is not the truth of a mathematical equation.

It is not the truth of reporting in good journalism.

Rather is it a deeper truth about the way things are, the way people are; in a word, a truth about the human condition; and a truth of such an order, both old and new, that one recognizes oneself in it. Therein lies the pleasure.

But what has this to do with the reader's pleasure, with the relationship between Christianity and the novel as an art form? Because it is no accident, as I have suggested, that the novel is almost exclusively a creature of Christendom.

The fact that novels are narratives about events which happen to people in the course of time is given a unique weight in an ethos that is informed by the belief that awards an absolute importance to an Event which happened to a Person in historic time. In a very real way, one can say that the Incarnation not only brought salvation to mankind but gave birth to the novel.

Judeo-Christianity is about pilgrims who have something wrong with them and are embarked on a search to find a way out. This is also what novels are about.

In a word, it is my conviction that the incarnational and sacramental dimensions of Catholic Christianity are the greatest natural assets of a novelist.

It is not too much to say, I think, that though most current novelists may not be believing Christians or Jews, they are still living in a Judeo-Christian ethos. If, in fact, they are living on the fat of the faith, so to speak, one can't help but wonder what happens when the fat is consumed. Perhaps there are already signs. Witness the current loss of narrative of character and events in the post-modern novel.

It is no accident that the novel has never flourished in the Eastern tradition. If Buddhism and Hinduism believe that the self is illusory, that ordinary life is misery, that ordinary things have no sacramental value, and that reality itself is concealed by the veil of *maya*, how can any importance be attached to or any pleasure be taken in novels about selves and happenings and things in an ordinary world?

Or take Marxism: if the events of history are seen as a remorseless dialectic whose outcome is inevitable, who wants to read a novel about it? Try to think of one good Marxist novel.

Or take behaviorism—which has had a tremendous influence on the scientific mind for the past fifty years. If all behavior is a psychological response to a stimulus, what happens to the freedom of choice which is the meat and bread of the novelist? Read any good behaviorist novels lately?

Same for Freudianism: if our actions, emotions, our very thoughts arise from unconscious conflicts and forgotten childhood traumas, how does one write a novel about anything but a psychoanalyst and his patient on the couch talking about her dreams? Have you ever noticed how boring it is to listen to somebody else's dreams, let alone read about them in novels?

In a word, it is you Catholic educators who are in the best position both to understand the special bearing of our own tradition on this unique art form—the good novel about life and how we live it—and to turn on your young charges to reading—and yes, to the fun of it.

That's the message in the bottle.

THE HOLINESS OF
THE ORDINARY

I suppose there are two ways of being both a Catholic and a writer. One is being a member of a society so thoroughly Catholic that it does not occur to one to write as a "Catholic." It is hard to think of a great writer more Catholic than Dante or Chaucer and less self-consciously "Catholic."

The other is being a Catholic in a hostile or indifferent society. Then one can hardly escape thinking of oneself, however indirectly, as choosing to be Catholic as an alternative, defending the one and opposing the other. Alternative to what? Protestantism? Humanism? Marxism? New Age Buddhism?

Yet, even now, one can think of a novelist like J. F. Powers who inserts his characters into such an exclusively Catholic milieu—priests in rectories, who have their troubles all right, but the troubles have little to do with the usual non-Catholic alternatives. It is difficult to imagine a depressed soul-searching humanist in a Powers novel.

Like most putative Catholic writers these days, I belong to the second group. That is to say, there is hardly a moment in my writing when I am not aware of where, say, my main character—who is usually some kind of Catholic, bad, half-baked, lapsed, whatever—of where he or she stands vis-à-vis the Catholic faith. It is a workable reference point. This doesn't mean that I feel obliged to make the good guys Catholic. No, it is much more fun to put a rotten Catholic down in a life crisis and see how he handles it. Maybe badly or well, but what makes him tick can usually be understood in terms of some reference, negative or otherwise, to his Catholic background. It's a tough birthright to shed. Love it or hate it maybe, but lukewarm seldom.

Nor, God forbid, do I feel obliged to write edifying tales where virtue wins out and the Catholic faith triumphs over high-class "secular humanists" or low-class Mafia types. It usually works better to let the latter win or think he wins. Novelists are a devious lot, Catholic novelists more than most.

While no serious novelist knows for sure where his writing comes from, I have the strongest feeling that, whatever else the benefits of the Catholic faith, it is of a particularly felicitous use to the novelist. Indeed, if one had to design a religion for novelists, I can think of no better. What distinguishes Judeo-Christianity in general from other world religions is its emphasis on the value of the individual person, its view of man as a creature in trouble, seeking to get out of it, and accordingly on the move. Add to this anthropology the special marks of the Catholic Church: the sacraments, especially the Eucharist, which, whatever else they do, confer the highest significance upon the ordinary things of this world, bread, wine, water, touch, breath, words, talking, listening— and what do you have? You have a man in a predicament and on the move in a real world of real things, a world which is a sacrament and a mystery; a pilgrim whose life is a searching and a finding.

Such a view of man as wayfarer is, I submit, nothing else than a recipe for the best novel-writing from Dante to Dostoevsky. Even an excellent atheist novelist like Sartre borrows from this traditional anthropology for the upside-down pilgrimage of his characters into absurdity.

It is no accident, I think, that the great religions of the East, especially Hinduism and Buddhism, with their devaluation of the individual and of reality itself, are not notable for the novels of their devotees.

Only recently, in so-called post-modern fiction, has the novelist abandoned this anthropology in favor of absorption with self or with the text, not the meaning, of words. The results are pre-dictable.

Show me a young California novelist raised in Taoism who spends his life meditating on the Way and I'll show you a bad novelist.

Show me a lapsed Catholic who writes a good novel about being a young Communist at Columbia and I'll show you a novelist who owes more to Sister Gertrude at Sacred Heart in Brooklyn, who slapped him clean out of his seat for disrespect to the Eucharist, than he owes to all of Marxist dialectic.

In the end, ten boring Hail Marys are worth more to the novelist than ten hours of Joseph Campbell on TV.

I have not mentioned the exceedingly important use of comedy in fiction—a different matter altogether—but there's not space here.

Anyhow, the notion of saying one's beads while watching Joseph Campbell is funny enough as it is.

1989

Epilogue

AN INTERVIEW

AND A

SELF-INTERVIEW

AN INTERVIEW
WITH ZOLTÁN
ABÁDI-NAGY

❧

How did you spend your seventieth birthday?

An ordinary day. I went with my wife and some friends to a neighborhood restaurant in New Orleans. I think I had crawfish. What distinguishes Louisianians is that they suck the heads.

You and your wife recently celebrated your fortieth anniversary. Is it easy, do you imagine, to be married to a writer?

Mine has been a happy marriage—thanks mainly to my wife. Who would want to live with a novelist? A man underfoot in the house all day? A man, moreover, subject to solitary funks and strange elations. If I were a woman, I'd prefer a traveling salesman. There is no secret, or rather the secrets are buried in platitudes. That is to say, it has something to do with love, commitment, and family. As to the institution, it is something like Churchill's description of democracy: vicissitudinous yes, but look at the alternatives.

What are the decisive moments, turning points that you regard as the milestones of those seven decades?

What comes to mind is something like this: (1) losing both parents in my early teens and being adopted by my Uncle Will, a poet, and being exposed to the full force of a remarkable literary imagination; (2) contracting a nonfatal case of tuberculosis while serving as an intern in Bellevue Hospital in New York, an event which did not so much change my life as give me leave to change it; (3) getting married; (4) becoming a Catholic.

If you had the chance, would you decide to be reborn or to flee back into William Blake's "the vales of Har"?

No vales of Har, thank you. No rebirth either, but I wouldn't mind a visit in the year 2050—a short visit, not more than half an hour—say, to a park bench at the southeast corner of Central Park in New York, with a portable radio. Just to have a look around, just to see whether we made it, and if so, in what style. One could tell in half an hour. By "we" of course, I do not mean just Americans, but the species. Homo sapiens sapiens.

Once you said that if you were starting over, you might like to make films. Would there be other decisions that would be different?

I might study linguistics—not in the current academic meanings of the word, but with a fresh eye, like Newton watching the falling apple: How come? What's going on here?

Apropos of your fascination with film, most of it finds its way into your novels on the thematic level, especially in The Moviegoer *and* Lancelot. *Does it happen that film or television influences you in less noticeable ways as well, such as cinematic structuring of material and so on?*

I can only answer in the most general way: that what television and movies give the writer is a new community and a new set of referents. Since nearly everyone watches television a certain number of hours a day (whether they admit it or not), certain turns of plot are ready-made for satirical use; namely, the Western shoot-out, one man calling another out, a mythical dance of honor. In my last novel I described one character as looking something like Blake Carrington. Now, you may not know who Blake Carrington is—though sooner or later most Hungarians will. A hundred million Americans do know. [He is John Forsythe's character in the television series *Dynasty*.]

Could you tell me how you feel about your inspiring beliefs, how faithful you have remained to them?

If you mean, am I still a Catholic, the answer is yes. The main difference after thirty-five years is that my belief is less self-conscious, less ideological, less polemical. My ideal is Thomas More, an English Catholic—a peculiar breed nowadays—who wore his faith with grace, merriment, and a certain wryness. Incidentally, I reincarnated him again in my new novel and I'm sorry to say he has fallen upon hard times; he is a far cry from the saint, drinks too much, and watches reruns of M*A*S*H on TV.

As for philosophy and religion, do you still regard yourself as a philosophical Catholic existentialist?

Philosophical? Existentialist? Religion? Pretty heavy. These are perfectly good words—except perhaps "existentialist"—but over the years they have acquired barnacle-like connotative excrescences. Uttering them induces a certain dreariness and heaviness in the neck muscles. As for "existentialist," I'm not sure it presently has a sufficiently clear referent to be of use. Even "existentialists" forswear the term. It fell into disuse some years ago when certain novelists began saying things like: I beat up my wife in an existential moment—meaning a sudden, irrational impulse.

Is it possible to define your Catholic existentialism in a few sentences?

I suppose I would prefer to describe it as a certain view of man, an anthropology, if you like; of man as wayfarer, in a rather conscious contrast to prevailing views of man as organism, as encultured creature, as consumer, Marxist, as subject to such-and-such a scientific or psychological understanding—all of which he is, but not entirely. It is the "not entirely" I'm interested in—like the man Kierkegaard described who read Hegel, understood himself and the universe perfectly by noon, but then had the problem of living out the rest of the day. It, my "anthropology," has been expressed better in an earlier, more traditional language—e.g., scriptural: man born to trouble as the sparks fly up; Gabriel Marcel's Homo viator.

You converted to Catholicism in the 1940s. What was the motive behind that decision?

There are several ways to answer the question. One is theological. The technical theological term is grace, the gratuitous unmerited gift from God. Another answer is less theological: What else is there? Did you expect me to become a Methodist? a Buddhist? a Marxist? a comfortable avuncular humanist like Walter Cronkite? an exhibitionist like Allen Ginsberg? A proper literary-philosophical-existentialist answer is that the occasion was the reading of Kierkegaard's extraordinary essay: "On the Difference between a Genius and an Apostle." Like the readings that mean most to you, what it did was to confirm something I suspected but that it took Søren Kierkegaard to put into words: that what the greatest geniuses in science, literature, art, philosophy utter are sentences which convey truths *sub specie aeternitatis*; that is to say, sentences which can be confirmed by appropriate methods and by anyone, anywhere, any time. But only the apostle can utter sentences which can be accepted on the authority of the apostle; that is, his credentials, sobriety, trustworthiness as a news bearer. These sentences convey not knowledge *sub specie aeternitatis* but news.

I noticed that you rarely refer to other converted novelists like Graham Greene and Evelyn Waugh when discussing your ideas. Or if you do, it is rarely, if ever, in this context.

Maybe it's because novelists don't talk much about each other. Maybe this is because novelists secrete a certain BO which only other novelists detect, like certain buzzards who emit a repellent pheromone detectable only by other buzzards, which is to say that only a novelist can know how neurotic, devious, underhanded a novelist can be. Actually, I have the greatest admiration for both writers, not necessarily for their religion, but for their consummate craft.

Can we discuss the "Los Angelized" and re-Christianized New South? Is there anything new in the way the South is developing in the 1980s or in the way you read the South or your own relation to it?

The odd thing I've noticed is that while of course the South is more and more indistinguishable from the rest of the country

(Atlanta, for example, which has become one of the three or four megalopolises of the United States, is in fact, I'm told by blacks, their favorite American city), the fact is that, as Faulkner said fifty years ago, as soon as you cross the Mason–Dixon Line, you still know it. This, after fifty years of listening to the same radio and watching millions of hours of *Barnaby Jones*. I don't know whether it's the heat or a certain lingering civility, but people will slow down on interstates to let you get in traffic. Strangers speak in post offices, hold doors for each other without being thought queer or running a con game or making a sexual advance. I could have killed the last cab driver I had in New York. Ask Eudora Welty, she was in the same cab.

Have your views concerning being a writer in the South undergone a change during the past decades? Is being a writer in the South in 1987 the same as it was when you started to write?

Southern writers—that's the question everybody asks. I still don't know the answer. All I know is that there is still something about living in the South which turns one inward, makes one secretive, sly, and scheming, makes one capable of a degree of malice, humor, and outrageousness. At any rate, despite the Los Angelization of the South, there are right here, in the New Orleans area, perhaps half a dozen very promising young writers—which is more than can be said of Los Angeles. It comes, not from the famous storytelling gregariousness one hears about, but from the shy, sly young woman, say, who watches, listens, gets a fill of it, and slips off to do a number on it. And it comes, not from having arrived at last in the Great American Mainstream along with the likes of Emerson and Sandburg, but from being close enough to have a good look at one's fellow Americans, fellow Southerners, yet keep a certain wary distance, enough to nourish a secret, subversive conviction: I can do a number on those guys—and on me—and it will be good for all of us.

Apropos of Southern writing, does regionalism still apply?

Sure, in the better sense of the word, in the sense that Chekhov and Flaubert and Mark Twain are regionalists—not in the sense that Joel Chandler Harris and Bret Harte were regionalists.

You studied science at Chapel Hill and became a medical doctor at Columbia. In your recently published essay "The Diagnostic Novel" you suggest that serious art is "just as cognitive" as science is and "the serious novelist is quite as much concerned with discovering reality as a serious physicist." Art explores reality in a way which "cannot be done any other way." What are some of the ways that are specific to an artistic as opposed to a scientific exploration of reality?

The most commonplace example of the cognitive dimension in fiction is the reader's recognition—sometimes the shock of recognition—the "verification" of a sector of reality which he had known but not known that he had known. I think of letters I get from readers which may refer to a certain scene and say, in effect, yes! that's the way it is! For example, Binx in *The Moviegoer* describes one moviegoing experience, going to see *Panic in the Streets*, a film shot in New Orleans, going to a movie theater in the very neighborhood where the same scenes in the movie were filmed. Binx tells his girlfriend Kate about his reasons for enjoying the film—that it, the film "certifies" the reality of the neighborhood in a peculiar sense in which the direct experience of the neighborhood, living in the neighborhood, does not. I have heard from many readers about this and other such scenes—as have other novelists, I'm sure—saying they *know* exactly what Binx is talking about. I think it is reasonable to call such a transaction cognitive, sciencing. This sort of sciencing is closely related to the cognitive dimension of psychoanalysis. The patient, let's say, relates a dream. Such-and-such happened. The analyst suggests that perhaps the dream "means" such and such. It sometimes happens that the patient—perhaps after a pause, a frown, a shaking of head—will suddenly "see" it. Yes, by God! Which is to say: in sciencing, there are forms of verification other than pointer-readings.

As for your view that it is a mistake to draw a moral and be edifying in art—is Lancelot's naïve-fascistoid idea of the Third Revolution illustrative of this?

I was speaking of the everyday use of the words "moral" and "edifying"—which is to say, preachy—in the sense that, say, Ayn Rand's novels are preachy, have a message, but may in the deepest sense of the word be immoral. So is Lancelot's "Third Revolution" in the deepest sense immoral and, I hope, is so taken by the reader. To tell the truth, I don't see how any serious fiction-writer or poet can fail to be moral and edifying in the technical nonconnotative sense of these words, since he or she cannot fail to be informed by his own deep sense of the way things should be or should not be, by a sense of pathology and hence a sense of health. If a writer writes from a sense of outrage—and most serious writers do—isn't he by definition a moral writer?

The influence of Dostoevsky, Camus, Sartre, and other novelists upon you has often been discussed. Is there any literary influence that joined the rest recently?

Chekhov reread—in a little reading group we have here in Covington. His stories "In the Ravine" and "Ward Number Six" are simply breathtaking. Also recently, the German novelist Peter Handke, whose latest, *The Weight of the World*, is somehow exhilarating in the spontaneity of its free-form diary entries. The accurate depiction of despair can be exhilarating, a cognitive emotion.

What is your attitude toward the reader?

I hold out for some sort of contractual relationship between novelist and reader, however flawed, misapprehended, or fragmentary. Perhaps the contract is ultimately narratological, perhaps not. But something keeps—or fails to keep—the reader reading the next sentence. Even the "anti-novel" presupposes some sort of contractual venture at the very moment the "anti-novelist" is attacking narrativity. Such a venture implies that the writer is up to something, going abroad like Don Quixote—if only to attack windmills—and that the reader is with him. Otherwise, why would the latter bother? The anti-novelist is like a Protestant. His protests might be valid, but where would he be without the Catholic Church? I have no objection to "anti-story" novels. What I object to is any excursion by the author which violates the novelistic contract between writer and reader, which I take to be an intersubjective transaction entailing the transmission of a set of symbols, a text. The writer violates the contract when he trashes the reader by pornography or scatological political assaults, e.g., depicting President Nixon in a novel buggering Ethel Rosenberg in Times Square, or L.B.J. plotting the assassination of J.F.K. Take pornography, a difficult, slippery case. It is not necessary to get into a discussion of First Amendment rights—for all I know, it has them. And, for all I know, pornography has its uses. All I suggest is that pornography and literature stimulate different organs. If we can agree that a literary text is a set of signals transmitted from sender to receiver in a certain code, pornography is a different set of signals and a different code.

Can it be said that in your case the primary business of literature and art is cognitive, whereas with John Gardner it is to "be morally judgmental"? It is clear that you and Gardner are not talking about the same thing.

I expect there is an overlap between Gardner's "moral fiction" and my "diagnostic novel." But Gardner makes me nervous with his moralizing. When he talks about literature "establishing models of human action," he seems to be using literature to influence what people do. I think he is confusing two different orders of reality. Aquinas and the Schoolmen were probably right: art is making; morality is doing. Art is a virtue of the practical intellect, which is to say making something. This is not to say that art, fiction, is not moral in the most radical sense—if it is made right. But if you write a novel with the goal of trying to make somebody do right, you're writing a tract—which may be an admirable enterprise, but it is not literature. Dostoevsky's *Notes from the Underground* is in my opinion a work of art, but it would probably not pass Gardner's moral test. Come to think of it, I think my reflexes are medical rather than moral. This comes, I guess, from having been a pathologist. Now, I am perfectly willing to believe Flannery O'Connor when she said, and she wasn't kidding, that the modern world is a territory largely occupied by the devil. No one doubts the malevolence abroad in the world. But the world is also deranged. What interests me as a novelist is not the malevolence of man—so what else is new?—but his looniness. The looniness, that is to say, of the "normal" denizen of the Western world who, I think it fair to say, doesn't know who he is, what he believes, or what he is doing. This unprecedented state of affairs is, I suggest, the domain of the "diagnostic" novelist.

Are there any trends or authors in contemporary American innovative fiction that you regard with sympathy?

Yes, there are quite a few younger writers whom I will not name but whom I would characterize as innovative "minimalist" writers who have been influenced by Donald Barthelme without succumbing to him, which is easy to do, or as young Southern writers who have been influenced by Faulkner and Welty without succumbing to them, which is also easy to do.

If I were asked whose work I feel to be closest to yours—the whole terrain of contemporary American fiction considered—I would choose Saul Bellow.

Why?

Because of the philosophical bent, because both of you are satirical moralists, because Bellow's is also a quest informed by an awareness that man can do something about alienation, and because philosophical abstraction and concrete social commentary are equally balanced.

I take that kindly. I admire Barth, Pynchon, Heller, Vonnegut—you could also throw in Updike, Cheever, and Malamud—but perhaps Bellow most of all. He bears the same relationship to the streets of Chicago and upper Broadway—has inserted himself into them—the way I have in the Gentilly district of New Orleans or a country town in West Feliciana Parish in Louisiana.

What exactly moves you to write? An idea? An image? A character? A landscape? A memory? Something that happened to you or to someone else? You have said about The Moviegoer *that you "liked the idea of putting a young man down in a faceless suburb."*

The spark might have come from Sartre's Roquentin in *Nausea* sitting in that library watching the Self-taught Man or sitting in that café watching the waiter. Why not have a younger, less perverse Roquentin, a Southerner of a certain sort, and put him down in a movie house in Gentilly, a middle-class district of New Orleans, not unlike Sartre's Bouville.

If every writer writes from his own predicament, could you give a few hints as to how The Moviegoer *illustrates this point?*

After the war, not doing medicine, writing and publishing articles in psychiatric, philosophical, and political journals, I was living in New Orleans and going to the movies. You can't make a living writing articles for *The Journal of Philosophy and Phenomenological Research.* The thought crossed my mind: why not do what French philosophers often do and Americans almost never— novelize philosophy, incarnate ideas in a person and a place, which latter is, after all, a noble Southern tradition in fiction.

Did you model any characters on your brothers, wife, children, grandchildren?

Not in any way anyone would recognize.

In connection with Message in the Bottle, *a collection of essays that had been published over two and a half decades, what attracted you to linguistics and semiotics, to the theories of language, meaning, signs, and symbols?*

That's a big question, too big to answer in more than a couple of sentences. It has to do with the first piece of writing I ever got published. I was sitting around Saranac Lake getting over a light case of tuberculosis. There was nothing to do but read. I got hold of Susanne Langer's *Philosophy in a New Key,* in which she focuses on man's unique symbol-mongering behavior. This was an eye-opener to me, a good physician-scientist brought up in the respectable behaviorist tradition of UNC and Columbia. I was so excited I wrote a review and sent it to *Thought* quarterly. It was accepted! I was paid by twenty-five reprints. That was enough. What was important was seeing my scribble in *print!*

Can you recollect what was involved in your getting started with The Last Gentleman?

I wanted to create someone not quite as flat as Binx in *The Moviegoer,* more disturbed, more passionate, more in love, and, above all, *on the move.* He is in pilgrimage without quite knowing it—doing a Kierkegaardian repetition; that is, going back to his past to find himself, then from home and self to the *West* following the summons of a queer sort of apostle, mad Dr. Sutter. "Going West" is U.S. colloquial for dying.

Love in the Ruins?

Love in the Ruins was a picnic, with everything in it but the kitchen sink. It was written during the Time of Troubles in the sixties, with all manner of polarization in the country, black versus white, North versus South, hippie versus square, liberal versus conservative, McCarthyism versus Commies, etc.—the whole seasoned with a Southern flavor and featuring sci-fi, futurism, and Dr. More, a whimsical descendent of the saint. After the solemnities of *The Moviegoer* and *The Last Gentleman*, why not enjoy myself? I did. Now I have seen fit to resurrect Dr. More in the novel I just finished, *The Thanatos Syndrome*. He is in trouble as usual and I am enjoying it.

Lancelot?

Lancelot might have come from an upside-down theological notion, not about God but about sin, more specifically the falling into disrepute of the word "sin." So it seemed entirely fitting that Lancelot, a proper Southern gent raised in a long tradition of knightly virtues, chiefly by way of Walter Scott, the most widely read novelist in the South for a hundred years, should have undertaken his own sort of quest for his own peculiar Grail, i.e., sin, which quest is, after all, a sort of search for God. Lancelot wouldn't be caught dead looking for God, but he is endlessly intrigued by the search for evil. Is there such a thing—malevolence over and beyond psychological and sociological categories? The miscarriage of his search issues, quite logically I think, in his own peculiar brand of fascism, which is far more attractive and seductive, I think, than Huey Long's.

Let me ask about The Second Coming, *too, since although it developed into a sequel to* The Last Gentleman, *originally it was not conceived as a sequel.*

The Second Coming was a sure-enough love story—a genre I would ordinarily steer clear of. What made it possible was the, to me, appealing notion of the encounter of Allie and Will, like the crossing of two lines on a graph, one going up, the other down: the man who has "succeeded" in life, made it, has the best of worlds, and yet falls down in sand traps on the golf course, gazes at clouds and is haunted by memory, is in fact in despair; the girl, a total "failure," a schizophrenic who has flunked life, as she puts it, yet who, despite all, sees the world afresh and full of hope. It was the paradox of it that interested me. What happens when he meets her? What is the effect on his ghost-like consciousness of her strange yet prescient, schizophrenic speech?

Nonfiction. Lost in the Cosmos?

Lost in the Cosmos was a sly, perhaps even devious, attempt to approach a semiotics of the self. Circumspection was necessary here, because semioticists have no use for the self, and votaries of the self—poets, humanists, novel readers, etc.—have no use for semiotics. It was a quite ambitious attempt actually, not necessarily successful, to derive the self, a very nebulous entity indeed, through semiotics, specifically the emergence of self as a consequence of the child's entry into the symbol-mongering world of men—and, even more specifically, through the acquisition of language. What was underhanded about the book was the insertion of a forty-page "primer of semiotics" in the middle of the book, with a note of reassurance to the reader that he could skip it if he wanted to. Of course I was hoping he, or more likely she, would be sufficiently intrigued to take the dare and read it, since it is of course the keystone of the book. Having derived the self semiotically, then the fun came from deriving the various options of the self semiotically—the various "reentries" of the self from the orbits most people find themselves in. Such options are ordinarily regarded as the territory of the novelist, the queer things his characters do. The fun was like the fun of Mendeleev, who devised his periodic table of elements and then looked to see if all the elements were there. Technically speaking, it was a modest attempt to give the "existentialia" of Heidegger some semiotic grounding—this, of course, in the ancient tradition of Anglo-Saxon empiricism administering therapy to the European tendency to neurotic introspection. It was also fun to administer a dose of semiotics to

Phil Donahue and Carl Sagan, splendid fellows both, but who's perfect?

Which of your novels do you expect to weather time best, and why?
I've no idea.

Would you rewrite any of your works from any aspect at any point if you could?
No, I hardly think about them. Sometimes in the middle of the night, however, something will occur to me which I would use in a revision. For example, in the chapter called "Metaphor as Mistake" in *The Message in the Bottle* I wish I had used this example. In Charity Hospital in New Orleans, which serves mainly poor blacks, the surgical condition fibroids of the uterus, an accurate if somewhat prosaic definition, is known to many patients more creatively as "fireballs of the Eucharist."

Is it correct to say that your oeuvre forms an organic whole and that there is a consistent logic that takes you from one work to the next as you explore reality step by step?
Yes, I hope so—though the organic quality, if there is any, occurred more by happenstance than by design. The "fruits of the search" are there—to the extent they are allowed in the modest enterprise of the novel. That is to say, the novelist has no business setting up as the Answer Man. Or, as Binx says in the epilogue of *The Moviegoer*: "As for my search, I have not the inclination to say much on the subject. For one thing, I have not the authority, as the great Danish philosopher declared, to speak of such matters . . ."
But the novelist is entitled to a degree of artifice and cunning, as Joyce said; or the "indirect method," as Kierkegaard said; or the comic-bizarre for shock therapy, as Flannery O'Connor did. For example, a hint of the resolution of Binx's search is given in a single four-word sentence on page 240 ["He'll be like you"]. The reader should know by now that Binx, for all his faults, never bullshits, especially not with children. In *Lancelot* the resolution of the conflict between Lancelot and Percival is given by a single word, the last word in the book. Which holds out hope for Lancelot.

Hope in what sense? Isn't he beyond reach for Percival anyway?

No, Lancelot is not beyond the reach of Percival and, accordingly, Lancelot is not beyond hope. The entire novel is Lancelot's spiel to Percival. Percival does not *in the novel* reply in kind. At the end Lancelot asks him if he has anything to say. Percival merely says yes. Lancelot, presumably, will listen. It is precisely my perception of the aesthetic limitations of the novel form that this is all Percival can say. But the novelist is allowed to nourish the secret hope that the reader may remember that in the legend it was only Percival and Lancelot, of all the knights, who saw the Grail.

I guess Lancelot *was meant as your bicentenary novel. But the two radical points of view, Lancelot's "pagan Greco-Roman Nazi and so on tradition" and Percival's orthodox Christianity, are unacceptable for most people, as you once explained. So, another guess, what you could teach America in* Lancelot *was what was wrong, and what you could work out in* The Second Coming *was what you could* recommend *to the nation.*

If you say so, though I had nothing so grand in mind as "recommending to the nation." I never lose sight of the lowly vocation of the novelist. He is mainly out to give pleasure to a reader—one would hope, aesthetic pleasure. He operates in the aesthetic sphere, not the religious or even the ethical. That is to say, he is in the business, like all other artists, of making, not doing, certainly not lecturing to the nation. He hopes to make well and so sell what he makes.

Isn't it safe to say, though, that Lancelot *and* The Second Coming *are twin novels in the sense that while Lance embarks on a quest to meet the devil, Barrett's quest is to meet God? The latter's physical journey downward seems to be an ironic counterpoint to his yearning, which is upward. Barrett's route leads him—through his fall into the greenhouse— to a different reality: perhaps the correction of direction you recommend to the South and to America. Is this stretching things too far?*

Yes, indeed. Will Barrett falls out of the cave into Allie's arms, i.e., out of his nutty Gnostic quest into sacramental reality. I liked the idea of falling out of a cave. I permitted myself a veiled optimism here, that one can in fact fall out of a cave; i.e., despair and depression, when aware of themselves as such, can be closest to life. From cave to greenhouse, courtesy of Søren Kierkegaard and Dr. Jung. Same reservation, however, about a "message to the South." The South is by and large in no mood for messages from Walker Percy, being, for one thing, too busy watching *Dallas, Love Boat*, and the NFL on the tube. Or Jimmy Swaggart.

Do the times have anything to do with your reaching this breakthrough to eros, affirmation, and celebration in 1980 and not before? In other words, could The Second Coming *have been written in the fifties or sixties? Or was your own age and life experience needed to reach this stage?*

Yes, no, yes. Also artistic development. Also luck—as I said before. You're sitting at your typewriter, nine in the morning, a bad time, or four in the afternoon, a worse time. Sunk as usual. In the cave. What's going to happen to these poor people? They're on their own. I'll be damned if I'm going to impose a solution on them, a chic, unhappy existential ending or an upbeat Fannie Hurst ending. What does this poor guy do? He falls out of the cave, what else?

Can we look at much of what goes on in innovative fiction, when it is not self-indulgent and cynical, in light of what you call "defamiliarization" in Lost in the Cosmos? *That is, the artist tries to "wrench signifier out of context and exhibit it in all its queerness and splendor"?*

Absolutely, but I would apply the principle even more broadly; indeed, to much that is beautiful in poetry. Take Shakespeare's lovely lines: "Daffodils / That come before the swallow dares, and take / The winds of March with beauty." Surely the wrenching-out of context and hence defamiliarization of such ordinary words as "daffodils," "swallow," "dare," "March," and even the curious use of "take," has something to do with the beauty. Obviously, Empson's theory of ambiguity in poetry is closely akin.

It is clear that once we are dealing with a "post-religious technological society," transcendence is possible for the self by science or art but not by religion. Where does this leave the heroes of your novels with their metaphysical yearnings—Binx, Barrett, More, Lance?

I would have to question your premise; i.e., the death of

religion. The word itself, "religion," is all but moribund, true, smelling of dust and wax—though, of course, in its denotative sense it is accurate enough. I have referred to the age as "post-Christian" but it does not follow from this that there are not Christians or that they are wrong. Possibly the age is wrong. Catholics—who are the only Christians I can speak for—still believe that God entered history as a man, founded a Church, and will come again. This is not the best of times for the Catholic Church, but it has seen and survived worse. I see the religious "transcendence" you speak of as curiously paradoxical. Thus, it is only by a movement, "transcendence," toward God that these characters, Binx et al., become themselves, not abstracted like scientists but fully incarnate beings in the world. Kierkegaard put it more succinctly: the self becomes itself only when it becomes itself transparently before God.

The second half of the question still applies: Is it possible to describe Binx and the others in terms of your semiotic typology of the self?

I would think, in terms of the semiotic typology of self described in *The Message in the Bottle.* The semiotic receptor or "self" described here is perceived as being—unlike the "responding organism" of Skinner or Morris or Ogden and Richards—attuned to the reception of *sentences,* asserted subject-predicate pairings, namings, etc. There is adumbrated here a classification of sentences—not grammatically but existentially; that is, how the semiotic self construes the sentences in relation to his "world" (*Welt,* not *Umwelt*), the latter itself a semiotic construction. Thus:

1. Sentences conveying "island news": There is fresh water in the next cove; the price of eggs is fifty cents a dozen; Nicaragua has invaded El Salvador; my head hurts; etc.

2. Sentences conveying truths *sub specie aeternitatis* (i.e., valid on any island anywhere): 2 plus 2 equals 4; $E = MC^2$ (mathematical sentences); to thine own self be true, etc. (poetic sentences); wolves are carnivorous (scientific sentences, true of all known wolves anywhere).

3. Sentences announcing news from across the seas: The French fleet is on its way to Saint Helena to rescue you (a sentence of possible significance to Napoleon). Or: A certain event occurred

in history, in the Middle East some two thousand years ago, which is of utmost importance to every living human. Presumably it was just some such sentence, however indirectly, obscurely, distortedly uttered, which might have been uttered or was about to be uttered to Binx Bolling, Will Barrett, at the end of these novels—by such unlikely souls as Sutter. Notice, too, that it is only this last sort of sentence, the good news from across the seas, which requires the credential of the news bearer. Or, as Kierkegaard phrased the sentence: Only I, an apostle (that is, messenger), have the authority to bring you this piece of news. It is true and I make you eternally responsible for whether or not you believe it. Certainly it is not the business of the novelist to utter sentences of class 3, but only a certain sort of class 2 sentence. Also, *mutatis mutandis*, it is Dr. Thomas More who, in *The Thanatos Syndrome*, hears the class 3 sentence as a nonsentence, devalued, ossified, not so much non-sense as part merely of a religious decor, like the whiff of incense or a plastic Jesus on the dashboard, or a bumper sticker common here in Louisiana: JESUS SAVES.

Is it possible that the idea central to your semiotic theory of the self—namely, that the self has no sign of itself—has something to do with Jung's idea in his Modern Man in Search of a Soul, *where he speaks about the difficulty man has expressing the inexpressible in his language?*

Actually, I would suppose that my notions about the "semiotic origins" of the self are more closely related, at least in my own mind, to the existentialist philosophers, Heidegger and Marcel and Jaspers, and to the existentialist school of psychiatrists. Some years ago I published a paper which sought to do precisely that: derive many of the so-called existentialia—anxiety, notion of a "world"—from this very structure of man's peculiar triadic relation to his environment: interpreter-symbol-referent.

The Jungian idea in The Thanatos Syndrome *is mentioned in the book—that anxiety and depression might be trying to tell the patient something he does not understand. Doesn't this contradict the "semiotic-predicament-of-the-self" theory in* Cosmos; *i.e., its unspeakableness in a world of signs?*

I don't think so. The concept of an unsignified self stranded in a world of solid signs (trees, apples, Alabama, Ralphs, Zoltáns) is very useful in thinking about the various psychiatric ways patients "fall" into inauthenticity, the way frantic selves grope for any mask at hand to disguise their nakedness. Sartre's various descriptions of bad faith in role-playing are marvelous phenomenological renderings of this quest of the self for some, any, kind of habiliment. This being the case, perhaps the patient's "symptoms"—anxiety, depression, and whatnot—may be read as a sort of warning or summons of the self to itself, of the "authentic" self to the "fallen" or inauthentic self. Heidegger speaks of the "fall" of the self into the "world." I am thinking of the first character you encounter in *The Thanatos Syndrome* through the eyes of Dr. More: the woman who lives at the country club and thinks she has everything and yet is in the middle of a panic attack. She is also the last person you encounter in the book—after being "relieved" of her symptoms by the strange goings-on in the book. So here she is, at the end, confronting her anxiety. She is about to listen to herself tell herself something. The next-to-the-last sentence in the novel is: "She opens her mouth to speak." Jung, of course, would have understood this patient as this or that element of the self speaking to itself, perhaps anima-self to animus-self. Perhaps he is right, but I find it more congenial and less occult to speak in terms of observables and semiotic elements. Perhaps it is the Anglo-Saxon empiricist in me.

One way to sum up The Thanatos Syndrome—*without giving away the plot—is to call it an ecological novel. What made you turn to the ecological theme?*

I wasn't particularly aware of the ecological theme. It is true that the Louisiana of the novel is an ecological mess—as indeed it is now—but this I took to be significant only insofar as it shows the peculiar indifference of the strange new breed of Louisianians in the novel. After all, chimp-like creatures do not generally form environmental-protection societies.

Novels like Cheever's Oh! What a Paradise It Seems, *Gardner's* Mickelsson's Ghosts, *and Don DeLillo's* White Noise *are about the contamination of the environment. Were you influenced by those novels or by any others with similar topics?*

Not really. If you want to locate a contemporary influence, it would be something like a cross between Bellow and Vonnegut—aiming at Bellow's depth in his central characters and Vonnegut's outrageousness and satirical use of sci-fi.

Did you make up the "pre-frontal cortical deficit," the Tauber test, and other things, the way you invented Hausmann's Syndrome for inappropriate longing in The Second Coming?

No, they're not made up. There is just enough present-day evidence to make my "syndrome" plausible, or at least credible. One advantage of futuristic novel-writing is that it relieves one of restriction to the current state of the art of brain function. Another way of saying this is that, fortunately, the present knowledge of cortical function is so primitive that it gives the novelist considerable carte blanche.

What about in The Thanatos Syndrome—*is the pharmacological effect of Na^{24} on the cortex known?*

Not that I know of, but perhaps some shrink will write me, as one did about Hausmann's Syndrome, and report that, sure enough, administration of Na^{24} to patients in the Veteran's Hospital in Seattle has been shown to reduce anxiety and improve sexual performance in both quantity and quality and variety (for example, presenting rearward).

What led you to the idea of cortex manipulation?

Well, of course, the cortex is the neurological seat of the primate's, and man's, "higher functions." But I was particularly intrigued by the work of neurologists like John Eccles who locate the "self" in the language areas of the cortex—which squares very well with the semiotic origins of the self in the origins of language—as that which gives names, utters sentences. It seems, despite the most intensive training, chimps do neither.

The idea of man regressing to a pre-lingual stage must be a satiric device to get at what you experience in human communicative behavior today?

Well, I might have had at the edge of my mind some literary critics, philosophers, and semioticians who seem hell-bent on denying the very qualities of language and literature which have been held in such high esteem in the past: namely, that it is possible to know something about the world, that the world actually exists, that one person can actually say or write about the world and that other people can understand him. That, in a word, communication is possible. Some poets and critics outdo me in regression. I was content to regress some characters to a rather endearing pongid-primate level. But one poet I read about claimed that the poet's truest self could only be arrived at if he regressed himself clear back to the inorganic level; namely, a stone.

When at the end of the book you hint that earlier poets wrote two-word sentences, uttered howls, or routinely exposed themselves during their readings, I thought you meant the counterculture.

I was thinking of Ginsberg and company—and some of his imitators who can be found in our genteel Southern universities. I do not imply that Ginsberg had been intoxicated by Na^{24}, but only that such poets might suffer cortical deficits of a more obscure sort. The fact that American writers-in-residence and poets-in-residence often behave worse than football players does not necessarily imply that they are more stoned than the latter. There is more than one way to assault the cortex.

You have said literature can be a living social force, that the segregationists could feel the impact of a satirical line about Valley Forge Academy in Love in the Ruins. *Do you expect* The Thanatos Syndrome *to be effective in that way?*

I would hope that it would have some small influence in the great debate on the sanctity of life in the face of technology. For one thing, I would hope to raise the level of the debate above the crude polemics of the current pro-abortion / pro-life wrangle. When people and issues get completely polarized, somebody needs to take a step back, take a deep breath, take a new look.

Aren't there more immediate ways besides writing satirical fiction? Have you ever been engaged in political activity?

Only in a small way in the sixties. For a while I had the honor of being labeled a nigger-lover and a bleeding heart. One small bomb threat from the Klan and one interesting night in the attic with my family and a shotgun, feeling both pleased and ridiculous and beset with ambiguities—for I knew some of the Klan people and they are not bad fellows, no worse probably than bleeding-heart liberals.

Is there any concrete issue that engages your attention most in con-nection with what is going on in America at the moment?

Probably the fear of seeing America, with all its great strength and beauty and freedom—"Now in these dread latter days of the old violent beloved U.S.A.," and so on—gradually subside into decay through default and be defeated, not by the Communist movement, demonstrably a bankrupt system, but from within by weariness, boredom, cynicism, greed, and in the end helplessness before its great problems. Probably the greatest is the rise of a black underclass. Maybe Faulkner was right. Slavery was America's Original Sin and the one thing that can defeat us. I trust not.

In connection with what is going on in the world?

Ditto: the West losing by spiritual acedia. A Judaic view is not inappropriate here: Communism may be God's punishment for the sins of the West. Dostoevsky thought so.

You have often spoken about the postpartum depression you are in when you finish a novel. To put the question in Lost-in-the-Cosmos *terms: Now that you have finished another novel, which reentry option is open to you?*

Thanks for taking reentries seriously. Probably reentry 3—travel (geographical—I'm going to Maine, where I've never been). Plus reentry 2, anaesthesia—a slight dose of Bourbon.

In 1981 you spoke about a novel you were writing about two amnesiacs traveling on a Greyhound bus. You also said that you had been at that novel for two years. Thanatos is obviously not that novel. Did you give up on that one?

I can't remember.

Do you have any plans for future works?

It is in my mind to write a short work on semiotics, showing how the current discipline has been screwed up by followers of Charles Peirce and Saussure, the founders of modern semiotics. The extraordinary insight of Peirce into the "triadic" nature of meaning for humans and of Saussure into the nature of the sign— as a union of the signifier and the signified—has been largely perverted by the current European tradition of structuralism and deconstructionism and the American version of "dyadic" psychology; that is, various versions of behaviorism, so-called cognitive psychology, artificial intelligence, and so on. It would be nice if someone pursued Peirce's and Saussure's breakthroughs. On the other hand, I may not have the time or the energy.

Are there hopes that you would like the eighth decade of your life to fulfill?

I was thinking of getting a word processor.

The minimum a seventy-year-old man deserves is a birthday present. Since the person in question happens to be a writer, and since he has shown in a self-interview that he is the best man to answer the questions, the birthday present is that he can ask the last question.

Question: Since you are a satirical novelist and since the main source of the satirist's energy is anger about something amiss or wrong about the world, what is the main target of your anger in *The Thanatos Syndrome?*

Answer: It is the widespread and ongoing devaluation of human life in the Western world—under various sentimental disguises: "quality of life," "pointless suffering," "termination of life without meaning," etc. I trace it to a certain mind-set in the biological and social sciences which is extraordinarily influential among educated folk—so much so that it has almost achieved the status of a quasi-religious orthodoxy. If I had to give it a name, it would be something like the "Holy Office of the Secular Inquisition." It is not to be confused with "secular humanism," because, for one thing, it is anti-human. Although it drapes itself in the mantle of the scientific method and free scientific inquiry, it is neither free nor scientific. Indeed, it relies on certain hidden dogma where dogma has no place. I can think of two holy commandments which the Secular Inquisition lays down for all scientists and believers. The first: In your investigations and theories, thou shalt not find anything unique about the human animal even if the evidence points to such uniqueness. Example: Despite heroic attempts to teach sign language to other animals, the evidence is that even the cleverest chimpanzee has never spontaneously named a single object or uttered a single sentence. Yet dogma requires that, despite traditional belief in the soul or the mind, and the work of more recent workers like Peirce and Langer in man's unique symbolizing capacity, Homo sapiens sapiens be declared to be not qualitatively different from other animals. Another dogma: Thou shalt not suggest that there is a unique and fatal flaw in Homo sapiens sapiens or indeed any perverse trait that cannot be laid to the influence of Western civilization. Examples: 1. An entire generation came under the influence of Margaret Mead's *Coming of Age in Samoa* and its message: that the Samoans were an innocent, happy, and Edenic people until they were corrupted by missionaries and technology. That this turned out not to be true, that indeed the Samoans appear to have been at least as neurotic as New Yorkers has not changed the myth or the mind-set. 2. The gentle Tasaday people of the Philippines, an isolated Stone Age tribe, were also described as innocents, peace-loving, and benevolent. When asked to describe evil, they replied: "We cannot think of anything that is not good." That the Tasaday story has turned out to be a hoax is like an erratum corrected in a footnote and as inconsequential. 3. The ancient Mayans are still perceived as not only the builders of a high culture, practitioners of the arts and sciences, but a gentle folk—this despite the fact that recent deciphering of Mayan hieroglyphs have disclosed the Mayans to have been a cruel, warlike people capable of tortures even more vicious than the Aztecs. Scholars, after ignoring the findings, have admitted that the "new image" of the Mayans is perhaps "less romantic" than we had supposed. Conclusion: It is easy to criticize the absurdities of fundamentalist beliefs like "scientific creationism"—that the world and its creatures were created six thousand years ago. But it is also necessary to criticize other dogmas parading as science and the bad faith of some scientists who have their own dogmatic agendas to promote under the guise of "free scientific inquiry." Scientific inquiry should, in fact, be free. The warning: If it is not, if it is subject to this or that ideology, then do not be surprised if the history of the Weimar doctors is repeated. Weimar leads to Auschwitz. The nihilism of some scientists in the name of ideology or sentimentality and the consequent devaluation of individual human life lead straight to the gas chamber.

1987

QUESTIONS THEY
NEVER ASKED ME

❧

Will you consent to an interview?
No.

Why not?
Interviewers always ask the same questions, such as: What time of day do you write? Do you type or write longhand? What do you think of the South? What do you think of the New South? What do you think of Southern writers? Who are your favorite writers? What do you think of Jimmy Carter?

You're not interested in the South?
I'm sick and tired of talking about the South and hearing about the South.

Do you regard yourself as a Southern writer?
That is a strange question, even a little mad. Sometimes I think that the South brings out the latent madness in people. It even makes me feel nutty to hear such a question.

What's mad about such a question?
Would you ask John Cheever if he regarded himself as a Northeastern writer?

What do you think of Southern writers?

I'm fed up with the subject of Southern writing. Northern writing, too, for that matter. I'm also fed up with questions about the state of the novel, alienation, the place of the artist in American society, race relations, the Old South.

What about the New South?

Of all the things I'm fed up with, I think I'm fed up most with hearing about the New South.

Why is that?

One of the first things I can remember in my life was hearing about the New South. I was three years old, in Alabama. Not a year has passed since that I haven't heard about a New South. I would dearly love never to hear the New South mentioned again. In fact, my definition of a New South would be a South in which it never occurred to anybody to mention the New South. One glimmer of hope is that this may be happening.

But people have a great curiosity about the South now that Jimmy Carter is President.

I doubt that. If there is anything more boring than the questions asked about the South, it is the answers Southerners give. If I hear one more Northerner ask about good ol' boys and one more Southerner give an answer, I'm moving to Manaus, Brazil, to join the South Carolinians who emigrated after Appomattox and whose descendants now speak no English and have such names as Senhor Carlos Calhoun. There are no good ol' boys in Manaus.

In the past you have expressed admiration for such living writers as Bellow, Updike, Didion, Mailer, Cheever, Foote, Barthelme, Gass, Heller. Do you still subscribe to such a list?

No.

Why not?

I can't stand lists of writers. Compiling such a list means leaving somebody out. When serious writers make a list, they're afraid of leaving somebody out. When critics and poor writers do it, they usually mean to leave somebody out. It seems a poor practice in either case.

Do you have any favorite dead writers?
None that I care to talk about. Please don't ask me about Dostoevsky and Kierkegaard.

How about yourself? Would you comment on your own writing?
No.

Why not?
I can't stand to think about it.

Could you say something about the vocation of writing in general?
No.

Nothing?
All I can think to say about it is that it is a very obscure activity in which there is usually a considerable element of malice. Like frogging.

Frogging?
Yes. Frogging is raising a charley horse on somebody's arm by a skillful blow with a knuckle in exactly the right spot.

What are your hobbies?
I don't have any.

What magazines do you read?
None.

What are your plans for summer reading?
I don't have any.

Do you keep a journal?
No.

But don't writers often keep journals?

So I understand. But I could never think what to put in a journal. I used to read writers' journals and was both astonished and depressed by the copiousness of a single day's entry: thoughts, observations, reflections, descriptions, snatches of plots, bits of poetry, sketches, aphorisms. The one time I kept a journal I made two short entries in three weeks. One entry went so: *Four p.m. Thursday afternoon—The only thing notable is that nothing is notable. I wonder if any writer has ever recorded the observation that most time passes and most events occur without notable significance. I am sitting here looking out the window at a tree and wondering why it is that though it is a splendid tree, it is of not much account. It is no good to me. Is it the nature of the human condition or the nature of the age that things of value are devalued?* I venture to say that most people most of the time experience the same four-o'clock-in-the-afternoon devaluation. But I have noticed an interesting thing. If such a person, a person like me feeling lapsed at four o'clock in the afternoon, should begin reading a novel about a person feeling lapsed at four o'clock in the afternoon, a strange thing happens. Things increase in value. Possibilities open. This may be the main function of art in this peculiar age: to reverse the devaluation. What the artist or writer does is not depict a beautiful tree—this only depresses you more than ever—no, he depicts the commonplaceness of an everyday tree. Depicting the commonplace allows the reader to penetrate the commonplace. The only other ways the husk of the commonplace can be penetrated is through the occurrence of natural disasters or the imminence of one's own death. These measures are not readily available on ordinary afternoons.

How would you describe the place of the writer and artist in American life?

Strange.

How do you perceive your place in society?

I'm not sure what that means.

Well, in this small Louisiana town, for example.

I'm still not sure what you mean. I go to the barbershop to

get a haircut and the barber says: "How you doing, Doc?" I say: "Okay." I go to the post office to get the mail and the clerk says: "What's up, Doc?" Or I go to a restaurant on Lake Pontchartrain and the waitress says: "What you want, honey?" I say: "Some cold beer and crawfish." She brings me an ice-cold beer and a platter of boiled crawfish that are very good, especially if you suck the heads. Is that what you mean?

What about living in the South, with its strong sense of place, of tradition, of rootedness, of tragedy—the only part of America that has ever tasted defeat?

I've read about that. Actually, I like to stay in motels in places like Lincoln, Nebraska, or San Luis Obispo.

But what about these unique characteristics of the South? Don't they tend to make the South a more hospitable place for writers?

Well, I've heard about that, the storytelling tradition, sense of identity, tragic dimension, community, history, and so forth. But I was never quite sure what it meant. In fact, I'm not sure that the opposite is not the case. People don't read much in the South and don't take writers very seriously, which is probably as it should be. I've managed to live here for thirty years and am less well-known than the Budweiser distributor. The only famous person in this town is Isiah Robertson, linebacker for the Rams, and that is probably as it should be, too. There are advantages to living an obscure life and being thought an idler. If one lived in a place like France where writers are honored, one might well end up like Sartre, a kind of literary-political pope, a savant, an academician, the very sort of person Sartre made fun of in *Nausea*. On the other hand, if one is thought an idler and a bum, one is free to do what one pleases. One day a fellow townsman asked me: "What do you do, Doc?" "Well, I write books." "I know that, Doc, but what do you really do?" "Nothing." He nodded. He was pleased and I was pleased.

I have a theory of why Faulkner became a great writer. It was not the presence of a tradition and all that, as one generally hears, but the absence. Everybody in Oxford, Mississippi, knew who Faulkner was, not because he was a great writer, but because he was a local character, a little-bitty fellow who put on airs, wore a handkerchief up his sleeve, a ne'er-do-well, Count No-Count they called him. He was tagged like a specimen under a bell jar; no matter what he wrote thereafter, however great or wild or strange it was, it was all taken as part of the act. It was part of "what Bill Faulkner did." So I can imagine it became a kind of game with him, with him going to extraordinary lengths in his writing to see if he could shake them out of their mild, pleasant inattention. I don't mean he wanted his fellow Southerners to pay him homage, that his life and happiness depended on what they thought of him. No, it was a kind of game. One can imagine Robinson Crusoe on his island doing amazing acrobatics for his herd of goats, who might look up, dreamily cud chewing for a moment, then go on with their grazing. "That one didn't grab you?" Crusoe might say, then come out with something even more stupendous. But even if he performed the ultimate stunt, the Indian rope trick, where he climbs up a stiff rope and disappears, the goats would see it as no more or less than what this character does under the circumstances. Come to think of it, who would want it otherwise? There is a good deal of talk about community and the lack of it, but one of the nice things about living an obscure life in the South is that people don't come up to you, press your hand, and give you soulful looks. I would have hated to belong to the Algonquin Round Table, where people made witty remarks and discussed Ezra Pound. Most men in the South don't read and the women who do usually prefer Taylor Caldwell and Phyllis Whitney to Faulkner and O'Connor.

No, it is the very absence of a tradition that makes for great originals like Faulkner and O'Connor and Poe. The South is Crusoe's island for a writer and there's the good and bad of it. There is a literary community of sorts in the North. The best Northern writers are, accordingly, the best of a kind. As different as Bellow, Cheever, Updike, and Pynchon are, their differences are within a genus, like different kinds of fruit: apples, oranges, plums, pears. A critic or reviewer can compare and contrast them with one another. But Faulkner, O'Connor, Barthelme? They're moon berries, kiwi fruit, niggertoes.

Niggertoes?
That's what we used to call Brazil nuts.

*How did you happen to become a writer? Didn't you start out as a
doctor?*
Yes, but I had no special talent for it. Others in my class were
smarter. Two women, three Irish Catholics, four Jews, and ten
WASPs were better at it than I. What happened was that I
discovered I had a little knack for writing. Or perhaps it is desire,
a kind of underhanded desire.

What do you mean by knack?
It is hard to say.

Try.
I suspect it is something all writers have in greater or lesser
degree. Maybe it's inherited, maybe it's the result of a rotten
childhood—I don't know. But unless you have it, you'll never be
a writer.

Can you describe the knack?
No, except in negative terms. It is not what people think it is.
Most people think it is the perfecting of the ordinary human skills
of writing down words and sentences. Everybody writes words and
sentences—for example, in a letter. A book is thought to be an
expanded and improved letter, the way a pro ballplayer is thought
to do things with a ball most men can do, only better. Not so. Or
if you have an unusual experience, all you have to do is "write it
up," the more unusual and extraordinary the experience the
better, like My Most Extraordinary Experience in *Reader's Digest.*
Not so. Psychologists know even less about writing than do laymen.
Show me a psychologist with a theory of creativity and I'll show
you a bad writer.

Can't you say what the knack is?
No, except to say that it is a peculiar activity, as little understood
as chicken fighting or entrail reading, and that the use of words,

sentences, paragraphs, plots, characters, and so forth, is the accident, not the substance, of it.

What is it if not the putting together of words and sentences?

I can't answer that except to say two things. One is that it is a little trick one gets onto, a very minor trick. One does it and discovers to one's surprise that most people can't do it. I used to know a fellow in high school who, due to an anomaly of his eustachian tubes, could blow smoke out of both ears. He enjoyed doing it and it was diverting to watch. Writing is something like that. Another fellow I knew in college, a fraternity brother and a trumpet player, could swell out his neck like a puff adder—the way the old horn player Clyde McCoy used to do when he played "Sugar Blues."

The other thing about the knack is that it has theological, demonic, and sexual components. One is aware, on the one hand, of a heightened capacity for both malice and joy and, occasionally and with luck, for being able to see things afresh and even to make things the way the Old Testament said that God made things and took a look at them and saw that they were good.

The best novel, and the best part of a novel, is a *creatio ex nihilo*. Unlike God, the novelist does not start with nothing and make something of it. He starts with himself as nothing and makes something of the nothing with things at hand. If the novelist has a secret, it is not that he has a special something but that he has a special nothing. Camus said that all philosophy comes from the possibility of suicide. This is probably not true, one of those intellectual oversimplifications to which the French regularly fall prey. Suicide, the real possibility of self-nihilation, has more to do with writing poems and novels. A novelist these days has to be an ex-suicide. A good novel—and, I imagine, a good poem—is possible only after one has given up and let go. Then, once one realizes that all is lost, the jig is up, that, after all, nothing is dumber than a grown man sitting down and making up a story to entertain somebody or working in a "tradition" or "school" to maintain his reputation as a practitioner of the *nouveau roman* or whatever— once one sees that this is a dumb way to live, that all is vanity sure enough, there are *two* possibilities: either commit suicide or not commit suicide. If one opts for the former, that is that; it is a *letzte Lösung* and there is nothing more to write or say about it. But if one opts for the latter, one is in a sense dispensed and living on borrowed time. One is not dead! One is alive! One is free! I won't say that one is like God on the first day, with the chaos before him and a free hand. Rather, one feels, What the hell, here I am, washed up, it is true, but also cast up, cast up on the beach, alive and in one piece. I can move my toe up and then down and do anything else I choose. The possibilities open to one are infinite. So why not do something Shakespeare and Dostoevsky and Faulkner didn't do, for, after all, they are nothing more than dead writers, members of this and that tradition, much-admired busts on a shelf. A dead writer may be famous but he is also dead as a duck, finished. And I, cast up here on this beach? I am a survivor! Alive! A free man! They're finished. Possibilities are closed. As for God? That's His affair. True, He made the beach, which, now that I look at it, is not all that great. As for me, I might try a little something here in the wet sand, a word, a form . . .

What's this about a sexual component?
I'd rather not say.

Why not?
Because no end of dreary bullshit has been written on the subject, so much as to befoul the waters for good. Starting with Freud's rather stupid hydraulic model of art as the sublimation of libidinal energies: libido suppressed in the boiler room squirts up in the attic. There followed half a century of dull jokes about x orgasms equals y novels down the drain, and so forth and so forth. Freud's disciples have been even more stupid about "creative writing." At least Freud had the good sense to know when to shut up, as he did in Dostoevsky's case. But stupider still is the more recent Hemingway machismo number. The formula is: Big pencil equals big penis. My own hunch is that those fellows have their troubles, otherwise why make love with a pencil? Renoir may have started it with a smart-ass statement: "I paint with my penis." If I were a woman, I wouldn't stand for such crap. No wonder women get enraged these days. Some of the most feminine women writers

have this same knack, or better, and can use it to a fare-thee-well—Southern women like K. A. Porter, Welty, O'Connor—look out for them!

The twentieth century, noted for its stupidity in human matters, is even stupider than usual in this case. And in this case Muhammad Ali is smarter than either Freud or Hemingway. Float like a butterfly, sting like a bee. Ali's exaltation and cunning and beauty and malice apply even more to writing than to fighting. Freud made a mistake only a twentieth-century professor would have been capable of: trying to explain the human psyche by a mechanical-energy model. Take away 450 psychic calories for love and that leaves you 450 short for art. Actually, it's the other way around. The truth is paradoxical and can't be understood in terms of biological systems. Psychic energy is involved here, but it follows a different set of laws. Like Einstein's theory, it at times defies Newton's law of gravitation. Thus, it is not the case that E minus one half E equals one half E (Newton, Freud), but rather E minus one half E equals six E. Or simply, zero minus E equals E—which is more astounding than Einstein's E equals MC squared.

I will give you a simple example. Let us say a writer finds himself at o, naught, zero, at 4 p.m. of a Thursday afternoon. No energy, depressed, strung out, impotent, constipated, a poet sitting on the kitchen floor with the oven door open and the gas on, an incarnated nothingness, an outer human husk encasing an inner cipher. The jig is up. The poem or novel is no good. But since the jig is up, why not have another look, or tear it up and start over? Then, if he is lucky—or is it grace, God having mercy on the poor bastard?—something opens. A miracle occurs. Somebody must have found the Grail. The fisher king is healed, the desert turns green—or better still: the old desert is still the old desert, but the poet names it and makes it a new desert. As for the poet himself: in a strange union of polarities—wickedness / good, malice / benevolence, hatred / love, butterfly / bee—he, too, comes together, sticks his tongue in his cheek, sets pencil to paper: What if I should try this? Uh-huh, maybe . . . He works. He sweats. He stinks. He creates. He sweats and stinks and creates like a woman conceiving. Then what? It varies. Perhaps he takes a shower, changes clothes. Perhaps he takes a swim in the ocean. Perhaps he takes a nap. Perhaps he takes a drink, flatfoots half a glass of Bourbon. Then, if he is near someone he loves or wants to love or should love or perhaps has loved all along but has not until this moment known it, he looks at her. And by exactly the same measure by which the novel has opened to him and he to it, he opens to her and she to him. Well, now, why don't you come here a minute? That's it. Give me your hand. He looks at her hand. He is like the castaway on the beach who opens his eyes and sees a sunrise coquina three inches from his nose. Her hand is like the coquina. What an amazing sight! Well, now, why don't we just sit down here on this cypress log? Imagine your being here at four-thirty in the afternoon. All this time I thought I was alone on this island and here you are. A miracle! Imagine Crusoe on his island performing the ultimate stunt for his goats, when he turns around and there *she* is. Who needs Friday? What he needs now is her, or she him, as the case may be.

Such is the law of conservation of energy through its expenditure: zero minus E equals E.

If writing is a knack, does the knack have anything to do with being Southern?

Sure. The knack has certain magic components that once came in handy for Southern writers. This is probably no longer the case.

Why is that?

Well, as Einstein once said, ordinary life in an ordinary place on an ordinary day in the modern world is a dreary business. I mean *dreary*. People will do anything to escape this dreariness: booze up, hit the road, gaze at fatal car wrecks, shoot up heroin, spend money on gurus, watch pornographic movies, kill themselves, even watch TV. Einstein said that was the reason he went into mathematical physics. One of the few things that diverted me from the dreariness of growing up in a country-club subdivision in Birmingham was sending off for things. For example, sending off for free samples, such as Instant Postum. You'd fill in a coupon clipped from a magazine and send it off to a magic faraway place (Battle Creek?), and sure enough, one morning the mailman would hand you a *box*. Inside would be a small jar. You'd make a cup and in the peculiar fragrance of Postum you could imagine an equally fragrant and magical place where clever Yankee experts ground up stuff in great brass mortars.

That was called "sending off for something."

It was even better with Sears, Roebuck: looking at the picture in the catalogue, savoring it, fondling it, sailing to Byzantium with it, then—even better than poetry—actually getting it, sending off to Chicago for it, saving up your allowance and mailing a postal money order for $23.47 and getting back a gold-filled Elgin railroader's pocket watch with an elk engraved on the back. With a strap and a fob.

Writing is also going into the magic business. It is a double transaction in magic. You have this little workaday thing you do that most people can't do. But in the South there were also certain magic and exotic ingredients, that is, magic and exotic to Northerners and Europeans, which made the knack even more mysterious. As exotic to a New Yorker as an Elgin pocket watch to an Alabama boy. I've often suspected that Faulkner was very much on to this trick and overdid it a bit.

You write something, send it off to a *publisher* in *New York*, and back it comes as a—book! Print! Pages! Cover! Binding! Scribble-scratch is turned into measured paragraphs, squared-off blocks of pretty print. And even more astounding: in the same mail that brought the Elgin pocket watch come *reviews*, the printed thoughts of people who have *read* the book!

The less the two parties know about each other, the further apart they are, the stronger the magic. It must be very enervating to be a writer in New York, where you know all about editing and publishing and reviewing, to discover that editors and publishers and reviewers are as bad off as anyone else, maybe worse. Being a writer in the South has its special miseries, which include isolation, madness, tics, amnesia, alcoholism, lust, and loss of ordinary powers of speech. One may go for days without saying a word. Then, faced with an interviewer, one may find oneself talking the way one fancies the interviewer expects one to talk, talking Southern— for example, using such words as "Amon": "Amon git up and git myself a drink." Yet there are certain advantages to the isolation.

At best, one is encouraged to be original; at worst, bizarre; sometimes both, like Poe.

It was this distance and magic that once made for the peculiarities of Southern writing. Now the distance and magic are gone, or going, and Southern writers are no better off than anyone else, perhaps worse, because now that the tricks don't work and you can't write strange like Faulkner, what do you do? Write like Bellow? But before—and even now, to a degree—the magic worked. You were on your own and making up little packages to send to faraway folk. As marooned as Crusoe, one was apt to be eccentric. That's why Poe, Faulkner, O'Connor, and Barthelme are more different from one another than Bellow, Updike, and Cheever are.

The Southern writer at his best was a value because he was somewhat extraterrestrial. (At his worst, he was overwhelmed by Faulkner: there is nothing more feckless than imitating an eccentric.) He was different enough from the main body of writers to give the reader a triangulation point for getting a fix on things. There are degrees of difference. If the writer is altogether different from the genus *Writer*, which is the only genus the reviewer knows, the reviewer is baffled—as New York reviewers like Clifton Fadiman were baffled by Faulkner; they were trying to compare him with such standard writers as Thornton Wilder, and it can't be done. But if the critic recognizes the value of difference, the possibility of an extraterrestrial point of view, he will be excited. That's why the French went nuts over Poe and Faulkner.

Meanwhile, Mississippians shrugged their shoulders.

Would you care to say something about your own novels?
No.

What about your last novel, Lancelot?
What about it?

What do you have to say about it?
Nothing.

How would you describe it?
As a small cautionary tale.

That's all?
That's all.

It has generally been well reviewed. What do you think of reviews?
Very little. Reading reviews of your own book is a peculiar experience. It is a dubious enterprise, a no-win game. If the review is flattering, one tends to feel vain and uneasy. If it is bad, one tends to feel exposed, found out. Neither feeling does you any good. Besides that, most reviews are of not much account. How could it be otherwise? I feel sorry for reviewers. I feel sorry for myself when I write a review. Book reviewing is a difficult and unrewarding literary form and right now no one is doing it. The reviewer's task is almost impossible. A writer may spend years doing his obscure thing, his little involuted sexual-theological number, and there's the poor reviewer with two or three days to figure out what he's up to. And even if the review is good, you're in no mood to learn anything from it. The timing is all bad. You're sick to death of the book and don't even want to think about it. Then, just when you think you're rid of this baby, have kicked him and his droppings out of the nest forever, along come these folks who want to talk about him.

Do you feel bad about a bad review?
Moderately bad. One likes to be liked. The curious thing is, I always expect people to like me and my writing and am surprised when they don't. I suffer from the opposite of paranoia, a benign psychosis for which there is no word. I say "curious" because there is a good deal of malice in my writing—I have it in for this or that—but it is not personal malice and I'm taken aback when people take offense. A rave review makes me feel even more uneasy. It's like being given an A+ by the teacher or a prize by the principal. All you want to do is grab your report card and run—before you're found out.

Found out for what?

Found out for being what you are (and what in this day and age I think a serious writer has to be): an ex-suicide, a cipher, naught, zero—which is as it should be, because being a naught is the very condition of making anything. This is a secret. People don't know this. Even distinguished critics are under the misapprehension that you are something, a substance, that you represent this or that tradition, a skill, a growing store of wisdom. Whereas, in fact, what you are doing is stripping yourself naked and putting yourself in the eye of the hurricane and leaving the rest to chance, luck, or providence. Faulkner said it in fact: writing a novel is like a one-armed man trying to nail together a chicken coop in a hurricane. I think of it as more like trying to pick up a four-hundred-pound fat lady: you need a lot of hands to hold up a lot of places at once.

There are four kinds of reviews, three of which are depressing and one of which is, at best, tolerable.

The first is the good good review. That is, a review that not only is laudatory but is also canny and on the mark. One is exhilarated for three seconds, then one becomes furtive and frightened. One puts it away quick, before it turns into a pumpkin.

The second is the bad good review. That is, it is the routine "favorable" review that doesn't understand the book. The only thing to say about it is that it is better to get a bad good review than a bad bad review.

The third is the bad bad review. It is a hateful review in which the reviewer hates the book for reasons he is unwilling to disclose. He is offended. But he must find other reasons for attacking the book than the cause of the offense. I don't blame this reviewer. In fact, he or she is sharper than most. He or she is on to the secret that novel writing is a serious business in which the novelist is out both to give joy and to draw blood. The hateful review usually means that one has succeeded in doing only the latter. The name of this reviewer's game is: "Okay, you want to play rough? Very well, here comes yours." A hateful reviewer is like a street fighter: he doesn't let on where he's been hit and he hits you with everything he's got—a bad tactic. Or he lies low and waits for a chance to blind-side you. A bad bad review doesn't really hurt. Getting hit by an offended reviewer reminds me of the old guy on *Laugh-In* who would make a pass at Ruth Buzzi on the park bench and get slammed across the chops by a soft purse. It's really a love tap. I can't speak for Ruth Buzzi, but I can speak for the old guy: all he wants to say is, "Come on, honey, give us a kiss."

The fourth is the good bad review, a rare bird. It would be the most valuable if one were in any shape to learn, which one is not. It is the critical review that accurately assesses both what the novelist had in mind, what he was trying to do, and how and where he failed. It hurts because the failure is always great, but the hurt is salutary, like pouring iodine in an open wound. Here the transaction is between equals, a fair fight, no blind-sliding. It makes me think of old-movie fistfights between John Wayne and Ward Bond. Ward lets the Duke have one, racks him up real good. The Duke shakes his head to clear it, touches the corner of his mouth, looks at the blood, grins in appreciation. Nods. All right. That's a fair transaction, a frontal assault by an equal. But what the hateful reviewer wants to do is blind-side you, the way Chuck Bednarik blind-sided Frank Gifford and nearly killed him. Unlike Chuck Bednarik, the hateful reviewer can't hurt you. He gives away too much of himself. The only way he can hurt you is in the pocketbook—the way a playwright can be knocked off by a *Times* reviewer—but, in the case of a book, even that is doubtful.

Even so, one is still better off with hateful reviewers than with admiring reviewers. If I were a castaway on a desert island, I'd rather be marooned with six hateful reviewers than with six admiring reviewers. The hateful men would be better friends and the hateful women would be better lovers.

The truth is, all reviewers and all your fellow novelists are your friends and lovers. All serious writers and readers constitute less than one percent of the population. The other ninety-nine percent don't give a damn. They watch *Wonder Woman*. We are a tiny shrinking minority and our worst assaults on each other are love taps compared with the massive indifference surrounding us. Gore Vidal and Bill Buckley are really two of a kind, though it will displease both to hear it. Both are serious moralists to whom I attach a high value.

Do you see the Jimmy Carter phenomenon as a revival of Protestant Christianity or as a renascence of Jeffersonian populism or the Southern political genius or all three, and if so, what is the impact on the Southern literary imagination and race relations?

How's that again?

Do you—

What was that about race relations?

How do you assess the current state of race relations in the South?

Almost as bad as in the North.

But hasn't there occurred a rather remarkable reconciliation of the races in the South as a consequence of its strong Christian tradition and its traditional talent for human relations?

I haven't noticed it. The truth is, most blacks and whites don't like each other, North or South.

But great changes have taken place, haven't they?

Yes, due mainly to court decisions and congressional acts and Lyndon Johnson. It was easier for the South to go along than to resist. After all, we tried that once. Anyhow, as Earl Long used to say, the feds have the bomb now.

Can you say anything about the future of race relations?

No.

Why not?

I'm white. It's up to the blacks. The government has done all it can do. The whites' course is predictable. Like anybody else, they will simply hold on to what they've got as long as they can. When did any other human beings behave differently? The blacks have a choice. They can either shoot up the place, pull the whole damn thing down around our ears—they can't win, but they can ruin it for everybody—or they can join the great screwed-up American middle class. Of course, what they're doing is both, mostly the latter. It is noteworthy that blacks, being smarter than whites about such things, have shown no interest in the Communist Party. Blacks seem less prone than whites to fall prey to abstractions. Comradeship and brotherhood are all very well, but what I really want is out of this ghetto, and if I can make it and you can't, too bad about you, brother. But that's the American dream, isn't it? It will even make them happy like it did us—for a while. It will take them years to discover just how screwed up the American middle class is. I visualize a United States a few years from now in which blacks and whites have switched roles. The pissed-off white middle class will abandon suburbia just as they abandoned the cities, either for the countryside, where they will live in RVs, mobile homes, converted farms, log cabins, antebellum outhouses, revolutionary stables, silos, sod huts, or to move back to the city, back to little ethnic cottages like Mayor Daley's, Victorian shotguns, stained-glass boardinghouses, converted slave quarters, abandoned streetcars—while the blacks move out to Levittown and the tracts, attend the churches of their choice, PTAs, Rotary, Great Books. In fact, it's already happening. The only danger is that this happy little switch may not happen fast enough and the young blacks in the city who have little or nothing to lose may say the hell with it and shoot up everything in sight.

There is a slight chance, maybe one in a hundred, that blacks and whites may learn the best of each other rather than the worst.

What is the worst?

Well, whites in the Western world don't know how to live and blacks don't know how to govern themselves. It would be nice if each could learn the gift of the other. But there are already signs in America that blacks are learning the white incapacity for life. For example, they've almost reached the white incidence of suicide and gastric ulcer and have surpassed them in hypertension. And some white politicians govern like Haitians and Ugandans. I've noticed that more and more blacks act like Robert Young as Dr. Marcus Welby, with that same tight-assed, suspect post-Protestant rectitude, while more and more white politicians act like Idi Amin.

Can you describe the best thing that could happen?

No. All I can say is that it has something to do with Southern good nature, good manners, kidding around, with music, with irony, with being able to be pissed off without killing other people or yourself, maybe with Jewish humor, with passing the time, with small, unpretentious civic-minded meetings. Some whites and blacks are sitting around a table in Louisiana, eating crawfish and drinking beer at a PTA fund-raiser. The table is somewhat polarized, whites at one end, blacks at the other, segregated not ill-naturedly but from social unease, like men and women at a party. The talk is somewhat stiff and conversation-making and highfalutin—about reincarnation, in fact. Says a white to a white who has only had a beer or two: "I think I'd rather come back as an English gentleman in the eighteenth century than in this miserable century of war, alienation, and pollution." Says a black to a black who has had quite a few beers: "I'd rather come back as this damn crawfish than as a nigger in Louisiana." All four laugh and have another beer. I don't know why I'm telling you this. You wouldn't understand it. You wouldn't understand what is bad about it, what is good about it, what is unusual about it, or what there is about it that might be the hundred-to-one shot that holds the solution.

Why do you leave Christianity out as one of the ingredients of better race relations?

Because the Christians left it out. Maybe Jimmy Carter and Andrew Young and a few others mean what they say, I don't know, but look at the white churches. They generally practice the same brand of brotherhood as the local country club. If Jesus Christ showed up at the Baptist church in Plains, the deacons would call the cops. No, the law, government, business, sports, and show business have done more here than the churches. There seems to be an inverse relationship between God and brotherhood in the churches. In the Unitarian Church, it's all brotherhood and no God. Outside the churches, the pocketbook has replaced the Holy Ghost as the source of brotherhood. Show me an A & P today that is losing money because it is not hiring blacks and I'll show you an A & P tomorrow that has hired blacks and, what is more, where blacks and whites get along fine.

But aren't you a Catholic?
Yes.

Do you regard yourself as a Catholic novelist?
Since I am a Catholic and a novelist, it would seem to follow that I am a Catholic novelist.

What kind of Catholic are you?
Bad.

No. I mean, are you liberal or conservative?
I no longer know what those words mean.

Are you a dogmatic Catholic or an open-minded Catholic?
I don't know what that means, either. Do you mean do I believe the dogma that the Catholic Church proposes for belief?

Yes.
Yes.

How is such a belief possible in this day and age?
What else is there?

What do you mean, what else is there? There is humanism, atheism, agnosticism, Marxism, behaviorism, materialism, Buddhism, Muhammad-anism, Sufism, astrology, occultism, theosophy.
That's what I mean.

To say nothing of Judaism and Protestantism.
Well, I would include them along with the Catholic Church in the whole peculiar Jewish–Christian thing.

I don't understand. Would you exclude, for example, scientific humanism as a rational and honorable alternative?
Yes.

Why?
It's not good enough.

Why not?
This life is much too much trouble, far too strange, to arrive
at the end of it and then be asked what you make of it and have
to answer, "Scientific humanism." That won't do. A poor show.
Life is a mystery, love is a delight. Therefore, I take it as axiomatic
that one should settle for nothing less than the infinite mystery
and the infinite delight; i.e., God. In fact, I demand it. I refuse to
settle for anything less. I don't see why anyone should settle for
less than Jacob, who actually grabbed aholt of God and wouldn't
let go until God identified himself and blessed him.

Grabbed aholt?
A Louisiana expression.

*But isn't the Catholic Church in a mess these days, badly split, its
liturgy barbarized, vocations declining?*
Sure. That's a sign of its divine origins, that it survives these
periodic disasters.

*You don't act or talk like a Christian. Aren't they supposed to love one
another and do good works?*
Yes.

*You don't seem to have much use for your fellow man or do many good
works.*
That's true. I haven't done a good work in years.

*In fact, if I may be frank, you strike me as being rather negative in
your attitude, cold-blooded, aloof, derisive, self-indulgent, more fond of the
beautiful things of this world than of God.*
That's true.

You even seem to take a certain satisfaction in the disasters of the twentieth century and to savor the imminence of world catastrophe rather than world peace, which all religions seek.
That's true.

You don't seem to have much use for your fellow Christians, to say nothing of Ku Kluxers, ACLUers, Northerners, Southerners, fem-libbers, anti-fem-libbers, homosexuals, anti-homosexuals, Republicans, Democrats, hippies, anti-hippies, senior citizens.
That's true—though, taken as individuals, they turn out to be more or less like oneself, i.e., sinners, and we get along fine.

Even Ku Kluxers?
Sure.

How do you account for your belief?
I can only account for it as a gift from God.

Why would God make you such a gift when there are others who seem more deserving, that is, serve their fellow man?
I don't know. God does strange things. For example, He picked as one of his saints a fellow in northern Syria, a local nut, who stood on top of a pole for thirty-seven years.

We are not talking about saints.
That's true.

We are talking about what you call a gift.
You want me to explain it? How would I know? The only answer I can give is that I asked for it; in fact, demanded it. I took it as an intolerable state of affairs to have found myself in this life and in this age, which is a disaster by any calculation, without demanding a gift commensurate with the offense. So I demanded it. No doubt, other people feel differently.

But shouldn't faith bear some relation to the truth, facts?

Yes. That's what attracted me, Christianity's rather insolent claim to be true, with the implication that other religions are more or less false.

You believe that?
Of course.

I see. Moving right along now—
To what?

To language. Haven't you done some writing about the nature of language?
Yes.

Will you say something about your ideas about language?
No.

Why not?
Because, for one thing, nobody is interested. The nature of language is such, I have discovered from experience, that even if anyone has the ultimate solution to the mystery of language, no one would pay the slightest attention. In fact, most people don't even know there is a mystery. Here is an astounding fact, when you come to think of it. The use of symbols between creatures, the use of language in particular, appears to be the one unique phenomenon in the universe, is certainly the single behavior that most clearly sets man apart from the beasts, is also the one activity in which humans engage most of the time, even asleep and dreaming. Yet it is the least understood of all phenomena. We know less about it than about the back side of the moon or the most distant supernova—and are less interested.

Why is that? Why aren't people interested?
Because there are two kinds of people, laymen and scientists. The layman doesn't see any mystery. Since he is a languaged creature and sees everything through the mirror of language, asking him to consider the nature of language is like asking a fish

to consider the nature of water. He cannot imagine its absence, so he cannot consider its presence. To the layman, language is a transparent humdrum affair. Where is the mystery? People see things, are given the names of things when they are children, have thoughts, which they learn to express in words and sentences, talk and listen, read and write. So where is the mystery? That's the general lay attitude toward language. On the other hand, there are the theorists of language, who are very much aware of the mystery and who practice such esoteric and abstruse disciplines as transformational generative grammar, formal semantics, semiotics, and who, by and large, have their heads up their asses and can't even be understood by fellow specialists. They remind me of nothing so much as the Scholastics of the fifteenth century, who would argue about the number of angels that could dance on the head of a pin.

Haven't you written something about a theory of language?
Yes.

Could you summarize your thoughts on the subject?
No.

Why not?
It is not worth the trouble. What is involved in a theory of language is a theory of man, and people are not interested. Despite the catastrophes of this century and man's total failure to understand himself and deal with himself, people still labor under the illusion that a theory of man exists. It doesn't. As bad and confused as things are, they have to get even worse before people realize they don't have the faintest idea what sort of creature man is. Then they might want to know. Until then, one is wasting one's time. I'm not interested in butting my head against a stone wall. I've written something on the subject. Maybe ten years from now, fifty years from now, some people will be interested. That's their affair. People are not really interested in science nowadays. They are interested in pseudo-scientific mysteries.

Like what?

Laymen are more interested in such things as the Bermuda Triangle, UFOs, hypnotic regression, Atlantis, astrology—pseudo-mysteries. Scientists are more interested in teaching apes to talk than in finding out why people talk. It is one of the peculiarities of the age that scientists are more interested in spending millions of dollars and man-hours trying to teach chimps to use language in order to prove that language is not a unique property of man than in studying the property itself. Scientists tend to be dogmatic about the nature of man. Again they remind me of the Scholastics battling with Galileo. Scholastics spent thousands of man-hours inside their heads trying to prove that Jupiter couldn't have moons and that the earth was at the center of the universe. To suggest otherwise offended their sense of the order of things. Galileo pointed to his telescope: Why don't you take a look? Today we have plenty of Scholastics of language. What we need is a Galileo who is willing to take a look at it.

You still haven't said what you think of Jimmy Carter.
No.

There is an extraordinary divergence of opinion. Some say he is the greatest of all Southern con artists, that everything he says and does in the way of humility, sincerity, honesty, love, brotherhood, and so forth, is an act, a calculated living-up to an image. Others say that these virtues are real. Which is it?
Is there a difference?

Moving right along . . . This is a pleasant room we're sitting in, overlooking a pleasant bayou.
Yes, it is. It is still a pretty country, despite the fact that the white man did his best to ruin it, ran the Indian off, cut down all the trees.

Is that a portrait of you over the fireplace?
Yes. It was done by an artist friend of mine, Lyn Hill. I like it very much.

I don't quite get it. What's going on there?

It shows me—well, not exactly me, a version of me—standing in front of what seems to be another framed painting. A picture within a picture, so to speak.

What does it mean to you?

I can only say what I see. The artist may very well disagree, but, after all, the subject and viewer is entitled to his own ideas—like a book reviewer. I identify the subject of the portrait as a kind of composite of the protagonists of my novels, but most especially Lancelot. He is not too attractive a fellow and something of a nut besides. As we say in the South, he's mean as a yard dog. It is not a flattering portrait—he is not the sort of fellow you'd like to go fishing with. He is, as usual, somewhat out of it, out of the world that is framed off behind him. Where is he? It is an undisclosed place, a kind of limbo. It's a dark place—look at that background; if one believed in auras, his would be a foreboding one. It is a kind of desert, a bombed-out place, a place after the end of the world, a no-man's-land of blasted trees and barbed wire. As for him, he is neither admirable nor attractive. Rather, he is cold-eyed and sardonic. There is a gleam in his eyes, a muted and dubious satisfaction. He is looking straight at the viewer, soliciting him ironically: *You and I know something, don't we? Or do we?* Or rather: *The chances are ninety-nine in a hundred you don't know, but on the other hand you might be the one in a hundred who does—not that it makes much difference. True, this is a strange world I'm in, but what about the world you're in? Have you noticed it lately? Are we on to something, you and I? Probably not.* But look at this apocalyptic world behind him. Something is going on. Is he aware of it? The dead blasted tree is undergoing a transformation. Into—? Into what? A bound figure? Figures? A woman? Lovers? The no-man's-land barbed wire is not really wire but a brier and it is blooming! A rose! Behind him there is a window of sorts, an opening out of his dark world onto a lovely seascape/skyscape. A new world! Yet he goes on looking straight at the viewer, challenging him: *Yes, I know about it, but do you? If you do, well and good. If you don't, there's no use in my telling you or turning around and pointing it out.* There's a limit to what writers can tell readers and artists can tell viewers. Perhaps he is Lancelot with the world and his life in ruins around him, but there is a prospect of a new world in the Shenandoah Valley. There was something wrong with the old world, the old things, the old flowers, the old skies, old clouds—or something wrong with his way of seeing them. They were used up. They have to be seen anew. Here is a new sky, a new sea, a new rose . . .

Could you say something about your debt to Kierkegaard?
No.

Could you at least explicate the painting in Kierkegaardian terms?
If I do, will you leave me alone?

Yes.
Very well, I see the painting as depicting the very beginning of the Kierkegaardian stages of life—which can apply to an individual, a people, an age. It is the dawn of the aesthetic stage, the emergence of life from death, of light from darkness, the first utterance of words between people. The desert is just beginning to flower and there is the possibility that there may be survivors after the catastrophe. He, somewhat sardonic and smart-assed as usual, knows it but does not want to give away the secret too easily. So he keeps his own counsel, except for the faintest glimmer in his eye—of risibility, even hope?—which says to the viewer: *I doubt if you know what's going on, but then again you just might. Do you?*
Do you understand?

No.

1977

BIBLIOGRAPHY
AND NOTES

❧

I. LIFE IN THE SOUTH

WHY I LIVE WHERE I LIVE, *Esquire* 93 (April 1980): 35–37.

NEW ORLEANS MON AMOUR, *Harper's* 237 (September 1968): 80–82, 86, 88, 90.

THE CITY OF THE DEAD, Lord John Press (19073 Los Alimos Street, Northridge, California), 1984.

GOING BACK TO GEORGIA, printed in pamphlet form by the University of Georgia, 1978.

MISSISSIPPI: THE FALLEN PARADISE, *Harper's* 230 (April 1965): 166–72. Reprinted with variants in *The South Today: 100 Years After Appomattox*, edited by Willie Morris (New York: Harper & Row, 1965), pp. 66–79 (text used here).

UNCLE WILL, originally entitled "Introduction" to *Lanterns on the Levee: Recollections of a Planter's Son*, by William Alexander Percy (Baton Rouge: Louisana State University Press, 1973), pp. vii–xviii.

UNCLE WILL'S HOUSE, *Architectural Digest*, October 1984: 44, 50, 54.

A BETTER LOUISIANA, originally entitled "Charting Our Future: Improving Education is the Key to a Better Louisiana," *The Times-Picayune / The States-Item* (New Orleans), May 23, 1985: A-25.

THE AMERICAN WAR, *Commonweal* 65 (March 29, 1957): 655–57.

RED, WHITE, AND BLUE-GRAY, *Commonweal* 75 (December 22, 1961): 337–39.

STOICISM IN THE SOUTH, *Commonweal* 64 (July 6, 1956): 342–44.

A SOUTHERN VIEW, *America* 97 (July 20, 1957): 428–29.

THE SOUTHERN MODERATE, *Commonweal* 67 (December 13, 1957): 279–82.

BOURBON, *Esquire* 84 (December 1975): 148–49. Recipe taken from the reprint of "Bourbon," Palaemon Press (Winston-Salem, North Carolina), 1981.

II. SCIENCE, LANGUAGE, LITERATURE

IS A THEORY OF MAN POSSIBLE? [Unpublished].

NAMING AND BEING, *The Personalist* 41 (April 1960): 148–57.

THE STATE OF THE NOVEL: DYING ART OR NEW SCIENCE? *The Michigan Quarterly Review* 16 (Fall 1977): 359–73.

NOVEL-WRITING IN AN APOCALYPTIC TIME (New Orleans, Louisiana: Faust Publishing, 1986).

HOW TO BE AN AMERICAN NOVELIST IN SPITE OF BEING SOUTHERN AND CATHOLIC, University of Southwestern Louisiana Printing Services (Lafayette, Louisiana), 1984.

FROM FACTS TO FICTION, *Washington Post Book Week*, December 25, 1966: 6, 9.

PHYSICIAN AS NOVELIST, *Chronicles: A Magazine of American Culture* (Rockford, Illinois: The Rockford Institute) 3 (May 1989): 10–12.

HERMAN MELVILLE, *The New Criterion* 2 (November 1983): 39–42.

DIAGNOSING THE MODERN MALAISE (New Orleans, Louisiana: Faust Publishing, 1985).

EUDORA WELTY IN JACKSON, *Shenandoah* 20 (Spring 1969): 37–38.

FOREWORD TO "A CONFEDERACY OF DUNCES" by John Kennedy Toole (Baton Rouge: Louisiana State University Press, 1980), pp. v–vii.

REDISCOVERING "A CANTICLE FOR LEIBOWITZ," orginally entitled "Walter M. Miller, Jr.'s *A Canticle for Leibowitz*: A Rediscovery," *The Southern Review* 7 (April 1971): 572–78.

THE MOVIE MAGAZINE: A LOW "SLICK," *Carolina Magazine* 64 (March 1935): 4–9.

ACCEPTING THE NATIONAL BOOK AWARD FOR "THE MOVIEGOER" [Unpublished].

CONCERNING "LOVE IN THE RUINS," talk at the 1971 National Book Award Spring Press Conference [Unpublished].

THE COMING CRISIS IN PSYCHIATRY, *America* 96 (January 5, 1957): 391–93, (January 12, 1957): 415–18.

THE CULTURE CRITICS, *Commonweal* 70 (June 5, 1959): 247–50.

THE FATEFUL RIFT: THE SAN ANDREAS FAULT IN THE MODERN MIND, excerpted as "The Divided Creature" in *The Wilson Quarterly* 13 (Summer 1989): 77–87 [Unpublished in final form].

III. MORALITY AND RELIGION

CULTURE, THE CHURCH, AND EVANGELIZATION [Unpublished].

WHY ARE YOU A CATHOLIC? first published in *Living Philosophies: The Reflections of Some Eminent Men and Women of Our Time*, edited by Clifton Fadiman (New York: Doubleday, 1990), pp. 165–76.

A "CRANKY NOVELIST" REFLECTS ON THE CHURCH, *The Quarterly* (St. Benedict, Louisiana: St. Joseph Seminary College) 1 (Summer 1983): 1–3, 6.

THE FAILURE AND THE HOPE, *Katallagete* (Journal of the Committee of Southern Churchmen) (Berea, Kentucky: Berea College) 1 (December 1965): 16–21.

A VIEW OF ABORTION, WITH SOMETHING TO OFFEND EVERYBODY, *The New York Times*, June 8, 1981: A-15.

FOREWORD TO "THE NEW CATHOLICS," edited by Dan O'Neill (New York: Crossroad, 1987), pp. xiii–xv.

IF I HAD FIVE MINUTES WITH THE POPE, *America* 157 (September 12–19, 1987): 127–29.

AN UNPUBLISHED LETTER TO THE "TIMES," *The Human Life Review* 14 (Spring 1988): 49–51.

ANOTHER MESSAGE IN THE BOTTLE ["From a Writer to Shipwrecked Teachers, or Why Should Students Read Novels Instead of Watching the Tube?" Unpublished].

THE HOLINESS OF THE ORDINARY, *Boston College Magazine* 48 (Summer 1989): 25–26.

EPILOGUE

INTERVIEW WITH ZOLTÁN ABÁDI-NAGY, *The Paris Review* 103 (Summer 1987): 50–81.

QUESTIONS THEY NEVER ASKED ME, *Esquire* 88 (December 1977): 170, 172, 184, 186, 188, 190, 193–94.

The dates at the end of each essay, speech, letter, or interview refer to initial dates of publication.